Using Groups to Help People

This new edition of *Using Groups to Help People* has been written with the interests, needs and concerns of group therapists and group workers in mind. It is designed to help practitioners plan and conduct therapeutic groups of diverse kinds and presents frameworks to assist practitioners in understanding and judging how to respond to the unique situations that arise during group sessions. It deals with issues such as:

- choosing group formats and structures to match the needs and capabilities of different populations of people;
- observing and listening to groups and making sense of what one sees and hears;
- problem situations and how they can be turned into opportunities;
- why, how and when to intervene in a group;
- events that may occur in therapeutic groups that cannot occur in individual psychotherapy and implications for the therapist;
- uses and misuses of theory when planning and conducting groups;
- planning and conducting research on one's own groups and those of colleagues.

This practical, up-to-date and readable book will prove valuable to all those involved in making use of small face-to-face groups to benefit their members. It takes into account new developments in the field during the past fifteen years, including new writing and the author's experiences and thinking during this time.

Dorothy Stock Whitaker is Emeritus Professor of Social Work at the University of York, England. She is a leading international figure in the field of group psychotherapy and group work.

Using Groups to Help People

Second Edition

Dorothy Stock Whitaker

First edition published in 1985
Routledge & Kegan Paul Ltd

Second edition published 2001
by Brunner-Routledge
27 Church Road, Hove, East Sussex BN3 2FA

Simultaneously published in the USA and Canada
by Taylor & Francis Inc.
325 Chestnut Street, 8th Floor, Philadelphia, PA 19106

Brunner-Routledge is an imprint of the Taylor & Francis Group

Typeset in Times by Keystroke, Jacaranda Lodge, Wolverhampton
Printed and bound in Great Britain by Biddles Ltd, Guildford and King's Lynn

British Library Cataloguing in Publication Data
A catalogue record for this book is available from the British Library

Library of Congress Cataloguing in Publication Data
Whitaker, Dorothy Stock, 1925–
    Using groups to help people / Dorothy Stock Whitaker.—2nd ed.
      p. cm.—(International library of group psychotherapy and group process)
    Includes bibliographical references and index.
    1. Group counseling. 2. Group psychotherapy. I. Title. II. Series.

  BF637.C6 W47 2000
  158′.35—dc21
                                            00-042497

ISBN 0–415–19562–4 (pbk)
     0–415–19561–6 (hbk)

To Galvin

Contents

Figures

Preface

When I was invited to prepare a second edition of *Using Groups to Help People* I asked myself the following questions: (a) What have I done or experienced or given special thought to in the past fifteen years which would warrant a second edition? (2) What has happened in the field during this same period which should be referred to and discussed? (c) In what ways ought a second edition therefore to differ from the first one?

In answer to the first question: every year for the past fifteen years I have participated as a member of staff in courses at the University of York about therapeutic groups, which have been attended by people who are currently engaged in practice. The members of the course are psychologists, social workers, psychiatrists, occupational therapists, and others. They work in diverse settings, with different populations of people, using different group structures and various leadership approaches. Some of the course members have had previous training in group psychotherapy or group work, but most of them have not. The course includes lectures and experiential groups. Time is also set aside for course members to share their experiences with one another and with staff, to examine episodes of practice, and to plan learning opportunities for themselves. Although I had taught about therapeutic groups for many years before this, it had been at postgraduate level with people with little or no practice experience. This past fifteen years' teaching has helped me to learn about a wider range of groups than those which I have worked with previously, and has put me in closer touch with the concerns and interests of practitioners, and with what they want to learn about.

During the past fifteen years I have also been engaged in 'learning programmes' for experienced practitioners and first-line managers, which helped participants to plan and conduct small-scale pieces of research on issues of special interest to them arising from their own work activity. The work done with participants on these programmes made evident the practical value of conducting research into issues arising in and from one's work, and moreover demonstrated that it is feasible to conduct such research whilst remaining engaged in the work itself.

During this same time I have found myself increasingly interested in connections between theory and practice. This interest goes back a long way, ever since I realised that group focal conflict theory and Ezriel's thinking about groups have much in common but have led to quite different forms of practice. I began to wonder why this happened. I found in the literature evidence that the connection between theory and practice is complex rather than direct. To prepare a second edition of *Using Groups to Help People* would provide an opportunity to explore the uses of theory and its connections with practice. All practitioners make use of theory, whether it be a formal theory or not. Any move towards understanding how group therapists may deploy theory in their work promised to be of considerable practical value.

In response to the second question – what has happened in the field during this same period which should be referred to and discussed? – I point first to increasing pressures on practitioners to conduct shorter-term groups, to use the time and resources available to them to reach more patients or clients, and to 'be efficient'. Such pressures have accompanied the advent of 'managed care' and of changes in management structures and procedures within service-providing organisations. Many practitioners are giving special thought to how they are to respond to such pressures without sacrificing the quality of treatment. The terms 'time-effective' and 'cost-effective' have entered the field. A second edition would need to acknowledge these pressures and events and to discuss some of their implications.

Still in response to the second question, a new edition would have to take new writing and thinking into account. There has been a substantial increase in publications since the time when the first edition of this book was being written. New theory is emerging, and many more accounts of examples of practice have appeared in print. There was bound to be much to be learned from this new literature.

My third question was: In what ways, therefore, ought a second edition to differ from the first one? I knew from the beginning that I wanted to incorporate into a new edition what I have learned during these fifteen years about types of groups and forms of practice, and about assisting practitioners to conduct research on issues arising from their own professional work. I wanted to take into account developments in the field and to pursue my long-standing interest in connections between theory and practice.

The second edition has accordingly been restructured. New chapters have been added. The table of contents shows the end result. I have retained a four-part structure, which concentrates, first, on what needs thinking about before any plans are made or actions taken; second, on planning; then on thinking and taking action during the life of a group; and lastly, on how practitioners can continue to learn. I have made changes within each part.

Part I has been reorganised. It now begins by discussing therapists' purposes in conducting a group. *Purpose* logically precedes what could be thought of as the *technology* of planning and conducting groups, and is fundamental to all else. I have stated a group therapist's overall purpose as being 'to enable and assist each individual in a group to achieve personal benefit through making as full use as possible of the potentials of the group as a medium for help'. The chapters in Part I pay attention to each of the main component parts of this statement. In Chapter 1, sub- or instrumental purposes contained within this overall purpose are named and discussed. In Chapter 2, the phrase 'each individual' is singled out by considering the diverse populations and sub-populations of people who might profit from a group experience. Chapter 3 defines benefit in terms which can be applied to any population or sub-population. Chapters 4 and 5 are about making as full use as possible of the potentials of the group as a medium for help. Chapter 4 summarises what is known, from work done within the field of group dynamics, about the properties and dynamics of small face-to-face groups. Chapter 5 discusses theory pertinent to psychotherapeutic groups, and begins to raise questions about connections between theory and practice.

Part II, on Planning, is more condensed than it was in the first edition and now contains two chapters. The first of these, Chapter 6, lists decisions which need to be made when planning a group. Chapter 7, which is new to the second edition, provides examples of different kinds of group structures for different populations of people, shows the versatility of groups, and discusses responses to pressures to be 'time-effective'.

Part III is about thinking and taking action during the life of a group. In restructuring this part, I have been much influenced by what I have learned through recent teaching. In the first edition I devoted separate chapters to successive developmental phases, and discussed other issues within this framework. In this second edition I have changed the framework, giving more prominence to situations and tasks which face group therapists, and to events and processes which they need to be alert to.

I have started Part III, as before, with a chapter on the internal 'think-work' which a therapist engages in while participating in group sessions (Chapter 8). Chapter 9 is titled 'Getting started: opening a group and responding to what happens next'. It concentrates on the first fifteen to twenty minutes of a new group. Chapter 10 brings together, from my own experience and from the literature, points about the development of a therapeutic group and the impact of changes in membership. Separate chapters are then devoted to problems and opportunities, and to how problems can often be turned into opportunities (Chapter 11); to personal gains and how they occur (Chapter 12); to little or no gain or actual harm (Chapter 13); to therapist errors (Chapter 14); and to intervening in groups (Chapter 15). Many examples of practice, from different kinds of groups, are presented and discussed. This reflects my conviction that those who conduct therapeutic groups learn best through the close examination of concrete examples. I refer to recent as well as to older literature whenever I consider that such references illuminate the issue under discussion. Some of the chapters in Part III cast up further issues concerning theory. When this is the case, I note them as questions at the end of the chapter, but reserve discussion of them until later.

Part III closes with two new chapters, which examine respectively the therapist in the group (Chapter 16), and theory and its connections with practice (Chapter 17). Chapter 16 draws attention to features of group psychotherapy which distinguish it from one-to-one psychotherapy. Situations are named and discussed that arise in groups and that do not and cannot arise in one-to-one psychotherapy. Implications for the group therapist's position, task, and intervention choices are considered. This chapter includes a discussion of what therapists can do to increase the likelihood that those participating in groups will gain from their experience. Thinking about these matters is essential if group therapists are to take advantage of the special potentials of a group as a medium for providing therapeutic help to individuals. Chapter 17, on theory and its connections with practice, examines diverse issues concerning theory and its uses. In this chapter I collect up all the questions concerning theory which were listed for future reference in earlier chapters, and examine each of them in turn. For instance, attention is paid to how therapists acquire theory, to mutual influences between theory and practice, to how therapists may make use of theory in their practice, and to what, besides theory, influences practice.

Part IV concentrates on how therapists may continue to learn, through careful examination of their own experience (Chapter 18), through taking advantage of the experience of others (Chapter 19), and through creating new opportunities to learn by planning and conducting research (Chapter 20). This part is expanded, compared with the first edition, and now includes two new chapters (19 and 20).

The book is meant to be of practical use. I did not want, however, to write a 'how to do it' book. Rules and prescriptions as to 'how to do it' are not likely to be helpful, since every situation which faces a practitioner is unique, and not like any other situation which it may resemble in some respects. A group therapist always faces the need to think out what is happening *this* time, and to choose an action fitted to *this* event, rather than to some other. I have sometimes offered frameworks for thinking – for instance, in Chapter 6, I list decisions which need to be made when planning a group. In Chapter 20, I name and discuss sequential steps in planning and conducting a piece of research. Often, I introduce sets of questions which practitioners can ask themselves and seek to answer in order better to understand themselves and the situations they face and, from this, see how to proceed. For instance, in Chapter 11 questions are listed which I believe will assist practitioners to think about problem situations and to work out ways of dealing with them. Chapter 14 lists questions which therapists can ask themselves and try to answer when thinking out whether they have made an error and if so what to do about it. Chapter 17 includes a sub-section titled 'How can practitioners make explicit to themselves the concepts which they *actually* use in their practice?' Here again, I suggest possible questions. Questions (as opposed to answers or prescriptions) have great utility because they direct attention to what it is useful to think about. They can be used by group therapists to arrive at their own conclusions and understandings.

A thread which recurs throughout the book has to do with the special properties of a *group* as a medium for help. This exploration begins in Chapter 4, which discusses small face-to-face groups, continues in Chapter 5 on theory, is taken forward through examples from practice presented in Part III, and culminates in Chapter 16, which examines how a therapist may make use of a group in order to benefit individual members.

The theme of theory and its connections with practice is also threaded through the book. Ideas helpful in defining 'benefit' are discussed in Chapter 3. Theory which pertains to small groups, without specific reference to therapeutic groups, is reported in Chapter 4. Group focal conflict theory is fully described in Chapter 5. The commentaries on the examples which appear in later chapters include reference to group focal conflict theory where relevant, and to other theories or single concepts when they illuminate aspects of an example. Certain terms – for instance, transference, counter-transference, insight – which are complex or else open to being understood in diverse ways, are defined and discussed in context. Broader issues concerning theory and its uses are discussed in Chapter 17.

I have tried to use plain language throughout. I have introduced technical terms only when it appeared economic of time and space to do so, taking care to define them. I have often used dictionaries in order to provide clear and explicit definitions of such commonly used and apparently obvious terms as 'opportunity', 'harm', 'spontaneous', 'intuition', 'insight', 'cohesiveness'. Plain language does not oversimplify. It avoids using abstract terms which may be understood differently by different readers, or misunderstood. It thus supports clarity and communicability.

Like the first edition, this book is titled *Using Groups to Help People*. The preface to the first edition began with the sentence: 'My greatest hope for this book is that it be of practical use.' My hope and my intentions remain the same.

DOROTHY STOCK WHITAKER

Acknowledgements

I wish to acknowledge my career-long indebtedness to Professor Herbert A. Thelen, who, when I was still a graduate student at the University of Chicago, made such a substantial contribution to my understanding of groups through including me in a research team which investigated and tried to operationalise the ideas of W.R. Bion. This research activity brought me into contact with Leland P. Bradford and other staff of the National Training Laboratories who were conducting group dynamics training programmes at Bethel, Maine, and elsewhere. The experiences of studying, and later of conducting, T-groups were important sources of learning.

My closest colleagues at the Veterans' Administration Hospital in Chicago, and later in the Department of Psychiatry at the University of Chicago, were Drs Roy M. Whitman and Morton A. Lieberman. I owe them much. I am grateful to Dr Thomas A. French, who joined us in testing whether his formulations of individual nuclear and focal conflicts could be extended to understanding inter-actions and processes in therapeutic groups, and connections between individual and group dynamics.

Becoming involved in the education of social workers at the University of York in England familiarised me with a broader range of groups than I had worked with before. Over the past fifteen years I have worked closely with two colleagues, Una McCluskey and Anne Harrow. Together we have conducted one-year courses in therapeutic group work for psychologists, social workers, psychiatrists, and others who were working with diverse patient and client populations in a range of work settings, making use of different group structures. I am grateful to Una and Anne, who shared their practice wisdom in our staff discussions and helped me to become more familiar with theoretical perspectives different from my own. I owe a great deal to discussions with course members who shared their practice experience with us and brought their own insights and views to the many examples of practice which we examined together.

During this same period of fifteen years or so, I have worked closely with Dr Lesley Archer in conducting courses which supported MA students in planning and preparing research dissertations. This activity was extended into devising and conducting 'Learning Programmes' to assist practitioners and managers in service-providing organisations to undertake research on issues which they chose themselves as being important to them in their work. I am grateful to Lesley Archer and to Dr Leslie Hicks, who joined us in this work, and to the participants in these learning programmes. They all contributed to my understanding of how research can be conducted by practitioners from a base in practice.

I have profited from discussions with other colleagues, encountered in other contexts, and particularly wish to mention Göran Ahlin, Siv Boalt-Boëthius, Graeme Farquharson, and Dave Pottage. I have learned different things from each of them, all valuable.

I am much indebted to my husband, Galvin Whitaker, who is a logician and linguist and has had extensive experience in consulting and teaching about organisations and work groups and in conducting T-groups. I have profited from the many discussions we have had about problems which I encountered in the course of preparing this second edition, especially those which had to do with ordering my thinking about theory. He has read some of the chapters and made invaluable comments which have assisted me in sharpening my thinking, and in moving towards clarity and simplicity in the use of language.

Permissions

I am grateful to the following for extending permission to quote from books published by them:

'Therapeutic Factors: Interpersonal and Intrapersonal Mechanisms', by E.D. Crouch, S. Bloch and J. Wanlass (1994), in A. Fuhriman and G.M. Burlingame (eds) *Handbook of Group Psychotherapy: An Empirical and Clinical Synthesis*. Copyright © 1994 by John Wiley & Sons. Inc. Reprinted with permission.

Koinonia: From Hate, through Dialogue, to Culture in the Large Group by P. de Mare, R. Piper and S. Thompson (1991). Published by H. Karnac (Books) Ltd (original publishers), reprinted with permission.

'Short-term Group Psychotherapy' by R.H. Klein;
'Psychoanalysis in Groups' by I.L. Kutash and A. Wolf;
'Integration and Nonintegration of Innovative Group Methods' by F.T. Reid Jr and D.E. Reid;
'Countertransference and Transference in Groups' by S. Tutman;
all in H.I. Kaplan and B.J. Saddock (eds) *Comprehensive Group Psychotherapy* 3rd edn. Copyright © 1993 Williams & Wilkins. Reprinted by permission of Lippincott, Williams & Wilkins.

'Notes on Help-rejecting Complainers' by M.M. Berger and M. Rosenbaum (1967) in *International Journal of Group Psychotherapy* 17(3): 357–70;

'On Interpretation in Group Analysis' by S.H. Foulkes (1968) in *International Journal of Group Psychotherapy* 18(4): 432–44;

'Comments on Issues Raised by Slavson, Durkin and Scheidlinger' by A. Fuhriman (1977) in *International Journal of Group Psychotherapy* 47(2): 169–74;

'Depth of Transference in Groups' by L. Horwitz (1994) in *International Journal of Group Psychotherapy* 44(3): 271–99;

'The Implications of Total Group Phenomena Analysis for Patients and Therapists' by Morton A. Lieberman (1967) *International Journal of Group Psychotherapy* 17(1): 71–81;

'Cultivating the Observing Ego in the Group Setting' by L.R. Ormont (1995) in *International Journal of Group Psychotherapy* 45(4): 489–506;

'Are there "Group Dynamics" in Therapy Groups?' by S.R. Slavson (1957) in *International Journal of Group Psychotherapy* 7(2): 131–54;

'Open Groups for Children of Holocaust Survivors' by E. Van der Hal, Y. Tauber and J. Gottesfeld (1996) in *International Journal of Group Psychotherapy* 46(2): 193–208;

all reprinted by permission of The Guilford Press.

The Anti-Group: Destructive Forces in the Group and their Creative Potential by M. Nitsun (1996). Published by Routledge, reprinted with permission.

Basics of Group Psychotherapy edited by H.S. Bernard and K.R. MacKenzie (1994). Published by The Guilford Press, reprinted with permission.

The Theory and Practice of Group Psychotherapy, 4th edn, by Irvin D. Yalom (1995). Copyright © 1970, 1975, 1985 and 1995 by Basic Books, Inc., reprinted with permission.

Part I

Thinking about groups before any plans are made or actions taken

Chapter 1

A therapist's purposes in conducting a group

WHY BEGIN WITH PURPOSES?

This is a book for practitioners, and practitioners are constantly engaged in making decisions. Amongst the decisions which face a group therapist are: Should this group proceed by open discussion, or by topics, or by activities, or by some combination? If topics are to be used, should I introduce them or should I encourage the group members to identify topics they wish to discuss? If activities are to be used, how should they be chosen? Should the group be time-limited or open-ended? How long should each session be, and how frequently should the group meet? What preparatory work do I need to undertake, if any? What shall I say and do when a group first meets? What should I be paying attention to while a group is in session? How and when should I intervene, and when is it best to say nothing? What should I say and do if the whole group turns on me? if one person gets extremely distressed? if two members attack one another?

Decisions and actions are guided by purposes. It is therefore reasonable to begin by thinking about the purposes which a therapist holds when planning and conducting a therapeutic group.

This chapter is organised as follows:

- A therapist's overall purpose.
- Instrumental or sub-purposes.
- Interconnections between instrumental purposes.
- A rationale for this way of formulating a therapist's purposes.
- Additional purposes likely to be held by a therapist.
- Distinguishing between purposes, goals, aims and tasks.
- Further questions arising from the statement of overall purpose.

A THERAPIST'S OVERALL PURPOSE

Anyone who conducts a therapeutic group, whatever its form, intends to make use of the group situation to benefit each person in it. This is an overall purpose. It can be stated more formally as:

A group therapist's overall purpose is to enable and assist each individual in a group to achieve personal benefit through making as full use as possible of the potentials of the group as a medium for help.

This overall statement of purpose needs to be spelled out, or 'unpacked'. A set of sub- or instrumental purposes is needed to help therapists to see what to work towards if the overall purpose is to be achieved. Such a set of instrumental purposes should suggest foci of attention and directions for a therapist's efforts. Instrumental purposes need to be more specific than the overall purpose but not so situation-specific that a vast number of them need to be stated, each applying only to a narrow range of tasks or situations.

The six sub- or instrumental purposes which follow are one way of factoring out the overall purpose.

INSTRUMENTAL OR SUB-PURPOSES

1   To plan and conduct the group so as to maintain a general sense of safety at a level at which members feel safe enough to stay in the group and to take personal risks.
2   To avoid the irredeemable collapse of structure.
3   To work towards the establishment and maintenance of norms, and shared beliefs and assumptions, which support the group as a positive medium for help.
4   To utilise events occurring in the group for the benefit of individual members.
5   To avoid harmful consequences for the members of the group, for oneself as therapist, and for the group's wider environment.
6   To avoid making errors as much as possible, and to discern such errors as occur and think out how to retrieve their consequences.

Each of these needs elaboration.

I Planning and conducting the group so as to maintain a general sense of safety at a level at which members feel safe enough to stay in the group and to take personal risks

If group members do not feel safe they will not involve themselves in the group. They will either flee, literally, or stay in the group but find ways to insulate themselves from the experience. Personal gains will not occur or will be limited.

Hardly anyone feels safe enough to take risks when first entering a therapeutic group. Most people who join a therapeutic group want to make positive use of the group experience but are also aware of, or sense, that there are hazards in participating. More often than not, becoming a member of a therapeutic group is a frightening prospect. Group members often anticipate that revealing themselves to others and exploring their own feelings and experiences carries risks of being ridiculed or criticised or shamed by other members, or of being overwhelmed by their own feelings or of being rejected by the therapist.

It is possible for members of a group to achieve a sense of safety by not taking any personal risks at all. In order to avoid pain or threat they may, individually or collectively, establish ways of participating which threaten no one but also reduce the likelihood that gains will occur. Individuals may sink comfortably into some familiar and customary way of behaving. Nothing new is experienced or tried. Collectively, members may establish collusive defences which render the group innocuous.

Feeling 'safe enough to take personal risks' falls somewhere between the two extremes of feeling so safe that personal gain does not occur, and feeling unbearably at risk. Feeling 'safe enough' does not mean the absence of all threat and challenge. On the contrary, it means feeling confident that threat and challenge can be borne and will be worthwhile.

A therapist, mindful of members' likely initial anxieties, will seek to avoid the group becoming either dysfunctionally threatening or so safe an environment that nothing of real importance is likely to occur. The middle ground – a group in which members feel 'safe enough to take risks' – is what is wanted.

2 Avoiding the irredeemable collapse of structure

By 'structure', I mean whether the group is to proceed by open discussion, topic-based discussion, activities or exercises, or some variation or combination of these; whether it is to be time-limited or open-ended, shorter- or longer-term, and meet at frequent or infrequent intervals.

Before a group begins, a therapist plans a structure which he or she predicts will fit the needs and capabilities of members. However, it is only when the group starts to meet that the suitability of the structure is put to the test. The structure introduced by the therapist may turn out to be manageable by the members. They 'take to it' and all is well. However, it is also possible that the structure does not mesh well with the members' needs and capacities. They are unable to use it or they resist using it, and the group is off to a difficult start.

Any structure needs to be given a fair chance to work as intended, with the therapist intervening in ways to help the members to work within it. Members often respond to such efforts, but sometimes they do not and cannot. A group whose members persistently fail to operate within the structure which the therapist has introduced may be experiencing intolerable distress brought about simply by being in the group situation. Or group members may lack skills in listening and communicating and, in consequence, cannot participate as the therapist hopes. If experience shows that members cannot work within the structure, the therapist will need to change or adapt it. The members cannot change, so the therapist must. The therapist's purpose is not to insist on maintaining the structure which he or she has planned, but to arrive at a structure which is manageable by the members of the group.

3 Working towards the establishment and maintenance of norms, and shared beliefs and assumptions, which support the group as a positive medium for help

All groups establish norms (or standards) which define acceptable and unacceptable ways of behaving in the group. Members also develop shared beliefs about themselves and the world around them. A group will be a more effective medium for help if its norms and shared beliefs support members in expressing feelings freely and frankly, sharing experiences, responding to one another's contributions and trying out new behaviours.

Norms which support the therapeutic process include, for instance, a mutual understanding that diverse opinions will be listened to and respected, that what members say about themselves inside the group will not be gossiped about outside, that individual differences will be accepted. Shared beliefs and assumptions which support the therapeutic process include, for instance, seeing each person as valuable and worthwhile, accepting as 'only human' feelings to which guilt or shame are often attached, accepting that it is a mark of personal courage to admit that one has personal problems and is prepared to discuss them.

Some norms and shared beliefs work against the effectiveness of a group, and some can do harm to individuals. Disadvantageous norms include, for instance, expressing hostile criticism in a sugary way, disguised as 'helping'; or regarding such feelings as anger or envy as unacceptable; or consistently behaving dismissively towards one person in the group. Shared beliefs which undermine the value of the group include assuming that all the members of the group are inferior beings because they cannot manage themselves without help; that all problems are due to outside agents or 'society'; that the therapist is likely to disapprove of members and use his or her power against them. Such norms and such beliefs and assumptions constrict what can be explored in the group and hence also constrict the gains which members can achieve.

A therapist can and should monitor the norms and beliefs which evolve through the members' interactions. If the therapist has introduced a norm in the form of a rule or a guideline, monitoring members' responses to it will show whether or not a guideline has been accepted as a norm. A therapist cannot, in fact, impose a norm on a group and be sure that it will stick. Whether or not a norm or a belief becomes an established feature of the group depends on the interactions of the members. A therapist who observes and listens with care may develop hypotheses about the nature of the norms, beliefs and assumptions which are in fact in operation, the function they are serving for the members and the forces which are holding them in place. On the basis of such provisional understandings, a therapist may intervene to encourage facilitative norms/beliefs to become established and discourage non-facilitative or destructive ones.

4 Utilising events occurring in the group for the specific benefit of individual members

To achieve this purpose, therapists need to understand each person well enough to form hypotheses about what, for each, would constitute benefit. They need to understand what it is about a *group* which can contribute to personal gain. In particular they need to appreciate that, in a group, benefit does not derive only and directly from the therapist, but from how members interact with one another. Under facilitative group conditions, members can share and compare feelings and assumptions and experiences; support one another in acknowledging feelings previously regarded as unacceptable by self or others; give and receive constructive feedback; try out new behaviours within the group; and, in general, feel supported in exploring dangerous territory.

In a group, themes emerge through the interactions of members, or else are given to the members by the therapist in the form of a topic and then accepted or transformed by the members. Individuals gain through exploring within a shared theme which means something to everyone, though the meaning will be unique for each person. As examples, themes which touch on anger and resentment, or envy, or feelings of deprivation or abandonment, or lack of self-worth, are likely to touch everyone in one way or another. It is to be expected that members relate to a theme in individual ways, seeing particular connections with current experiences outside the group and/or past experiences within the family or with significant other people, for instance in school, the neighbourhood, the armed forces, and so on. Exploring within themes provides therapeutic opportunities for more than one person at the same time. Sometimes there are special resonances between group and individual dynamics, or two or more persons become especially important to one another. These, too, offer opportunities for profitable exploration.

Many benefit-producing situations are generated by interactions amongst members. The therapist does not need to intervene, apart from offering general support and encouragement. At other times therapist interventions are crucial and can make the difference between exploiting a situation for the benefit or one or more members or letting it slide by without it having much impact. At times, it is useful or necessary to intervene in order to support therapeutic work, or forestall harm, or turn difficult situations into opportunities for gain. For this, a therapist needs a repertoire of interventions to select from when faced with particular circumstances. A therapist also needs a sense of when not to intervene. It is often appropriate to allow the therapeutic potentials of interactions amongst members to occur without interfering too much or at the wrong times. When a therapist chooses to intervene, he or she may direct an intervention to one person, or to two people in interaction with one another, or to several people in order to emphasise their different reactions to a theme. Sometimes the therapist will address the members in general, encouraging mutual exploration, or trying to ensure that members have noticed and registered significant events.

Adopting a monitoring stance towards events arising in the group is essential for intervening in order to benefit individuals. The therapist needs to note the themes which emerge and how members contribute to and respond to them. He or she needs to listen with care to what members reveal about themselves, how they interact with one another, how they feel about and respond to the therapist, and who comes to have a special meaning for whom.

Seeing how to make use of a group for the benefit of individual members includes being sensitive to its destructive as well as its constructive potentials. On the positive side, group members can be effective helpers to one another; the group itself can be a benign and supportive environment; and individuals may create opportunities to explore issues important to themselves. On the other hand, members sometimes behave in ways which damage or threaten others or prevent the group from becoming a gain-promoting environment. Some group processes can do harm. It follows that a therapist needs to monitor a group with its potentials for helping and harming in mind, intervening in order to support the former and to interrupt and reverse the consequences of the latter. This brings us to the next instrumental purpose:

5 Avoiding harmful consequences for the members of the group, for oneself as therapist, and for the wider environment in which the group is operating

Everyone knows that harm can come to people through their being in a group. Anyone who has been bullied at school, or seen it happen, knows this. So does anyone who (as leader or as member) has been excluded from a group, or become the target of direct or subtle ridicule or criticism, or been made uneasy by being drawn by others into behaviours usually avoided or kept under control, or been told by others some 'truths' about themselves which are hard to bear.

All of these potentially harm-generating events can occur in therapeutic groups. Members may be pressed into participating in ways which generate excessive threat. They may be unable to stop themselves from revealing personal matters which stir up unmanageable anxiety. They may find some long-held view of themselves abruptly jarred. Personal defences could be rendered inoperable at a time when they are still needed. An individual's *model of self and surroundings* could be challenged or overturned, with consequent upsurges of hard-to-manage anxiety.

Sometimes harm-inducing events, and the feelings of distress and hurt which follow, are temporary. If well explored and utilised they can eventuate in personal gain. A person may experience distress and pain, but pain is not necessarily harm.

Of course, it is too simple to say that participating in groups leads to harm or can 'cause' harm. Potentially harmful events do occur in groups, but what is critical is how these interact with the fears and vulnerabilities and defensive strategies which each person brings to a group, and how the therapist and others respond to the potentially harm-generating event. What is overwhelmingly threatening to one person is bearable and manageable by another. Abiding harm follows when some threat occurs *and* an individual has no defence against it *and* nothing happens to assist the person to recover from the impact of the event and make good use of it.

A therapist, too, can experience harm through participating in a group. It is to be expected that, in therapeutic groups, there will be times when events occurring in the group touch the therapist personally, stirring up feelings which are painful and hard to manage. A therapist can experience severe threat if he or she comes under persistent attack, or feels out of control or helpless in the face of some group event, or if some aspect of the therapist's model of self and surroundings is challenged or undermined. Especially if there is no one to turn to for consultation, a therapist may be left with a sense of confusion and helplessness, and may make matters worse by his/her responses to group events. If co-therapists have incompatible ideas about how to proceed, and if they persistently behave in ways which undo one another's efforts, then harm or at least substantial discomfort may ensue.

Harm can also come to the wider organisation. Many therapists work in settings in which a group is only one of a number of therapeutic activities which take place, alongside individual psychotherapy, task or planning groups, or a programme of activities. This is the case, for instance, in day centres, psychiatric hospital wards, hostels, and residential care settings for children or old people. Unless care is taken, staff may work at cross-purposes or competitiveness and envy may spring up. There may be confusion or conflict over who holds responsibility for what. Members of a therapeutic group may experience powerful feelings which spill out into other parts of the helping programme and cause problems for others.

A therapist who is aware of potentially harm-provoking situations can often avoid harm occurring, or else can turn a potentially harmful situation into a positive opportunity. A therapist who is not in touch with potential hazards may, without being aware of it, behave in ways which lead to or exacerbate harm, either directly or by failing to intervene when a harm-generating situation is occurring or building up.

6 Avoiding making errors as much as possible, and being ready to discern such errors as occur and think out how to retrieve their consequences

An error is something which a therapist does or doesn't do which has undesirable consequences for individual members or which works against the group becoming or sustaining itself as a positive therapeutic environment.

Therapists can and do make errors: in planning; by actions taken while a group is in session; or by failing to take useful action. Of course it is better not to make errors, but they do occur from time to time and cannot really be avoided altogether, given the often complex and rapidly moving events during group sessions. Although a therapist cannot avoid making errors entirely, he or she can learn to reduce their frequency. Therapists can also learn to recognise errors soon after they have occurred and take steps to correct for their undesirable consequences.

Some not unusual errors are: colluding with a group in maintaining some interactive pattern which makes everyone feel comfortable but which avoids facing some important issue; supporting an interactive pattern which is causing harm to some one person but which is rationalised by all (except the victim) as 'help'; or failing to notice opportunities for benefiting an individual or furthering the development of the group.

The undesirable consequences of errors are likely to persist if the error is not discerned, or not discerned in time for the therapist to do something about it. Some errors have consequences which are extremely difficult if not impossible to reverse or to turn into something positive. For instance, a therapist who has shown him- or herself to be untrustworthy or harshly invasive will very likely have stirred up defensive responses in members which they cling to for a long time.

Errors which a therapist repeats over and over again are of course the worst of all.

Interconnections between instrumental purposes

It is evident that these six instrumental purposes are interconnected. Assisting members to feel 'safe enough to take risks' paves the way for experiences likely to benefit individuals. Colluding with group members in attacking one person is an error which, if not retrieved, can lead to harm for that person. If the therapist repeats certain errors and does not recognise and try to deal with their negative consequences, potentially beneficial events and interactions will be less likely to occur; and so on.

A RATIONALE FOR THIS WAY OF FORMULATING A THERAPIST'S PURPOSES

The purposes which I have presented are purposes *held by the therapist*. The overall purpose includes a reference to what the therapist hopes will occur as outcomes for individuals ('to achieve personal benefit'). It also refers to (but does not as yet name or spell out) the processes by which this may occur ('by making as full use as possible of the potentials of the group as a medium for help').

The overall purpose refers to hoped-for personal benefits in general terms. It does not refer to such specifics as achieving insight, or increasing self-understanding, or developing practical skills, or recovering from the effects of a crisis, or becoming better able to relate to others. Any of these more specifically stated benefits could be important for some individuals, or for some populations of people, and not for others.

The sub- or instrumental purposes can be thought of as *way-points*. They are processes and/or states which, if achieved, will contribute to benefits for group members. They have to do with what a therapist can aim for which is likely to assist individual group members to achieve personal gain.

The first three instrumental purposes have to do with *encouraging a group to develop into an environment in which potentially beneficial interactions and experiences can occur.* The fourth has to do with *utilising situations arising in groups for the specific benefit of particular members.* The remaining sub-purposes support the first four: the fifth has to do with avoiding harmful consequences for the members and for others connected with or affected by the group, and the sixth and final sub-purpose has to do with avoiding making errors and retrieving them if they occur.

I have tried to formulate sub- or instrumental purposes at a level which lies somewhere between the overly general and the overly situation-specific. I have made a deliberate decision to use plain language and to avoid technical terms from the world of psychotherapy. In part, this is because technical terms are likely to be differently understood by different people, and in part it is because it seems so easy to hide behind language, falling into the trap of believing that one has understood something because one has given a name to it.

ADDITIONAL PURPOSES LIKELY TO BE HELD BY A THERAPIST

A therapist may well hold purposes additional to those which have to do with assisting individual members to achieve personal gain. For example, a therapist might want to establish a group programme in his or her work setting, or expand and develop own experience by taking on more groups or different kinds of groups, or contribute to the education and training of others by bringing them in as co-therapists, and so on. Some of these purposes are pursued through associated activities such as providing supervision to others or devising and running training programmes. These purposes are additional to that of benefiting members and, on the whole, mesh well with it.

Some kinds of additional purposes are likely to work against the core purpose of benefiting group members. A therapist might be motivated by personal interests and needs: for instance, to display own skills to others (either group members or colleagues), or to establish a reputation which will assist in gaining promotion or a new job, or to protect the self from anxieties stimulated by certain kinds of group events, or to show oneself to be superior to colleagues. Problems arise if a therapist pursues these personal needs in ways which work against the best interests of group members. The risk of this is greater if the therapist is unaware of these further purposes, for covertly held purposes risk being expressed in behaviour which interferes with the therapeutic process or does actual harm.

DISTINGUISHING BETWEEN PURPOSES, GOALS, AIMS AND TASKS

When writing this chapter the word 'purpose' seemed to me to be better than 'goal' or 'aim', but I had to consult dictionaries to find out why. Of the several definitions of *purpose*, the one which fits my thinking is 'intention, resolution, determination'. *Purpose* is thus different from *goal*, which is defined as an end-point: 'the end toward which effort is directed': literally, 'the finishing point of any race'. *Aim* refers to channelling one's efforts: 'to have the intention to direct at or towards a specified goal'; 'to endeavour earnestly'. (Dictionary sources are the *Longman Dictionary of the English Language* and the *Shorter Oxford English Dictionary*.)

'Task', by dictionary definition, is 'a duty, function' (*Longman*); or 'any piece of work that has to be done' (*Shorter Oxford English Dictionary*). 'Task' has a connection with 'purpose', if thought of as 'any piece of work that has to be done'. When discussing sub-purposes I have sometimes referred to 'purposes or tasks', or tasks attached to purposes. From a certain point of view, purposes can be thought of as tasks. For instance, it is not only a purpose to avoid the irredeemable collapse of structure: it is also a task. One of the therapist's tasks is to encourage favourable conditions in the group within which gain-promoting experiences are more likely to occur (which is also one of his/her purposes). It is the therapist's task to avoid making errors. It is the therapist's task to perceive and use opportunities arising in the group for benefiting individuals.

Some tasks belong only to the therapist, such as avoiding the irredeemable collapse of structure or avoiding making errors. Sometimes, both the therapist and the members pursue a task. For instance, it is not only the therapist who utilises events occurring in the group for the specific benefit of members. Members themselves often take initiatives which promote gain. For instance, a member may grasp the opportunity provided by a general discussion about angry or envious feelings to explore such feelings in him- or herself, or one member may support another by showing empathy and understanding. A therapeutic or working alliance may become established in which the therapist and the members work together collaboratively to achieve benefit.

Maintaining a sense of safety in the group is somewhat different. Both the therapist and the group members have an interest in maintaining a sense of safety in the group, and both work towards this. However, the therapist will want members to feel safe enough to take personal risks, while members may (especially at first) try to feel safe by *not* taking risks. In other words, there are times when members try to achieve a sense of safety by means which the therapist considers work against the therapeutic process. It then becomes a part of the therapist's task to assist members to achieve a sense of safety while at the same time being ready to take personal risks in the group.

When scanning the literature for what therapists say about goals, purposes or tasks, I find that the term 'purpose' is not much used. Some writers refer to goals, and some to tasks with goals implied. Some writers do not refer to goals explicitly, though goals can be inferred from what they say about how a therapist might best proceed.

For example, when discussing short-term group psychotherapy, Robert H. Klein (1993: 258) names four goals: the amelioration of distress, re-establishing a previous equilibrium, promoting the efficient use of personal resources, and increasing understanding and coping skills. These are hoped-for positive consequences for the patients. As stated, they also contain the idea that there is an agent (or some process) which supports achieving them. Malcolm Pines (1993a: 100), referring to long-term groups conducted in line with the theory and practice put forward by S.H. Foulkes, names the therapist's primary task as being to facilitate the communicative capacities of group members. I take this to mean that improved communicative capacities are personal gains in themselves and also are processes by which further gains may be achieved. Irvin Yalom (1995: xii–xiii) refers to the goals of symptomatic relief *and* characterological change which mark intensive long-term therapy groups, heterogeneously composed with respect to presenting problems. He refers also to more limited goals in shorter-term therapeutic groups composed of people who face similar problems (ibid.). These goals are preferred end-states or hoped-for positive consequences. Yvonne Agazarian (1997: 18) names, as the goal of her systems-centred therapy, enabling patients to manage their everyday lives. This statement, like Yalom's, refers to a preferred end-state.

These different conceptualisations of goals, aims and/or tasks are not alternatives to one another. One could hardly say that some are correct while others are incorrect. Each is a way of saying something about what human beings *are* and what a therapist hopes that human beings will be able to achieve or become. Some statements refer to the means by which hoped-for outcomes may be achieved, while others do not.

FURTHER QUESTIONS ARISING FROM THE STATEMENT OF OVERALL PURPOSE

The overall statement of purpose with which this chapter began refers to three issues which need further consideration: Who are these individuals whom one hopes will benefit (what kinds of people become members of groups)? How can 'benefit' be defined and conceptualised? And what it is about small face-to-face groups and what happens in them which makes a group a context in which, potentially, personal benefit can occur? These are the subjects of the next three chapters.

Chapter 2

Who are groups for?

In the preceding chapter, the overall purpose held by group therapists was stated as:

> *to enable and assist each person in a group to achieve personal benefit through making as full use as possible of the potentials of the group as a medium for help.*

One of the issues raised by this statement is: which persons? what kinds of people, how situated, can be brought into a group with the expectation that they will benefit personally? The answer, of course, is that very different kinds of people can benefit from a group experience – so many that it is helpful to have in mind some way of categorising individuals into populations and sub-populations.

Although every person, and every person's circumstances, are different from every other, populations of people can be named whose members have certain characteristics and needs in common. The categories which I shall shortly present are based on my own experience and that of members of courses on group psychotherapy and therapeutic group work. The latter were educated and trained in different parent disciplines and worked in a wide range of settings with diverse patient and client groups. A wide range of experience could thus be drawn upon when devising categories. I have tried to be as comprehensive as possible. There will always, of course, be more than one way to sort people into population categories and sub-categories. This chapter presents one way of doing so and then points to alternative ways. There are two sections: the first suggests a way of placing individuals into categories of people who might benefit from a group experience; the second indicates other ways of categorising individuals into populations.

A SUGGESTED WAY OF PLACING INDIVIDUALS INTO CATEGORIES OF PEOPLE WHO MIGHT BENEFIT FROM A GROUP EXPERIENCE

I Persons who have been functioning adequately and who would be described as 'normal' by ordinary standards but who are facing or experiencing some traumatic event which carries a threat to life or identity, and/or who continue to be affected by trauma suffered in the past

In this category are persons facing major surgery or debilitating or terminal illnesses; amputees and other accident victims; burns victims; persons who have lost hearing or vision; and so on. It also includes victims of terrorism, crime or violence; holocaust survivors and children of holocaust survivors; those who have suffered sexual abuse or violence in childhood; and those who have witnessed especially distressing events. Such people are 'victims of fate' or, if one prefers, 'victims of bad luck'. The traumatic event may have occurred recently or at some considerable time in the past with ongoing consequences, or it may not yet have occurred although those concerned know that it soon will.

Such people need opportunities to face and express their feelings about the traumatic event and its impact. They need time and space to think about how they are now placed, or will soon be placed (if the event is still in the future). They need to maintain or recover a sense of continuity of self despite current or past threats to it. They need opportunities to retrieve for themselves what it is possible to retrieve from their previous lives, and at the same time face losses which are irrecoverable. Some will need to make practical decisions. If the trauma has been very recent, some people may still be in a state of crisis and may need one-to-one support. Having emerged from this state, they may benefit from a group experience.

2 Persons who have been functioning adequately and who would be described as 'normal' by ordinary standards but who are in a close relationship with one or more others who make considerable demands on them and generate special stress

Included in this category are parents of children with physical or mental handicaps or a chronic or progressive illness; spouses or partners of persons with a terminal illness, a life-threatening illness or a chronic debilitating physical condition; spouses or partners of prisoners; adolescent children of alcoholic parents; wives of abusing husbands; parents or spouses of schizophrenics or schizoid persons living at home; adults looking after a relative with Alzheimer's disease; and so on. This is a 'linked-fate' category.

Such people need opportunities to face and express the feelings they have about themselves, the person with whom they are linked, the position they are now in and its special stresses and its rewards. Some will need to think out whether they can extricate themselves from the linked-fate relationship. Some will not wish to extricate themselves or feel able to do so. All will need to give thought to their current day-by-day life and how best to cope with its demands. Many will need to think about the future and prepare themselves for it as best they can. Some will need to make practical plans. All will profit from forming realistic judgements about their situation, finding the best possible ways to cope with it, and alleviating the stresses associated with it.

3 Persons experiencing or anticipating some life transition

This category includes people about to be discharged from psychiatric hospitals or prison; adolescents about to leave residential care; persons entering residential care or confinement in a prison or secure unit; older persons who have just retired or are about to retire from their jobs; middle-aged people who have lost their jobs and are unlikely to find another one; recent immigrants; recently divorced or bereaved people; and people who have been forcibly separated from their families or communities and have thus lost the support and the anchorage on which their identity depends.

Another kind of transition involves moving from one life stage to another, with its associated new demands, opportunities and stresses. Simply by virtue of growing older, individuals move from adolescence to early adulthood, from early adulthood to middle age, from middle age to old age, from vigorous old age to decrepit old age. Changes in life circumstances may be a part of such life transitions, such as where one lives and who one lives with, and demands on one's time, day by day. Sometimes circumstances remain essentially the same, yet a significant transition is taking place in the form of changes in internal feelings and expectations. Many people negotiate life-stage transitions seamlessly and smoothly. Others encounter problems and setbacks. Erik H. Erikson's ideas about developmental tasks associated with different life stages help one to see what successful and unsuccessful negotiation of successive life stages is about: generativity versus self-absorption in adulthood; integrity versus disgust or despair in old age; intimacy versus isolation in young adulthood; and so on (Erikson 1950).

Some transitions are self-sought, some are thrust upon people, and some are simply a part of growing older. Some can be anticipated while others are triggered by unexpected events. Many people cope well with transitions with the support of family or friends. Others need further forms of support in order to acknowledge and cope with their feelings and the new demands and stresses (or opportunities) which the transition brings. For them, a group experience may be suitable. They may need to learn new skills or acquire new information. Above all, they need to find ways to remain essentially themselves despite the changes which the transition brings or requires. Some people who face transitions are rather like those in the first category, in that they are experiencing severe discontinuity with their previous lives and a sense that their established identity is under threat.

4 Persons who may appear to outside observers to be functioning adequately but who are anxious or depressed, dissatisfied with their lives, and seen by self or others as functioning below capacity and/or behaving repeatedly in self-defeating ways

This category includes many persons who seek help from counselling centres, out-patient clinics or private practitioners. It also includes people who do not see themselves as needing help but are referred by others who regard them as functioning below capacity.

People in this category are likely to be suffering from long-term problems which have their roots in relationships and experiences in earlier life. They repeatedly find themselves in disadvantageous positions, somehow never gaining for themselves what they most want. They repeatedly engage in self-defeating behaviours. Such people need to undergo experiences which will free and unlock them from possibly life-long dysfunctional feelings, images of self, assumptions about self and others, and behaviours and choices which are repeated again and again and have become part of a firmly established life style. They need to undergo experiences which render their dysfunctional behaviour no longer necessary to them – experiences which demonstrate to them that they can safely give up behaviours, ways of presenting the self, noxious feelings and so on, which work against their own best interests. They need opportunities to follow through – that is, to practise new behaviours in diverse interpersonal settings in order firmly to establish changes in feelings, self-concept and associated behaviour.

5 Persons who need help with reference to some specific, ongoing problem, such as bulimia, anorexia, gross overweight or disabling phobias or compulsions

Some people in this category do not regard themselves as having a problem at all (for example, some anorexics) while others yearn for symptom relief.

With reference to people in this category, some therapists think primarily in terms of symptom relief and will recommend behaviour therapy or life-management approaches. Others assume that specific symptoms mask something more fundamental and longer term and/or are a way of expressing (or acting out) relationship problems. They take the view that in order to achieve symptom relief it is necessary to get in touch with and address underlying problems. If the latter view is adopted, people in this category resemble those in population category 4, just discussed.

Whether or not people in this category recognise that they have a problem, outside observers perceive that some symptom is present which is interfering with achieving life satisfactions or maintaining physical health.

6 Persons who are experiencing or have recently experienced a breakdown in functioning. Within a relatively short period of time they have become unable to function at home or at work in their customary ways

People in this category may have become acutely anxious, depressed, self-preoccupied or immobilised, to the point where they cannot carry out their ordinary activities. They have experienced some form of overload or added stress which their existing strengths and resources could not cope with, and have fallen into a seriously disadvantageous and dysfunctional emotional or mental state. Some may have been functioning well or well enough, previously, but have experienced trauma so severe that it has been impossible for them to avoid being severely affected by it. For instance they may have witnessed a serious crime or an accidental death. Others have been more fragile all along, and have been triggered into a breakdown by events which sturdier people might take in their stride. Some fragile people experience breakdown after breakdown. Such persons may be found in the reception wards of psychiatric hospitals, in the psychiatric ward of a general hospital, in residential retreats, or at home where they are supported by family members and/or a general practitioner. People in this category are in a state of acute disturbance.

One hopes that such people will achieve (or re-establish) a level of functioning which is more advantageous to them than their current state. They may need a period of protection from the stresses of everyday life and, possibly, treatment by drugs. During the period immediately following a breakdown, a group experience may be contraindicated on the grounds that events in groups cannot be controlled closely enough to avoid placing additional stresses on people who are already in a fragile state. However, once such persons have emerged from a state of acute disturbance, a group experience could prove helpful. Some people in this category may prove to need ongoing support, through a group experience on its own or through a group experience combined with or alternating with other forms of help. Some will need further help intermittently as they move through subsequent ups and downs.

7 Persons who have lost or never fully acquired basic social, interpersonal or practical skills of living

Such people characteristically and over long periods of time function at some low and unsatisfactory level. They are to be found both inside and outside institutions. This category includes some long-stay psychiatric hospital patients, 'drifters', some alcoholics, chronic offenders, and ex-psychiatric patients who have been discharged 'into the community' and are now living on their own in bed-and-breakfast accommodation or a hostel. Some live on the streets. Some drift from one emergency shelter to another.

Also in this category are physically or mentally handicapped people who have been in institutional care for long periods and for whom semi-independent life in the community is now being sought. Alternatively, one might consider that such individuals fit better into category 3, above, since they are facing a major transition.

People in this category need to move in a positive direction beyond their current level of skills, whatever that may be. Some are regarded by their carers as capable of developing useful practical and interpersonal skills. Others are judged to have sunk too far into a dysfunctional state for positive movement to occur. It can be hard to predict what a particular person can achieve until some form of help is tried. The most useful form of group will most likely employ activities and exercises directed to skill development. Responses to opportunities to develop practical and social skills provide further information about personal potentials. Some people seem to reach their limit very soon, while others show a capacity to go on changing and learning. Many people in this category require ongoing support from professional helpers who are prepared to see them through many ups and downs. Some may need practical help to extricate themselves from an unsatisfactory life style, alongside psychological help.

Some of the people described as belonging in category 6 may slip into category 7.

8 People who are regarded by others as having or being problems because they are disruptive, unruly, break laws or offend commonly held standards, or are destructive in their relationships

People in this category tend not to see themselves as having problems and typically do not seek help of their own volition. The category includes some adolescent and adult offenders, disruptive children or adolescents in schools, parents suspected of having harmed their children physically or sexually, and so on. Professionals such as social workers, health visitors, or the police have identified them as people who have already done harm to others, or are likely to do harm, or are dangerously unpredictable. Some appear to be unaware of or unconcerned about the consequences of their behaviour for others. In the language of social scientists, they violate social norms: they offend against the law, or against commonly held customs or standards.

Some of the people who fall into this category will be regarded by professionals as needing 'resocialising' – that is, they need to adopt values and norms more in line with the majority culture. Opinions will differ as to what has caused them to be in their current state: perhaps some form of developmental arrest, or brain dysfunction, or previous socialisation into a delinquent sub-culture. Whatever the antecedents, many such people are in an ongoing cycle of behaving unacceptably and thus eliciting rejection or punishment from others, especially people in authority, which in turn often leads to further unacceptable behaviour, and so on. Some may be loners, while others belong to and are supported by a deviant subculture. Individuals differ in that they may display anger, or defiance, or uncaring indifference, or pride in their deviancy. Such behaviours may mask and overlie profound insecurity and neediness.

For such people, the vicious circle needs somehow to be interrupted, and the task is an exceedingly difficult one. A group might or might not be able to provide the experiences which are needed. A great deal depends on the group's composition. If the group is homogeneously composed of similar people, then a consensus will quickly develop amongst the members that the characteristic behaviours which each displays are normal, ordinary and acceptable. There needs to be a countervailing perspective within the membership: a few people who are nearer to the majority culture or who are to some degree uneasy or ambivalent about their own behaviour or attitudes. If this is the case there is some chance that a working alliance between the therapist and the members can be established and that a group can be helpful.

9 Persons who are training to become therapists or professional helpers and who expect to make use of groups in their work

Such persons may be group workers or therapists or care workers who want to learn more about how groups function, how they themselves function in groups, and how participation in a group can help people in personal ways. They are not generally regarded by others as being in need of personal help, and may or may not so regard themselves. They need to undergo a group experience in order to gain a qualification or for the sake of professional development. Their reason for entering a group is to learn about groups. However, some people of the people in this category may have similar needs to those described under category 4, above, or they may be facing a transition or be in a linked-fate relationship. Therefore, what has been said with respect to categories 2, 3 or 4 might also apply to certain of them.

OTHER WAYS OF CATEGORISING INDIVIDUALS INTO POPULATIONS

Out in the real world there are no categories: there are only actual people, each unique and uniquely placed. When sorting people into categories, one makes judgements about perceived commonalities and gives a name to the category which summarises the presumed commonality. Categories, in other words, are not a fact of nature. They are created by people as a convenient way of organising thinking – in this case about the kinds of people who might benefit from a group experience.

It follows that there will be different ways of categorising populations. One approach, different from that presented above, would be to classify on the basis of diagnostic categories: for example, affective disorders, personality disorders, schizophrenia, the neuroses, the chronically mentally ill, and so on. Anyone choosing this route would be greatly helped by a number of contributions which appear in Kaplan and Sadock (1993): Brook on group psychotherapy with anxiety and mood disorders; Kanas on schizophrenia; Stone on the chronically mentally ill; and Azima on personality disorders. Those whose work involves them with that large and rather diverse population which lies between psychosis and neurosis (the personality disorders) may wish to think in terms of sub-categories. Roth (1982) offers six sub-categories of borderline and narcissistic patients. Azima (1993) discusses borderline personality disorder, narcissistic personality disorder, paranoid personality disorder, schizoid personality disorder, and others which belong within the general term 'personality disorder'.

Some of those who prefer to categorise in this way will accept the general term 'mental illness' as the parameter within which categorising is done. Others may wish to expand their system to include essentially 'normal' populations composed of people facing some difficult life circumstance (as in categories 1, 2 and 3, above.)

Another way to categorise people is on the basis of life stage. In broad terms one would think in terms of children, adolescents, younger and older adults, and old people. A number of sub-categories would be required to accommodate the many different states which characterise people within any life stage and the different situations in which they find themselves. Probably, transitions from one life stage to another would be included.

Any system for categorising populations will have some advantages and some disadvantages. Any set of categories will draw attention to some phenomena and give less prominence to others. For instance, because the categories I have put forward do not relate primarily to life stage, old people and adolescents do not appear as named categories. Particular adolescents, particular old people could fit into a number of the categories named above, depending on their circumstances.

Practitioners may well want to work out a categorisation system of their own. Taking the populations categories which I have described as a point of departure, they might wish to add further population categories, or sub-categories. Or they might find it useful to sub-divide further, into sub-sub-categories. Alternatively, they might wish to work out a different set of categories altogether. For instance, those whose work involves them primarily with medically ill people will most likely want to make this a major category with a number of sub-categories. They will find Spira's (1997) book on group therapy for medically ill patients useful. Those whose work involves them with women's groups, or problems associated with position in society, or conflicts between ethnic groups may wish to devise a set of categories which gives prominence to these populations. Some will wish to make race, colour, gender or culture a basis for categorising populations.

However it is done, thinking in terms of categories and sub-categories assists in seeing the wide range of people who might possibly benefit from one or another form of group experience. It is worth pointing out that, although categories are useful, two unjustified assumptions need to be avoided: first, that every person within a category will profit from a group experience; and second, that groups should invariably be composed of people who belong in the same category or sub-category. These are planning issues, and will be taken further in Chapter 6.

Chapter 3

Defining 'benefit'

It was said in Chapter 1 that:

> *a group therapist's overall purpose is to enable and assist each individual in a group to achieve personal benefit through making as full use as possible of the potentials of the group as a medium for help.*

One of the issues raised by this statement is, of course: what is benefit? how can benefit best be defined for broad populations of people, for sub-populations, and for individuals?

References to 'benefit' have already been made in the previous chapter. With respect to each population category, comments were made about what members of the population 'need' in order to achieve the kind of gain most relevant to them. Such statements were made as: 'They may need to learn new skills or acquire new information'; 'they may profit from exploring what the transition means to them'; 'they may need to undergo experiences which render their dysfunctional behaviour no longer necessary to them'. These statements refer to what 'benefit' can be said to consist of for people in particular population categories.

In this chapter I shall look more closely at 'benefit' and 'gain', beginning by presenting a list of personal gains which individuals could, possibly, achieve through participating in one or another kind of therapeutic group. Such a list shows that potential gains are quite diverse. One sees immediately that what would be a significant gain for one person, or one population of people, is irrelevant to others. After a list of potential gains has been presented, a framework is introduced for thinking about what constitutes 'benefit' for particular populations of people, sub-populations and individuals.

This chapter is organised into the following sections:

- Potential personal gains.
- Thinking about benefit in terms of 'current state' and 'preferred state'.
- Three useful concepts for thinking more specifically about benefit: 'life space'; 'preoccupying concern' and 'frontier'.

- Thinking in terms of what is *potentially achievable* for particular populations, sub-populations and individuals.
- Recognising that a fuller understanding of what would constitute benefit for each individual necessarily has to be postponed until after a group comes into being, when more information becomes available.

POTENTIAL PERSONAL GAINS

- Feeling less isolated – that is, reducing the sense of being alone with respect to own feelings or circumstances or history, feeling that no one else experiences anything similar and that no one else can really understand.
- Getting things 'off one's chest': experiencing catharsis.
- Feeling more acceptable to others.
- Feeling more hopeful about the future: developing a sense that things can change for the better, or that it will become possible to cope better with that which will not change.
- Maintaining a sense of being the person one has always been and still is, even though personal circumstances may have changed drastically; experiencing continuity of the self.
- Facing what requires facing; facing the previously unfaceable; strengthening one's resolve to acknowledge and deal with difficult real-life circumstances; gaining courage.
- Revising previously held assumptions about oneself and/or others; thinking differently and more realistically about oneself and about people in one's salient world; revising one's model-of-self-and-surroundings.
- Developing a more positive view about oneself: feeling better about oneself; appreciating oneself.
- Developing an understanding, or a fuller and more accurate understanding, of the consequences of one's own behaviours, for oneself and for others.
- Experiencing fear, guilt or shame when appropriate to circumstances, and not experiencing them when not appropriate. For many people this will mean feeling less anxious, less fearful, less guilty, less ashamed. For others, who have disregarded the impact of their behaviour on others, it will mean feeling more guilt or shame at times.
- Developing an understanding, or a fuller and more accurate understanding, of how past experiences have, up to now, influenced the present.
- Owning feelings and experiences which have previously been denied or pushed aside. Accepting parts of the self or of past experience which have been felt, previously, to be unacceptable or intolerable.
- Learning new ways and acquiring new skills. Finding better ways to cope with practical tasks and everyday encounters with others.
- Seeing new possibilities: realising that one does not have to go on as one always has; becoming able to relinquish disadvantageous or self-defeating behaviours

and life styles; freeing oneself from 'the tyranny of the past': turning oneself around and heading in some other, more advantageous direction.
- Trying out new behaviours more advantageous to self and others and making them a part of one's repertoire.
- Experiencing personal gratification through being helpful to others.

For certain populations and for particular individuals, some gains will be more important than others. For some people, for instance, relief from a sense of isolation or learning new practical skills are substantial gains in themselves. For others, such gains will not be at the cutting edge of their needs, for they do not feel particularly isolated and they already have satisfactory practical skills. For some, a particular kind of gain might be an interim achievement needed in order to move towards further forms of gain.

It is evident that in addition to having in mind potential gains, one needs to think out *which* gains or benefit are relevant to *whom*.

THINKING ABOUT BENEFIT IN TERMS OF 'CURRENT STATE' AND 'PREFERRED STATE'

The population categories presented and discussed in the previous chapter include very different kinds of people in quite different circumstances. Some have considerable personal resources and some have few. All can be thought of as being in some less than satisfactory 'current state'. For each population category, another, different state can be imagined which would place those concerned in a better position. This better position can be referred to as a 'preferred state'. Because the 'current state' is different, the 'preferred state' will also be different for different population categories.

For instance, for one population the current state can be described as being without satisfactory ways of coping with some new and unusual stress-generating circumstance. The preferred state can be thought of as the expansion of coping skills to meet the requirements of the new situation. 'Benefit' will consist of acquiring new coping skills. New understandings and/or new ways of thinking about the self may also be involved.

For other populations, the current state consists in being locked into anxiety or depression, or chronically low levels of self-esteem, or self-defeating behaviours which are repeated again and again and which work against achieving personal rewards and satisfactions. The preferred state is, clearly, extrication from such personally disadvantageous feeling states or behaviours. Depressed individuals would become less so; persons who persistently behave in self-defeating ways would manage to abandon such behaviour; self-deprecating persons would learn to value themselves; phobic people would relinquish their fears.

For still other populations, the current state can be described as lacking practical or interpersonal skills for everyday living – skills which have never developed in the first place or which have been lost following a personal breakdown or prolonged mental illness. The preferred state can be defined as establishing or re-establishing necessary skills and making them a firm and accessible part of a personal repertoire. Such people need to learn how to prepare meals for themselves, use money, converse with shop-keepers, hold down a job without spoiling things for themselves. They need to feel more comfortable and be more competent in their personal worlds.

Some people are in a very precarious current state. They are very vulnerable and at risk of deterioration or fragmentation. 'Benefit' consists in forestalling further deterioration or fragmentation and, if possible, achieving more satisfactory levels of functioning.

Some people are caught up in whole life styles which incline them towards violence or crime. They damage others, or terrorise them, or cause them misery. They may draw down upon themselves punitive responses from others, including the courts. They may in consequence lose their personal liberty. For them, the preferred state consists of a shift away from a whole life style.

It will be seen from the above discussion that 'benefit' can consist of (a) moving from some current state which works against a person's well-being and effectiveness to something more advantageous for that person; (b) expanding coping skills for dealing with stress generating circumstances and/or experiencing relief and support through sharing feelings and experiences with others who are similarly placed; or (c) maintaining a current state which, while unsatisfactory, is at risk of becoming worse.

The terms 'current state' and 'preferred state' are applicable to broad categories of people as well as to population sub-categories and individuals. They should, however, be thought of as a first approximation, for when planning a group and then working with the people in it, one needs to conceptualise benefit in more detail.

THREE USEFUL CONCEPTS FOR THINKING MORE SPECIFICALLY ABOUT BENEFIT: 'LIFE SPACE', 'PREOCCUPYING CONCERN' AND 'FRONTIER'

Life space

The term and concept *life space* is taken from the work of Kurt Lewin. It is a concept with wide application: to individuals, to social groups, and to different social groups in contact with or in conflict with one another. When applied to individuals it refers to a person's contemporary experiential world (which includes representations of the past and representations of and hopes for the future) (see Lewin 1951: 188–207, and references to 'life space' in Marrow 1969.) Lewin depicted life space graphically as an oval, with sub-spaces within it.

When conceptualising 'benefit' for members of a sub-population or for individuals, it is useful to focus on what lies inside the life space, what lies outside it, and the nature of the boundaries between what is inside and outside the life space.

Inside are particular skills, understandings and personal capacities; prevailing feelings, hopes, expectations, fears; images of self and of significant other people; diverse personal and social resources; and certain life circumstances, some of which may be stress-generating. 'Current state' is defined by what is inside the life space.

Outside the life space are skills, understandings and so on not yet achieved or not yet accessible. Some of these define benefit. When thinking of an individual, there is something outside the life space which the person does not have yet, but would benefit from acquiring. When thinking collectively about sub-populations, there is something outside the life space of its members which they do not yet have but likewise would benefit from acquiring. Some of what lies outside the life space is not related to benefit. For instance, a particular skill or capability, such as climbing a mountain, may lie outside a person's current capacities but achieving that skill would not be a benefit since it is irrelevant to the person's sense of well-being and outside his or her personal ambitions and hopes.

Boundaries exist between what is inside and outside the life space. Some of these boundaries are easy to cross, others difficult, still others impossible. Thinking in terms of physical analogies, some boundaries are like an open field, others are like a thick forest, while still others are like a cliff edge. Because there is virtually always more than one significant boundary, I find it useful to represent life space as a multiple-sided figure – for instance a hexagon or pentagon. Each of the lines marks a part of the boundary between what is inside the life space and what is outside it.

With this image in mind, one could think of benefit as crossing a boundary into some area currently beyond the life space, which would bring advantage to an individual, or to a sub-population of people similarly placed. Another way of putting this is to think of extending a boundary so that the new boundary includes, and brings into the life space, something new which was not previously there. One could also think of thrusting something which is currently inside the life space (an unwanted stressor) outside it, into territory beyond the boundary.

Preoccupying concern

Inside the life space there may be preoccupying concerns. This term refers to any situation, worry or issue which is never far from a person's thoughts. Sometimes such a preoccupation arises in response to some event or circumstance which is new to the person, which is outside his or her life experience so far. Or the preoccupation is long-term and ongoing. Or the preoccupation could be about something which has not occurred yet but which a person has good reason to believe will occur. An event could be positively sought after and anticipated with pleasure (for example, emigration) and still be a preoccupying concern. Not everyone has a preoccupying concern in the sense meant here, but many do.

A severely preoccupied person may experience worries or concerns which are more than he or she can manage, or which are managed only at great cost. He or she may feel and be immobilised and may have lost any sense of being able to cope. Being dominated by a preoccupying concern soaks up time and energy, and often confronts an individual with tasks or feelings which are beyond his or her current coping capacities. For individuals beset by a preoccupying concern, benefit will consist of finding better and more effective ways of dealing with it. Thinking in terms of life space, some skill, some new understanding, some practical resource may need to be acquired and made a part of the life space.

Frontiers

The lines in a multi-sided figure which mark the boundaries of a life space can be thought of as *frontiers*. The term *frontier* is of course a metaphor. In its literal sense it is applied to political or natural boundaries which may be easy or difficult to cross for a variety of reasons: the political boundary is undefended and unmanned; the mountain range is rugged and presents difficult obstacles; some counter-force such as a border patrol prevents easy movement across the boundary.

As a metaphor, the term frontier can be applied to individuals and to collectivities of people similarly placed. Individuals faced with a personal frontier or boundary may want desperately to cross it or may not care at all about doing so, or there may be someone else who thinks they *ought* to cross it. They may find the frontier easy to cross or enormously difficult, have the equipment necessary to cross the boundary or lack it. There may be strong counter-forces which get in the way of moving beyond a frontier.

For any individual, or any sub-population, there will most likely be multiple frontiers, with still more frontiers beyond. This is the reason for adopting a multi-sided figure to represent the life space. As an example, for people about to be released from prison, one important frontier to cross might be acquiring new skills which would increase employability. Another might be moving towards getting re-established in day-to-day living within the family. Still another might be finding a peer group which supports law-abiding behaviour. For some, avoiding slipping back into alcoholism might be a frontier in the sense that a gain already achieved needs to be maintained in a new social context where counter-forces might be present.

Further frontiers may exist beyond the ones immediately in view. That is, certain frontiers, once crossed, may reveal some further frontier which it would also be beneficial to move beyond.

These three concepts – life space, preoccupying concern and frontier – help us to see in more detail what is meant by current and preferred state. Of these three concepts, life space and frontier have broader application than preoccupying concern. Every individual can be described in terms of his or her life space, and frontiers can likewise be identified for everyone. Only some individuals, however, can be said to have a preoccupying concern in the sense meant here.

THE IMPORTANCE OF THINKING IN TERMS OF WHAT IS POTENTIALLY ACHIEVABLE FOR PARTICULAR POPULATIONS, SUB-POPULATIONS AND INDIVIDUALS

Some of what lies beyond a frontier is so far beyond it that it is unrealistic to think that it can be reached, at least not in a single move. Other skills, understandings and so on which are *just* beyond a frontier are potentially achievable, nearly within grasp. Thinking in terms of life space, boundaries or frontiers and preoccupying concerns draws attention to the next most useful and potentially achievable step for members of a sub-population and for each individual. Thinking in these terms guards against applying universal criteria which may be pertinent to some populations (or sub-populations or individuals) but not to others. It guards against harbouring unrealistic hopes and thinking too idealistically.

Most people have the capacity to move beyond current frontiers or find better ways to deal with a preoccupying concern. For many people it is important to try, for *where they are now* – their current state – is unsatisfying, dysfunctional, gets them into trouble or is dangerous to others.

What has been said here about how benefit can be conceptualised has implications for planning. Once one has decided on the sub-population with which one intends to work, one can think about that sub-population in terms of current and preferred state, life space, frontier and preoccupying concern. Usually, one knows enough about a sub-population, through previous experience or through reading, to make provisional formulations in these terms. This should assist in thinking about whether or not a group is likely to be a useful and usable route towards achieving benefit, and if so, the sort of group structure likely to be suitable.

RECOGNISING THAT A FULLER UNDERSTANDING OF WHAT WOULD CONSTITUTE BENEFIT FOR EACH INDIVIDUAL NECESSARILY HAS TO BE POSTPONED UNTIL AFTER A GROUP COMES INTO BEING, WHEN MORE INFORMATION BECOMES AVAILABLE

When a therapist gets to know individual group members better through their participation in a group, it becomes possible to think much more specifically about what might constitute benefit for each. The concepts introduced in this chapter remain useful. One can begin to think about just what, beyond a current frontier, it would be useful for each group member to move towards. One can begin to identify just which aspect of an hypothesised preoccupying concern is important for a particular individual. Ideas about what is likely to constitute benefit for each group member will be held provisionally at first. As time goes on, more information usually becomes available and the therapist's understanding of each person expands.

Formulations of 'benefit' can be revised and updated. Improving one's understanding of each person and of what would constitute benefit for him or her is one of the issues discussed in Chapter 8, which has to do with a therapist's internal 'think-work' while conducting a group.

There are two further issues which require attention before moving into planning and conducting groups: the nature of small face-to-face groups and what happens in them (to be discussed in Chapter 4); and sets of ideas – that is, theory – which can be applied to understanding groups (the subject of Chapter 5).

Chapter 4

Small face-to-face groups

The statement of overall purpose put forward in Chapter 1 included making *as full use as possible of the potentials of the group as a medium* for help. This clearly points to a need to understand the properties and characteristics of small face-to-face groups as a preliminary to understanding how a group can be used to help people in personal ways.

Group dynamics, as a field of study, focuses on the properties of groups and on interactive events which occur within groups. Interest in the dynamics of groups was at its height in the later 1940s, the 1950s and 1960s. It was spearheaded by Kurt Lewin (1948, 1951), the 'father of group dynamics', and was carried forward by his students and colleagues and, later, by others. Those who sought to understand small groups were, for the most part, interested in work groups, task groups and working teams – that is, groups which had some external goal. Some focused on classroom groups, neighbourhood groups or groups of children in summer camps.

This chapter discusses some of what has been learned through investigations of small face-to-face groups. It is organised as follows:

- Group level phenomena: goals; norms and shared beliefs; themes, agenda items, and the idea of the 'hidden agenda'; moods, atmospheres and emotional contagion; cohesiveness; and change and development.
- Inside the group: leaders and leadership functions; personal roles; sociometric choice and sub-grouping; communication patterns, cueing and altercasting.
- The group dynamics literature and summaries written for group therapists.
- Further theory needed by group psychotherapists.

GROUP-LEVEL PHENOMENA

Goals

Those who participate in work groups will have some agreed, external goal, such as developing a curriculum or planning a marketing strategy. These are usually referred to as goals *of the group*. More precisely and accurately, they are goals held in common by the members and explicitly acknowledged by them. Such goals are often stated in a group's constitution, or 'mission statement'. They pertain to what the members hope to accomplish in the outside world.

In addition to declared and agreed external goals, members may hold in common goals pertaining to the internal functioning of the group, such as making good use of the expertise of individual members, maintaining a supportive atmosphere, developing satisfactory ways of dealing with internal conflict, working efficiently, and so on. Goals which have to do with how groups function are not always articulated explicitly and they are unlikely to be referred to in a mission statement.

Sub-groups do not always form within a group; but if they do, the members of one sub-group may hold goals which are different from, and sometimes in conflict with, goals held by members of other sub-groups. Individuals in a group also hold personal goals which may or may not fit well with the group's publicly stated goals or the goals of any sub-group. An individual might, for instance, want to get ahead in the organisation, or get some particular item on to the agenda, or show him- or herself to be superior to the others, or be well regarded by the chairperson. Personally held, individual goals are unlikely to be stated publicly and they may or may not be recognised and acknowledged by those who hold them.

Goals and motivation are linked. Individuals, and members collectively, hold certain goals and are motivated to try to achieve them. Conflict – either overt or covert – may occur when certain individuals or sub-groups pursue their goals in ways which make it difficult for other individuals or sub-groups to achieve *their* goals.

Because so many different kinds of goals can be present simultaneously, the term *goal system* is often employed.

Norms and shared beliefs

The term norm refers to behaviours regarded by members as either acceptable and appropriate, or unacceptable and inappropriate. For instance, a norm might exist in a group that everyone should have a chance to talk and express an opinion. Or a norm might pertain to how anger may be expressed: directly, or through sarcasm, joking or some other means. Some norms are explicit, some implicit. Some are brought into the group from the wider culture. If members belong to different outside sub-cultures, incompatible norms may be brought into the group. Many norms are specific to a particular group. They emerge through interaction and may take time to evolve.

The term 'shared belief' refers to points of view, opinions, attitudes and versions of 'reality' accepted by group members as 'truth'. Shared beliefs may be about what 'we' are like, what others are like, what can be expected from others and so on. As with norms, some shared beliefs are brought in from cultures outside the group while others evolve through members' interactions. A shared belief may or may not be a good fit with 'reality' as understood by people outside the group. For instance, members of a cult may firmly believe that the world will end on a certain date, a belief which will seem bizarre to outsiders but entirely plausible to members of the in-group.

Both norms and shared beliefs have regulatory functions in groups. Once established, they declare what is acceptable and unacceptable behaviour, what is 'true' and what is 'untrue'. If norms and shared beliefs are supported by a firm consensus they have considerable force and power. They can be very difficult to dislodge because the norm or the belief becomes a 'given' which is taken for granted. The norm or the belief is experienced as a fact of nature or a universal truth and is not recognised as something created and maintained by members. When everyone believed that the sun revolved around the earth, this was experienced not as a belief, but as a fact. Consensus lends force to a norm and validity to a belief.

Members who deviate from a norm or an otherwise accepted belief are commonly put under pressure to conform.

Themes, agenda items and the idea of the 'hidden agenda'

Work groups usually proceed by working through a list of agenda items. These may have been formulated by the chairperson or worked out collaboratively by the members. Agenda items are stated explicitly and everyone knows what they are.

In addition to explicitly stated agenda items, themes may evolve in a group which may coincide with agenda items, be present side by side with them, or conflict with them. A theme is an issue or a concern which dominates the attention of group members for a period of time, during a part of a session or over several sessions. It is *about* something. All themes have content and most also involve feelings of one kind or another.

Some themes are covert and are not recognised by members as being present or an influence on the group. A covert theme can intrude into a discussion meant to be focused on some agenda item. Anyone who has ever been in or heard about a staff group which spent twenty minutes discussing who should make the coffee knows that this can happen. Sometimes a covert theme is expressed through the manner in which an agenda item is discussed. For instance, in and through a discussion of some item of business, any of the following could be expressed: competitive feelings amongst the members; collusive attempts to place blame on one person; anger with the chairperson. In work groups, norms are usually present which prevent covert themes from being acknowledged and discussed openly. The expression 'hidden agenda' is sometimes used to refer to a covert theme. An issue which is important to the members but not acknowledged by them, is 'hidden' behind some manifest content which on the face of it is different from the theme which is preoccupying members.

Moods, atmospheres and emotional contagion

It is part of our ordinary use of language to make such comments as: 'It was a tense meeting', or 'The class was in a rebellious mood', or 'Apathy hung in the air'. It cannot literally be the case that a group has a mood since a group is not an organism capable of feeling. Yet such comments are in some sense correct in that there are times when particular moods or atmospheres develop in a group which are prevalent or widespread.

Group moods and atmospheres are expressed in what is said, how things are said and how people behave non-verbally. A mood or atmosphere builds up from the interactions of members. It may or may not be triggered by an outside event.

One can judge that there is a rebellious mood in a group (or one that is confident, depressed, apathetic, panicky and so on) without necessarily assuming that every single person present is experiencing the same feelings. One judges that there is a *prevailing* mood in the group, being expressed in behaviour by a number of persons. Some members may not participate actively but may nevertheless share in the mood (as might be shown by non-verbal behaviour). Some may not share in the mood but at the same time do not counter it through their behaviour.

Some moods are transient. Some become an abiding feature of a group. Individuals both influence and are influenced by a group's atmosphere or prevailing mood. One frightened person or one very excited person can trigger similar feelings in others. Many people have had the experience of entering a group in which a tense atmosphere was already established, and soon found that they were beginning to feel tense themselves. The same can be said of such atmospheres and moods as depression, fearfulness, hopefulness and so on.

Sometimes, in a group, moods and associated behaviours spring up so quickly as to seem instantaneous. The term *contagion*, which strictly speaking refers to the spread of a disease, is often used as a metaphor to refer to the rapid spread of a mood or a form of behaviour in a group. Fritz Redl observed this in groups of children. He accounted for it as follows: when contagion occurs in a group there is an initiator and there are imitators. In order for contagion to occur there must exist an acute conflict area within the imitators which involves strong impulses towards expressing some feeling and at the same time strong pressure from ego or superego forces to suppress the impulse. The impulse towards expressing the feeling is barely held in check by the pressures to inhibit it. Within the initiator there must be a similar strong urge towards the expression of an impulse but at the same time weak inhibiting forces. If this combination occurs, then the initiator who expresses some strong affect releases others to express the same feeling without fear or guilt, through a little understood process which Redl calls 'magical exculpation through the initiatory act'. It is generally recognised that the one who casts the first stone is commonly held to be more guilty than those who follow with exactly the same behaviour. (The frequently heard childhood plaint, 'but s/he did it first', is well known to parents and teachers.) Another way of stating Redl's argument is that in order for feelings and behaviours to become contagious, the same impulse must be present in at least a latent form in everyone in a group but one member must have a lower threshold for expressing it than the others. Under these conditions, that person functions as a trigger for the others, giving 'permission' to others to express the same feeling or behaviour (Redl 1966b).

Cohesiveness

The word cohesiveness is not in either of the two dictionaries which I regularly consult (*Shorter Oxford English Dictionary* and *Longman's Dictionary of the English Language*). Cohesion and cohesive both appear, but the meanings assigned to them are from physics and biology. To cohere is defined (*Longman*) as 'to hold together firmly as parts of the same mass, *broadly*, stick or adhere'. Dictionary definitions make it clear that when the idea of 'cohesiveness' is applied to groups, it is being used as a metaphor. When a term is transposed from the realm in which it originated to some other realm, one has to ask oneself: In what sense does the original definition apply to this new situation to which it is being applied? In this case, one needs to ask: In what sense do members of groups 'hold firmly together as parts of the same mass'?

I have started with dictionary definitions because the phenomenon of cohesiveness, while generally acknowledged to be a characteristic or a property of groups, appears to be complex and hence open to different definitions and interpretations.

Cartwright and Zander (1960) use the term 'cohesiveness' and speak of 'groupness' and 'we-ness'. They refer to such indicators of cohesiveness as loyalty to the group and readiness to work towards group goals, taking responsibility for group tasks, and defending the group against attack or criticism by outsiders. They suggest that three different meanings can be distinguished: attraction to the group; members' motivation to participate; and coordination of members' efforts.

Yalom places great emphasis on cohesiveness as a phenomenon and as a concept relevant to group psychotherapy. He regards cohesiveness in group therapy as the analogue of relationship in individual therapy. He refers to it as a complex and abstruse variable and defines it as:

> the resultant of all the forces acting on all the members to remain in the group, or, more simply, the attractiveness of a group for its members. It refers to the condition of members feeling warmth and comfort in the group, feeling they belong, valuing the group and feeling, in turn, that they are valued and unconditionally accepted and supported by other members.
>
> (Yalom 1995: 48)

By this definition, cohesiveness refers to the phenomenon and the experience of sticking together as members of a group, as well as to associated emotional states of members.

The core idea of cohesiveness seems to be the attractiveness of the group for its members. Different writers, however, draw into this concept many or fewer associated phenomena. In other words, different writers locate the boundary around the concept differently. Thus, different emphases and glosses have been put on the term.

My particular gloss is that a cohesive group is one in which the members experience a clear sense of belonging to the group, find the group appealing and attractive, and are quite clear as to who is and who is not a member. In such groups the boundary around the group is clear and relatively impermeable. Insiders stay in and outsiders stay out. Members feel that they belong to the group and they distinguish themselves from outsiders who do not belong. Leaving the group is a visible and noted act and entry into the group is likewise visible and noted.

In contrast to this, a group marked by low cohesiveness has more permeable boundaries. It is less obvious to the members and to others just who is a member of the group and who is not, who belongs in the group and who does not. The group means less to the members. It is easy to leave the group, and if someone leaves it is regarded by all concerned as an event of relatively little importance. Similarly it is a relatively unremarked event when someone new comes into the group. Being absent or late is not only tolerated but may hardly be noticed.

Cohesiveness is not, of course, a fixed characteristic: a given group may exhibit different degrees of cohesiveness in the course of its life.

Change and development

Utter stability in a group over time – that is, no change at all – is unlikely because groups are never entirely free of influences from events in the environment, changes in the membership, and changes in the state and circumstances of individual members.

Although all groups tend to change over time, only some groups can be said to 'develop'. The term *change* refers to shifting from one state to another, and then perhaps back again or to still another state, without any detectable overall direction. The term *development*, in contrast, implies change in some identifiable direction, even if temporary reversals occur. One usually thinks of development as being from some unformed state to some more coherent state supportive of the group's task. If all goes well in a work group, it becomes a more effective instrument for getting tasks done, with less 'wheel-spin'. However, it should be kept in mind that a group could also develop towards some unfavourable state, analogous to the development of a disease.

There have been many attempts to describe developmental stages in groups. Bales and Strodtbeck (1951) worked out a phase theory of group problem-solving. They posit a movement from *initiating* a discussion of a problem which requires a group decision to *completion* of it. This is a continuous process, yet phases can be identified within it which move from orientation, then evaluation, and then control. Bales and Strodtbeck worked out a twelve-category observation system which they used to track a group through the problem-solving process. Another formulation of group development was worked out by Bennis and Shepard (1956). They posit an overall movement from dependence to interdependence. Each of these two main phases includes sub-phases. The final sub-phase of phase II is named as 'consensual validation', in which interdependency problems are resolved.

Some comments about the six group-level properties just discussed

All these terms used in the previous sub-sections are *concepts*. They are not directly observable phenomena. What can be observed about a group consists of sequences of verbal and non-verbal behaviour. From such observations one can infer that certain norms are in operation, that cohesiveness is high or low, and so on. Norms, cohesiveness and the like are ways of conceptualising events. They are not the events themselves.

These six properties differ somewhat in their complexity and in how easy or difficult it is to see their connections with observable events. Norms, for instance, can be fairly readily grasped by observing consistencies in members' behaviours. Some goals are quite visible, being overtly expressed and publicly acknowledged. Others can be fairly readily inferred from observed behaviour. Still others remain concealed and inaccessible to an observer except by inferential leaps which may be hard to defend. Group development is so complex and multi-faceted that different theorists can and do define and conceptualise development differently.

Although these group properties and processes have been discussed separately, they interact with and influence one another. For instance, a group marked by low cohesiveness will develop differently from a highly cohesive group and indeed may fail to 'develop' at all, though it certainly will change. Norms which place narrow boundaries around what may be acknowledged and discussed constrain both the themes which emerge and the manner in which members explore them. A group which is stuck in a mood of apathy is unlikely to develop in a favourable way. And so on.

It should be pointed out that group properties could be categorised differently. At one stage in writing this chapter, I made norms and shared beliefs separate categories, and then decided later that they belonged together. Had they remained separate, there would have been seven properties of groups, not six. Scheidlinger has provided a list of 'group dynamics (process) factors in small groups' which includes twelve items. He includes four of the six which I have presented above (cohesiveness, norms, climate, development); does not include goals or themes; lists values (defined as beliefs and myths) as a separate category rather than together with norms, as I have done; and adds the further categories of individual person-alities in interaction; group boundaries; leadership; role differentiation; patterns of communication; and sub-groupings (Scheidlinger 1997: 153). I have preferred to locate some of Scheidlinger's latter categories under a different heading (see following section).

I call attention to these differences to show that the 'pie' of group-level phenomena can be cut in a number of different ways. Indeed, there can be differences of opinion as to what belongs inside and outside the pie. Different ways of classification emphasise different aspects of groups and represent different perceived connections amongst them.

INSIDE THE GROUP

Leaders and leadership functions

Most groups have an official or designated leader. Certain responsibilities are attached to this role, but how individual leaders carry out their responsibilities differs widely. It is a matter of observation that different people occupy the leadership role in different ways – hence, the phenomenon of leadership styles. The style adopted by the leader of a group influences the character of the group and the experiences which individuals have in groups. This was demonstrated early in the history of group dynamics as a field of study. In a now-classic series of experiments, Lewin, Lippitt and White studied three leadership styles – autocratic, democratic, and *laissez faire* – and their effects on climate, member behaviour and member satisfaction (see Lewin *et al.* 1939, White and Lippitt 1960).

How a person functions as a leader is a product of demands which derive from his or her official role in interaction with personal preferences and needs. Leaders may or may not recognise that they *have* a style, though others can discern their style by noting consistencies in their behaviour. Personal needs which influence style may operate outside awareness.

Those interested in group dynamics distinguished between 'the leader' – that is, the person who is the official and recognised leader of the group – and 'leadership behaviour or functions' which might be carried out by the official leader or by others in the group. Leadership behaviour, if factored out, includes summarising, encouraging participation, testing for consensus, supporting morale, dealing with intra-group conflict, providing information, keeping members focused on the task, and so on. It will be seen that certain leadership behaviours pertain directly to working on the task while others pertain to supporting the group as an instrument for getting work done. Leadership behaviour of one sort or another can be performed by members as well as by the designated leader of the group – hence the term 'distributed leadership'. In a group, it is not only the leader who leads. Different members at different times also perform leadership functions.

The official leader nevertheless retains special influence. Reasons include: the leader holds real power over members in the form of 'fate-control'; members make assumptions about the leader's power and expertise and how he or she will use it, and then behave in line with their assumptions; and the leader often holds information unavailable to the members.

Sometimes an individual, whether the official leader or a member, comes to occupy a central position in a group. Fritz Redl (1966a) developed the idea of the 'central person' – the person around whom emotional processes coalesce and who is central to some dynamic which currently prevails in a group. Redl, who was working with groups of children, identified ten types of central person, and emphasised that it is sometimes the official leader of the group who functions as a central person but that, often, it is one or another of the members. Amongst Redl's list of central persons are 'the central person as object of aggressive drives'; 'the seducer' (who is the first to behave in some unacceptable and usually suppressed way and by so doing permits or makes it safe for others to behave similarly); and 'the hero', who dares to be the first to take a risk, again allowing others to take similar risks.

Personal roles, cueing and altercasting

In any group, individuals try to find a niche for themselves in which they feel comfortable and safe and, if possible, rewarded. For instance, some persons immediately seek a position of power and influence and quickly make themselves and their views known to the others. Others seek a peripheral position and only feel comfortable if they are allowed to occupy it. Individuals may be allowed by others to occupy their preferred position in a group, or they may be challenged by others or prevented by them from being the kind of person they want to be in the group.

When seeking to occupy some particular interpersonal role or position in a group, individuals engage in 'cueing' behaviour. These cues, which are conveyed in what they say and how and when they say it, direct others to 'think of me in *this* way, not in *that* way'; 'allow me to behave in *this* way, not in *that* way'; 'support me in who I want to be in this group and in how I want to participate'. Of course, no one says such things directly or overtly. Instead, 'messages' are sent to others through what a person says and does. A person can engage in cueing behaviour without being aware of doing so. Others may respond to cues or else ignore or fail to register them.

Some people are quite consistent in the cues they offer to others. For instance, they persistently present themselves as knowing all that needs to be known, or as needing advice, or as being very touchy and sensitive to any hint of disapproval.

Sometimes an individual is pressed into some role or position by others – for instance, into the role of scapegoat, or expert adviser, or person-of-no-account. This is sometimes referred to as 'altercasting'. One person, the 'alter', is cast into some position by the behaviour of others. That person may relish the role and may even have invited it, or may desperately want to escape from it. Complex dynamics are involved, for it is not simply a matter of others 'doing something' to the person who is so cast. The person may, through his or her own cueing behaviour, invite the altercasting which occurs or, though not initiating it, may accept the role and behave in line with it. Roles and positions may be transient or more abiding.

Sociometric choice and sub-grouping

As group members get to know each other, they develop particular feelings towards one another, both positive and negative, and particular preferences. Social psychologists refer to interpersonal preferences as 'sociometric choice'. Such preferences may or may not be reciprocated. They may involve just two people in pair relationships, or they may bind people together into clusters (for example, sub-groups).

When participating in a work group, one often comes to realise that one can count on certain people for support, while others are virtually certain to raise questions about one's suggestions, opposing them or criticising them either directly or in some subtle way. One may notice preferences in oneself. For example, one may realise that one listens carefully to certain people and takes their comments seriously, while paying less attention to others and expecting little of them.

Interpersonal affinities and antagonisms may lead to the establishment of sub-groups: three or more persons who, as it were, cluster together because they share personal goals, or assumptions about how a group should proceed, or similar or complementary role-preferences. Sub-groups may exist in harmony with one another, or they may compete and conflict with one another. In work groups, intra-group conflict often focuses around disagreements about policy or over strategies for achieving external goals. Some groups are seriously split in ways which make it difficult for the group as a whole to work effectively in pursuit of its official goals.

Communication patterns

Alex Bavelas (1950) identified a number of communication patterns which can occur in groups. For instance, each member may address him- or herself exclusively to the designated leader, or members may freely address one another, or one member may occupy a central position in a communication network: others address comments to him or her, or to others *through* the person who is in the centre. Bavelas conducted experiments in which communication patterns were constrained by allowing communication between some members and preventing it between others. This was done by erecting physical barriers between some group members while allowing others to have open access to one another. Through such experiments, Bavelas studied the effects of different communication patterns on problem-solving, member morale and commitment, and individuals' insight into the problem confronting the group. Although the communication patterns which Bavelas studied were contrived, comparable patterns arise in groups which operate in natural settings.

Bavelas concentrated on the *structures* within which communication occurs. One can also examine communication *processes*. When one looks closely at successive comments and contributions in groups by different group members, one often sees that communication occurs in chains. Each person is influenced by what has gone before: adding something, ignoring some part of preceding comments, selecting something to respond to and to emphasise. Sometimes, members respond primarily to the emotion contained in a contribution rather than to its content. Sometimes a comment harks back to something which has been said earlier. Sometimes a person says something which seems unrelated to anything that has gone before. If this happens, it may initiate a shift in the conversation or it may be lost in the group because no one responds to it.

Such sequences of interactions are summarised by the term 'associative processes' or 'associative flow'. Comments within an associative flow may pertain to the avowed task. They may also refer to, or reveal, affective issues within the group, such as conflicts or alliances between members.

Each individual contributes to associative processes in his or her own way, driven by personal interests, concerns and needs. They will seek to influence the group in particular directions, sometimes realising that they are doing so, sometimes not.

Recognising that associational processes occur in groups helps one to see how it is that what emerges as features of a group are the product of the interactions of individuals. Of the group properties discussed earlier, themes, acknowledged shared goals, norms, shared beliefs, and moods and atmospheres are all generated by associative processes amongst members. So also are level of cohesiveness and the course of a group's development, but as these are more complex processes, they are less easy to track.

THE GROUP DYNAMICS LITERATURE AND SUMMARIES WRITTEN FOR GROUP THERAPISTS

The literature on group dynamics is vast, rich and varied. Those who are interested in original sources may want to read Lewin's own writings (1948, 1951), or compendia such as those compiled by Cartwright and Zander (1960), P.B. Smith (1970), and Gibbard *et al.* (1974), which include articles reprinted from their original sources. Marrow's (1969) biography of Lewin provides a full account of his life and work.

A number of accounts of the principal developments in group dynamics have been written especially for group therapists. Helen Durkin in her book, *The Group in Depth* (1964: 6–35), provides an account of principal developments within the field, and then addresses the issue of integrating individual and group dynamics (ibid.: 36–111). Ken Heap (1977) has written a book titled *Group Theory for Social Workers*. His discussions of group structures and processes are enriched by examples drawn from the wide activities of social workers, which include, for instance, working with youth clubs and neighbourhood associations as well as with therapeutic groups. Although published so long ago, neither of these books is out of date, since many of the most crucial developments in this field occurred from the late 1940s through to the 1950s and early 1960s. A more recent account of group dynamics has been written by Richard L. Munich (1993). It includes more up-to-date references than either Durkin or Heap, but it is less detailed, so it is a good idea to read these sources together.

FURTHER THEORY NEEDED BY GROUP PSYCHOTHERAPISTS

As we have seen from this chapter, much theory has been developed within the field of group dynamics which sheds light on properties of groups and on interpersonal dynamics which occur in them. Group therapists need such understandings, but they also need more: they need an integrated understanding of individual and group dynamics, how they bear on one another, the *processes* which connect group, intra-personal and interpersonal dynamics. They need conceptual tools – *theory* – to help them to understand the multitude of events which occur in groups, how individuals contribute to them and how they in turn bear on individual experience, for good or for ill.

The next chapter is devoted to theory directed to understanding therapeutic groups and processes affecting individual experience within them. It offers definitions of theory, presents one theoretical framework in detail, refers to others, and raises some questions about connections between theory and practice.

Chapter 5

Theory

The previous chapter presented some understandings about small face-to-face groups derived from the study of non-therapeutic groups – especially work groups whose members work towards some goal external to the group itself. Therapeutic groups are both similar to and different from such groups. They are similar to them in that comparable events and processes occur in both. They are different in that the goal is different. Therapeutic groups are not directed to effecting some change in the outside world. Rather, the whole point of therapeutic groups is that they are meant to benefit individual members in personal ways. The point was made at the end of the previous chapter that group therapists need theory which includes but is not restricted to the dynamics of groups. They need theory which integrates group and individual dynamics, and which deals with the processes by which benefit may occur for individual members.

This chapter begins with two premises. The first is that every practitioner needs theory in the form of a set of explanatory ideas to assist in making sense of the many complex events which occur in therapeutic groups. The second is that every practitioner actually holds some form of theory, perhaps explicitly, perhaps implicitly. It is impossible to do otherwise. The unimaginable alternative is forever to be faced with a myriad of unrelated and non-understandable events whose import for therapeutic work remains a mystery.

The theoretical framework with which I am most closely familiar and use as a point of departure for my work with groups is group focal conflict theory. I shall describe it in some detail, emphasising the procedures used when developing it and some of the ways in which I have modified it over the years. I do not wish to convey that this theory (or any other) should be regarded as a finished product – a kind of entity not open to examination or to further modification. This chapter will go on to refer to other theories to be found in the literature and to problems inherent in comparing and classifying theories. Some questions concerning connections between theory and practice are raised towards the end of the chapter.

The chapter is organised as follows:

• Definitions of 'theory'. How theory is ordinarily developed and tested.
• Group focal conflict theory: antecedent experiences and influences; the theory itself and how it was developed.

- Subsequent modifications and additions to the theory.
- Applications and limitations of group focal conflict theory.
- Understanding some of the phenomena described in Chapter 4 in group focal conflict terms.
- The wide range of theories available to practitioners, and some problems inherent in classifying theories.
- Evidence that a theory influences but does not determine a therapist's way of practising.
- Theory and its connections with practice: some questions.

DEFINITIONS OF 'THEORY'; HOW THEORY IS ORDINARILY DEVELOPED AND TESTED

The *Shorter Oxford English Dictionary* offers, amongst its definitions of theory, 'a scheme or system of ideas or statements held as an explanation or account of a group of facts or phenomena'; and 'in a loose or general sense: A hypothesis proposed as an explanation; hence, a mere hypothesis, speculation, conjecture'. *Longman* offers: ' a plausible or scientifically acceptable principle or body of principles offered to explain a phenomenon'; and 'an unproved assumption or conjecture'.

What one seeks, and hopes to find, in a theory is a coherent set of ideas which fits observable events and explains and accounts for some phenomenon: the solar system, or the respiratory system, or therapeutic groups. This fits the first dictionary definition of theory. However, the second dictionary definition of theory – that it can be mere speculation – is a reminder that a theory may be plausible or else far-fetched; well rooted in observable phenomena or only loosely related to them.

Usually, a theory is developed step by step, by painstaking efforts. Many repeated observations of a phenomenon are undertaken, possible explanations come to mind, and statements are formulated which define, describe and offer an explanation of the phenomenon in question.

Once devised, a theory will be tested through further observations. Sometimes further observations are supported by new technology or new information-gathering methods. In consequence of further testing, a theory may be supported, or extended, or revised. New observations test the limits of its applicability. Sometimes a theory is abandoned altogether if new observations show that the theory does not fit the phenomenon or account for all aspects of it.

History is full of examples of theories which have been abandoned or modified. It is also full of examples of people clinging to a theory in the face of new observations and evidence which refute it or point to its inadequacies. Sometimes one sees resistance to a new theory because to accept it would mean overturning some previously established and strongly held view of 'reality'. This points to the importance of trying to maintain an open-ended attitude towards theory, reminding oneself that it fits with what has been observed, or has been observable, so far.

As we have said, a theory is a set of ideas considered useful for understanding some phenomenon. It is not the phenomenon itself. A theory is not found in nature. It is a construction: a set of meanings which someone attributes to events with the intention of assisting in understanding them. This is a fundamental point sometimes lost sight of. It is important to hold in mind the distinction between a theory and the observable events it purports to explain, lest a theory, or the terms it uses, comes to be regarded as part of the real, observable world, which it is not. A theory is a cognitive convenience for making sense of complexity.

Most theories have identifiable antecedents, which may lie in the thinking of particular others or in tradition; that is, in generally held assumptions which come to be taken as axiomatic.

GROUP FOCAL CONFLICT THEORY

Group focal conflict theory is the body of theory in which I am most fluent. I was involved in devising it and have made use of it for many years, selecting from it in different ways for its relevance to different kinds of groups, modifying it and bringing in concepts from elsewhere as circumstances seemed to require, and sometimes setting it aside altogether when it did not fit circumstances encountered in practice.

One reason for presenting this theory in some detail is to make clear the baseline from which I have thought about groups and operated in them. When I refer to this theory later, it will be easier, I hope, for readers to see what I am extracting from the totality of the theory, or how and why I am departing from it, or adding to it.

Group focal conflict theory was developed in the late 1950s and early 1960s by a group of colleagues who worked first at the Veterans' Administration Research Hospital in Chicago and subsequently in the Department of Psychiatry, University of Chicago. Drs Roy M. Whitman, Morton A. Lieberman and Dorothy Stock (later, Whitaker) were involved throughout. Dr Thomas M. French, whose ideas about the nuclear conflict and focal conflicts, as applied to individuals, stimulated this theory-building effort, participated during the VA hospital days. Dr Martin M. Lakin became involved after the move to the University of Chicago. Many others joined in the effort for shorter periods of time, while working in one or another of these two settings.

Antecedent experiences and influences

The thinking of Dr Thomas M. French was the most immediate influence on the development of group focal conflict theory. Dr French was a consultant to the psychiatric service at the VA hospital at the time that theory-building began. He had devised a theory, applicable to individual personality dynamics and individual psychotherapy, which utilised the concepts of individual nuclear and focal conflicts (French 1952). This was a version of psychodynamic theory which accepted many of its basic tenets, including unconscious processes, personal defences and their relation to underlying conflicts, and connections between current behaviour and earlier, usually intra-family, experiences. Those involved in theory-building found French's ideas congenial, since all already accepted the broad precepts of psychodynamic theory.

Each of those principally involved brought his or her personal backgrounds and previous experiences to the task. Roy Whitman was a psychiatrist with substantial clinical experience of individual and group psychotherapy. He had also worked as a T-group leader in group dynamics laboratories conducted at Bethel, Maine. Morton Lieberman and Dorothy Stock were psychologists with an interest in group dynamics and personality theory. Both had been research assistants to Dr Herbert A. Thelen at the University of Chicago. There, they had worked within a team of researchers who were working out ways to operationalise the ideas of W.R. Bion (1959) about small face-to-face groups.

Bion's basic concepts were the three 'basic assumption' cultures: dependency, pairing and fight-flight; the work culture (all of which referred to group-level dynamics); and 'valency', which refers to tendencies within individuals that account for how they participate in the various group cultures. Sources of data for the research were T-groups conducted by staff of the National Training Laboratories, at Bethel, Maine. A number of assessment and measurement devices were developed to assist in studying communication within groups, predispositions on the part of individuals to participate in particular ways, sociometric choice, developmental stages and so on. The research instruments included a behavioural rating scheme which paid attention both to the content of successive comments during a group session and to associated 'affective messages'; a sentence completion device for assessing individual members' predispositions to behave and respond in particular ways with respect to the prevailing basic assumption; and a Q-sort (see Stephenson 1953; Brown 1997) for identifying individuals' perceptions of their actual and ideal role-behaviour in the group and their perceptions of other members. All these instruments incorporated Bion's concepts: for instance, the 'stems' in the sentence completion device referred to group situations dominated by fight, or flight, or dependency, and so on. These devices were used in conjunction with one another in different ways: for instance, to assess connections between self-percepts and behaviour; to identify and also try to account for sociometric preferences within the group; to track individual change; and to track group development. The research methods have been described in Thelen and Stock et al. (1954), and substantive findings have been reported in Stock and Thelen (1958). A summary of substantive findings appears in Rosenbaum and Berger (1963).

Through this research, both Stock and Lieberman acquired invaluable experience in closely observing and analysing interactions in groups and in examining connections between individual and group dynamics. During this same period and afterwards, both conducted T-groups themselves. Both moved to the VA hospital at the same time, after the research project with Thelen had been completed. This move brought a shift in emphasis from groups intended to support learning about groups (the T-groups), to groups intended to provide personal benefit to members. (In those days the Bethel T-groups were directed to helping group members to understand the dynamics of groups. Encounter groups and other forms of experiential groups intended to support personal development were still in the future.) At the VA hospital both Lieberman and Stock conducted individual as well as group psychotherapy.

Why did we not simply make use of Bion's ideas rather than try to develop a different framework? Truth to tell, I cannot remember. Perhaps it was because Roy Whitman was keen to test the relevance of French's ideas to therapeutic groups. Perhaps it was because we perceived that something further, beyond Bion's concept of 'valency', was needed to understand connections between individual intrapsychic dynamics and group-as-a-whole dynamics. The research team under Thelen had differentiated the concept of 'valency' into three related but distinguishable elements: area of concern, culture preference, and affective approach. These elaborations helped with understanding the ways in which individual dynamics connected with group dynamics, but they did not explain why and how these individual dynamics developed in the first place, nor why and how they were maintained. Something more was needed when the purpose of the group was to benefit individual members.

Group focal conflict theory and how it was developed

At the time that theory-building began there was already an active programme of group psychotherapy going on at the VA hospital. Most patients on the psychiatric ward were in concurrent group and individual psychotherapy. There were always a number of groups to observe and to study. Usually, seven or eight or nine people were involved in theory-building at any one time. Drs Whitman, Stock, Lieberman and French participated throughout, and other members of staff participated for shorter periods of time.

We undertook two activities. First, we observed one another's groups from behind a one-way screen. This made it possible for the observers to discuss group events with one another as they occurred. Immediately after each session, the therapist (or co-therapists) joined the observers for further discussion. The second activity consisted of regularly timetabled discussions attended by the same members of staff, joined by Dr French. In these discussions we painstakingly examined verbatim transcripts made from audio-tapes. By these means, ideas gradually took shape about the applicability of French's formulations to groups, and to ways in which those ideas would have to be modified or extended to fit group *and* individual dynamics, rather than individual dynamics alone.

To make clear the theory itself and how it evolved, I will divide the discussion which follows into (a) the theory as applied to individuals, and to individuals in groups; (b) testing the applicability of French's ideas to group-level dynamics; (c) how individual and group dynamics connect; and (d) published accounts of group focal conflict theory.

The theory as applied to individuals and to individuals in groups

Dr French had formulated the idea that, for individuals, one or several 'nuclear' conflicts developed in early life. He postulated that a nuclear conflict consisted of some 'disturbing motive' in conflict with some 'reactive motive', which requires the young child to establish one or several 'solutions' which would deal with the conflict in some way. In the first instance, the reactive motive would have been a 'reality factor' – for example, a mother who really was unresponsive and prevented the child's need for emotional nurturance from being satisfied. Such a reality factor soon becomes transformed into an internalised feeling – some fear or guilt experienced by the young child, such as a fear of being altogether abandoned by mother.

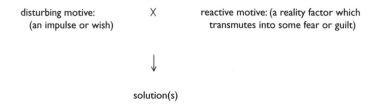

Figure 5.1 A generalised diagram of an individual nuclear/focal conflict

The two elements of the conflict – the disturbing and the reactive motives – persist as time goes on and retain their emotional power. The personal solutions, arrived at early on, also persist, often in modified forms as the individual matures. A personal solution might be some behaviour pattern, or stance towards the world, or assumption about self and surroundings. The individual experiences these as necessary to psychic survival and continues to make use of them, even though some of them may have disadvantageous consequences. The nuclear conflict is re-experienced in many contemporary social and interpersonal settings in the form of a derived individual focal conflict, related of course to the earlier nuclear conflict but also coloured by the character of the current situation. Nuclear and focal conflicts include the same three elements of a 'disturbing motive' (an impulse seeking expression or gratification), which was in conflict with a 'reactive motive' (some fear or guilt which opposed or was in conflict with the disturbing motive), and one or more 'solutions' (the person's attempts to deal with the underlying conflict). Figure 5.1 shows the three features of the theory as they apply to individuals. A concrete example is shown in Figure 5.2.

As this person grows older, the disturbing motive persists, for he or she continues to be motivated by a need for nurturance, though not necessarily from mother. The reactive motive – the fear of being rejected or abandoned – also persists, though it has most probably become internalised and lost to awareness. The solution becomes habitual and is reinvoked when something happens to intensify reactive fears. However the habitual solution may also be utilised when the realities of the situation do not require it: the person acts the clown with persons who do not need him or her to be one in order to elicit the response he or she craves. The manner in which an habitual solution is expressed in adult life is influenced by maturation as well as circumstances. A small boy may think it very funny to stand on his head. As an adult, he may tell sophisticated stories, but the same basic solution is operating and is fulfilling analogous functions.

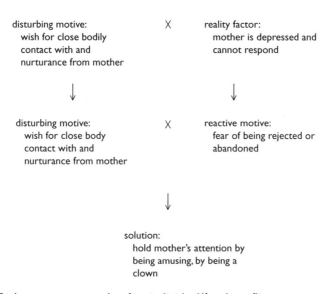

Figure 5.2 A concrete example of an individual/focal conflict

Some solutions are defences in the usual sense of the term (denial, rationalisation, avoidance and so on) but others take the form of habitual ways of presenting the self, or preferred interactive styles. They might be expressed in occupational choice or even whole life styles. An individual will most likely have developed two or three or more solutions to the same underlying conflict.

When theory-building started, French had already established to his satisfaction that individuals could be understood in these terms. He considered that individuals experience their nuclear conflicts in a derived form in many contemporary settings. They were then called 'focal' conflicts. Focal conflicts take on colour from the character of the contemporary setting, but are the same in their essentials as the nuclear conflict. It was reasonable to suppose that a group situation would be one of the contemporary interactive situations in which an individual focal conflict could surface.

Through observing group sessions we tested whether individuals revealed enough about themselves in a therapeutic group to enable nuclear conflict and focal conflict formulations to be made concerning them. We found that it was virtually always possible to identify individuals' preferred personal solutions. These were shown in the content of a member's contributions or in interpersonal interactions or in responses to and participation in themes arising in the group. Underlying wishes and fears were less visible. Sometimes they could be inferred, but sometimes there was no evidence on which to base a formulation or it took considerable time for evidence to emerge. Some individuals were less visible than others within the group. As was the case in individual psychotherapy, an emerging understanding of an individual in group focal conflict terms had to be held tentatively at first, as an hypothesis. As further events occurred, the formulation might be supported, or added to, modified or adjusted.

Observation showed that, in a therapeutic group, each member can be expected to establish, or try to establish, habitual personal solutions. He or she will seek to occupy a particular position in the group, or present him/herself as a particular kind of person, or establish a particular kind of relationship with others which is consistent with previously established personal solutions.

Testing the applicability of French's ideas to group-level dynamics

Could French's theory be applied to group-level dynamics and, if so, how would it have to be adjusted or elaborated? The groups which we were studying were open discussion groups – that is, topics or activities were not introduced by the therapists. It became evident very quickly that under these conditions associational processes occur. These could be tracked. Over a period of time, a theme was built up which occupied the attention of members. Most members, sometimes all members, participated, each in his or her own way. Successive contributions pushed and pulled and influenced the theme in one direction or another. A theme might be supported or opposed. Some aspect of it persisted while others dropped out of sight. Over a relatively short period of time – fifteen to twenty minutes or so – a theme became evident.

Sometimes the manifest content of a discussion referred directly to a theme, but sometimes it was a vehicle for carrying an underlying, unstated theme. For example, members of a group might be criticising the cleaners and the maintenance staff for their carelessness. This was the manifest content which could actually be observed and heard. We judged it to be a means for expressing concerns about whether the therapist really cared about the group members. A theme would typically hold sway in the group for a period of time – for a session or part of a session – and then give way to something else.

A theme could be understood in French's terms. The terms *disturbing motive*, *reactive motive* and *solution* could be applied to group-level dynamics. To carry on with the example, introduced above, of a group whose members criticised the carelessness of the maintenance staff: we postulated an underlying impulse or wish to be supported, cared for and helped by the therapist. In focal conflict terms this was the *disturbing motive*. Such impulses and wishes were not and could not be expressed directly. The evidence for this was the use of a metaphor to express (and also to conceal) feelings. Making use of a metaphor functioned as a *solution* for the members. A solution to what? The metaphor must be needed by the members as a protective device, for if it were not needed, they would be able to express their feelings directly. It was hypothesised that the disturbing motive was in conflict with some *reactive motive* which according to theory would consist of some fear or guilt. We judged in this case that the reactive motive had to do with fears of what would happen if the members criticised the therapist directly – possibly a fear of abandonment or of retaliation. From this example it can be seen that a group had to be observed over a period of time in order to form hypotheses about group-level dynamics in group focal conflict terms. We defined a theme formally as 'a series of group focal conflicts linked by similar disturbing motives' (Whitaker and Lieberman 1964: 64).

Observing many diverse instances of group life supported a growing conviction that French's three interrelated concepts – the disturbing motive, the reactive motive and the solution – had explanatory power with reference to the group, but that certain adjustments and extensions were required. It was obvious from the start that French's concept of the *nuclear* conflict could not be applied to a group, for the group did not have a history which pre-dated the members assembling for the first time. We could, however, think in terms of *a group focal conflict*, occurring in the here-and-now of the group. Because, in a group, prevailing feelings and/ or behaviour patterns are built through the interactions of a number of people, we began to think in terms of *shared* feelings being involved in the disturbing and reactive motives, and *mutually maintained* behaviours or beliefs or assumptions being involved in the solution. This did not necessarily mean that everyone felt or behaved in the same way or made the same assumptions, but it meant that there was a convergence in the group towards something held in common – shown in the behaviour of most of the members. There was no way of knowing whether silent members concurred in whatever was emerging (perhaps they were paying no attention at all), but one could see that they were not countering or interfering with it. If some issue was introduced by one person and not supported and developed by others, it would become 'lost' in the group. Similarly, if what could potentially become a 'solution' was introduced by one person and not supported by others, it did not become established.

Theory began to take shape as follows: we retained the idea of the disturbing motive, but began to think of it informally as some shared impulse or wish. We retained the idea of the reactive motive, and began to think of it informally as some fear or guilt. The disturbing and the reactive motives (the wish or impulse versus the fear or guilt) were the two elements of a prevailing group focal conflict. In response, group members sought to establish solutions to the currently prevailing conflict. Observation showed that solutions could be of two kinds: 'enabling' solutions, which dealt with fears and also allowed for the expression of associ-ated wishes; and 'restrictive' solutions, which only dealt with fears. For instance, intellectualising about something protected members from facing their fears. However, neither the fears nor the associated impulses could be acknowledged or discussed in direct terms. On these grounds intellectualising was regarded as a 'restrictive' solution. In contrast, an 'enabling' solution might for instance consist of an explicitly stated shared view that the members of a group were courageous because they acknowledged their problems. Members regarded it as a personal virtue to reveal problems and acknowledge anxieties and guilts. This mutually held point of view – 'we are courageous' – supported the direct expression and exploration of feelings contained in both the disturbing and the reactive motives.

Observation also showed that solutions constructed through interaction in the group could involve either homogeneity within the group or role differentiation. This was another extension of theory. A solution could consist of similar behaviours or a mutually supported belief. At other times, a solution involved different members occupying different roles. For instance, one person might become the patient while the others became the helpers. This placed one person in an exposed position and protected the others from the presumed risks of self-exposure. It thus functioned as a solution to an underlying conflict which could be hypothesised to be a 'wish to benefit by revealing oneself' versus 'fear of eliciting criticism or ridicule from others'. As another example, one person might occupy the role of advice-giver while the others sought his or her advice. This could function as a solution to the underlying conflict 'anger at the therapist for not being helpful in the ways expected' versus 'fear of retaliation from the therapist should such anger be expressed'. The solution consisted of finding a substitute therapist within the group. Both these examples would be regarded as restrictive solutions, since they alleviated fears but did not allow the associated impulse to be acknowledged or expressed. The elements of group focal conflict theory as developed so far are shown in Figure 5.3.

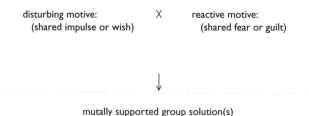

Figure 5.3 A generalised diagram of a group focal conflict

The idea of 'solutional conflict' and the 'deviant' member had to be invented and brought into the emerging theory, since it sometimes happened that most of the members could support an emerging solution but one could not, thereby placing him/herself in a 'deviant' position in the group. The group was then said to be in a state of 'solutional conflict'. This dynamic is illustrated in Chapter 12, where a patient referred to as Arnold is described. Arnold could not accept an emerging point of view which was supported by all the others – namely, that 'everyone has faults'. This was a belief which, if it came to be shared, would constitute an enabling solution because it would make it easier for the patients to acknowledge 'faults' without fearing criticism or some other form of punishment. Arnold insisted that, as for him, he was perfect. This made it impossible for the solution 'everyone has faults' to become established. Arnold clung to this point of view in the face of many attempts on the part of the others to persuade and coax him to change his mind. Eventually the members worked out a revised solution which everyone, including Arnold, could accept, and which fulfilled the same function as the one which had been abandoned. It was: 'everyone *tries* to be perfect'. For a full account, see the second example in Chapter 12. When a solutional conflict is present, the diagram is extended, as is shown in Figure 5.4.

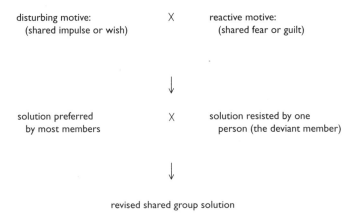

Figure 5.4 A generalised diagram of a solutional conflict

The concepts central to group focal conflict theory, as applied to group-level phenomena, can be summarised as follows:

- *group focal conflict*, comprised of disturbing motive (a shared impulse or wish) in conflict with a reactive motive (a shared fear or guilt);
- *solution*: a mutually supported norm or belief which functions to resolve the underlying conflict;
- two forms of solution: *restrictive solutions*, which alleviate underlying fears but do not allow for acknowledgement or expression or satisfaction of the associated impulses or wishes; and *enabling solutions*, which deal with both aspects of the underlying conflict (either form of solution can involve unanimity within the group, or else role differentiation);
- *solutional conflict*: a situation in which some members press for a particular solution to become established while others fight against it.

These basic ideas could be applied to the development of a group over time. Observation showed that particular group focal conflicts take time to emerge, or at least to become discernible. Often it was the solution which could be detected first, and often the first detectable solution was a restrictive one. If a group could move from a restrictive to an enabling solution, more profitable exploration of the prevailing theme could take place, with individuals gaining from expressing feelings ordinarily censored, comparing their own experiences and feelings with those of others, and giving and receiving feedback freely. We found that an enabling solution could prevail for some time but tended to give way to a restrictive solution as explorations reached a point where anxieties began to build up which could not be contained by the current solution or set of solutions. The theme tended to be abandoned. Over a period of time, some other theme emerged.

The development of the group (if it was going well) had the character of a deepening spiral in which particular themes recurred from time to time and were explored in a further or different way each time. When the theory was later set down in formal terms, one of the propositions was that 'the development of a therapy group from its inception to its termination is characterized by the recurrence of basic themes under progressively expanding cultural conditions' (Whitaker and Lieberman 1964: 117). 'Progressively expanding cultural conditions' referred to the group's movement from predominantly restrictive solutions to predominantly enabling solutions. Observation showed that groups do not arrive at a set of enabling solutions and then maintain them consistently. Rather, groups had recourse from time to time to restrictive solutions in the face of intensified anxieties. Overall, however, in a well-functioning group the movement was towards operating mainly on enabling solutions.

The idea emerged that diverse 'group cultures' could become established in therapeutic groups. In group focal conflict terms, the culture of a group refers to the solutions which have become established over a period of time and remain available to the members as resources for containing anxiety and, sometimes (if a solution is an enabling one), for exploring issues important to members. The culture will differ from group to group. A well-functioning group will have established a repertoire of enabling solutions but will also have restrictive solutions to fall back on when anxieties intensify. A poorly functioning group will rely mainly on restrictive solutions, or will have few solutions available to it and thus be impoverished.

How individual and group dynamics connect

Sometimes an individual's preferred personal solutions are expressed in the group without opposition or interference. They fit the other members' needs, or at least do not interfere with them. One can say that they are allowed, even supported, by the dynamics of the group. Sometimes, however, the dynamics of the group are such that a preferred personal solution cannot operate. These are two ways in which individual and group dynamics may connect.

Another kind of connection has to do with how individual nuclear/focal conflicts relate to the prevailing shared group focal conflict. There are times when the connection is a close one: the disturbing and the reactive motives in the *group focal conflict* are closely related to the disturbing and the reactive motives in the *individual focal conflicts* of some of the members. One could say that they resonate with, or are isomorphic with, one another. Sometimes this is easily perceived. For instance, a group focal conflict might involve a wish for support and nurturance from the therapist versus a fear of not getting it because of not deserving it. For some individual group members, this could be close to a long-standing personal conflict, deriving from earlier experiences within their families. In such a case, a significant individual focal conflict could be reactivated, and re-experienced in the group.

Such re-experiencing is important for the therapeutic process, for such experiences occur 'live' in the here-and-now of the group and can be examined. It sometimes becomes possible to see connections between the 'here-and now', the 'there-and-then' (significant events in the individual's personal past history) and the 'there-and-now' (significant events in the individual's current outside life). 'Corrective emotional experiences' can occur in the course of such re-experiencing.

The concept of the corrective emotional experience is not intrinsic to group focal conflict theory but it is compatible with it and was built into it from the beginning. The essence of the concept is that individuals maintain behaviours, feelings and ways of thinking about themselves and others which are disadvantageous to themselves but also serve a protective function. The unrecognised fear is that disaster will follow if the behaviour, percept or whatever is yielded up. The behaviour, the perception of self, the assumptions about others therefore persist. If an individual can experience that *disaster will not follow* if the behaviour is expressed (or the belief or assumption or feelings acknowledged) the way is open for personal change. Fear no longer holds the disadvantageous patterns in place. In group focal conflict terms, one would say that a corrective emotional experience consists in the emotional learning that it is possible to abandon some disadvantageous personal solution because the feared disaster (the reactive fear or guilt) will not occur if the associated impulses (the disturbing motive) are acknowledged and expressed. The solution is no longer necessary, or not as necessary as before. The dynamic of the corrective emotional experience was originally recognised in and seen to occur in one-to-one psychotherapy. It can also occur in the context of a group.

The concept of the corrective emotional experience has had a somewhat curious history. It was put forward in a somewhat nascent form by Alexander and French (1946) as an explanatory principle for understanding how personal gain occurs in individual psychoanalysis. Alexander (1956) subsequently recommended a particular way of using this theory in psychoanalytic practice which some psychoanalysts found difficult to accept. He recommended that the analyst deliberately behave in ways which would support showing the patient that he (the analyst) was *not* behaving or feeling or manifesting opinions which were similar to those of the family member (usually a parent) who had stirred up the fears in the first place. This way of practising was regarded by mainstream psychoanalysts as contrary to the accepted assumption that the analyst must maintain a neutral position in order to be the recipient of transference reactions. Alexander's recommendations, in other words, were inconsistent with prevailing assumptions about what constitutes helpful interventions. Considerable controversy followed. Some analysts rejected the concept as well as the practice, even though accepting the concept does not in fact require accepting Alexander's particular use of it. This controversy persisted for some time, and is well described in a special issue of the *Psychoanalytic Quarterly* (1990). Especially useful are articles by Wallerstein, Casement, Bacal, Miller, and Pines.

Frank and Ascher (1951) had stated the concept of the corrective emotional experience in a way which was faithful to its original formulation and did not include the prescriptions for practice put forward by Alexander. Those who were building group focal conflict theory found Frank and Ascher's formulation congenial, and used it.

Nowadays the concept of the corrective emotional experience is quite widely accepted and has been built into a number of different theoretical frameworks. Some practitioners remain suspicious of it and do not use the term. Even so, they seem to be familiar with the dynamic. I have heard the same dynamic referred to as a 'crucial emotional experience' rather than a 'corrective' one.

Published accounts of group focal conflict theory

Published accounts can be divided into three time periods: the years during which the theory was being developed, up to 1964; the publication in 1964 of a book which set the theory down in formal terms; and the period following 1964 when further articles appeared which summarised the theory or emphasised certain aspects of it or explored its further applications. The first time period saw the publication of Whitman and Stock (1958); Stock *et al.* (1958); Whitman *et al.* (1960); Stock (1962); and Stock and Lieberman (1962). A point was reached when the theory seemed sufficiently well worked out to warrant pulling together what had emerged so far. Morton A. Lieberman and I undertook the task of setting down the elements of the theory in formal terms. Certain omissions became evident which then had to be thought about and dealt with, in order for the theory to approach completeness. This led to the book, *Psychotherapy through the Group Process* (Whitaker and Lieberman 1964), in which the theory was set out in a series of propositions. This book was a definitive statement of the theory as it had developed up to that point. Subsequent to the publication of that book, other articles appeared which either emphasised certain aspects or applications of the theory or undertook to compare it with other theories: Whitaker (1965); Lieberman (1967); Lieberman, Lakin and Whitaker (1968); Lieberman, Lakin and Whitaker (1969); Whitaker (1982); Whitaker (1987a, 1987b); Whitaker (1989); and Whitaker (1992b). Two of the later publications discussed applications beyond therapeutic groups: Whitaker (1987a) focused on intervening in personal networks, and Whitaker (1992b) on transposing learnings from group psychotherapy to work groups.

SUBSEQUENT MODIFICATIONS AND ADDITIONS
TO THE THEORY

Group focal conflict theory was first developed some forty years ago. Since then, those principally concerned have gone their separate ways and have had diverse further experiences. In referring to subsequent modifications and additions to theory I can therefore speak only for myself. Modifications which I have made to the theory stem from two kinds of further experience. First, I have worked with groups other than those on which the original theory was based, especially groups composed of people facing particular stress-generating situations. Second, I have participated in training courses for people who come from diverse professional backgrounds and work in diverse practice settings. Through them, I have become familiar with a wider range of types of groups, for a wider range of populations, than is represented in my direct practice experience.

The principal modification which I have found necessary is the redefinition of the term theme. Originally, a theme was defined as 'a series of group focal conflicts linked by similar disturbing motives' (Whitaker and Lieberman 1964: 64). In consequence of further experience of my own and that of students and course members, I have retained the idea of theme but now define it in more general terms than before. This redefinition includes but is not restricted to the original definition. At some times, in some groups, a theme emerges in a way which fits the 1964 definition. At other times a theme might refer to the reactive motive (the shared fear or guilt), or else to both aspects of the underlying conflict. When no underlying covert conflict can be identified, theme is indistinguishable from topic. The redefinition of theme as an issue which commands the attention of group members for a period of time makes it fit a wider range of groups than those on which the theory was originally based.

As my experience has expanded, I have found it useful to make use of certain additional concepts which are not intrinsic to group focal conflict theory itself but are compatible with it and could also be used in conjunction with other theories. For example, when defining benefit, in Chapter 3, I brought in ideas of current and preferred state, and of life space, frontier and preoccupying concern (some of this is from the thinking of Kurt Lewin). In Chapter 4, when discussing moods and atmospheres, I brought in the concepts of cueing and altercasting, to assist in understanding how individuals come to occupy particular positions in groups. The concept of central person was imported from the thinking of Fritz Redl (1966a) to assist in seeing the complexities and subtleties of leadership in groups. Theory useful in understanding processes of contagion was also brought in from Redl. In subsequent chapters, especially in Part III, further concepts will be drawn upon when needed.

Those who constructed group focal conflict theory did not use the term transference. The reason is that at the time that group focal conflict theory was being developed, transference, for most psychotherapists, had a very specific meaning associated with individual psychotherapy. It referred to feelings and assumptions, derived from early experiences with significant figures (usually within the family), which a patient projected on to the therapist, who presented him- or herself as a neutral figure. Applying the term to interactions within groups would imply that transference *in a group setting* involves and is restricted to the same dynamic. This would be misleading. Although patient–therapist transferences can and do occur in groups, transference can also take quite other forms. We were particularly aware that certain patients could become transference figures for other patients, and that re-experiencing significant earlier life events can occur when there is a 'resonance' between group-level shared conflicts and individual focal conflicts. Later in this book (in Chapter 16), I examine the complexities of the term transference when it is applied to therapeutic groups. Counter-transference is discussed in some detail in Chapter 8 and is referred to again in Chapter 14 as one source, but not the only source, of therapist errors.

APPLICATIONS AND LIMITATIONS OF GROUP FOCAL CONFLICT THEORY

Group focal conflict theory is particularly applicable to therapeutic groups in which associative processes occur. Such processes occur in their most unfettered form in open-discussion groups, but can also occur in more heavily structured groups, where chains of associations occur inside or despite the structure. In topic-orientated therapy groups, for instance, associative processes influence how the members develop a topic, how they deviate from it and what they deviate to.

In some groups, associative processes do not and cannot occur; for instance, because the members are so self-preoccupied or so lacking in communication skills that they cannot listen to one another and build on one another's comments. Group focal conflict theory cannot then be applied. It also cannot be applied, or has limited usefulness, in groups whose members are capable of associative processes but where such processes are suppressed by a very firm structure or by an authoritarian, directive therapist.

Group focal conflict theory was worked out through observing groups made up of people drawn from two of the population categories described in Chapter 2. These were people recovering from a serious breakdown in functioning (category 4) and people who might appear to outside observers to be functioning adequately but who were anxious or depressed or behaving in self-defeating ways (category 6). Subsequent experience shows that the theory is also applicable, or applicable in part, to other population categories, especially people facing particularly challenging circumstances (as is the case for the first three population categories). There are two population categories for which the theory is a poorer fit. These are category 7 ('persons who have lost or never fully acquired basic social, interpersonal, or practical skills of living') and category 8 ('people who are regarded by others as having or being problems because they are disruptive, unruly, break laws or offend commonly held standards, or are destructive in their relationships').

People in category 7 tend to lack communication skills and therefore often do not build on one another's contributions. Associative processes do not occur. People in category 8 can often be more fully understood if one thinks in terms of peer-group dynamics rather than in terms of intra-psychic conflicts.

UNDERSTANDING SOME OF THE PHENOMENA DESCRIBED IN CHAPTER 4 IN GROUP FOCAL CONFLICT TERMS

Norms and shared beliefs, as described in Chapter 4, are referred to in group focal conflict theory as solutions. This term emphasises that norms and beliefs fulfil functions for the members of a group. They serve the purpose of establishing the boundaries within which the group operates and constructing a safe environment for the members. Group focal conflict theory contains the idea that some solutions are 'restrictive' while others are 'enabling'. Both kinds of solution protect members from undue anxiety, but *enabling* solutions support the therapeutic process by allowing relatively wide explorations while *restrictive* solutions constrain and constrict what can be examined and explored.

In group focal conflict terms, a particular mood or atmosphere can be understood to arise for different reasons and serve different functions. For instance, an apathetic atmosphere could function as a restrictive solution which protects members from the hazards of directly experiencing feelings or impulses involved in the underlying disturbing motive. Panic or depression could be regarded as manifestations of an underlying shared fear, in other words of feelings contained in a prevailing reactive motive. Emotional contagion can sometimes be seen to function as a restrictive solution. For instance, the rapid escalation of silliness or of joking might function to distract members from very serious feelings which they feel it dangerous to face. At other times, emotional contagion denotes a (usually temporary) absence of any form of solution. Impulses break out into action without any restraining force in the form of a mutually maintained solution.

Group focal conflict theory accepts that whatever level of cohesiveness becomes established in a group is the product of the interactions of the members through associative processes. In a therapeutic group, cohesiveness can be dysfunctionally high or dysfunctionally low. In group focal conflict terms, very high cohesiveness could be functioning as a restrictive solution, buying comfort but constraining explorations. Under conditions of dysfunctionally high cohesiveness, group members do not engage in interactions which threaten the degree of cohesiveness which they have achieved. Under some circumstances low cohesiveness can also function as a restrictive solution, protecting members from the presumed dangers of close involvement. Under other circumstances, however, low cohesiveness and permeable boundaries constitute a preferable and necessary solution in that they make it possible for particularly vulnerable people to remain in the group. (See the striking example in Chapter 7 of open groups for adult children of holocaust survivors.)

Change and development can be understood in group focal conflict in terms of the kinds of solutions which prevail. In many groups, early sessions are marked by a preponderance of restrictive solutions. As fears about the likely negative consequences of participating in the group became alleviated, restrictive solutions are replaced by enabling ones. A shift in the character of prevailing solutions marks the boundary between the formative and the established phase of a group. Later in the life of a group, members sometimes resort to restrictive solutions temporarily, to cope with upsurges in reactive fears. As fears again become alleviated, the restrictive solution is abandoned and some enabling solution is established or re-established. This way of looking at development is detailed in Chapter 10.

In group focal conflict terms, the roles and positions which individuals come to occupy in groups can be understood to result from two dynamics which often operate simultaneously: attempts on the part of individuals to establish preferred personal solutions in the group; and pressures on the part of others to fix individuals in positions which satisfy solutional needs for the group as a whole. For instance, members of a group may *need* a substitute therapist or a scapegoat in order to feel reasonably comfortable. Individuals are likely to feel personally comfortable if a prevailing group solution allows them to maintain an habitual personally preferred solution. They are likely to experience personal threat under two conditions: first, when a solution being maintained in the group as a whole makes it impossible for them to maintain some favoured personal solution; and second, when they are pressed into occupying some position within a restrictive solution which generates hurt or harm, such as becoming the displaced object of attack.

THE WIDE RANGE OF THEORIES AVAILABLE TO PRACTITIONERS, AND SOME PROBLEMS INHERENT IN CLASSIFYING THEORIES

Editors of large compendia about group psychotherapy have had, perforce, to think about how to organise the sections of their books and the chapters within them. Kaplan and Sadock, in their large compendium titled *Comprehensive Group Psychotherapy* include a very long section titled 'Specialized group psychotherapy techniques' (Kaplan and Sadock 1993: 126–312). Included are accounts of different theories and their associated practices. Those which pertain to small face-to-face groups composed of people who are strangers to one another and where a therapist is present are:

- Psychoanalysis in groups (Kutash and Wolf);
- Psychoanalytic group psychotherapy (Rutan);
- Group analysis (Pines and Hearst);
- Group-centered models of group psychotherapy (Horwitz);
- Object relations theory and group psychotherapy (Kibel);
- Self psychology and group psychotherapy (Baker);

- Interpersonal group psychotherapy (Yalom and Vinogrador);
- Transactional analysis in groups (O'Hearne);
- Cognitive-behavioural group psychotherapy (Rose);
- Psychodrama (Sacks);
- Gestalt group psychotherapy (Greve);
- Existential-humanistic approach to group psychotherapy (Rosenbaum);
- Integration and non-integration of innovative group methods (Reid and Reid); and
- Short-term group psychotherapy (Klein).

By using the term techniques in their section-title, which I imagine was done with care and forethought, Kaplan and Sadock allow their various contributors to emphasise theory or practice or both. A chapter on systems theory and small groups, by Agazarian and Janoff, appears in another section of this volume.

Dies (1992), in his nicely titled article, 'Models of group psychotherapy: sifting through confusion', took an empirical approach to the same task. He conducted a postal survey, asking senior clinicians within the American Group Psychotherapy Association to say what they considered to be the main theoretical orientations in the field, and who they regarded as representing each. This survey yielded the following ten models of group psychotherapy: psychodynamic/psychoanalytic; group as whole/systems; TA/gestalt/redecision; interpersonal/interactional; cognitive/behavioural; object relations; group analysis; psychodrama; existential/humanistic; and self psychology. The four 1992 issues of the *International Journal of Group Psychotherapy* contain articles describing these various approaches (see Rutan on psychodynamic group psychotherapy; Leszcz on the interpersonal approach; Ellis on rational-emotive and cognitive behaviour therapy; Agazarian on a systems approach; Ganzarain on object relations group psychotherapy; Gladfelter on redecision therapy; Stone on self psychology; Mullan on existential therapists; Roberts and Pines on group-analytic psychotherapy; and Kipper on psychodrama).

It is clear that there are more ways than one of classifying theory and that the task is not a straightforward one. One cannot list theories without deciding which to include or exclude, and one cannot classify without comparing theories and deciding which ones belong together. Dies points to some of the problems involved in classifying theories. In the first few pages of his article he refers to different dimensions used by his respondents to differentiate between different theoretical positions. There were differences in the relative emphasis placed on the individual, the interpersonal and the group-as-a-whole; therapist style; the therapeutic factors emphasised in the theory, and others. Dies's own system was produced by combining the opinions of a number of practitioners – a difficult task when one has to cope with quite different points of view. He reports, for instance, that respondents placed Yalom (1970, 1995) in six different categories. Further problems are revealed when one compares Dies's table of models of group psychotherapy and their principal proponents (Dies 1992: 3) with the actual articles included in the four

1992 issues of the *International Journal*. Sometimes there is a close correspondence between an article and the category of theories it was meant to describe; sometimes there is not. This can also be observed in articles included in the Kaplan and Sadock (1993) compendium. This is not a criticism, for there are inescapable difficulties inherent in the task of describing and categorising theories. It can be difficult to give proper attention to all the theories within a category when they resemble one another in some respects but diverge in others. Whenever theories are grouped together, oversimplification may occur.

The theories, or clusters of theories, named by Kaplan and Sadock and by Dies are, for the most part, theories which approach comprehensiveness. There are also theories which pertain to particular aspects of groups and can be considered sub-theories. Theories about group development, discussed in Chapter 10, are an example. In addition, there are individual concepts which are in themselves complex and have been built into diverse theories. Examples are transference, counter-transference, and the corrective emotional experience.

New theory continues to be developed, or previously worked out theories are re-examined, often by comparing theories and trying to see how they bear on one another. It is therefore difficult to be entirely up to date when describing and classifying theories. For instance, criticisms of Foulkesian group analysis by Nitsun (1996) and Dalal (1998) are too recent to have been included by Kaplan and Sadock or by Dies, or in recent historical accounts (for example, those by Scheidlinger 1993: 2–10; Rutan and Stone 1993: 9–29; Ettin 1992: 27–110; and MacKenzie 1990: 3–18). Theory based on Kohut's self psychology is developing rapidly: an updated understanding of it would have to include articles in a recent book edited by Harwood and Pines (1998). Ahlin (1996) has developed a matrix theory of processes in therapeutic groups, drawing substantially on S.H. Foulkes but also bringing in thinking from Stern (1985), Whitaker and Lieberman (1964), and others. He has clarified the concept of 'the group matrix' and developed a 'matrix representation grid' consisting of eight group determinants which operate at five possible levels.

Long-established theory continues to be further illuminated by recent thinking. For instance, Hinshelwood (1999) has recently published an article titled 'How Foulkesian was Bion?', which examines anew the thinking of these two significant figures during their respective (and non-overlapping) days at the Northfield Hospital during the Second World War.

EVIDENCE THAT A THEORY INFLUENCES BUT DOES NOT DETERMINE A THERAPIST'S WAY OF PRACTISING

Theory ought to bear on practice, and it does, but the relationship does not seem to be a direct one. Theories which have much in common are used differently in practice by different therapists. Proponents of the same theory operate differently in their groups.

Henry Ezriel's concept of the common group tension has much in common with the concept of the group focal conflict. However, Ezriel and those who devised group focal conflict theory operated quite differently in their groups. Commonalities between the two theories are evident. With reference to the components of the common group tension, Ezriel's *required relationship* is equivalent to the concept of the *solution* in group focal conflict theory (= feelings, beliefs, behaviours, relationships which the individual feels, usually without being aware of it, that s/he *must* maintain in order to feel personally safe). Ezriel's *avoided relationship* is equivalent to the *disturbing motive* (= the impulses and wishes which drive an individual but which s/he experiences as dangerous to acknowledge or express). Ezriel's concept of *calamity* is equivalent to the *reactive motive* (= the fears and guilts which would follow from an acknowledgement or expression of the disturbing motive).

With reference to practice, Ezriel argued that the therapist should restrict her- or himself to 'here-and-now interpretations', first pointing to the common group tension and then to individual reactions to it (Ezriel 1959). Those who devised group focal conflict theory allowed themselves a wider range of interventions, directed sometimes to the group and sometimes to individuals. Interpretations were seen as just one form of intervention and were de-emphasized. Ezriel tended to intervene relatively infrequently, since it usually took some time to grasp all aspects of the common group tension. Therapists making use of group focal conflict theory probably intervene more frequently than Ezriel did, though there can be longish periods in which the therapist chooses not to intervene on the grounds that the members are doing good therapeutic work on their own.

Leonard Horwitz, following experience with Ezriel's methods, accepted the usefulness of group-centred formulations and interventions but regarded Ezriel's intervention style as excessively rigid, with the consequent relative neglect of individual members in favour of interpretations at the group level. Horwitz (1977), accordingly, arrived at an intervention style which attended first to individuals, only afterward showing how individual contributions converge to generate phenomena common to the group. Horwitz also attends to member interactions – which Ezriel tended not to do.

Further evidence that therapists use theory differently in their practice derives from observing how group analysts who in general accept the thinking of S.H. Foulkes intervene in groups. In their book, *A Work Book of Group-analytic Interventions*, Kennard et al. (1993) presented a large number of group analysts with eight group situations which might be encountered in practice, and asked each how they would understand and respond to them. There were comparabilities but there was also diversity. Farhad Dalal (1995), in giving an account of his initiation into group analysis from a background in humanistic psychology, described very large differences in the purposes which group analysts pursued and in how they intervened in groups, despite subscribing to a group-analytic perspective.

All of this calls attention to the fact that therapists make active decisions as to how to use theory in practice, and that the resulting practice can differ from therapist to therapist. Such observations raise questions about how therapists make use of theory and about connections between theory and practice.

THEORY AND ITS CONNECTIONS WITH PRACTICE: SOME QUESTIONS

From what has been presented in this chapter, some questions can be raised about theory and its connections with practice:

1   What is theory *for*? What functions does it fulfil for the practitioner?
2   How is it that some theories are closely connected with a particular practice approach while others are not?
3   Which comes first: theory or practice? Does a therapist's preferred theory influence how or she operates in a group? Does practice experience influence theory development? Or do theory and practice influence one another?
4   Why are there so many theories? Can they be reconciled? What function is served by seeking to reconcile theories?

Some of the chapters which follow cast up further questions about theory, and its connections with and uses in practice. These will be named in context. A series of questions concerning theory and practice will be accumulated by this means and will be discussed in Chapter 17.

Part II

Planning

Chapter 6

Necessary decisions when planning a group

The following list spells out decisions which need to be taken when planning a group. They are presented in the order in which they need to be made:

1   What population of persons shall I work with?
2   Is a group experience suitable for the population I intend to work with or should I choose some other way of helping?
3   If I decide to form a group, shall I work alone or with one or more co-therapists?
4   Which group structure is likely to benefit the persons to be brought into the group? What are the implications of structure for therapist style?
5   What steps do I need to take to increase the likelihood that the group will fit within its wider environment without damage ensuing either for the group or for parts of the environment?
6   What further practical decisions have to be made before the group can start?
7   How shall I monitor and assess the group and my own behaviour as therapist? How shall I find support and consultation for myself?
8   Who will be invited to join the group as members? How do I select members and compose a group? Do members need to be prepared for participating in the group, and if so, by what means?
9   What shall I say when the group first meets?

Some of these decisions matter a good deal, others not so much, but all have to be taken. Some decisions, once made, cannot be unmade without serious cost. For instance, once it is decided to bring a particular person into a group, one cannot decide later that this had been an error and exclude that person from the group. Rather, one can do this, but should not do it lightly because of the likely damaging consequences for the person and for the group. Other decisions are open to amendment in the light of further experience, and no bad consequences are likely to follow. For instance, a therapist may have decided on an open discussion group, only to realise when the sessions begin that the members cannot listen to each other and build on one another's contributions. It is not too late too change the structure and no harm will occur if one does so.

I have listed nine decisions, but there could have been more or there could have been fewer, depending on how they are grouped together or separated out. I make this point to avoid implying that there is something fixed and official about this list of nine. The order in which they are presented, I believe, makes sense. Some decisions need to be made early because they influence other decisions which can only be made as one gets nearer to finalising a plan.

Each of the decisions will be discussed in turn. A brief final section discusses bases for making decisions.

WHAT POPULATION OF PERSONS SHALL I WORK WITH?

The setting of one's work limits the kinds of people with whom one can work but certain choices usually remain. A psychiatric out-patient clinic attached to a hospital, for instance, is likely to include some people suffering from acute anxiety or depression though still managing their day-to-day lives, others on the verge of a severe breakdown, others in a crisis triggered by some change in life circumstances, and still others who have been discharged from an in-patient facility and are now living in the community. As another example: if a therapist is in private practice, potential patients tend to be managing day-to-day life (some of them, just barely) but may be experiencing different kinds and levels of anxiety, depression, isolation, uncertainty or dissatisfaction with their lives. As still another example, a centre for homeless men in a large city defines a population but, again, there is diversity. Some of the men may have been fixed in a homeless life style for a long time; others will only recently have emerged from a mental institution or prison; still others will have recently been wrenched or expelled from a family. Within each pool of potential clients or patients there is a degree of diversity. It is virtually always the case that the work setting limits but does not determine choice.

A therapist's level of experience and confidence may influence the choice of population with which to work. Some populations are much easier to work with than others, because members drawn from it can be expected to be well motivated, eager to take advantage of opportunities for sharing experiences and ventilating feelings, and unlikely to be disruptive and difficult to manage. If a group therapist is relatively inexperienced it makes sense to start with an 'easy' group, or arrange to work in the first instance with a more experienced colleague. I have been told many times in recent years, by members of training courses, that they have been pressed by their managers to take on groups which they do not feel equipped to work with. Managers are likely to want to provide for the full range of people served by the unit, to generate a 'fair' work-load, and so on. They may not take adequately into account practitioners' needs to avoid excessive anxiety, preserve their own sense of competence, and at the same time develop their skills. Negotiation is of course needed, with reference both to the sorts of people to be worked with, and forms of support through supervision or consultation. To support their point, practitioners can emphasise longer-term benefits in the form of confident, motivated and increasingly skilled staff. Pressure from managers on staff to take on more and more difficult groups seems more prevalent now than it was fifteen or so years ago, when the first edition of this book was being written. Then, practitioners often reported that their managers and supervisors were wary of making use of groups, considering one-to-one work preferable. Those who wanted to work with groups had to make a case for doing so, and did not always succeed.

When choosing who to bring into a group, one decision is whether to draw the members of a prospective group from the same population or sub-population or from several. Often it makes sense to create a relatively homogeneous group by drawing from a single population. For instance, persons who have lost practical skills of living and are at about the same level of skill can usefully be brought together since members will be comparable with respect to current state; a preferred state can be identified which applies to all of them; and a programme can be devised which is likely to suit them all. Persons who belong to particular sub-populations within the larger 'victims of fate' or 'linked-fate' populations (categories 1 and 2 in Chapter 2) can be expected to understand what others who are in a similar situation are facing. On the other hand, bringing people together who have a particular physical handicap may be counter-productive because a group experience (especially a lengthy one) could support an identity based on the handicap. Young offenders brought together into a group may be so similar in outlook that they mutually support a world view which maintains them in their delinquent behaviours. If this is likely, special care needs to be taken to bring diversity into the group.

IS A GROUP EXPERIENCE SUITABLE FOR THE POPULATION I INTEND TO WORK WITH OR SHOULD I CHOOSE SOME OTHER WAY OF HELPING?

A group experience is just one of a number of ways of providing help. Others include one-to-one psychotherapy of various kinds; informal support provided in the course of group living; informal support through visits to patients or clients in their own homes; chemotherapy; or practical rather than psychotherapeutic help.

People are unlikely to profit from a group if they are unable to listen to and interact with others, or at the very least derive some comfort from being in physical proximity with others. These can be regarded as minimal criteria for the use of groups. By these criteria one might rule out the floridly psychotic, the most severely mentally handicapped, those so sunk in mental illness that close physical proximity with others is in itself profoundly threatening, and those so beset by internal concerns that they have virtually tuned out the outside world.

Sometimes it is appropriate to defer providing any form of help but simply to keep in touch with an ongoing situation. Sometimes it is appropriate to concentrate on supporting and strengthening personal networks rather than working directly with patients or clients.

It should be emphasised that at this stage in planning one is thinking about the suitability of groups for whole populations or sub-populations, which means for persons who fit into some large category. It is often the case that a group experience is correctly judged to be potentially useful for a population *in general* but that nevertheless there are some people within the population for whom a group experience is contraindicated. Selection and preparation become important – points which are discussed later in this sequence (pp. 75–8).

IF I DECIDE TO FORM A GROUP, SHALL I WORK ALONE OR WITH ONE OR MORE CO-THERAPISTS?

This decision could be made later and is sometimes made earlier. I have placed it here because it is at this point that one is ready to think more specifically about the shape and character of the group. If there are to be co-therapists, there are advantages in collaborative planning from this point onwards. Both therapists can influence further decisions and the two together can test their potential compatibility and prepare themselves for working with the group.

Some group structures require more than one therapist. This will be the case, for instance, if a relatively large group of adolescents or latency-age children are to spend part of the time in sub-group activities. In other situations, working alone or with a colleague is a matter of choice and preference. Sometimes there is no choice, either because a co-therapist is not available and one therefore must work alone, or because the service-providing organisation has a policy of pairing a less experienced with a more experienced therapist for training purposes.

There are potential advantages and potential disadvantages in working together with someone else. Whether advantages outweigh disadvantages or vice versa depends very much on the persons concerned and whether or not they can find ways to work in a complementary, congenial and mutually supportive way. If all goes well between co-therapists, one of them may notice and act on some event which escapes the notice of the other. One may participate in a way which cues the other into understanding what is going on. Co-therapists can engage in post-session discussions. On the other hand it is both painful and counter-productive if co-therapists are incompatible to the point of undermining one another's efforts. It is a good idea to keep the possibility of working together open for a time before making a final decision. Potential co-therapists can share their views about how the group can and should operate. They can discuss and compare their personal styles when working with a group. If discussions reveal likely compatibility and complementarity, prospective co-therapists can move ahead with greater confidence. If, in contrast, discussions reveal unresolvable conflicts or very divergent thinking, it is not too late to decide not to work together.

I do not of course mean that in order to work well together co-therapists need to share precisely the same views or take a comparable stance towards the group. In fact, the advantage of co-therapy lies in a certain divergence with respect to skills, sensitivities and intervention styles. However, serious incompatibilities can occur. Acknowledging these and deciding not to work together may be painful, but not nearly so painful as trying to work, session after session, with a seriously incompatible co-therapist.

Roller and Nelson (1993) have written a useful article on co-therapy in which they discuss some of the benefits which may accrue to both the therapists and the group members, and some of the problems which may arise.

WHICH GROUP STRUCTURE IS LIKELY TO BENEFIT THE PERSONS TO BE BROUGHT INTO THE GROUP? WHAT ARE THE IMPLICATIONS OF STRUCTURE FOR THERAPIST STYLE?

Groups can be structured to rely on open discussion, topic-orientated discussion, activities or exercises, or some combination of these. Structure also includes the expected duration of the group in terms of number of sessions, whether it is to be time-limited or not, and the duration and frequency of sessions.

There are a large number of possibilities: for example, a time-limited group which is to meet for one-and-a-half hours per week and is to go on for, say, twenty sessions and rely on open discussion; a 'slow-open' group which relies on open discussion and is expected to go on indefinitely, with most patients remaining for very long periods; a short-term time-limited group which is to meet once a week for twelve weeks and discuss a different topic each time, set by the therapist; a short-term time-limited group which is to meet for eight sessions and make use of open discussion; a group which is to meet once a month indefinitely, with each session devoted to a particular topic; a group which is to meet daily for five days, two hours at a time, with each session pre-planned to include periods of exercises or activities followed by periods of discussion; an activity-based group which is to meet once a week for two-and-a-half hours with no planned termination date; and so on.

It should be mentioned parenthetically that open-discussion groups are sometimes referred to as 'unstructured'. This is not accurate, for open discussion is as much a structure as any other, though the structure is not as 'heavy' as in, for instance, a group in which the therapist expects to lead people though pre-planned activities.

With reference to time span, I have the impression (no proof) that many therapists assume that very long-term groups are 'deeper' and therefore better than short-term groups, which are regarded as more 'superficial'. Such an assumption misses the point that the duration of the group, along with other elements of structure, ought to match the situation and needs of the prospective members. Some people (especially those drawn from a population of people who share some preoccupying

concern) are essentially psychologically healthy. They are not in need of fundamental personality change, are able to move quickly into discussing significant
personal material, and do not need a very lengthy therapeutic experience. People
who persistently engage in self-defeating behaviours, become involved in destructive or unfulfilling relationships and/or have adopted unsatisfying life styles are
likely to need a longer-term therapeutic experience. Very damaged people also may
need a longer term of experience which offers ongoing support, or they may profit
from a number of short-term group experiences dispersed over time.

In making decisions concerning a group's structure, one is aiming for internal
viability: a group which will function reasonably well, most of the time, as a
therapeutic environment suited to and usable by its members. Arriving at a suitable
structure is an act of the informed imagination. It requires the forecasting of the
likely consequences of one set of decisions rather than another, on the basis of
one's understanding of a population or sub-population; awareness of the range of
groups which *can* be designed; and an appreciation of the demands which different
structures make on group members. Sometimes a choice needs to be made between
alternative structures which are judged to be equally suitable. A structure is not
desirable or undesirable on its own, but only in the light of the needs and capabilities
of the population it is intended to serve.

The structure decided upon will have implications for therapist style. Open
discussion groups, for instance, require the therapist to be inactive enough to allow
themes to arise in the group, yet ready to be active when members need support or
encouragement to explore further, or when members run out of their own resources.
Activity-centred groups require a more active style in which the therapist introduces
activities and guides members through them. A time-limited group requires the
therapist to remind members of time constraints at the beginning of the group and
again towards the end, and to support as full use as possible of the termination phase
of the group. Co-therapists who discuss such matters beforehand are more likely to
work effectively together.

WHAT STEPS DO I NEED TO TAKE TO INCREASE THE LIKELIHOOD THAT THE GROUP WILL FIT WITHIN ITS WIDER ENVIRONMENT WITHOUT DAMAGE ENSUING EITHER FOR THE GROUP OR FOR PARTS OF THE ENVIRONMENT?

Internal viability is of course essential but a group also has to survive in its
environment. Few if any groups are isolated and insulated from a wider environment
– usually a service-providing organisation of some kind and a network of outside
organisations and/or individuals. Within a service-providing unit or organisation,
diverse activities for patients (or clients or attenders) may be combined into a
programme including, for instance, one-to-one psychotherapy, community or ward
meetings, a programme of activities and outings and so on, and one or more

therapeutic groups. A therapeutic group for patients or clients or residents may exist side by side with groups for relatives. A network of outside individuals and organisations often bears on work with a group: for instance, schools, the police, probation officers, and so on. Even therapists in private practice – a work setting which may appear to be independent – are likely to rely upon a network of referrers.

A group is not always a good fit with the larger organisation of which it is a part. Especially if conducting groups is a new venture within an organisation, the very fact that there *is* a group may upset established ways of thinking about accountability, of allocating work, of using space. There may be conflicts or potential conflicts among staff over jurisdiction and responsibility. One part of the programme could undermine the effectiveness of another, or members of staff might fear that this could happen. A patient or client who is in both individual and group therapy could behave in ways which set the therapists against one another. Managers may require forms of record-keeping which the group therapist considers likely to interfere with maintaining confidentiality within the group. And so on.

At this stage in planning, the prospective group therapist(s), other staff directly involved with people likely to become group members, and managers need to communicate with one another over planning decisions, so that the impact of the group on the organisation, and vice versa, can be anticipated in so far as this is possible before the group actually begins. Decisions need to be made about what kinds of ongoing communication, with whom, need to be provided for. The aim of course is to achieve complementarity, and to avoid working at cross-purposes or allowing one part of a programme to sabotage another part of it.

Inter-organisational and network dynamics can easily involve conflicts of interest. This is understandable when one considers that organisational or professional cultures differ one from the other with respect to goals, procedures, and world view, including assumptions about what is good for people and how staff should operate. It is not unusual for a school, for example, or the police to pursue policies or take actions which work against what the staff of a residential facility consider to be the best interests of those in their care. Some inter-organisational problems are ongoing. They are never really solved, but need constant attention to keep them under a degree of control.

WHAT FURTHER PRACTICAL DECISIONS HAVE TO BE MADE BEFORE THE GROUP CAN START?

Further practical decisions have to do with the number of persons to be included in the group, venue, the arrangement of the room, and the records which are to be kept.

The size of the group will influence the experiences of its members. A large group allows some members to locate themselves at the periphery of the group (which may be suitable for some populations and not others). A very small group loses opportunities for exchange and interpersonal comparison. There are differences of opinion in the literature as to how big is too big, and how small is too small, but usually a membership of six to nine or so is regarded as about right.

Sometimes there is choice as to venue and sometimes there is not. A group needs to meet *somewhere*, but less-than-ideal meeting places can be tolerated and do not necessarily work against the viability of the group. This was brought home to me on an occasion when the only place available to me to conduct a group composed of psychiatric inpatients was an alcove at one side of a large ward. Everything that went on in the group was open to view, and if non-members were near enough they could hear the conversation. This struck me as a serious disadvantage, for how could privacy and confidentiality be maintained? Yet things turned out well and the setting proved to be an advantage. A few of those who had declined to join the group stationed themselves just outside the alcove, where they could hear all that occurred. One person changed her position each time, sometimes approaching, sometimes moving away. I judged that these 'non-members' might be achieving some benefit, although there was no evidence one way or the other. It seemed reasonable to suppose that they were regulating their degree of exposure to the group, possibly gaining some benefits through watching and listening, while avoiding direct participation.

The arrangement within the meeting room – for instance, whether there is to be a table or an open circle of chairs – matters and can be influenced by the therapist. Some people feel safer and less exposed if they are sitting at a table. Others can tolerate an open circle. All the chairs should be the same.

A decision will also have to be made about whether to keep written records and if so, what kinds. Some forms of record-keeping may be required by managers or heads of units. In addition or instead, therapists may decide to keep certain forms of records to support their own learning both while the group is going on and afterwards (see the next sub-section, below, and Chapter 18, where this point is developed in further detail).

HOW SHALL I MONITOR AND ASSESS THE GROUP, AND MY OWN BEHAVIOUR AS THERAPIST? HOW SHALL I FIND SUPPORT AND CONSULTATION FOR MYSELF?

Structures and procedures for monitoring and assessing a group need to be decided upon before a group actually begins. It is no use deciding by the sixth or eighth session that it would have been interesting and useful to have notes of each session, or that co-therapists could profitably have engaged in post-session discussions, or that it would have been valuable to have assessed, at the start of the group, each member's current state in order to help in making judgements later on about gains. Monitoring and assessing will not happen unless planned from the start.

I take it for granted that some form of monitoring and assessing should go on as the group proceeds, and also that much can be gained by reviewing a group after it has ended. I will not go into further detail here, because structures and procedures and how they may actually be used is discussed in detail in Chapter 18, which is about learning from one's own practice experience.

WHO WILL BE INVITED TO JOIN THE GROUP AS MEMBERS? HOW DO I SELECT MEMBERS, AND COMPOSE A GROUP? DO MEMBERS NEED TO BE PREPARED FOR PARTICIPATING IN A GROUP, AND IF SO, BY WHAT MEANS?

Selection and composition are important tasks which influence how well the group is likely to operate once it gets going. Preparation is useful for some kinds of groups and populations; not so crucial for others.

With regard to selection, it seems best not to bring into a group anyone in an acute state of crisis or anyone who displays profound dread of entering a group and is unable to articulate anything further about the nature of the dread, or reasons for it. Dread is not the same as fear, and still less is it the same as having reservations about being in a group. Many people have reservations about entering a group but are nevertheless prepared to join one, especially if their reservations can be aired in a preliminary interview.

With regard to composition, groups seem to work best if they are *homogeneous* with regard to level of vulnerability, and *heterogeneous* with regard to preferred defences. If a group contains one or a few people who are much more personally vulnerable than the others, the majority will move relatively quickly into areas which the more vulnerable ones find intolerably threatening. The risk is that some individuals will become over-faced and withdraw literally or psychologically from the group.

Heterogeneity with respect to preferred defence is desirable because it lessens the risk that individual preferences will be mutually supported and reinforced through the group interaction, thus becoming established as collusive defences (in group focal conflict terms, as restrictive solutions). One need only imagine a group made up of intellectualisers or of deniers to see the point of this. If *everyone* intellectualises or denies there will be no one within the group membership to challenge the defence or provide any contrast with it. There is a risk of the group getting stuck in some unprofitable or constricted way of interacting.

In general, it is best to avoid including anyone who stands out in comparison with the others by virtue of age, sex, race, level of education and so on. This point of view is supported by theory. If there is just *one* person who is much older or is noticeably better educated than the others, it becomes easy for the members to locate such a person within some restrictive solution (such as making use of the person as a substitute therapist). This holds the person in a position or role within the group which tends to insulate him or her from potentially beneficial experiences associated with sharing and comparing. There is also a risk of one member becoming stereotyped. If there is, say, only *one* man in a group otherwise composed of women, he may become the repository of attitudes towards men in general. He may be deprived of opportunities to be seen for what he is. Instead, he is seen as what others assume he must be. The same point can be made, of course, if there is just one woman in an otherwise all male group, or one black in a group otherwise composed of whites, or vice versa. This principle of composition can be understood in group focal conflict terms but one can arrive at the same point of view by different routes. This same principle is referred to by MacKenzie (1990) as the 'Noah's Ark' principle and by Pollack and Slan (1995) as the 'sore thumb' principle.

Selecting members with an eye to the composition of a group is one of the more important planning decisions, judged by potential consequences. The question remains as to the means by which a suitable composition can be achieved. Since composing a group is a somewhat inexact art, it would be better to say that the question is how to avoid the most dysfunctional compositions. There are two main courses of action open to a therapist. The first is to accept members on a first come, first served basis. The second is to carry out selection interviews. Either course of action can be justified, depending on circumstances.

Consider the first alternative: sometimes selection is not possible, for instance if one must work with, or at least extend invitations to, all the residents of a hostel or other residential facility. Sometimes selection is possible but unlikely to have a better result than bringing people into a group on a first-come, first-served basis. For instance, membership might be formed by open invitation to a potential population of participants – for example, to all parents of physically handicapped children attending an out-patient clinic. The group will be composed of individuals who opt in to the activity. This route can be chosen if there is no reason to believe that the homogeneity–heterogeneity principles named above will be violated.

Sometimes one wishes to take a more active part in decisions about selection and composition by conducting selection interviews. This will be the case if it cannot reasonably be assumed that virtually any member of a population will be a suitable candidate for a group experience, or if it is judged that there is a risk of ending up with an unbalanced composition.

A selection interview serves multiple purposes: it can provide information which helps one to decide whether or not to invite a person into a group; it can constitute preparation for prospective group members; and it allows a therapist to build up a group composition person by person, and so have some control over the balance in the membership.

If possible, it is best to begin a selection interview by getting to know the person without immediately bringing up the possibility of a group. As the discussion proceeds, one might judge that the person should not be brought into a group, for instance if he or she appears to be seriously threatened by the prospect of being in a group, or in a state of crisis. If so, one looks for alternative forms of help. The person need not feel that s/he failed some sort of admission test, because a group has not been mentioned. Taking this approach in a selection interview obviously depends on there being alternative forms of help available in the setting, or alternative sources of help to which an individual can easily be referred.

If, as the interview proceeds, one judges the person to be a potentially suitable candidate, one mentions the possibility of a group experience, and the person will respond with enthusiasm (not so frequent), with some reservations (quite frequent), or with dread (again, not so frequent).

Suppose that a person expresses fears and reservations. These can then be explored. Amongst the reservations which people express are fearing that others will look down on them or criticise or ridicule them; or that they will experience shame; or that there are personal matters which they could never bring up; or that they will say things about themselves which will upset them or which they will regret having said; or that everyone will know more than they do or be better off than they are; or that topics will come up in the group which will be upsetting. The therapist will of course acknowledge and discuss whichever worries surface. If fears can be named, and if the interviewer respects them and seeks to explore and understand them, this in itself is often enough to tip the balance and bring the person to the point of feeling ready to try a group. Some people will say that they prefer individual psychotherapy. When asked why, they may refer to some of these same fears and reservations, and/or they may say that in a group they will not have the exclusive attention of a therapist (which is of course true). The assumption that one needs the specific and exclusive attention of one professionally trained helper in order to achieve personal gains is widespread in the broader culture and it is no surprise that many people share it. If anyone makes this point one might say: 'Of course that is true, because the therapist has to listen to and try to understand everyone, but on the other hand the group creates opportunities to discuss common concerns with others in a similar situation, and to share and compare one's own situation and feelings with those of others.' This may or may not lead a person towards being ready to join a group. Sometimes one can alleviate fears by assuring people that they can decide for themselves what to say and what not to say.

Some people express dread when the possibility of a group is mentioned. Dread, by dictionary definition, is 'to look forward to with terror' (*Shorter Oxford English Dictionary*). Dread – really profound and unarticulated fear – is different from nameable fears and reservations. People who dread groups are often quite unable to say just what it is about a group that is so dreadful. They are alarmed at the prospect of being in a group in some gross, profound, and often inchoate way. When invited to give examples of the bad things that could happen, they are unable to do so. They are utterly convinced that they will be unable to cope. They cannot say more about it, and cannot name or examine their fears. Such people are most likely sensing something in themselves which makes being in a group somehow terribly dangerous. One does not encounter dread so very often but when one does it seems to me best to find some alternative form of help. The person concerned is sensing a personal vulnerability which may well make being in a group a damaging rather than a helpful experience.

After an interview has gone on for some time it is usually possible to form a view as to whether or not the person is a suitable candidate for the group one is forming. If one judges that the person could manage and profit from the group, and will fit into the composition, one can ask: 'What do you think? Join a group?' If the person says: 'Yes, o.k.' it is likely to mean that he or she feels that certain fears, though quite possibly still present, will prove to be manageable. If one judges that the person is likely to be overwhelmed by group events, or will not fit the emerging composition, one can quietly drop the matter and offer some alternative form of help.

A selection interview of the kind just described can constitute useful preparation for a group experience. The individual rehearses, for him- or herself, what a group is probably going to be like, what could or could not easily be said and shared in it, and what fears and anxieties are likely to be experienced. Some therapists recommend much more elaborate and extended forms of preparation. MacKenzie (1990) suggests several individual preparatory interviews, and/or one or two pre-therapy group discussions. He points out that individual sessions help a person to find a focus for his or her participation in the group, especially useful for short-term groups. Preparation which consists of pre-group meetings may include structured exercises, or discussion based on a rather lengthy information handout which MacKenzie gives to prospective group members beforehand. This includes sections titled 'Do groups really help people?'; 'How group therapy works'; 'Common myths about group therapy'; 'How to get the most out of group therapy'; 'Common stumbling blocks'; and 'Group rules' (see MacKenzie 1990: 107–14). When the group meets for its preparatory work, MacKenzie takes those present through the handout, paragraph by paragraph. Budman does something similar though not so elaborate. He and his colleagues prepare people for membership through individual interviews lasting 30–60 minutes, plus participation in a one-and-a-half hour pre-group workshop (Budman *et al.* 1996). (See the first example in Chapter 7.)

Decisions about what whether or not to offer preparation, and the sort of preparation to offer, are based on one's understanding of the population to be worked with, and also on the expected duration of the group. Those who, like MacKenzie, expect to work in relatively short-term time-limited groups often emphasise the usefulness of preparatory work which makes a 'jump-start' more likely.

One more decision needs to be made before the group actually starts.

WHAT SHALL I SAY WHEN THE GROUP FIRST MEETS?

There are many ways to open a group. Amongst these are referring to what the members have in common, referring to opportunities to share and compare experiences, describing the procedures to be followed (for example, open discussion, exercises, and so on), reminding members of meeting times, introducing the members, not introducing the members, getting members started with an exercise or activity if one is to be used, or saying nothing.

In general, whatever one does to open a group should support the structure one has in mind and make it easier for people to begin to participate. The structure is more likely to work as intended if it is described at the beginning even if members already know about it through an individual interview or other preparatory work. Thus one might refer to meeting times and places, the duration of sessions, the duration of the group, and expected procedures.

Is it appropriate to say nothing at all? This is recommended by some therapists who work with long-term ongoing groups in which 'uncovering' is to be emphasised. Saying nothing places responsibility for getting started squarely on the members. It also tends to stir up anxiety so, if considering getting started by saying nothing, one has be fairly sure that group members can tolerate anxiety and not respond by fleeing from the group. On the grounds that, in many groups, saying nothing generates unmanageable levels of anxiety and does not help a group to get started, I favour some sort of opening comment. Most people tend to feel reassured if they at least hear the therapist's voice.

Some group therapists or workers lay down ground rules about, for instance, attending regularly, coming to sessions on time, maintaining confidentiality, or avoiding contact with one another outside the group. Some make use of written contracts. Reminding members of the structure is in itself a mild form of pressure (for example,'We will meet on Monday and Thursday nights, beginning at 7.30 pm, for one-and-a-half hours'). Some therapists introduce not only rules, but sanctions if rules are broken. For instance, members may be told at the start that overt violence will be followed by expulsion from the group.

Decisions about whether or not to state guidelines, make rules, and introduce and utilise sanctions have to be made with reference to each group, taking into account its structure and the population being served. Stating rules and guidelines does not guarantee conformity to them. Group therapists cannot control punctuality and so on. Rather than stating rules prescriptively, a therapist may decide to say that 'a group usually works best if . . .'. Or a therapist may decide to say nothing at all about such matters on the grounds that, if members are concerned about, for instance, confidentiality, they will bring up the matter themselves. If attendance, tardiness, or outside contacts occur and interfere with the effectiveness of the group, that may be the time to pay attention to them.

Very lengthy opening statements are to be avoided on grounds that they unnecessarily postpone the start of the group.

BASES FOR MAKING DECISIONS

Decisions should be made in the light of anticipated consequences. When planning a therapeutic group, the best decisions are those which tilt the probabilities towards benefiting the individuals who are to become members. One constantly asks oneself: When making this particular decision, what alternatives are possible and what are the most likely consequences of each?

Decisions which need to be made when planning a group are interrelated. If one decides to conduct a short-term group, one will want members to move into productive work as quickly as possible. Consequently one will need to decide whether members' own strong motivations will move them into useful exchanges quickly, or whether preparation is needed to make a 'jump-start' more likely. If the population one intends to work with is inherently homogeneous with respect to traits likely to influence the work of therapy, one will need to make a specific effort to balance the composition. And so on.

A therapist's freedom of choice when planning a group may be restricted by circumstances outside his or her own control, located in policies and practices in the work setting. Some populations will be available, others will not. A therapist may be obliged by organisational policy to work with a co-therapist. Policy may favour short-term groups. And so on. Despite limitations on choice, and despite not being able always to predict the consequences of one decision over another, careful attention to planning has pay-offs for the group. Decisions made during planning cannot guarantee a viable and benefit-promoting group, but they can influence probabilities in a positive direction.

Chapter 7

Examples: different groups for different populations

This chapter draws upon the literature on group psychotherapy and group work for examples of the end-products of planning and for guidance in planning for particular populations. It includes five main sections:

- Six examples of groups designed for different populations of patients or clients.
- Appreciating the range and variety of groups by sampling the recent literature.
- Responses to recent pressures to conduct short-term and other forms of time-effective psychotherapy groups.
- A second look at some of the planning decisions set out in the preceding chapter.
- Further guidance to be found in the literature.

The first three sections could be presented in any order. They are three different approaches to understanding varieties of small therapeutic groups. Taken together, they show the versatility of the small group as a medium for help. They also provide more detailed comment on some of the planning decisions discussed in the preceding chapter.

SIX EXAMPLES OF GROUPS DESIGNED FOR DIFFERENT POPULATIONS OF PATIENTS OR CLIENTS

Example 1: groups for people with personality disorders, structured in terms of six-month contracts, renewable twice

Budman and his colleagues (1996) describe groups especially designed for people at the top end of the personality disorder continuum: people who are holding down jobs (or flit from job to job) but are nevertheless isolated, behave maladaptively, and in general are unsettled in their lives. Six-month contracts are used, renewable twice, so that members can be in a group for up to eighteen months. Budman *et al.* emphasise the importance of structuring the group experience for these relatively severely impaired patients. Pre-group preparation is offered which consists of individual interviews lasting 30–60 minutes, plus participation in a one-and-a-half hour pre-group workshop. In the individual interview the prospective group member is helped to identify specific goals which he or she would like to work towards, and is encouraged to discuss any anticipated difficulties or obstacles. The workshop is a structured experience which includes, first, introductions; second, role-paying in small groups of three or four, in which a member describes and role-plays a problematic interpersonal situation, followed by other members role-playing alternative ways of responding to the situation; and third, a whole-group exercise in which everyone works on some group task. A leader is present who summarises, requests feedback from the members, and actively shapes and guides the experience. These pre-group experiences are also a screening device, for on the basis of what the therapist observes and hears, he or she may decide that a particular person is unsuited to the group.

When the group actually begins, the therapist is fairly active but not coercive, focusing mainly on here-and-now interactions within the group, striving to show members how their behaviour has an impact on or is received by others, helping them to see and try alternatives and, in general, seeking to improve interpersonal skills. Interpretations may be offered at the individual, sub-group or group-as-a-whole level. The time-limited nature of the group is frequently called to the members' attention, in order to support focused work. Members are encouraged to set their own goals and to set bench-marks by which they can evaluate their own progress. As the termination date approaches, the therapist writes a letter to each group member which focuses on what each person has accomplished. These letters are brought to group sessions, read within the group, and feedback is elicited from both the recipient of the letter and other group members.

Example 2: a group for parents of children with progressive diseases, which met for four sessions at a time, at year-long intervals

Engebrigtsen and Heap (1988) describe a group for parents of children with a progressive inherited disease which leads to loss of physical and mental functioning and then inevitably to death by, at best, the late twenties. The condition is rare, affecting (at that time) a total of only thirty children and young people in the whole of Norway. Work was carried out at the Frambu Health Centre south of Oslo, which provides services to children with a wide range of handicaps and progressive diseases. Children and members of their families were admitted for a period of two weeks, once a year. As the families lived in all parts of Norway, many of them travelled long distances to attend the Centre. They typically knew no one else in their home communities who was similarly affected. The authors describe the families as being in a state of chronic sorrow.

During their two-week stay, parents were offered four group sessions of one-and-a-half hours' duration each. A year later, when they returned, they again participated in a group, with many of the same members as before. Groups were homogeneous with respect to the illness suffered by the children but the ages of the children differed, as did the stage of deterioration. In some families, more than one child was affected.

The authors describe the groups as supportive in character. Those conducting the groups chose not to press members beyond the limits which they themselves showed they could tolerate. Themes were allowed to emerge through the interactions of members. On the basis of analysing a number of such groups, themes were named by the therapists as: the impact of the illness on family culture and organisation; ways of coping; the loneliness of caring; uncertainty; the Frambu experience; and ambivalence toward the sick child. Although the time was so limited, family members often emerged feeling satisfied with how they coped with their difficult situations, at the same time becoming able to expand ways of coping and admitting to feelings previously concealed or denied. Sharing and comparing had positive consequences. During the year-long interval between face-to-face sessions, group members contacted one another by telephone. By this means they maintained interpersonal support. Their sense of being isolated with a problem which no one understood or shared was alleviated.

Example 3: open groups for adult children of holocaust survivors

Van der Hal *et al.* (1996) describe groups composed of adult children of holocaust survivors. They knew from their own work and that of others that such people can experience a wide range of problems in adult life, deriving from their parents' ways of responding to being survivors. For instance, holocaust survivors may find it difficult to allow their children to grow up as individuals and to separate themselves from the family, because this is experienced as yet another loss. They may place a thorough taboo on discussing any aspect of their holocaust experience or else never cease to talk about it. Either way, they convey an ongoing sense of horror to their offspring. They may insist that all is now 'normal', making it difficult if not impossible to face problems or difficulties within the family. They may expect their children to lead the kind of life they themselves feel they have been deprived of. Consequences for the offspring include guilt at *not* having experienced the same horrors as their parents, or feeling pressed into a degree of loyalty to the parents which makes it difficult for them to lead their own lives, or taking on their parents' sense that no one can understand them or the experiences they have had, or general insecurity, low self-esteem, and anger.

A group experience seemed ready-made to help the children of survivors to deal with the problems they were left with. The authors emphasise that:

Groups provide various opportunities for expressing feelings, for naming and verbalizing experiences. They permit the children of survivors to clarify fragmented knowledge and compare experiences. Finally, groups offer a sense of collectivity and community that are necessary to permit expressions of grief and anger, while also fostering a separate sense of identity.

(Van der Hal *et al.* 1996: 195)

Groups were set up, but the therapists found that commitment and attendance were low, and that few groups became established as an ongoing activity. They judged that frequent meetings, with the expectation that members would attend regularly, generated a too-intense experience. They therefore decided on another group structure altogether. They established a series of monthly meetings, each to last for one-and-three-quarters hours. People were informed through newspaper advertisements that such meetings were to take place, and the series of meetings was given the title 'Communication in survivor families'. There was no 'membership' as such, and no pressure to attend regularly. The authors report that attendance ranged from three to sixty, averaging out at about twenty-five. There were three therapists, in case individuals experienced crises during sessions which would require the attention of one person. Topics were introduced for each session, such as 'friendship', 'communication with parents', 'religious holidays'. Those attending were allowed freedom to pursue matters outside the declared topic.

This structure, so different from what is usually considered appropriate for therapeutic groups, worked well. There was a small core group of relatively regular attenders, but some people attended only once, and some attended for short sequences of sessions and might or might not return later. Some individuals took months to decide to come to a meeting after first hearing about them. Despite shifts in attendance and a continually changing group composition, some continuity became established in the group. The authors report that those who attended opened up quickly, and were ready to talk about their experiences.

It seems clear that many individuals were able to attend these group sessions precisely because choice was placed in their own hands. They were not required to commit themselves to the group and they could regulate their attendance, thus controlling their exposure to the group and to the stresses generated by attending. The authors point to one particular and special advantage of a group structured in this way which is specific to the offspring of survivors: namely, that the group continues to exist whether or not any particular individual attends. The therapists learned that many children of holocaust survivors feel that their presence in the family is necessary to its survival: the family has suffered many losses and is already fragmented in that there is no extended family. In consequence the family unit is tiny. Adult offspring fear that a further loss, in the form of their establishing a life of their own, would be intolerable to the parents. The offspring are, in consequence, deeply conflicted about separating enough from their parents to lead a life appropriate to an adult. The fact that the group goes on, whether the individual is present or not, is a relief for them. The authors report that many of those who attended came to feel that the survival of the family of origin was no longer dependent entirely on them. A healthy separation from their own families, into more independent adulthood, was facilitated.

Example 4: a task-orientated group for people living in a home for the elderly

Staff in this residential home for elderly people in the north-east of England organised 'reminiscence sessions' which were held once a week and were open to any resident who wished to attend. Residents were told that the meetings would be opportunities to think back to what life was like when they were growing up. No instructions or directions were presented and for the most part none was needed. Staff were ready with prompts in case the conversation died down, such as: 'What about travel? How did you get around and where did you go?' Some members brought photographs and, in a few cases, household objects. A picture began to build up of what life was like fifty, sixty or seventy years ago in and around this small market town. Almost forgotten features of that life were recalled – such as the 'Tom Pudding' barges that operated on a nearby canal. The old people as well as the staff enjoyed these sessions. The meetings led to an associated activity, in which members of a local folk club were invited in to lead residents in singing old-time songs.

In describing this activity, staff emphasised that the sessions were popular, and experienced by both residents and staff as 'fun'. One member of staff said: 'I strongly believe that many elderly people die because they have lost the will to live. They can't see the point in having to get up morning after morning to face a day which lacks purpose or meaning.' This, plus a wish to avoid the grimness of inactive old people sitting in chairs in a row, with their backs against a wall, was what motivated staff to plan for and work with this group.

A 'reminiscence' group fits Erik Erikson's ideas about life stage. Erik Erikson (1950) named the developmental task of the final life stage as 'Ego Integrity vs Despair'. Negotiating this life stage successfully means being, on the whole, satisfied with one's life and experiencing it as having had coherence and meaning. As is the case for all life stages, old people need to maintain a sense of identity – that is, the sense that despite changes associated with old age, they are still essentially the same person they were in earlier life.

Reminiscing with contemporaries during the last stage of life assists in avoiding despair and achieving integrity, and maintaining a sense of ego identity. This was recognised intuitively by those who planned and conducted these groups. In the group meetings, individuals recognised the good and the bad, the hardships and the pleasures. They supported one another by valuing and indeed celebrating aspects of earlier life in which all had shared.

Example 5: short-term time-limited groups for people who have suffered personal losses

Piper *et al.* (1992) offer a practice model for people who have suffered personal losses. Groups consist of a series of twelve weekly sessions of one-and-a-half hours each. They see such groups as moving through three stages: a beginning stage (sessions 1–3); a middle stage (sessions 4–8); and a termination stage (sessions 9–12). The duration of each stage differs somewhat from group to group.

To support the effectiveness of such short-term time-limited groups, Piper *et al.* emphasise the importance of selection and preparation, and of the therapist's intervention approach. Care is taken to include members likely to be able to move quickly into productive work. Criteria for inclusion are that there be a demonstrable pathological grief reaction, 'psychological mindedness', and a willingness to enter a short-term group. Assessing suitability for group membership is done in a series of individual interviews, which also constitute preparation for participating in the group. These practices help members to move through the beginning stage relatively quickly.

As to therapist approach: Piper and colleagues report focusing on the here-and-now and relying substantially on group-level interpretations. For the latter, they give as reasons that group interpretations emphasise the commonalities amongst the members, are often combined with individual interpretations, and can be presented in ways which enhance receptivity. They also say that there needs to be a balance between interpretations directed at the group and interpretations directed at individuals (Piper 1995).

Example 6: a multiple group therapy programme for adolescent substance abusers who also have psychiatric problems

Pressman and Brook (1999) describe a day-hospital programme for adolescents aged 14–18 who are substance abusers and also have mental health problems. Participants attend daily from 8.30 am to 2.30 pm, five days a week. Mondays through Thursdays are structured similarly, with members attending an on-site school in the mornings, a daily community meeting, and a range of further kinds of groups in the afternoons. The latter include a once-a-week forty-five minute psychotherapy group; a once-a-week forty-five minute self-awareness group which makes use of activities; a one-and-a-half hour multiple family group which meets once a week and includes the adolescents plus one or two parents of each, making a group of from ten to twenty-five people; a once-a-week forty-five minute substance abuse group which focuses both on altering substance-abuse behaviour and exploring factors associated with relapses; and a once-a-week forty-five minute health group which offers structured input, for instance on coping with withdrawal symptoms, preventing HIV infections, and avoiding pregnancy. The groups are conducted by different members of the staff, appropriate to the special focus of each group. Friday is reserved for outings which serve both educational and recreational purposes. Use of drugs is monitored through regular urine tests. Participants are also seen individually, to assess symptoms and provide a venue for bringing up matters which they feel they cannot bring up in the groups. Daily staff meetings are held after the adolescents leave for the day.

Selection criteria are strict. Mentally retarded adolescents are not brought into the programme because facilities for providing education are not available. Adolescents with a severe history of violence are referred to more supervised settings, and intravenous heroin users are referred to detoxification centres. Those already in the programme may be expelled from it if they repeatedly break the rules, which require regular attendance, remaining abstinent, and reporting any lapses into renewed drug-taking. If anyone takes drugs on the premises or offers drugs to others, they are expelled immediately. Entry criteria are thus quite strict and so are conditions for remaining in the programme. While the programme is quite structured, there is flexibility within group sessions. Pressman and Brook report that much cross-fertilisation occurs: issues arising in one part of the programme are often carried into and worked on in other parts of it.

APPRECIATING THE RANGE AND VARIETY OF GROUPS BY SAMPLING THE RECENT LITERATURE

There is a very large literature on types of groups planned for different populations of people. I sampled this literature by examining all the issues of the *International Journal of Group Psychotherapy* from January 1995 (an entirely arbitrary starting point) through to the end of 1999. This examination yielded the following:

*   Geczy and Sultenfuss (1995) on group psychotherapy on psychiatric hospital admission wards;
*   Belfer *et al.* (1995) on cognitive-behavioural group psychotherapy for agoraphobia and panic disorder;
*   Kleinberg (1995) on the group treatment of adults in midlife;
*   Aronson (1995) on groups for adolescent daughters of parents with AIDS;
*   Benjamin and Benjamin (1995) on working with mothers with dissociative disorders;
*   Stewart *et al.* (1995) on a support groups for dialysis and transplant patients;
*   Eliasoph and Donnellan (1995) on group therapy for individuals identified as autistic who are without speech and use facilitated communication;
*   Sultenfuss and Geczy (1996) on group psychotherapy on chronic wards in psychiatric hospitals;
*   Nightingale and McQueeny (1996) on group therapy for schizophrenics;
*   Budman *et al.* (1996) on time-effective group psychotherapy for patients with personality disorders;
*   Fenster (1996) on group treatment for 'people of color' (blacks and Latinos in the USA);

- Zamanian and Adams (1997) on group psychotherapy with sexually abused boys;
- Johnson (1997) on an existential model of group therapy for chronic mental conditions;
- Lubin and Johnson (1997) on working with traumatised women in groups (victims of sexual abuse and violence);
- Gartner (1997) on an analytic group for men who had been sexually abused as children;
- Goodman and Weiss (1998) on group therapy for Vietnam veterans suffering from war and childhood trauma;
- Kelly (1998) on group psychotherapy for persons with HIV and AIDS-related illnesses;
- Abbey and Farrow (1998) on group therapy with organ transplant patients;
- Allan and Scheidt (1998) on group psychotherapy for patients with coronary heart disease;
- Toner *et al.* (1998) on group therapy for patients with irritable bowel syndrome;
- Leszcz and Goodwin (1998) on group psychotherapy for women with metastatic breast cancer;
- Longstreth *et al.* (1998) on group psychotherapy for women molested in childhood;
- Müller and Barash-Kishon (1998) on psychodynamic-supportive group therapy for elderly holocaust survivors;
- Tantillo (1998) on group therapy for women with bulimia nervosa;
- Carbonell and Parteleno-Barehmi (1999) on psychodrama for girls coping with trauma; and
- Roller and Nelson (1999) on group psychotherapy treatment of borderline personalities.

Taken as a set, these articles describe a wide range of groups which differ from one another with respect to the kind of person served, the setting, and the approach taken by the therapist.

RESPONSES TO RECENT PRESSURES TO CONDUCT SHORT-TERM AND OTHER FORMS OF TIME-EFFECTIVE PSYCHOTHERAPY GROUPS

The term 'managed care' is now widely used to refer to management structures and procedures, both inside and outside service-providing organisations, which place considerable power for controlling access to treatment and the duration of treatment into the hands of managers and take power out of the hands of practitioners. The objective is cost containment. Managers put pressure on practitioners to serve more people than before, without additional resources.

Some group therapists have seen this as a boon and a potential support for group psychotherapy, for it is obvious that more people can be reached if they are worked with through groups rather than through individual psychotherapy. Others are much concerned that they will be unable to provide the treatment which patients and clients need. As it seems impossible to reverse this trend, it is forcing practitioners to reconsider the issue of duration: how long is long enough, for which populations and which kinds of problem? Could dispersed group experiences be as effective as a single, longer-term experience? Could other forms of 'time-effective' group psychotherapy be devised? Can it be argued that longer-term psychotherapy is more time-effective than shorter-term psychotherapy in some instances because it reduces the likelihood of problems recurring, with greater costs overall? What are the ethical implications of constricting access to treatment?

Much attention has been paid to these developments in recent issues of the *International Journal of Group Psychotherapy*. An article by Roy MacKenzie examined (1994b) implications for the field. This article was based on MacKenzie's presidential address to the American Group Psychotherapy Association in February 1994. In the same issue, Helfmann (1994) and Mone (1994) provided responses to MacKenzie's article. In the following year Rosenberg and Zimet (1995) reviewed research on brief group psychotherapy; and Gross (1995) provided a commentary on points made by Helfman and by Mone. The July 1996 issue of the journal was almost entirely devoted to 'managed care' arrangements in the USA and the consequent need to examine the potentials of short-term, time-limited groups and other time-effective group structures (see Piper (1996); Budman (1996); and articles by Steenbarger and Budman (1996); Piper and Joyce (1996); Budman *et al.* (1996a, 1996b)) The January 1997 issue of the same journal returns to this issue, concentrating this time on implications for delivery systems, ethical issues, and threats to the therapeutic alliance. Articles include Tutman (1997) on protecting the therapeutic alliance; Zimet (1997) on the impact on the profession and how services can be delivered; and Spitz (1997) on effects on treatment, training, and therapist morale.

Short-term time-limited groups and other time-effective structures are not a recent phenomenon, but it is probably fair to say that less status has been accorded them than traditional longer-term forms of group psychotherapy based on psychoanalytic principles. In consequence of these recent pressures, shorter-term formats are receiving increasing attention and attracting more respect.

The term time-effective, as used by Budman (1996), refers to (a) short-term, time-limited therapeutic groups; (b) groups which meet intermittently over longer time spans; and (c) longer-term time-limited groups which can be regarded as time-effective because they can make unnecessary still greater investments of time and money due to patient relapses or the need for repeated hospitalisation.

Rosenberg and Zimet (1995) provide a useful review article of brief group treatment. They emphasise that short-term groups are typically organised around specific treatment goals, which means that groups are composed homogeneously with respect to members' life circumstances or type of problem: for instance, specific medical illness or having been a victim of incest or being an abusing husband. Homogeneity of this kind is understood to support rapid movement towards cohesiveness. Goals are likely to be limited in scope. The therapist is more active than in traditional, longer-term forms of therapy, and is more likely to focus on current life situations rather than on the impact of early life experience. Rosenberg and Zimet comment sympathetically on how difficult it can be for group therapists accustomed to long-term open-ended groups, intended to effect basic personality change, to adapt to working with shorter-term groups. Quite significant shifts are required in how one thinks about therapeutic goals, experiences considered necessary to effect personal change, and oneself as therapist.

MacKenzie (1990) has provided a general text on time-limited group psychotherapy. His discussion includes groups which meet for as few as eight sessions and as many as thirty or forty. MacKenzie's groups have a definite termination date known by everyone from the beginning. Procedures are adopted which make it more likely that a group will move through its early stages quickly, and make the most of the time available. MacKenzie points out that homogeneity of composition assists rapid movement, as does preparation for group participation. To assist in the latter, he provides prospective members with a patient information handout (described in the previous chapter). The intention is to establish realistic expectations and a readiness to participate in potentially productive ways.

MacKenzie's (1995) edited book on using group therapy in managed care regards it as a foregone conclusion that the future of group psychotherapy lies in short-term groups for specific populations. A number of practice models are described by different practitioners, to illustrate possibilities.

Klein (1993) provides a comprehensive account and critique of short-term group psychotherapy which includes attention to time management, patient selection, composition, preparation, contracts with individuals and with the group, and the role of the therapist. Klein, like others, emphasises that short-term group therapy is a distinct modality and not merely an abbreviated form of more traditional, longer-term forms of group psychotherapy or group analysis. He points to further necessary thinking:

> Can the therapist, for example, maintain a neutral position, despite assuming an active stance? What about the frequency and the timing of therapist interventions in a group treatment context in which the therapist cannot afford to wait to accumulate substantial evidence before interpreting? When do therapist interpretations based on considerable inference shade over into persuasion, rather than psychoanalytic work?
>
> (Klein 1993: 267)

Some of the examples provided earlier in this chapter are time-effective in that they require relatively little investment of time on the part of the therapist, yet meet the needs of the group members. Short-term time-limited groups for people who have suffered personal losses are described by Piper *et al.* (fifth example). The second and third examples are of groups which met at longer than usual intervals. Engebrigtsen and Heap (second example) met with their groups for four sessions during a two-week period at yearly intervals. Van der Hal *et al.* (third example) designed a group for adult children of holocaust survivors which met just once a month. Neither Engebrigtsen and Heap nor Van der Hal and his colleagues had time-effectiveness in mind when they planned their groups. The structures they adopted suited the members' needs and, in the case of Engebrigtsen and Heap, were also influenced by practical considerations.

It should be noted that the most time-effective groups of all are self-help groups which do not require the presence of a therapist. Group therapists need to be informed about self-help groups, partly in order to refer patients to them when this is suitable, and partly to assist in judging whether a therapist-led group could usefully continue as a self-help group. (See Lieberman 1993 and Goodman and Jacobs 1994 for overview articles with substantial bibliographies.)

A SECOND LOOK AT SOME OF THE PLANNING DECISIONS SET OUT IN THE PRECEDING CHAPTER

This chapter sheds further light on certain of the steps in planning discussed in the preceding chapter – especially those which have to do with the structure of the group, the preparation of members, and monitoring and evaluating a group experience.

The fourth step in planning was stated as: 'Which group structure is likely to benefit the persons to be brought into the group?' Under that heading it was said that decisions about structure are made 'on the basis of one's understanding of a population or sub-population, of awareness of the range of groups which *can* be designed, and of an appreciation of the demands which different structures make on group members'. Some of the examples provided in this chapter show that the therapist's understanding of the population needs to be very close indeed, based on own and others' experience, and on material to be found in the literature. The second and fourth of the detailed examples presented in the first section of this chapter illustrate this point well. In Engebrigtsen and Heap's (1988) work on parents experiencing 'chronic sorrow' it was necessary to understand the impact of such an unusually powerful stressor, the personal resources which parents could bring to bear, and limits on what they could tolerate in the way of 'uncovering'. In their work with the adult children of holocaust survivors, Van der Hal *et al.* (1996) needed to understand the special pressures on such people to protect the fragmented family from any further loss.

Groups can be structured in their detail in many, many ways. An initial decision may be made about type of structure, but then further decisions may be needed *inside the parameters decided upon*. For instance, Van der Hal *et al.* decided on a structure in which groups met once a month and attendance was likely to be variable.

This required a topic-based approach, which in turn required careful consideration of topics which could frame group discussions while still allowing individual choice about how to participate.

In planning a structure for a group, practical considerations often have to be taken into account, such as members' physical distance from the therapeutic facility, or length of stay in a psychiatric hospital or hostel, or limitations on the availability of financial support if members must pay fees.

For many populations, it is worth considering whether structures can usefully be combined. Again, there are many possibilities. For instance, in working with schizophrenic patients, Nightingale and McQueeny (1996) combined a psychoeducational model with supportive psychotherapy. Pressman and Brook (1999) made use of a traditional form of psychotherapeutic group as just one part of a much wider programme which used different kinds of groups.

Several of the articles listed in the second section of this chapter show the importance of being prepared to depart from orthodoxy or tradition, if the needs of the prospective members require it. Eliasoph and Donnellan (1995) worked in groups with individuals identified as autistic who were without speech and used facilitated communication. Into a group of five members they brought a leader, an assistant leader, and a communication facilitator for each member, making seven staff or auxiliary staff in all. In this case there were good reasons for staff members to outnumber patients, something one would ordinarily avoid. Geczy and Sultenfuss (1995) were prepared to use very short (thirty-minute) but frequent (three times a week) sessions with in-patients to accommodate the patients' short attention spans.

Time constraints, as referred to in the third section in this chapter, require special attention to the fourth and the eighth planning steps – working out a structure, and preparing people for membership. With reference to structure, one suggestion is that many people could profit from a number of spaced group experiences, rather than one extended one. This requires changing one's thinking about what one expects people to achieve through a group experience. Rather than thinking in terms of fundamental change, which is associated with long-term intensive group treatment, therapists think in terms of specifically defined, shorter-term goals. Associated with this is being ready to work with the same patients again, in future groups as circumstances require. With respect to preparation, many therapists are working out quite elaborate forms of preparation in the expectation that this will assist members to get into meaningful discussion more quickly and reduce the number of group sessions required. Examples of time-effective groups show that external constraints on how much time individuals can spend in a group is not always or necessarily a matter for despair. Caution is indicated, however, for as Klein (1993) points out, short-term approaches cast up issues which need thought and investigation.

Pressures towards time-effectiveness also emphasise the importance of monitoring and assessing the group (the seventh step in planning). If one is moving into time-saving structures it will be important to assess the outcomes achieved and compare groups which use different structures or different ways of preparing members. Comparing groups places the practitioner in the position of researcher – a matter which is discussed in detail in Chapter 20, the final chapter in this book.

An overall point which can be drawn from this chapter is that effective planning requires both imagination and disciplined thinking. It is important to be able to imagine the unlikely: to be ready, when conditions require it, to depart from traditional assumptions and usual practices. It is equally important to be disciplined in one's thinking: to anticipate as carefully and closely as possible the likely consequences of making use of one group structure or one practitioner style rather than another.

FURTHER GUIDANCE TO BE FOUND IN THE LITERATURE

In planning, thinking out a structure likely to suit members' needs and capabilities is centrally important. If this can be done in a time-effective manner, so much the better. In some cases, however, 'short' may be 'too short'. Budman (1996) cautions that 'short' is not necessarily 'effective'. It is crucial to distinguish between efficiency and effectiveness. If 'efficiency' is mistakenly understood to mean 'using fewer resources', then one might end up making use of a structure which is not effective for the population concerned.

Schoenholtz-Read (1994) offers guidance for matching the potential group member with the most appropriate kind of group. She takes into account severity of problem or level of functioning; motivation for change; and individuals' expectations and goals. With reference to kinds of groups, she refers to in-patient and partial hospitalisation groups, out-patient groups, and 'other-than-therapy groups', by which she means self-help groups, '12-step groups' such as Alcoholics Anonymous, and psychoeducational groups.

In addition to articles and books already mentioned, the following are useful: Vannicelli (1992) on group psychotherapy with substance abusers and their family members; Yalom and Vinogradov (1988) on bereavement groups ; Harper-Giuffre and MacKenzie's (1992) edited book on group psychotherapy for people with eating disorders; Frankel's (1993) book on working with chronic mental patients; Spira's (1997) edited book on group therapy for medically ill patients; and Seligman and Marshak's (1990) edited book on group psychotherapy with special populations.

Kaplan's and Sadock's edited book, titled *Comprehensive Group Psychotherapy* (3rd edition, 1993), includes articles on group psychotherapy with the following special disorders and populations: anxiety and mood disorders; personality disorders; schizophrenia; the chronically mentally ill; alcoholics, substance abusers, and adult children of alcoholics; eating disorders; the medically ill; HIV-infected persons and their caregivers; cancer patients and the terminally ill; sexual dysfunctions; gender-dysphoric patients; gay men and lesbians; adults with a history of incest; rape victims and battered women; sexually abused children; post-traumatic stress disorder; children; adolescents; and the elderly.

Part III

Thinking and taking action during the life of a group

Chapter 8

'Think-work'

Listening, observing, and attributing meanings to what one hears and sees

In taking on the task of conducting a group, a therapist assumes the dual responsibility of saying and doing (a) that which will help the group to become, and remain for as much of the time as possible, a positive medium for help; and (b) that which will help each person to benefit from being in the group. Internal think-work – listening, observing, and trying to make sense of what one sees and hears – is a necessary part of this task.

Think-work occurs inevitably. Therapists are bound to form suppositions about the state of individual members, the state of the group, and the import of observed behaviour. Only a fraction of what a therapist thinks is actually expressed overtly in a group. The two are of course related but think-work goes on all the time while a therapist intervenes overtly in the group only from time to time. Therapists form hypotheses about the meaning of events and then make a separate decision about whether and how to act on them in the group. This chapter focuses on internal think-work.

Think-work is done in the face of situations which can be quite complex. A great deal may be happening all at once. Members do or do not build on the thread of the discussion, interrupt, change the subject, behave 'characteristically' or 'uncharacteristically', become irritated, get upset, make jokes, withdraw, and so on. They form alliances, shift alliances, support or don't support one another, display different and sometimes contradictory feelings towards the therapist. Individuals respond to others with sympathy, impatience, boredom, anger, bafflement, and much else. The general atmosphere may be depressed, excited, sullen, flat, or other. The conversation may be focused or scattered or halting. The therapist sometimes finds events hard to follow and understand. Sometimes there are undertones of affect which seem inconsistent with what is actually being said. Sometimes group members construct metaphors through which they both express and conceal their feelings or opinions. Topics may shift in unexpected ways. Long periods of laboured and apparently fruitless discussion may occur. When the structure planned for a group involves discussing successive topics, members may stick to the topic, drift away from it, or ignore it altogether. When an activity, game or exercise is introduced, members may work hard at it, or resist and query it, or slip into chaotic behaviour. The therapist may feel pleased, despairing, confused, excited, impatient, angry, approving or disapproving of the group or of particular members. Co-therapists may work in complementary ways, or they may undermine one another's efforts. They may enjoy working together, or feel irritated and impatient with one another.

How is a therapist to make sense of such many-faceted events? With so much going on, what does he or she particularly need to pay attention to? seek to understand? Any therapist will pay special attention to certain events and let others slide into the background. One cannot notice everything. Any therapist will make use of some set of ideas – some theory – when trying to understand the complex and often fast-moving events in a group session. Whatever these ideas are they may be held explicitly or implicitly.

This chapter is organised into the following sections:

- Developing, refining and expanding one's understanding of each person in the group.
- Keeping in touch with the state of the group as a whole within each session and as the group develops over time.
- Keeping in touch with one's own feelings as therapist and noting one's own behaviour and its consequences.
- Doing all this listening and observing at the same time.
- Attributing meanings to what one hears and sees. Relevant realms of theory.
- When listening, observing, and attributing meanings, getting one's thinking as right as possible.
- The place of intuition.
- Theory and its connections with practice: some further questions.

DEVELOPING, REFINING AND EXPANDING ONE'S UNDERSTANDING OF EACH PERSON IN THE GROUP

Therapists begin to form hypotheses about what group members are like even before anyone has been specifically selected for a group. They will have provisional ideas about the needs and characteristics of people drawn from the population they intend to work with. Of course, one can think only in broad terms before actually meeting and getting to know the persons who will become members. Still, one will have some ideas about likely current and preferred state, preoccupying concerns and the like, as discussed in Chapter 3.

In many though not all groups, understanding each individual person begins when working out a group membership. A therapist begins to build a picture of each person through one or several preliminary individual interviews or other forms of preparation, or referral notes, or discussions with colleagues. This, however, is only a start. A fuller understanding begins to develop once the group begins to meet.

Some of what one learns about individuals occurs through hearing what they say about themselves. As members begin to interact, they begin to offer factual information about themselves. Such information tends to emerge in bits and pieces, often widely spaced, during group discussions or in the course of participating in activities. An individual may begin a personal account and get interrupted. He or she may provide only hints by saying: 'It's the same with me', or: 'I have never felt that way'. In other words, information revealed in the *content* of what individuals say about themselves is likely to appear in scattered, fragmentary and unordered forms. A therapist can begin to patch together an understanding of an individual by bringing together, in his or her mind, these scattered self-revelations.

Systematic history-taking is not appropriate in a group. If a therapist literally goes round the room, interviewing each person in turn, he or she is introducing a model of turn-taking into the group, which precludes exchanges amongst the members, one of the main sources of personal help in a group. Nor is it advisable for the therapist to respond to some personal self-revelation by probing for further information – especially when the group first starts. One cannot interview an individual in a group as one might in one-to-one therapy or in a diagnostic interview. Or rather, one *can*, but undesirable consequences are likely to follow. In a group, one never *only* speaks to an individual. One is always also conveying something to others as well. If the therapist encourages one person to continue talking about his or her own feelings and experiences, others will be placed in a passive, listening position. Concentrating on one person can generate envy in others, or provide others with a hiding place behind whoever is at the centre of attention. For these reasons, systematic history-taking within group sessions is not a good idea. Therapists who feel that they need to understand an individual's life course sometimes conduct individual diagnostic interviews before the group starts. This too has its consequences: every group member knows that the therapist has information about them which they themselves do not want to reveal in the group, and everyone knows that the therapist holds secrets about each person in the group.

What people say about themselves is by no means the only source of information available to a group therapist. A group is a superb medium for learning about a person through noting the manner and pattern of his or her participation. A therapist can pay attention to non-verbal behaviour, to individuals' contributions and reactions to successive themes, to responses to particular others, to characteristic ways of presenting themselves, and to cues which encourage others to think about them and respond to them in particular ways.

For instance, in a time-limited group for mothers of learning-disabled children, one woman offered to get the group started by providing an account of her son's difficult birth and early years. She proceeded to do so in a manner which called attention to her patience and skill in handling him. In another group, for adults with a range of personal problems, a youngish woman sat silently, staring at her hands. Her whole manner conveyed: 'Leave me alone; don't press me.' Both of these women were presenting themselves as particular kinds of persons and sending out signals and cues about how they wished others to think about them or respond to them.

Therapists build an understanding of each group member through what members say about themselves and their personal circumstances, *and* by how they behave in the group. The information acquired by these two means is brought together and built into a developing understanding of each person. I sometimes think of there being, in my mind, a space for each person: a 'Mary-shaped space', a 'Chris-shaped space', a' Roger-shaped space', and so on. As new information of many kinds emerges, it is tucked into that space. As time goes on, an understanding of each individual is gradually expanded, corrected and refined.

An understanding of each person includes developing a sense of what, for each, would constitute a benefit or gain. One can reinvoke the ideas of current and preferred state; 'life space', 'frontier' and 'preoccupying concern', introduced in Chapter 3. Sometimes, though not always, one can form a view of just what, beyond a person's current frontier, it would be most beneficial for that person to achieve, or which aspect of a preoccupying concern needs to be better dealt with. One can think in terms of 'red-letter' days – for example: 'It will be a red-letter day for Peggy when she realizes her daughter's condition is not her fault'; 'It will be a red-letter day for Julia when she sees that she does not have to be trapped forever into feeling useless because she has not done as well academically as her brilliant brother'; 'It will be a red-letter day for Bernard when he can walk down the street without the terrible fear that he is being followed'; 'It will be a red-letter day for Jack when he can prepare his own lunch'. And so on.

In developing an understanding of each person in a group, the therapist has to be careful not to foreclose too quickly – to remain aware that emerging ideas might be incomplete or require revision. In fact, it is best not to foreclose at all, for one continues to develop one's understanding of each person throughout the life of a group.

KEEPING IN TOUCH WITH THE STATE OF THE GROUP AS A WHOLE WITHIN EACH SESSION AND AS THE GROUP DEVELOPS OVER TIME

The group is both the context and the means for personal benefit. It is important, therefore, for therapists to keep in touch with group-level dynamics. How can a therapist grasp the norms and beliefs, shared themes, moods and atmospheres, levels of cohesiveness which prevail in a group at any given time? How can a therapist keep in touch with development and change over time?

Moods and atmospheres are typically grasped through the content of what is being said, together with tone of voice, slowness or rapidity of pace, fluid versus halting speech, and high or low volume of conversation. In addition, therapists often get in touch with a prevailing mood through sharing in it emotionally.

Grasping a theme requires paying attention to the associational flow. When listening to successive comments in a group one typically notices that, as the conversation proceeds, members hear and respond selectively. They emphasise some bits, ignore others, nudge the group in one direction or another, and build or do not build on one another's comments. Individual contributions begin to come together, forming some thread or theme. Some members may remain silent, perhaps listening attentively, perhaps tuning the group out, but in any case not interfering with the emerging theme. By tracking the sequence of associations, a therapist forms an understanding of an emerging theme.

Some themes are easy to grasp because they are expressed directly. The members talk about what they will do when they leave hospital, or how they still resent their fathers because of how they were treated as children, or how the other children in the family are influenced by the presence of a severely physically handicapped child. At other times the manifest content of a conversation conceals and is, at the same time, a vehicle for expressing or hinting at some underlying issue. The theme is expressed indirectly, or in terms of a metaphor. It underlies the content rather than being expressed explicitly in it. Paying attention to the feelings or attitudes which are being expressed through the content helps to grasp an underlying theme. If, for example, members are complaining about the government, which in their view does not care about people like them, one may note to oneself that the members are expressing a sense of being uncared for by people in authority who ought to have their interests at heart. One may hypothesise that the feeling of being uncared for might refer to people important in each person's current or earlier life, or to the therapist, or to both. A therapist needs to go on listening in order to gather further evidence to discern which hypothesis is the more justified.

It can take some time for a theme to emerge clearly enough to be recognised. A concern expressed by one person is not of course a shared theme. One has to wait to see how members build upon one another's contributions over a period of time before one can judge whether or not an individual contribution triggered a shared theme or whether it became lost in the group. If someone expresses a concern which is not, at the time, picked up by others, a shared theme does not develop. However, the therapist learns something about the person who has introduced an apparently idiosyncratic concern. Also, it is possible that others share in the concern but are not ready to pursue it at the moment. A therapist has to keep these possibilities in mind, and await further evidence.

Norms and shared beliefs are best grasped through noting patterns and consistencies in behaviour amongst members. Degree of cohesiveness is best grasped through noting individuals' attitudes to the group, responses to absences or lateness, and responses to members who leave and new members who join the group.

Perceiving development and change over time requires backing away from specific events enough to perceive swings in a group. A group may shift from periods of productive work into periods of desultory conversation and back again. A group may shift from one theme to another and then another, and then back again to a theme previously explored, tackling it now in a different way. Sometimes one forms the view that a turning-point has occurred in a group – for instance, members may have become noticeably freer to express themselves. Sometimes a group seems to 'regress'. From having been able to express themselves freely, members somewhat abruptly become guarded or defensive. Some changes are precipitated by easily observable events, such as someone dropping out or a new person entering, or by some event in a group's environment. Some changes evolve gradually through the interactions of members.

KEEPING IN TOUCH WITH ONE'S OWN FEELINGS AS THERAPIST AND NOTING ONE'S OWN BEHAVIOUR AND ITS CONSEQUENCES

Even before a group begins, a therapist is likely to harbour certain hopes and fears for persons in the group, for the group enterprise in general, and for him- or herself. Especially if working with groups is a new venture within the agency or institution, a therapist may have staked a good deal on the group's success: own reputation, and the likelihood or not that working with groups will become an established part of the organisation's work. Hopes may be high and worries substantial. If therapeutic work with groups is well established in the work setting an inexperienced therapist or worker may feel that he or she has a lot to live up to. In settings in which a therapeutic group is just one part of a larger programme, the therapist is likely to be aware that colleagues form opinions about how the group is going, its impact on its members, and how and whether the group meshes well or else interferes with other helping efforts.

Once a group begins to meet, specific events may stir up particular feelings. There will almost certainly be times when the issues and themes with which members of the group are struggling resonate with a therapist's personal concerns. From time to time a therapist may be challenged or attacked by the members. There will be times when the therapist feels confused and at a loss to understand what is going on. A therapist can feel hopeless when a group gets stuck in an unproductive patch, helpless when thoroughly confused by events, or exhilarated when a group does well and then disappointed when it does not keep up its good work. Some feelings are about individual members. A therapist can feel angry with someone who seems to be spoiling the group, or worried when someone is being pushed into more than he or she can handle, or excited when someone achieves something of great personal importance.

Based on his experience in training group therapists, Meyer Williams (1966) identified a number of 'fearful fantasies' amongst trainees. These included fears of encountering unmanageable resistance; of losing control of the group; of excessive hostility from or among members; of acting out by group members; of powerful dependency demands from members; and of group disintegration. Experience helps to remind one that many 'fearful fantasies' do not materialise and that if they do they can in fact be dealt with. However, experienced as well as inexperienced therapists and workers can worry: 'What if no one comes next time?' 'What if no one says anything?' 'What if they gang up on me?' And so on.

Therapists can cultivate the habit of noting their own feelings and observing their own behaviour and its consequences. By so doing, they build up an understanding of themselves: of feelings likely to be triggered by different kinds of group events, of characteristic ways of responding to them, of favoured ways of protecting the self, of blind-spots, and the like. For instance, a therapist may learn that he (or she) can manage overt attacks from group members but feels threatened when attacked covertly. Or a therapist may feel particularly disturbed by situations which seem chaotic and for which no ready explanation comes to mind.

Self-awareness has great practical use when conducting a group. A therapist who is aware of personal feelings and preferences and vulnerabilities will have more choice over whether and how to express them in the group. For instance, suppose that a therapist notices that he or she feels especially gratified when someone expresses appreciation of the group, and in consequence is inclined to favour that person. Realising this will help the therapist to maintain better control over actually expressing favouritism in behaviour. Being aware of own feelings helps a therapist to avoid expressing them impulsively or allowing them to 'leak out' in the group without being aware that this is what is happening.

The term counter-transference is often used to refer to therapists' personal feelings and responses in a group which are rooted in his or her personal needs. Hayes (1995: 521–2) has defined counter-transference as 'therapists' cognitive, affective, and behavioral reactions to clients that are grounded in therapists' unresolved intrapsychic conflicts'. He organises his discussion of counter-transference in terms of origins, triggers, manifestations, effects, and management factors, and provides a large bibliography. Hahn (1995), writing about therapist anger in group psychotherapy, distinguishes between *counter-transference anger* and *realistic therapist anger*. He sees the former as a defence against the experience of shame, which occurs in response to a therapist's need to live up to the expectation that he (or she) will understand everything and be able to benefit everyone. Hahn points out that such idealised expectations are built up by a combination of therapist's and patients' expectations. Realistic therapist anger, in contrast, does not have its roots in shame or in narcissistic and idealised expectations of what the therapist can accomplish. I infer from what Hahn says that realistic anger is an understandable response to group events which is not contaminated by unrealistic expectations of oneself as therapist. Ormont (1991), following Winnicott (1949), distinguishes between 'subjective counter-transference' and 'objective counter-transference'. Ormont says that subjective counter-transference is highly individual and idiosyncratic. It refers to some bias in the therapist deriving from experiences in his or her individual past which leads him/her to respond to the patient in some way which is different from the response which would be elicited from most others. Objective counter-transference refers to non-idiosyncratic responses to the patient's behaviour: the therapist responds as most others would, for instance, with irritation if one group member deliberately harms or shames another, or sadness when a group member experiences a personal loss. Ormont's point is that it is subjective counter-transference which tends to be injurious, first, to the therapist, who, in Ormont's words, has been 'thrown off center' and second, also to the patients.

Thus, 'counter-transference' is a collective term and it is useful to distinguish between the various forms it can take. It is a mistake to assume that all emotional reactions on the part of the therapist are rooted in 'unresolved intrapsychic conflicts'. As both Ormont and Hahn remind us, some may be understandable as usual human responses to events in the group.

Ormont makes the interesting point that the patients themselves can help the therapist to become aware of behaviours rooted in subjective counter-transference. For instance, if the group members begin to behave in some atypical way, the therapist might ask himself if his own behaviour has stimulated this shift. Or a therapist might ask the members if they have noticed any change in the group lately, and then ask whether they think the therapist has had anything to do with it. Or a therapist might note members' criticisms of him/her. A valuable lesson which can be learned from Ormont's discussion is to take members' criticisms of oneself seriously: not all criticisms are rooted in members' own transference reactions. Some of their criticisms may follow from accurate observations of the therapist's behaviour. Ormont reckons that a therapist who becomes aware of a subjective counter-transference bias (an inappropriate perception or piece of behaviour) can resolve to keep it under control and not show it in behaviour, but will find it hard to do this consistently unless s/he also understands the feelings which underlie the bias. It is this kind of understanding which can free the therapist from perceiving inaccurately or behaving inappropriately. The members will also benefit, of course, since they are no longer subjected to a bias which is off the point as far as their own behaviours and feelings are concerned.

DOING ALL THIS LISTENING AND OBSERVING AT THE SAME TIME

Although I have discussed attending to each group member, keeping in touch with the state of the group as a whole, and noting own feelings and behaviours separately, it is obvious that a therapist has to think about all these at the same time, since all of them interact. In the real world of practice, one cannot 'factor out', but must attend to everything all at once. One sees that individuals influence the group, that the group has an impact on individuals, and that pair interactions influence not only those principally concerned but also those who are watching and listening. One tries to observe the group and the group members from a therapist's vantage point, while at the same time observing oneself in the group.

ATTRIBUTING MEANINGS TO WHAT ONE HEARS AND SEES; RELEVANT REALMS OF THEORY

By 'attributing meanings' I have in mind what is referred to in ordinary language as making sense of something. Attributing meanings to what one sees and hears in a group is an inextricable part of listening and observing. Everyone wants to make sense of their surroundings and of themselves in their surroundings. It follows that every therapist will make use of some set of ideas for ordering their understandings of what they see and hear.

To introduce a metaphor: every therapist needs to have a knapsack of ideas available when conducting a group. What needs to be inside the knapsack? What realms of theory are relevant? I suggest that therapists need sets of concepts (= theory) (a) for understanding how a group can function as a medium for personal benefit; and (b) for understanding the population being worked with. In addition, they may need (c) certain bodies of information, depending on the population.

Theory which pertains to how a group can function as a medium for personal benefit

One necessary realm of theory has to do with what can occur within a group which facilitates personal benefit. Useful theory will encompass individual dynamics, communication processes and interaction patterns within the group (including the participation of the therapist), dynamics of the group as a whole, and connections amongst them.

A satisfactory theory will pay attention to individual dynamics but not *only* to individual dynamics. It will pay attention to group dynamics but not *only* to group dynamics. Lieberman, referring collectively to Bion (1961), Foulkes and Anthony ([1957] 1965), Ezriel (1950a, 1950b), and Whitaker and Lieberman (1964) put it this way:

> Although it would be an error to imply congruence among these theorists, collectively they address themselves to these areas: (1) What are the special characteristics of the psychotherapeutic enterprise as a social system, and how is this system created? How does it develop, and what are the effects of its past history on its current operation? (2) How does the social system influence the behavior of the patients and therapists and what are reciprocal influences between the individual and group? (3) How does the social system influence individual change? (4) What elements of the social system can the group therapist influence to maximize therapeutic potential?
> (Lieberman 1967: 71–2)

Although this statement was written more than thirty years ago, it remains sound and comprehensive. Nowadays, one would refer to many more theorists than Lieberman did, given that the importance of integrating group and individual dynamics is so much more widely accepted.

What Lieberman has said provides a *framework* for thinking about the group, the members, and oneself as therapist in the group. It does not say what, exactly, needs to be inserted into the framework. This is a decision which has to be based on the kind of population one is working with and the group structure one has decided to use. For instance, with respect to individual change and how it is influenced by the social system (Lieberman's third point) one would have to think more specifically about the kind of individual change regarded as relevant and the kind of group experience likely to generate it. For some populations, it will be appropriate to think in terms of individuals' yielding up virtually life-long self-defeating behaviours, and of group conditions under which corrective emotional experiences are likely to occur. For other populations, it will be appropriate to think in terms of developing practical skills and group experiences which encourage practising them.

This realm of theory will necessarily include ideas about the position and role of the therapist in the group – that is, levels of activity, focus of the therapist's efforts, the therapist's internal reactions to events arising in the group, and his or her actual actions and behaviours in the group. Also included will be members' attitudes towards and feelings about the therapist and their expectations of the therapist.

Theory which pertains to the population one is working with or expects to work with

A second realm of theory has to do with characteristics of particular populations of people. For instance, depending on the population, a therapist might profit from familiarity with theories pertaining to bereavement and grief, or transition experiences, or the lingering effects of trauma, or developmental tasks associated with different life stages, or antecedents of delinquency, or processes whereby self-defeating behaviours and relationships come to be established and maintained.

Often, a number of different theories need to be drawn upon in order to understand the population one is working with. For instance, suppose a practitioner is working with unaccompanied adolescent asylum-seekers recently arrived in the UK. He or she will profit from familiarity with theory about life stages, transition experiences, loss and bereavement, and culture and culture clash.

Davidsen-Nielsen and Leick (1989–90) provide a concrete example of drawing from diverse theories to construct a theoretical grounding for one's work – in this case for working with people who have experienced severe personal losses. Davidsen-Nielsen and Leick brought together ideas from Bowlby (1969, 1973, 1980) about attachment; Erikson (1950) about the development of basic trust and of a sense of independence early in life, with attendant risks of failing to achieve optimum closeness with/distance from significant people in later life; Parkes (1972) about bereavement and grief; and Yalom (1980) about existential experiences, with emphasis on conflicts concerning death, freedom, isolation and meaninglessness. They also refer to Miller (1986, 1987) and her hypothesis that individuals who experience the complex and apparently contradictory feelings involved in grief become able to move beyond (and 'undo') the effects of emotional deprivation during childhood. From these sources, they developed ideas about the tasks involved in grief work and about procedures likely to be helpful.

Relevant information

Certain kinds of information – as distinct from theory – are also relevant, depending on with whom one is working. For example, it could be useful to be informed about the character and progression of certain diseases or conditions (for example, Alzheimer's disease, renal failure, HIV and AIDS, bulimia), or about certain congenital conditions (for example, Down's syndrome), or about typical ups and downs experienced by people who are seriously and chronically mentally ill. Where a group is made up of people drawn from a culture other than that of the therapist, it will be useful to become informed about features of that culture.

WHEN LISTENING, OBSERVING AND ATTRIBUTING MEANINGS, TRYING TO GET ONE'S THINKING AS RIGHT AS POSSIBLE

Getting one's thinking as right as possible is supported if one regards every person, every situation, as unique, and not 'the same as' some other person or situation. The understandings which one builds up about each individual are an accumulation of what one has heard and seen which sheds light on *this* person, at *this* time, as related to *this* person's past life and experiences and current interactions and behaviours. What one judges about the state of the group or of interpersonal interactions within the group needs to be based on what is being observed *now*, taking into account understandings which have been built up about *this* group and *these* group members.

It is useful to hold explanations in mind provisionally, remaining ready to revise them as new information, new evidence, surfaces. Initial hypotheses may be upheld, but on the other hand it may become clear that they need to be revised or abandoned. Another way of saying this is that one should avoid foreclosing prematurely on an explanation of some run of events.

Notions about the meaning of events in groups often pop into mind apparently spontaneously. Yet they are based on *something*. Notions need to be taken seriously, for they may be based on something which has been going on but which has not been registered altogether consciously: some idea of what an event might mean has crept into the edges of one's mind. Such notions need to be regarded as hypotheses to be examined against subsequent evidence. As before, one holds on to an hypothesis if one finds grounds for supporting it, and discards it if not.

It is helpful to appreciate common pitfalls and habits of language and thought which can lead one astray, so that they can be better avoided. These include: (a) jumping to the conclusion that an explanation based on some previous, similar (but not of course identical) experience will fit the current situation; (b) thinking in abstract terms which obscure rather than illuminate what is happening and put a halt to further thinking; and (c) accepting a concept as a reality rather than as a possibly useful way of thinking about a situation (that is, mistaking a piece of theory for reality).

THE PLACE OF INTUITION

Those who conduct groups may consider that they do not have time, in the hurly-burly of a group, to do the kinds of thinking discussed here. Is all this thinking necessary, or even possible? It may all seem too intellectual. What about grasping the meaning of events intuitively?

By dictionary definition, intuition refers to 'knowledge gained from immediate apprehension or understanding; the power of attaining direct knowledge or under-standing without evident rational thought and the drawing of conclusions from the evidence available' (*Longman's Dictionary of the English Language*). There are certainly times when a therapist immediately grasps the meaning of some event, and is confident in being right. The problem is that the therapist may be right but, then again, may be wrong.

An intuitive grasp of the meaning of some event which is also right, or right enough, is probably based on a combination of accumulated practice wisdom and of empathy aroused by the current situation. An intuitive grasp of the meaning of some event which is wrong, or partial, or skewed is probably based on unrecognised assumptions and projections rooted in own needs.

There are times in a group when the therapist is faced with a rapidly developing situation in which some action needs to be taken and there is literally no time to think. The therapist perforce relies on intuition and bases action on it. At other times there is plenty of time to think, as for instance when a situation regarded as a problem has rumbled on for a long time with no sign of it shifting, or when a shared theme evolves slowly over time. In such situations, an explanation may come to mind 'intuitively', but there is time to test it as an hypothesis. One can wait for further information, or take active steps to acquire further information, and then make use of that information to test the hypothesis before firmly accepting it.

When there is no time to think, a therapist's intuitive understandings are likely to be more reliable if he or she has been in the habit of noting the consequences of his or her actions and of thinking ahead to the likely consequences of interventions. Informed intuition is better than uninformed intuition. This is not meant to deprecate the value of 'soaking up' the flavour and atmosphere of a group, using one's 'anten-nae' (or whatever other metaphor one prefers for intuitively grasping the meaning of events). Thinking *and* feeling are involved in watching, listening, and meaning-making. If one takes a stand against thinking in order to ensure spontaneity, one loses self-discipline and increases the risk of distorted or filtered listening. If one overvalues a cognitive stance one increases the risk of missing significant events (some of which can only be detected by using one's 'antennae') and one also risks forcing events rigidly into some preconceived conceptual framework.

THEORY AND ITS CONNECTIONS WITH PRACTICE: SOME FURTHER QUESTIONS

This chapter raises some further questions about theory and how practitioners select, understand, and use theory. They can be added to the four which were named at the end of Chapter 5 (I am continuing the numbering). They are:

5 How do practitioners acquire theory? Where do they start from?
6 How can practitioners make explicit, to themselves, the ideas or set of concepts which they actually use in their practice? Why is it useful to do this?
7 By what criteria may a therapist judge the merits and demerits of a theory, and its usefulness and applicability?

These questions, together with some others still to come, will be discussed in Chapter 17.

Chapter 9

Getting started

Opening a group and responding to what happens next

It was pointed out towards the end of Chapter 6 that the last decision which a therapist can make before a group actually begins is to think out what he or she will say or do when the group first assembles. After that, it is a matter of responding to events as they arise.

It was said that 'in general, whatever one does to open a group should be planned to support the structure one has in mind and make it easier for people to begin to participate'. A number of points were made about what may usefully be included or excluded in an opening comment. This decision, like all others, should be made on the grounds of anticipated likely consequences. The best decisions are those which tilt the probabilities towards benefit occurring for group members. What one says at the start needs to be in line with one's understanding of the needs and capabilities of the members and with what one hopes individuals will achieve through participating in the group.

This chapter is organised as follows:

- Some examples of opening statements.
- Diverse possible responses on the part of group members to a therapist's opening comment, and what a therapist might then do.
- Quick starts and slower starts.
- Helping members to move beyond a halting or defensive or obstructive start.

SOME EXAMPLES OF OPENING STATEMENTS

For an outpatient group I have talked with each of you individually but this is the first time we are meeting as a group. We expect to meet on Tuesdays and Fridays starting at 4 o'clock for an hour-and-a-quarter each time. During that time we expect to discuss whatever concerns the people here. The idea is to reflect on one's own experience and that of others, and hear one another's opinions and points of view.

For a group of learning-disabled adults attending a day centre, living either with their families or in small group homes We are going to meet every

Wednesday for an hour and we'll do something different each time. Today we are going to talk about this neighbourhood and where this day centre is, and where each person here lives. Perhaps we will mention places in the neighbourhood that people know about and sometimes go to. (The conductor then begins to involve those present in the task.)

For a group of recently orthopaedically impaired patients soon to be discharged from hospital   This is the first of four one-and-a-quarter hour discussions. They are intended to give each of you an opportunity to anticipate what may happen after you leave the hospital and to think about the best ways to cope with your new situation. Everyone here has a physical handicap of one sort or another, relatively recently acquired either through illness or accident. Let's start.

For a group of people aged about 50–70, each of whom is looking after a relative with Alzheimer's disease at home   Everyone here is looking after a relative with Alzheimer's disease. We intend to meet once a week on Thursday nights from 7.30 to 9.00 for eight weeks, to discuss and share experiences. Towards the end of that period, we will decide whether or not to continue, and if so, in what way.

DIVERSE POSSIBLE RESPONSES ON THE PART OF GROUP MEMBERS TO A THERAPIST'S OPENING COMMENT, AND WHAT A THERAPIST MIGHT THEN DO

When the therapist stops speaking, something else will happen. The 'something else' cannot be precisely predicted but, whatever it is, the therapist's subsequent behaviour must take it into account and be a response to it.

The following are instances of what may happen following the therapist's opening statement:

The opening comment is followed by discussion of an issue important to all the members

In a group for parents of learning-disabled children, the opening comment was followed by members asking one another for, and receiving, factual information about the ages of the learning-disabled child and the other children in the family. This was soon followed by a discussion about discipline: Is it fair to discipline a learning-disabled child when he or she may not be able to distinguish right from wrong? Different opinions were expressed.

It may be noted that the first part of this discussion (about ages and so forth) carried little or no risk: no one minded providing this information and everyone participated. The discussion then moved to the issue of disciplining a learning-disabled child. Most members had evidently pondered this on their own and were now expressing and hearing different views and opinions. Most, though not everyone, participated. The therapist showed interest in what was being said but did not direct the discussion, on grounds that the members were doing well on their own.

The opening comment is followed by a discussion about members' hopes and fears about being in the group

In a group for young adults who were dissatisfied with how their lives were going, the therapist's opening statement was followed by one member saying: 'Now that I'm here I'm not sure that I want to be here.' Several others expressed hopes and worries about what might happen. The therapist acknowledged the feelings that were being expressed and encouraged further discussion of here-and-now feelings.

The opening comment is followed by a conversation about some topic of no apparent personal relevance to the members

This is not an unusual occurrence. Group members begin to talk about a programme that was on television the previous night, or about a forthcoming football match, or about favourite sports. Everyone seems interested and keeps the conversation going but, from the therapist's point of view, the discussion is off-target.

Quite understandably, the therapist or worker considers that the group was not brought together in order to pursue such topics and may therefore feel that s/he ought to move the group on to something more personal. I am going to suggest, however, that in the first instance it is best to do nothing at all. The reason for this is the likelihood that while the *content* is apparently trivial, the *interactive process* could be moving the group along.

For example: during the first session of a group of psychiatric in-patients the members spent thirty minutes or so talking about baseball. The discussion turned to which teams various members supported. Members said that each of the teams mentioned was good in its own way, or was good but had been having bad luck, or had some good players, and so on. The therapist did not intervene. After twenty minutes or so, one person said: 'We didn't come here to talk about baseball.' The conversation turned to more personal matters.

Whilst listening to this conversation the therapist formed the view that the talk about baseball was a low-risk way for members to test out whether individual differences would be tolerated within the group and whether members would be sympathetic and supportive of one another. Members were showing that they could accept one another's preferences and find something to value about them. The therapist judged that this was likely to increase the general sense of safety even though everyone was 'only' talking about baseball. This judgement was confirmed when one person said: 'We didn't come here to talk about baseball', and the members moved to a topic nearer to their own concerns. In this situation and others like it, it would be against the members' best interests if the therapist interrupted this useful process by prematurely pressing the group to talk about 'important' matters.

This kind of situation can be understood in group focal conflict terms. One can hypothesise that there is, on the one hand, a wish to make positive use of the group by sharing personal feelings and experiences. On the other hand (and in conflict with this wish) members fear that others will reject or criticise them. Neither the wish nor the fear is expressed directly in the content. What is visible and manifest is that the members are engaged in a discussion about something remote from their personal concerns. In group focal conflict terms, this is a restrictive solution. It protects members from their fears, but does not allow for the discussion of more personal matters. It is obvious that if the members did no more, session after session, than talk about baseball, no meaningful personal gain would occur. However, they are unlikely to do so, for, although fears are present, so also are wishes to use the group for personal gain. The wishes as well as the fears drive the discussion.

In situations of this kind, the therapist needs to judge whether the members are interacting in ways likely to lead to the alleviation of initial fears, whatever the content of their conversation. If they are, it is better not to interrupt what is in fact constructive work.

The opening comment is followed by a conversation amongst members which the conductor judges to be a metaphor for feelings about the group or about being in the group

It is not unusual for group members, through their interaction, to construct a metaphor through which feelings about the group are expressed in a safe way.

For example: three or four of the members of a seven-member in-patient group began to discuss recordings which are compilations of different pieces of music. They speculated as to whether the selections really fit together, whether they would meet the taste of anyone who bought the record, or whether such records included some 'junk'. One or two members mentioned records of this kind which they had enjoyed. As the conversation proceeded, someone said: 'Records like that can be a really good buy', and several others agreed. The conversation shifted to talking about feelings members had about being in a psychiatric ward.

The therapist understood the content about recordings to be a metaphor for the group: will the members of the group fit together? will the combination make sense and be pleasing? will the group serve its intended purpose? The therapist concluded that the metaphor was being used by members to express their reservations and concerns about the group, and that as the conversation went on, feelings shifted towards more optimistic expectations. Perhaps the group would, after all, prove to be a 'good buy'. The therapist judged that good work was being done within and through a metaphor. This judgement seemed to be confirmed when the members left the metaphor behind. The therapist did not participate while the discussion focused on recordings, and did not interpret the metaphor.

The opening comment is followed by a long and increasingly anxious silence

If this occurs, it is a reasonable guess that the members are feeling uneasy or confused. As long as the silence persists, the therapist has no way of knowing just what feelings are present or whether or not members have similar feelings. He or she therefore needs to encourage members to talk. The first question is how soon to interrupt the silence, and the second question is how to do so.

It is a mistake to break a silence too soon because this does not allow the group members to do so themselves. It is a equally a mistake to allow a silence to run on for so long that the members become more and more anxious, or else become more and more fixed on silence as a way of going on in the group. To keep oneself from intervening too soon it is useful to remember that even a brief silence can seem a very long time indeed. I always sit where I can see a clock on the wall, to remind myself without being conspicuous about it that a silence which feels to be very long has in fact lasted for only one or two or three minutes. On the other hand, one does not want to wait too long before intervening. To avoid this, it is helpful to notice non-verbal behaviours and postures which suggest an escalating sense of threat amongst the members, or else a creeping sense of apathy.

If an intervention seems to be in order, what might be said or done? Often, as one scans the group, one notices someone who seems to be on the verge of speaking. A nod or a smile can offer support. Sometimes a question is helpful: 'What is making it difficult to talk?' or 'It is hard to get started. How is that?' Such questions usually make it possible for someone to say something; perhaps: 'We don't know where to start', or 'I had a lot of things to say before I came but now I can't remember any of them', or 'I thought you would tell us what to talk about'. One needs to find out whether the feelings reflected by such statements are held by only one member of the group, or are shared by others. Subsequent comments, or else non-verbal participation, provide clues. The problem shifts from being 'no one is talking' to 'members have expectations of the therapist which are not being fulfilled' or 'people don't know where to start and need help with this'. The therapist then has some idea of how to proceed.

If the members need help from the therapist as to how to get started, why not offer it? One need not do this by offering a prescription or giving an order. It is better to offer a menu of possibilities from which patients may choose. One might say, for instance: 'It's understandable that people are not sure how to start. Well, we could start by talking about how each person feels now, or by talking about what brought people here, or by introducing ourselves.' Such a comment provides guidance without imposing any single course of action. In my experience a silence does not persist beyond such an intervention unless one has thoroughly misjudged the capacities of the members.

The opening comment is followed by an extended abstract or intellectual discussion

For instance, the members talk about the plight of the single parent, or loneliness, or the sense of the lost self in contemporary society. No one refers to personal feelings or experiences. In group focal conflict terms, using abstract terms or intellectualising is a restrictive solution. It protects against the presumed dangers of self-revelation.

As with discussions about apparently trivial topics, the ways in which members interact *while* speaking in such intellectual terms may lead to the alleviation of fears and to a discussion of more personal matters. It is sensible therefore to avoid interrupting such a conversation for some time, to allow such processes to occur (if they are going to). Sometimes members go on and on in the same vein. If so, the therapist may judge that an intervention is indicated. The therapist might try extracting from the conversation its emotional quality and putting this before the group: for example, 'We have been reflecting on how hard it is to bear loneliness' or 'You are saying that people just don't understand what single parents are up against'. Such comments sometimes help members to shift into something more personal. If this does not happen, the therapist might try something a little stronger, such as: 'What about this loneliness? We have been saying that it is pretty universal. Has anyone here *not* experienced it?' This intervention attempts to sanction experiencing loneliness and reduce the fear of owning it. If the group still continues in the same manner one could try: 'What would happen if we talked about our own feelings of loneliness?' As the therapist tries one intervention and then (after an interval) another, he or she avoids putting direct pressure on the members to stop their intellectualising, and is not judgemental.

One or another of these interventions is likely to lead to a shift away from intellectualising *providing* that intellectualising is not very firmly fixed in each member as a favoured personal defence. If this is the case, the therapist is facing a difficult composition. He or she will be the only person who wants to depart from an interactive style which everyone else finds congenial or even necessary, in order to maintain a personal sense of safety. In such a situation it is easy to fall into becoming the members' antagonist. This, however, would interfere with establishing a working alliance in the group. Also, the members would win the battle. It is better to get on the same side as the members rather than to quarrel with them. By 'getting on the same side' I do not mean joining in with the intellectualising or letting it run on indefinitely. Rather, the therapist can acknowledge the prevailing preference for intellectualising in a sympathetic way and put the issue to the members as a shared problem for all to address: 'I can see that everyone enjoys talking about this issue in very broad terms. Yet we also want our discussions to have meaning for each person here. How are we going to manage this?' Such an intervention can shift the situation from one in which the therapist is (or soon will be) the group's adversary to one in which all are facing the same problem.

The opening comment is followed by a long series of questions directed to the therapist about record-keeping, the use of audio-tapes, or case conferences

The therapist might judge that the members are asking such questions because they are worried about confidentiality or fear that what they say about themselves in the group will somehow be used to their disadvantage. They are unable to express their fears directly, and apparently do not perceive that their queries about record-keeping and so on have anything to do with here-and-now concerns about the group. In response to such questions it seems best to provide clear and concise information, but not to explain at length or get defensive. If the members persist with such questions, one could enquire about why it is important to have this information. Or one could ask: 'What bad things could happen through record-keeping or case conferences?' Such questions are aimed at getting underlying fears out into the open, where they can be discussed.

When a therapist or worker is required to keep or contribute to formal records, he or she has real power over members in the form of fate-control. It may be tempting to try to conceal one's real power, or to offer false reassurances, out of a fear that group members will otherwise censor their participation. This would amount to deception, which is never advisable, not least because it is virtually certain to come to light and show that the therapist is not to be trusted or is inclined to avoid difficult situations. One might instead say something like: 'I think it is important that each person here decides for himself or herself what to say and what not to say in the group. You will know better than anyone else what it feels OK to talk about.' Such a comment makes it clear that control over self-revelations is in the hands of members (where it lies in any case). It tends to have a freeing as well as a reassuring effect. I am aware that not all therapists agree with this, and that some regard it as appropriate to encourage or even direct members to express feelings and describe experiences openly. I doubt that this really accelerates the process. The approach I am recommending is likely to reduce members' fears and not add to them, thus making it easier for them to begin to share own experiences.

The opening comment is followed by direct, aggressive challenges to the therapist's competence

One or several members ask, in a somewhat belligerent tone: 'What has your training been for conducting groups?' or 'How many groups have you led?' or 'You look too young (or too old) to be able to help people like us.' It is reasonable to assume that such challenges mask fears – for instance, about what might surface in the group and whether the therapist will be able to handle emotionally loaded situations.

It is as well to be aware that such comments and questions can occur, so as to be forearmed and not taken by surprise. Probably the best reply is to give matter-of-fact information in a neutral tone and then wait to see what happens. One might say, for instance: 'This is the third group I have conducted in this day centre'; or 'This is the first group of this type that I have conducted.' Such comments could be followed by a question: 'In what way is this important?' Whatever follows should provide more information about the members' feelings. If the challenges persist and members begin to ask: 'How could you possibly handle a group like this?' one could ask what sorts of things might emerge that would be difficult to handle. The aim is to get the members' fears out into the open where they can be examined. A defensive response (which is easy to fall into) is best avoided because it shows the members that the therapist is *not* capable of handling difficult situations. Such a response increases rather than alleviates fears.

A variation of this pattern consists of someone, sometime during the first session, making it clear that he or she considers group psychotherapy second-best compared with one-to-one psychotherapy. If this happens there is no point in defending group therapy or trying to persuade people to think otherwise. Instead, one needs to take such comments seriously and try to understand them. One could ask what it is that group members expect in a one-to-one situation that they are unlikely to get in a group. The answers provide information for all to see about expectations, assumptions, hopes and concerns, which can then be explored and discussed. The principal error would be to get into an adversarial exchange with the members of the group – that is, as members insist more and more strongly that the group cannot be of any use, the therapist insists more and more strongly that it can, perhaps even citing evidence from research. This is fruitless and places the therapist and the members in opposing camps. It works against members and therapist becoming engaged in a mutual enterprise.

The opening comment directs the members to engage in some activity, or discuss some topic, and the members do not follow the instruction: they do something else, or nothing

For example, the therapist asks for volunteers for role-playing and no one volunteers, or asks accident victims to tell about the circumstances surrounding their accident, and no one does so. If this happens, the therapist needs to try to understand what underlies the members' unwillingness (or inability?) to work to the structure. One could ask the reluctant role-players: 'What is getting in the way of volunteering?' One could explain to the accident victims one's reasons for asking the question – for example, 'I was assuming that talking about the accident would be a way to start. Does it seem different to you?' If resistance persists, it is better to avoid pressing members further, towards doing something they have shown they cannot do or are fearful of doing. It is better to turn the situation into a shared problem which all can face together. This can be done by restating the purpose one had in mind for the group and asking for suggestions about alternative ways of pursuing it. One could say, for instance: 'Our real interest today is in working out new ways of dealing with conflicts and quarrels. If we don't use role-playing, let's think of another way to go about it.' Or to the accident victims: 'Our real interest is in helping people in this group to deal with any changes in their lives that their accident might require of them. We don't necessarily have to start by talking about the accident. I wonder how we *might* start?' These suggestions are consistent with the view that it is less important to hold on to the planned structure than it is to find *some* structure which members can use.

The opening comment is followed by one person talking about his/her problems while the others ask questions and act as therapist or helper

This interactive pattern, when it occurs at the very start of a group, is likely to be functioning as a restrictive solution. One person is prepared to talk about him- or herself and all the others are thus protected from putting themselves at risk. Keeping such a pattern going requires the cooperation of everyone in the group. It is incorrect or at least an oversimplification to think of it as one person monopolising the group, since others are permitting and even encouraging one person to be the centre of attention. Even if that person is benefiting in some way, the therapist is unlikely to want to see this interactive pattern persist, because opportunities for more than one person to benefit, through sharing and comparing, are precluded.

Sometimes the person who is at the centre of attention becomes uneasy and stops talking. He or she might say: 'That's enough about me', or 'It's someone else's turn'. Someone else may then come forward for his or her turn. A pattern of turn-taking can become established, which is undesirable for the same reasons as before: opportunities for sharing and comparing do not occur. If no one else comes forward and a silence occurs, members may put pressure on the person who has been 'the patient' by returning to his/her problem, asking further questions, and the like. If so, the person who has been acting as the patient is likely to become more and more anxious. The therapist will need to intervene, probably by commenting that members seem to want X to continue to talk about him- or herself and wondering why this should be the case.

A variation on this pattern consists in one group member directly addressing the therapist, describing a personal problem and clearly expecting a helpful response. If the therapist responds in line with the member's wishes, s/he will be falling into conducting one-to-one psychotherapy with an audience. This is undesirable for the same reasons already mentioned. Where are the other members? Nowhere: it is as if they do not exist. A therapist who is being insistently addressed by one person could of course break up the pattern by saying nothing at all. This would force a change but it is inadvisable because it could so easily be experienced as rejection by the person concerned. Others too may note the therapist's non-response, and come to feel that the therapist is uninterested or that little can be expected of him or her. A general mood of anger, despair, or lassitude could follow.

The therapist might, instead, respond briefly but refer to what has just been said in a way which turns it into something which others might also be experiencing. For instance, the therapist might say: 'It is worrying to keep looking for a job and never find one', and then look around expectantly to see if others can join in. If they do not and the first person continues to address himself to the therapist, the therapist might say something like: 'Jerry is telling us that he has been looking for a job this past week and is worrying about not having found one. This *is* worrying, isn't it?' Or the therapist might say, explicitly: 'I have been wondering what others have been thinking while Jerry has been talking.' Such interventions sometimes lead to more general discussion, providing the members are capable of it.

If the pattern does not change in response to these various interventions, one might begin to conclude that it is unrealistic to expect the persons in this particular group to interact directly with one another. Events begin to show that one has planned a structure which the members are unable to use. Rethinking and replanning needs to be done in the light of this new information. Perhaps a different structure needs to be introduced. Or perhaps the therapist needs to change his or her style and become much more active in linking members' communications with one another – for instance, by such interventions: as 'Tom is telling us that he wonders if he is being given the right medication. Who else has wondered about that?'

The opening comment is followed by a brief silence and then members break into sub-groups and speak only to their neighbours

If this happens, one might decide not to interrupt for a short while on the grounds that the persons in the group are at least speaking to *someone*, even if they are unable or unwilling to engage in general discussion. However, one does not want sub-group discussions to persist for very long, for two reasons: first, it precludes sharing across the group, and second, while it goes on it is unlikely that events will occur which could pave the way for yielding it up. For these reasons it seems appropriate to interrupt after some minutes, perhaps by calling the members together again and asking whether they can share with the whole group anything discussed with their neighbours. Often, at least someone will be able to respond to this through having gained some confidence by talking initially to only a few others. If anyone says: 'We were just talking about unimportant things', this makes an opportunity for the therapist to say something like: 'Well, that's all right. We don't have to talk about important things all the time. We can start wherever we like.' Such a comment gives permission to begin in some way which feels comfortable to members but which they may have thought was unacceptable to the therapist. Once a reasonable sense of safety is established in a group, sub-group discussions are less likely to occur.

QUICK STARTS AND SLOWER STARTS

Some groups begin in a promising way, right from the start, while others begin in a hesitant or defensive or obstructive manner.

In the first two examples, the members moved quite quickly into direct explorations. In the first example, members began to explore an issue important to most: whether and how to discipline a learning-disabled child. In the second example, when one person said: 'Now that I'm here I'm not sure that I want to be here', it soon became evident that others felt similarly. Others joined in, acknowledging some of their own fears and expressing some of their own hopes. As members come to feel less alone with their fears, those fears tend to subside. It will very likely soon become possible to talk about personal matters.

In both these examples, the group was off to a good and quick start. In both cases, group composition played a part. In the first example – the group composed of parents of learning-disabled children – members explored an issue important to most of them. They were in the same boat, knew they were in the same boat, and had something to say about the issue. In the second example, the composition included one person who was able to voice fears which others also experienced. This triggered (or permitted) others to acknowledge comparable feelings.

Quick starts occur when motivation is high to begin with, and where individual members have been waiting for an opportunity to tell their stories and share their feelings. A quick start is also facilitated if one person shows him- or herself to be able to be more forthright than others. Such a person is the first to take a risk, and paves the way for others to do the same.

The remaining examples show that a therapist cannot count on members moving immediately into sharing personally meaningful material. There are three possible explanations. The first is that members share certain fears about being in the group, and act in ways to protect themselves. The second is that the members do not have the personal and interpersonal skills needed in order to work within the structure which the therapist has introduced. Both of these possibilities were illustrated in this chapter. There is a third possible explanation not shown in any of the examples in this chapter, which is illustrated by the third example in Chapter 7. In the group described there, which was for adult children of holocaust survivors, members were severely threatened and overwhelmed by their powerful feelings. They did not lack interpersonal skills but could not tolerate the intensity of frequent meetings. So many dropped out that the group quickly lost viability. A different, more manageable structure was needed.

In my experience the first explanation accounts for many difficult starts, while the other two explanations do not apply so often.

HELPING MEMBERS TO MOVE BEYOND A
HALTING, DEFENSIVE OR OBSTRUCTIVE START

A halting, defensive or obstructive start may persist beyond the first session. A therapist's intervention strategy when this happens is based on his or her understanding of what is getting in the way of a good start. If the therapist judges that the members lack the skills necessary for working within the introduced structure, it will be up to the therapist to change the structure or else adopt a different and more active leadership style. If the therapist judges that the members have the necessary interpersonal skills but are unbearably threatened by the intensity of the group, he or she will again have to change the structure, or even abandon the group effort altogether.

If the therapist judges that fears of the consequences of participating in the group and revealing themselves are the root cause of a difficult start, then an appropriate strategy is to seek to alleviate fears. How this may be done is discussed in the next chapter, in the sub-section on a group's formative phase.

Chapter 10

Subsequent events

Developmental stages and goings and comings

This chapter is concerned with how groups move on, after their very beginnings. Most groups develop towards being a satisfactory and facilitative environment within which personal benefit can occur. Some get stuck in an early stage of development, or change and fluctuate without developing. Some are interrupted by the goings and comings of members or by a change of therapist.

Group development has been conceptualised in quite a number of ways, not all of them compatible with one another. I will begin by describing how development can be understood in group focal conflict terms, first with reference to medium-term groups which proceed by open discussion and which have a beginning, a shorter or longer ongoing life, and a definite end-point. From this as a kind of base-line, other forms of development and of change, in differently structured groups, will be discussed. Then, some of the other ways in which development has been conceptualised will be described.

The chapter is organised as follows:

- A three-phase model of group development, within which themes may recur.
- Differences in developmental patterns.
- Groups which fluctuate and change, but cannot be said to develop.
- Drop-outs and other changes in membership. A change in the therapist.
- The literature on termination.
- The literature on developmental stages.
- Choosing from among different theories of development.

A THREE-PHASE MODEL OF GROUP DEVELOPMENT, WITHIN WHICH THEMES MAY RECUR

This model of group development posits a 'formative', an 'established', and a 'termination' phase, and at the same time recognises that certain themes may recur throughout the life of a group and be dealt with somewhat differently at each recurrence.

The formative phase

It is generally recognised in the literature that all groups move through a formative phase and that, if all goes well, they move from being a collection of strangers to being a coherent group. The formative phase begins with, but does not consist only of, what the therapist says when opening a group and what happens next, as discussed in the preceding chapter. The duration of the formative phase differs from group to group. Questions which need thinking about are: What characterises the formative phase? What marks the shift from being a new, unformed group to becoming established as a viable group within which productive work can take place? By what processes does desirable movement or development occur? What can a therapist do to assist a group to move beyond a halting or defensive or obstructive start? How long does it take for a group to move out of its formative phase?

In the discussion which follows, I shall omit reference to situations in which the structure proves to be unsuitable and has to be changed, and shall concentrate on situations in which members are capable of using the structure but nevertheless do not move easily or quickly into productive work.

What characterises the formative phase?

Members usually know that in order to gain from the group experience they will need to reveal personal feelings and experiences but they may also fear that doing so will elicit rejection, criticism, or ridicule from other members or rejection or abandonment by the therapist. They may fear that what they reveal and learn about themselves will be more than they can bear.

That individuals may have fears connected with being in a group is under-standable. Many people who enter groups feel uncomfortable or downright fearful at the prospect of revealing personal concerns to strangers. They harbour certain fears. Will others accept them? Will they be criticised or ridiculed? Will they themselves be able to tolerate the feelings stirred up in them by what they or others say? In the face of such fears, individual members do what they can to feel comfortable. Each person tries to find a place in the group which is comfortable, safe, and manageable. This 'preferred niche' will differ from person to person. It can be hypothesised in general terms that each will try to re-establish in the group habitual ways of behaving and relating to others. Individuals often collide with one another while trying to establish preferred niches within the group. What one person presses for makes it difficult for one or more others to achieve what *they* are pressing for. Members sometimes manage to occupy exactly their preferred niche, but it is more often the case that they do not. Yet the need to feel safe persists. Interactions during the early sessions of a group are often understandable as efforts to establish safe conditions in the group. 'Safe' does not necessarily mean 'productive' or 'facilitative'. What often emerges is a collusive defence, erected in the face of fears of what might happen if personal concerns and feelings and experiences are revealed in the presence of strangers. The members might for instance discuss safe topics remote from their personal concerns, or fall into long silences, or allow one group member to be 'the patient', thus protecting everyone else from exposing themselves. These are mutually maintained defences which develop from and are sustained by interactions amongst the members. Such events can be conceptualized in group focal conflict terms as in Figure 10.1.

disturbing motive:	X	reactive motive:
(shared impulse or wish) wish to benefit by revealing oneself in the group; discussing one's own problems		(shared fear or guilt) fear of being criticised, ridiculed, etc. or of being overwhelmed by own feelings

$$\downarrow$$

mutually supported group solution(s):
e.g. talking off-target; utilising a metaphor;
intellectualising; turn-taking; attacking the
therapist or group therapy; etc.

Figure 10.1 A generalised diagram showing group focal conflicts likely to be in operation during the early sessions of a therapeutic group

Some restrictive solutions involve all or most of the members doing much the same thing – for instance, all or most engage in casual conversation, or talk in terms of a metaphor, or discuss an issue in abstract or intellectual terms. Alternatively, a restrictive solution may involve role differentiation – for instance, one person becomes 'the patient' and others act as therapists. Restrictive solutions have in common that they protect against fears but do not allow associated impulses and feelings to be expressed and examined.

Behaviour which is understandable as a mutually supported group solution is directly observable. Underlying fears are not directly expressed but can be inferred from the content of the conversation or the interactive pattern being maintained. The underlying impulse or wish also is inferred.

What marks the shift from being a new, unformed group to becoming established as a viable group within which productive work can take place? Thinking in terms of group focal conflict theory, a collection of individuals becomes established as a viable group when members shift from operating on restrictive solutions to operating, most of the time, on enabling solutions. Restrictive and enabling solutions both deal with underlying fears. However, enabling solutions allow for explorations of personal feelings and experiences, while restrictive solutions do not. When enabling solutions are in operation, members feel safe enough to take risks. When restrictive solutions are in operation, members feel safe because they do not take personal risks. Enabling solutions are thus more facilitative of the therapeutic process. Sometimes the point at which the shift occurs is easily noted, almost dramatic. Someone says: 'I suddenly feel I can tell you what *really* brought me here', proceeds to do so, and others follow. Sometimes the shift is not signalled so clearly, but the therapist becomes aware that there is more self-revelation and mutual exploration in the group than before. The therapist may also notice a personal feeling of relief, and greater confidence that the group will 'work' – will be a going concern. When enabling solutions begin to predominate, one can say that the group has moved beyond its formative phase, and has become viable. The arena within which the group can operate expands, and more personally meaningful issues begin to be explored.

By what processes does desirable movement or development occur? What can a therapist do to assist a group to move beyond a halting or defensive or obstructive start? If initial fears of the consequences of being in the group can be alleviated, members can move beyond the need to defend against the experience. In group focal conflict terms, if reactive fears are reduced, it is not so necessary to maintain restrictive solutions. Sometimes fear alleviation occurs through the efforts of the members themselves. Sometimes the therapist can intervene in a way which helps the members to acknowledge, examine, and test whether their fears are justified. Sometimes a therapist *must* intervene if the restrictive solution which is in operation is causing harm to someone.

It follows that if a therapist judges that fears of the consequences of participating in the group and revealing themselves are the root cause of a difficult start, he or she will first monitor events in the group in order to form an opinion of the nature of the fears and to judge whether members are interacting in a way likely to reduce those fears. The therapist will then judge whether an intervention on his/her part could help the process along or is necessary because the group seems to be stuck or one person is being harmed. Diverse routes towards fear alleviation have been illustrated in the previous chapter.

Some group conductors or leaders, anticipating a difficult or a slow start, make use of special instructions, exercises, or games as short-cuts intended to help members to move more quickly into useful forms of participation. Some of these are helpful and others are not. In general, helpful devices are those which take the needs and capabilities of members into account, provide a manageable way into participating in the group, and do not generate anxieties which would not otherwise be present. Therapists sometimes introduce themes as a way of focusing attention and giving members something to talk *about*. Whether this is effective or not depends on how carefully and sensitively the theme was chosen and how much individual choice is allowed when responding to it. A therapist may bring in props to support discussion of a theme. For instance, in a skill-development group for long-term hospitalised mental patients who were soon to move out into the community, the therapist brought along to a session a number of coins and spread them out on the table. This stimulated members to say which they recognised and which they didn't, what could be bought with them, and so on. The device directed members to a theme the therapist had in mind, helped to focus the discussion, and did no harm. A therapist might introduce a device which protects members but nevertheless allows for interaction. For instance, a therapist might place paper and pencil in front of each participant, to be used or not in any way preferred – perhaps for doodling. The pencil and paper stand between the member and the group, and offer something to concentrate on if a person cannot tolerate direct interaction.

In contrast, some short-cuts do not, in the event, function as short-cuts at all, but set the group back. Consider a therapist who, intending to accelerate matters, asks members of a group for anxious or depressed adults to say why they came to the group. Some members may be ready to do this but others may feel threatened. Those who feel threatened may be fearful of complying yet feel that they must. Some may evade the pressure by responding trivially. Some may reveal more about themselves than feels safe to them. The short-cut does not accomplish what it was intended to accomplish, since fears of being in the group are intensified rather than alleviated. As another example, consider a therapist who asks each member to name three things which he or she hopes to get out of participating in the group. Members may not feel safe enough to respond yet feel obliged to. The same kinds of consequences may follow. These kinds of instructions risk placing some persons in a worse rather than a better position to make use of the group.

In general, instructions, activities, exercises or games which preserve a degree of personal choice are more likely to be helpful than prescriptive ones. Prescriptions allow little or no choice. If an individual cannot bring him- or herself to participate as instructed, the only choice is to opt out or tune out, neither of which is desirable. As an example of a non-prescriptive instruction, Ruth Cohn (1971) advises her group members to be their own chairman, and to make their own choices as to whether to speak or not, and about what. This ground rule encourages members to assume control over their own participation. At first glance it may seem to restrict participation but in fact it is likely to have a freeing effect because it helps members to feel safe in the group and reduces the need for personal defences.

Therapists do not like to see members operating in terms of one restrictive solution after another, but it should be pointed out that restrictive solutions have the great advantage of making it possible for members to stay in the group rather than flee from it. A restrictive solution which keeps people feeling safe is preferable to a group which disintegrates because a number of people drop out.

How long does it take for a group to move out of its formative phase?

As the examples presented in the previous chapter show, some groups move very quickly into being an established, well-functioning group. A formative phase, as described here, can hardly be observed at all or is very brief. More frequently (in my experience) the formative phase goes on for four or five or six sessions. Some writers on groups refer to the early stages as going on for much longer. Nitsun (1991: 12), for example, refers to mistrust prevailing in a new group for several months. One of the situations presented by Kennard *et al.* in *A Work Book of Group-analytic Interventions* (1993) describes a pattern of turn-taking which was still going on in the sixth session of the group. In group focal conflict terms, this would be regarded as a restrictive solution. Day (1981), writing about 'classical' psychodynamic groups (that is, long-term, slow-open groups), refers to the 'group envelope', which he equates with the formation of a cohesive group. Day says that it takes between thirty and forty meetings for such a group to form. In my experience it does not take so long for a group to become formed. It is, however, hard to judge whether or not different writers are referring to comparable dynamics when they speak of achieving mutual trust, or 'maturity', or the establishment of a 'group envelope', and so on. Different theorists name different achievements which, for them, mark the completion of the formative phase. For Yalom, for instance, it is the achievement of cohesiveness which marks the onset of the 'mature' group.

The established phase

The established phase of a group is longer or shorter depending on the overall duration of the group. Initial fears about the consequence of participating in the group have been allayed, and enabling solutions are in operation most of the time. Energy can be put into exploring a range of issues. In an atmosphere of (relative) safety and confidence, themes emerge which are important to the members in personal ways.

Themes are many and varied. They include, for instance, feelings and experiences of envy, or of resentment, or of having been abandoned; anger and hatred; despair and hopelessness; mistrust or fear of people who hold power; fears connected with getting too close to others; a sense of guilt, or unworthiness, or isolation; and many others. Sometimes a theme is explored through here-and-now interactions within the group. Sometimes it is explored through members relating experiences from past life or current outside life. A theme can be important to almost everyone and yet mean different things to different people. Explorations within themes provide opportunities to express feelings ordinarily censored, compare own experiences and feelings with those of others, and give and receive feedback freely.

Sometimes themes emerge gradually through an associative flow to which most members contribute. Sometimes themes are triggered by some external event known to all the members, or by someone leaving or someone entering the group.

Members do not usually deal exhaustively with one theme and then move on to another. A well-functioning open-discussion group tends to move in a kind of deepening spiral. One theme comes into focus, is worked on for a while, is dropped, another takes its place, and so on. From time to time the members return to an issue or theme which was in the forefront earlier, usually taking it a bit further and exploring it in a somewhat different way. They may leave it for something else and return to it yet again, still later.

In a group which is working well, the overall trend is 'upward', or 'forward', or perhaps it would be better to say that the trend is 'outward', since there is an expansion in the themes or issues which can be discussed. One might also say that the trend is 'downward', in the sense of 'deeper'. These words are all metaphors which refer to the group developing towards being, most of the time, an environment in which themes important to members arise and are explored and feelings and experiences can be shared freely.

The phrase 'most of the time' needs to be inserted because an established group goes through its ups and downs. Thinking in group focal conflict terms, it is not the case that the members arrive at and operate consistently within some enabling solution which renders the group, henceforward and without exception, a satisfactory environment in which benefit can take place. Development is not uniformly 'forward' or 'deeper', though the overall trend may be positive.

What happens is that the members explore some theme, within some enabling solution, to the point where anxieties began to build up which cannot be contained by the current solution or set of solutions. Members arrive at some sort of limit and have, in a sense, over-reached themselves. The theme is abandoned and members stop their explorations and begin to interact in some more superficial, self-protective way. Within this more protective cocoon, interactions of course continue. Fears again abate, and profitable work resumes, most probably with respect to a different theme. The issue which the members fled from will very likely emerge again later, and be taken further (providing the group goes on long enough for this to happen).

A group therapist may feel disappointed when he or she sees a group, which has been functioning well, seem to retreat. However, such periods are a part of the process, and in a sense are even to be welcomed, since they show that the members have been working well. Otherwise, they would not have taken their explorations to a (temporary) limit.

The therapist's purpose and task during the established phase is double-pronged. Many opportunities arise during this phase for individual benefit to occur. A therapist who is alert to these opportunities can intervene in ways which increase the likelihood that they will be exploited and utilised. At the same time, it remains important for the therapist to monitor the state of the group and to be aware of periods in which members slip back into (and need to slip back into) making use of restrictive solutions. Attention needs to be paid to individuals *and* to the dynamics of the group.

The termination phase

The termination phase is that period towards the end of a group's life when the therapist and all the members know that the group will cease meeting on a specified date in the near future.

Themes especially associated with termination include the sense that time is running out, experiences of separation and mourning, self-assessment and stock-taking, and planning for the future.

With respect to 'time running out', it is not unusual for persons in a group to delay certain forms of risk-taking out of a sense that there will be time later to go into certain matters and therefore no particular need to explore a potentially painful or difficult issue just yet. If this has happened, and a termination date is now looming, members know that there is a limited and finite period of time still available to them. If they are to examine certain issues they must do so soon. There may be a sense of unfinished business in certain individuals or in the group. The impending end of the group exerts pressures on group members to explore themes which have been avoided previously or not taken as far as they might have been.

With respect to experiences of separation and mourning, it is obvious that as the termination date approaches, members know that they will soon lose the group. For virtually every adult, the experience of separating from the group, or losing it, will be the most recent of a number of separation experiences. Thus the prospect of losing the group (or specific members or the therapist) may stimulate re-experiencing earlier separations and provide opportunities to work on them and through them.

With respect to self-assessment, stock-taking, and planning for the future, many members recognise the period immediately before termination as a time for looking at what has been achieved, at where each now stands, who each now is, and what still needs to be worked on. They may focus on how gains may be maintained after the group ends. They may reflect on what has *not* been achieved and sort out realistic hopes from unrealistic ones. They may acknowledge that some of their life circumstances will not change, or may even get worse, and give thought to how to face them.

DIFFERENCES IN DEVELOPMENTAL PATTERNS

Groups whose formative phase is vanishingly short are usually composed of people who have in common some life circumstance which preoccupies them (population categories 1, 2 and 3 in Chapter 2). Members of such groups often have built-up feelings and accumulated experiences which they want and need to get off their chests. They are often ready to do so quite quickly. Members of such groups may assume right from the start that the others will understand what they are faced with. For these reasons they begin to share experiences with one another quite quickly, offer sympathy and acceptance to one another, and are not beset with the kinds of fears which mark the formative stage in many other kinds of groups.

Some groups do not go through a termination phase because there is no fixed termination date. When a person leaves the group he or she is replaced by someone new. Such groups may go on virtually indefinitely, with individual members staying for varying lengths of time. Disregarding for the moment those who drop out early, members may remain in the group from two or three months, or up to two or three years, or even more. Although there is not a termination phase during which all the members know they will be leaving at the same time, individuals will of course each have their own personal termination dates. When one person leaves it has an impact on that person and also on the other members.

Some individuals leave such groups at a time which seems appropriate to all concerned: to the member him- or herself, to the therapist, and to other members.

Sometimes, however, departures are abrupt and/or unexpected: a member drops out without notice, or someone's attendance becomes more and more sporadic and then stops altogether. If fees are required of members, a person might be forced to leave before he or she or anyone else thinks the time is right, because financial support is no longer available. Sometimes a departure is announced in advance. However a departure occurs, it is likely to be a significant event for the person leaving and for those who remain in the group. When notice of a departure has been given, the person about to leave as well as the other members can explore the meaning of the event for themselves. As in time-limited groups with a definite termination date, themes are likely to include time running out, separation and mourning, personal stock-taking, and planning for the future. When the departure is abrupt or unexpected, similar themes are likely to surface. However, those who have departed cannot participate in the exploration of such themes, and those who have been left so abruptly are likely to speculate about the reasons for the person leaving. There tends to be a vacuum of information, and into this vacuum speculations are introduced about 'the reasons why'. Not infrequently, those who remain behind feel bereft or angry or guilty about possibly having driven the member away. Whenever someone leaves or is about to leave, opportunities are present for members to explore other losses they have experienced in their own lives, and the feelings associated with them.

If a group is very short-term and also in time-limited groups, one can detect a formative, established, and termination phase but the established phase will be shorter. When this is the case, one does not always see a recurrence of themes, for a theme will be taken as far as the members can manage in the time available, and they may not return to it.

Therapists who use a topic-based structure will introduce topics which they predict are important to members, in a particular sequence. There may be logical or psychological reasons for ordering the sequence in some particular way. For instance, the therapist may choose to start with relatively non-threatening topics. Towards the end of the group the therapist may introduce topics or themes usually associated with a group's termination phase: for instance, 'what has been accomplished in this group so far'; or 'how each person intends to take what they have learned here into the future'.

One sometimes observes, in topic-orientated groups, that development-related dynamics 'leak through' a topic or influence and colour how it is explored. Members' fears and preoccupations infuse the structure and influence how topics are dealt with. For instance, a theme which is introduced early in a group's life may be explored only superficially because members do not as yet feel comfortable in the group.

Sometimes members give a topic a twist of their own or depart from it altogether. They may return to an earlier topic, and depart from the one just announced. This is akin to what happens in open-discussion groups, where topics and themes emerge through the interactions of members. Associative processes occur despite or in the context of topics. The therapist who has worked out and announced a topic may regard a departure from it as a failure or a problem, but departures from, or transformations of, topics are virtually bound to happen from time to time and can be regarded as advantageous. The members are making the group more relevant to their own concerns, or they may be distancing themselves from a threatening topic. By noting what the group shifts to and the processes by which this occurs, the therapist is likely to learn more about the members and what concerns them.

GROUPS WHICH FLUCTUATE AND CHANGE BUT CANNOT BE SAID TO DEVELOP

Some groups get stuck early in their development, and some are marked by irregular attendance and/or rapid changes in membership.

Groups which get stuck somewhere in the formative stage

When a group gets stuck in its formative stage and hardly seems to move at all, it appears to be for one of two reasons: either the members cannot manage the structure which the therapist has planned for them, and are immobilised; or else the members establish and then cannot extricate themselves from some restrictive solution and are fixed in an unproductive way of going on.

If the members are unable to make use of the structure planned for them, it is up to the therapist to change the structure. In effect, he or she helps the group to start again, with a new way of going on, a new procedure. Several examples of this were provided in Chapter 7. One may recall that Geczy and Sultenfuss (1995) used very short sessions for hospitalised psychiatric patients with very short attention spans, and that Van der Hal *et al.* (1996) scheduled meetings at monthly intervals for the adult children of holocaust survivors, with no pressure to attend regularly.

Another way in which a group may get stuck has to do with being capable or interacting but nevertheless maintaining some restrictive solution more or less indefinitely. Some given solution, or small set of restrictive solutions, does not yield or shift. This can occur for at least two reasons: the composition of the group; or the behaviour of the therapist.

A group may be composed homogeneously such that each person's preferred personal solution closely resembles that of everyone else. Members support one another's individually preferred restrictive solution and make it a characteristic of the group. For instance, if virtually everyone relies on intellectualising as a personal defence, this will very likely become established in the group as a mutually maintained defence. The same can be said of other defensive patterns; for instance, blaming others for their plight, or maintaining a rosy view and denying that any problem exists. Sometimes what is held in common is some shared assumption; for instance, that breaking the law is an expected and acceptable way to behave.

In all such cases, the therapist is up against unanimity and consensus in the group. There is nothing in the group composition to support any shift from the prevailing defence or point of view. The therapist is alone against the group. Such situations follow from an error in composing the group or from an unfortunate accident of composition: the members are too much like one another. Behaviours and assumptions inimical to the therapeutic process become so firmly established through unanimity and consensus that there is no point of entry for the therapist and no way of influencing unanimously held views.

A group may get stuck for quite a different reason which has to do with the behaviour of the therapist. A therapist can, for instance, drive a group into a defensive silence through repeatedly offering interpretations which are unacceptable or threatening to members. Or members may respond by playing at therapy, making what seem to be profound comments but in reality remaining untouched. In group focal conflict terms, these are restrictive solutions. A therapist could extricate a group from such a state but will not do so if he or she remains convinced of both the correctness and the appropriateness of his or her interventions. A therapist can also constrain a group by maintaining a cold, distant stance towards the members, such that members do not feel supported in their difficult explorations, and therefore avoid them. (These points are discussed at greater length in Chapter 14, on therapist errors.)

Bernard (1994) reports that, in his experience with groups homogeneously composed with respect to some real-life problem or circumstance, members can begin in a lively way, comparing experiences and related feelings connected with the problem they hold in common. Then, however, they seem to run out of material, slow down, and do not seem to know what to do next. This tended to occur in Bernard's groups which were made up of patients with genital herpes. In one of his examples, after the first few sessions one member began to repeat herself, and others became irritated but did not express their feelings. Bernard judged that the group needed to be encouraged to talk about their feelings about one another; up to then this had been outside the boundaries of the group. He made the point that, in general, groups get stuck because feelings have developed which are not expressed and explored. Group focal conflict theory would suggest that certain feelings remain unexpressed because of members' fears of the consequences of doing so. Some restrictive solution has been constructed which protects the members from anxiety but constrains the issues or feelings which can be acknowledged and explored. Moving on would require making more explicit and exploring the inhibiting factors, and testing whether the feared consequences of exploring the avoided feelings are in fact likely to occur.

Change but not development in groups in which attendance is irregular and sporadic, or members go and come with great frequency

In some groups, attendance is so irregular and comings and goings so frequent that the group is, effectively, fragmented and has little continuity. It is unusual for exactly the same people to turn up for successive sessions. Some members may stay for long periods, but they frequently experience the group dissolving and reforming around them as members go and come. Because of the nature of the population from which members are drawn, the therapist cannot expect regular attendance. The group seems continually to be restarting. Such groups cannot be said to develop, though they do of course change.

If the nominal membership remains the same but there are frequent absences, a structure is needed which takes the attendance pattern into account. Perhaps the therapist announces a topic at the start of each session, or members are invited to suggest topics for the day. More regular attendance might be supported by a nurturing stance on the part of the therapist: he or she might provide nurturance literally by offering food or snacks.

If the nominal membership changes in consequence of a member leaving for good, the therapist has two choices. The first is to replace each departing member immediately with a new person. The second is not to replace immediately but to allow the membership to dwindle and then to introduce a number of people into the group at the same time, bringing the membership up to strength again. If the turnover can be more or less predicted (for instance, on the basis of average length of hospital stay) it is possible to fix the point at which new members will be brought in – perhaps every six or eight weeks. If this is done, both the therapist and the group members will know when to expect a period of stability and when to expect changes. The period over which stability in membership can be sustained can be increased by increasing the frequency of sessions – for instance, twice a week rather than once.

Groups composed of certain populations or conducted within particular settings are especially prone to be or to become fragmented. It is unrealistic to expect anything like regular attendance. Thinking back to the populations named and discussed in Chapter 2, one probably cannot expect regular attendance or commitment to a group from persons who, through life circumstances, have lost or never fully acquired basic social, interpersonal, or practical skills of living (category 7), and people who are regarded by others as having or being problems because they are disruptive, unruly, break laws or offend commonly held standards (category 8).

DROP-OUTS AND OTHER CHANGES IN MEMBERSHIP

To be considered here are early drop-outs; a mass exodus or a number of drop-outs in quick succession; later drop-outs; absences; new members; and groups which dwindle in size because members who leave are not replaced.

Early drop-outs

When someone drops out early, sometime during a group's formative stage, one may assume that the person has experienced unusual threat or found the group irrelevant. Sometimes dropping out is, on balance, a good decision. A person who drops out may have sensed, correctly, that he or she will be unable to cope with feelings likely to be stirred up by participating in the group and that the group will prove to be an intolerably overwhelming experience. In such a case, dropping out is an appropriate protective measure. It is hard to be certain about this, because it is also possible that the person has not given himself enough time, or has not been encouraged to do so. It is possible that group processes have placed the person in a particularly threatening position early on, and that the therapist has not detected and dealt with this.

Some people who drop out early feel that the group is not relevant to their interests or needs. It is hard to make out what this might mean, for the person is gone and the matter cannot be explored directly. It *could* mean that the group's composition is such that the person quite quickly feels that s/he is an outsider, or that the person cannot connect with the early themes emerging in the group, or that the judgement that the group is irrelevant masks some sense of personal threat. Sometimes a therapist can develop a better understanding of why someone has dropped out by reviewing the immediately preceding events.

Sometimes an early drop-out seems hardly to affect the others at all. This is likely under conditions of low cohesiveness. Sometimes, however, others are powerfully affected. One person leaving may confirm the sense that the group is a dangerous place. It may be taken as evidence that the group is not worthwhile, or that attendance does not matter. If members do not comment on a drop-out themselves, the therapist should refer to it in order to make an opportunity for members to explore their reactions.

A mass exodus or a number of drop-outs in quick succession

In my experience this is unusual but it does sometimes happen. When it does, it tends to have a powerful negative effect. Those who remain may lose confidence in the group, the therapist, and the likelihood that they will gain from their group experience. The therapist too may lose confidence and hope. It requires considerable resolve on the part of a therapist to face such an event without evading it or passively allowing its consequences to persist.

Direct and specific attention needs to be paid to the event. The therapist needs to help members to express and examine their feelings and assumptions. Members may profit from testing the reality base for their assumptions. For instance, members sometimes feel guilty: they assume that something they did or said led people to drop out. Often, such assumptions are not justified, in which case, it is advantageous to realise this and explore why feelings of guilt so readily surfaced.

Sometimes, on reflection, a therapist sees that it was his or her behaviour which drove people out. If so, s/he can avoid making the same kind of error again.

Later drop-outs

If someone drops out later in the group, it is almost certain that something has happened which has generated unusual stress. It might be the entry of a new member or some new personal crisis which the individual cannot bear to explore in the group. A person may sense that he or she is getting too close to dangerous territory, such that anxiety escalates. One hopes that the therapist has noticed prodromal signs, for instance in the form of a shift from customary behaviour. If so, there may be time either to encourage explorations or else give permission for the individual to lie low for a while.

Sometimes, as with early drop-outs, the therapist has precipitated the drop-out by behaving in a way which has intensified stress for the person concerned. One hopes that this can be avoided or quickly noted and corrected for if it has happened.

Absences

Different dynamics underlie absences. Perhaps a member needs protection or relief from a particularly intense or disturbing group event, and is regulating his/her exposure to the group. Perhaps a member is using an absence to call the therapist's or the members' attention to him- or herself: an absence can be a call for help, or a way of acting out rather than acknowledging a need for attention and nurturance. Perhaps the person is absent casually, because he or she feels no attachment or obligation to the group. Perhaps the person forgot that the group was to meet (and why should *that* happen?). Perhaps the absent member's car broke down.

An absence which occurs early in a group could lead to the member dropping out altogether. Suppose that someone fails to turn up for the first session or comes the first time but then misses a session. Perhaps the member's child was ill and s/he was needed at home, and is now wondering uneasily whether s/he is still welcome in the group. It would be too bad to lose a group member for such a reason. I would be inclined to allow, say, two consecutive absences but then get in touch with the person. In the course of a phone call, the reasons offered by the person for non-attendance could be ascertained and discussed. It may be enough simply to say that the person is welcome to come back to the group. By this means, fears might be alleviated to a point where the person could resume attending. On the other hand, fears might prove to be massive and intractable. If so, the therapist might feel it appropriate to sanction dropping out, helping the person to leave the group with dignity.

New members

A colleague, Murray Horwitz, once likened joining a new group to entering a completely dark room: you know there are various pieces of furniture, some with sharp corners, but you don't know where they are. You also know that there is a light switch but not how or where to find it. The only way to find your bearings in this new setting is by stumbling against obstacles and quite possibly getting hurt in the process. The new person in the group is in this position. Like anyone else, he or she will try to find a place in the group which is comfortable. Such attempts may or may not fit in with the group's way of operating (its culture, or the prevailing set of solutions on which it operates). He or she may learn about the norms operating in the group by stumbling against them. In short, a new member may behave in a way which is unusual for the group, which offends or distresses or startles the others. This presents a problem for both the new member and the group. It presents a new task which needs to be addressed.

From the point of view of the existing members, a new person joining a group is an unknown quantity. He or she can become a figure on to whom all sorts of fantasies are projected: 'Here is someone who will know all the answers'; 'Here is someone who will dislike and despise us', and so on. Sometimes, simply by having been brought in by the therapist, the entering member is cast by the others into the role of unasked-for sibling. A new member can constitute new 'raw material' for the existing members.

If a number of new people are brought into a group all at once, the group may split into 'old members' and 'new members'. New members may constitute some sort of threat to the old members. New members may feel uneasy through having entered an unfamiliar world. Like other situations arising in groups, conflict or tension between old and new members can be an opportunity. Members can be encouraged to reflect on: 'What do we old members think the new members might do?' 'How does it feel to be a new member in a group and why do we new members huddle together?' 'What do we need to find out about one another?' And so on.

Groups which dwindle in size because members who leave are not replaced

If members terminate or drop out and are not replaced, a group may dwindle to three or perhaps four members. This may be by the direct choice of the therapist, or else the remaining members argue against new people being brought in and the therapist acquiesces. A group can actually become so small that it lacks useful diversity. It becomes too easy for members to collude in some self-protective way of going on. Little give-and-take, little challenging, little introduction of alternative points of view occurs. Opportunities diminish for personal gain through interpersonal comparison, feedback, and the like. On these grounds, dwindling to a very small number should be avoided. This point is discussed again in Chapter 13, for it is one of the circumstances in which little or no gain is likely to occur for members. I believe most group therapists consider that a group can become too small to be useful, though I have heard it argued that a three-member group has the advantage of replicating the nuclear family.

A change in the therapist

In a group being conducted by co-therapists, one may leave while the other stays. Usually, this is because trainees rotate through the setting, or students may be attached to the unit from time to time in order to gain experience. When this happens, an experienced member of staff stays with the group throughout, but co-therapists or co-workers come and go, staying for shorter periods of time – often six weeks or eight weeks. Because the therapists know that this will happen, it can be mentioned to the members in the opening statement the first time the group meets.

Sometimes there is a change in the principal therapist, although this is to be avoided if possible. If there is only one therapist, and he or she has to leave for some reason, it is obvious that the members face a major change. Sometimes there is an interruption caused by the therapist being away on holiday or ill.

Such changes often trigger themes of separation and loss, with possibly attendant feelings of grief, fear, anger, disappointment. Because exploration within such themes carries therapeutic benefit, it is advantageous to give members notice of any such changes, if possible, and encourage discussion. If no notice can be given, someone will have to step in to help the members with their feelings.

THE LITERATURE ON TERMINATION

'Termination' can refer to the termination of the whole group, imposed by its structure from the beginning, or imposed by the therapist, or arrived at by agreement amongst the members (often after considerable struggles). It can also refer to termination by individual members who leave the group under a very wide range of circumstances, and to therapist termination – that is, one therapist leaves the group and is replaced by another.

Lothstein (1993) offers an extensive review of the literature on termination, both of the group and on the part of the therapist or of individual members. When thinking of individuals who terminate (= leave) Lothstein organises his discussion in terms of premature termination (dropping out, either early in the group or later on); forced or enforced termination (the therapist decides unilaterally that someone must leave); circumstantial termination (a change in a patient's personal circumstances, such as taking a job in another city, which makes it necessary for him or her to leave); and planned termination (the patient, the therapist, and others see the person as being ready to leave).

The January 1996 issue of the *International Journal of Group Psychotherapy* includes a lengthy section on termination. It includes articles by Rice on premature termination; Fieldsteel on termination in long-term psychoanalytic group therapy; MacKenzie on time-limited group psychotherapy, where the termination date is fixed in advance and is known to all members from the beginning; Joyce *et al.* on therapist decisions to terminate a long-term open-ended group; Brabender and

Fallon on aspects of patient-termination in in-patient groups; and Schermer and Klein on two theoretical perspectives on termination: object relations theory and self-psychology.

The literature on theories of group development

MacKenzie (1994a) provides a 45-page account of the history of theories of group development, starting from the early 1900s, citing 117 different authors and examining theory based on the study of work groups and experiential groups as well as therapeutic groups. This represents a very large amount of work done on just this one aspect of small groups. Formulations of development differ: many more stages are posited in some than in others, and different aspects of groups are emphasised.

To give some idea of the diversity of theory, I will describe conceptualisations put forward by Piper *et al.* (1992); Budman and Gurman (1988); MacKenzie (1990); Beck and her associates (articles produced from 1977 through to the present; references are given on p. 140); and Yalom (1995).

Piper *et al.* (1992), in their book *Adaptation to Loss Through Short-term Group Psychotherapy*, posit a beginning, a middle and a termination stage in their short-term time-limited groups (twelve sessions) and say that each stage presents the group with particular tasks and obstacles which require different strategies and responses on the part of the therapist for goal attainment. These are then illustrated by means of a detailed example which includes verbatim excerpts from all three stages of a single group. In this group, themes which emerged in the beginning stage included: the issue of trust; dependence on the therapist, who was expected to provide answers and advice; and preoccupation with an absent member (who had in fact dropped out after the first session) and which included guilt and anger. A recurrent theme which appeared in the middle stage was frustration with the therapist for interpreting rather than giving advice, and turning to one another and ignoring the therapist. Patients were preoccupied with 'the empty chair' if someone was absent. Anger was expressed towards members who had been absent and then turned up, which made an opportunity to explore anger directed towards lost family members or other significant losses. Themes appearing in the termination stage included patients evaluating their progress, evaluating the therapist, and 'saying goodbye'. In such groups, the authors point out that some themes were recurrent while others were stage-specific or situation-specific.

Budman and Gurman (1988) posit five phases in short-term, time-limited group psychotherapy: the start of the group, early therapy, middle, late, and termination. They list issues likely to arise in each of these phases, the foci of work, and the aims and participation of the therapist. What goes on in each stage is much influenced by the patients' awareness of how much time is left. In the beginning, when members are new to one another and termination is felt to be far in the future, members are likely to be concerned with issues of safety and the therapist will be seeking to support the development of cohesion and to clarify themes. In the middle stage, frustration and loss of confidence in the group may occur, with attendant disappointment in or criticism of the therapist. This is precipitated by an increased awareness of the limited time left to the members. In the penultimate phase, members are motivated by time pressure to engage in intensive work.

MacKenzie (1990), also with reference to time-limited groups, named six stages: engagement, differentiation, individuation, intimacy, mutuality, and termination. These terms refer to tasks which are in focus during each of the stages:

1   *engagement*: achieving engagement with the group;
2   *differentiation*: recognizing differences amongst members and working out ways of resolving conflicts;
3   *individuation*: seeking to understand the complexity of each individual;
4   *intimacy*: opportunities to explore relationships arising from the increased intimacy in the group and members' knowledge of one another; and
5   *mutuality*: appreciating the uniqueness of each person while at the same time establishing mature relationships based on mutual agreement and consent.

These first five are seen as occurring in sequence. Within each, particular polarities are posited, and the work achieved in each makes it possible for the group to move on to the next. 'Termination' is different in kind for it can occur at different points in a group's development. Whenever it occurs, termination too carries its particular task, which is to disengage comfortably from the group. Themes of loss prevail, and aspects of loss have to be worked through. In each of the six stages, particular tasks face the therapist.

Ariadne Beck and her associates have identified nine developmental phases (eight plus a termination phase) based on their empirical studies of therapy groups and encounter groups. These are:

1   creating a contract to become a group;
2   survival: personal influence and survival in group/the resolution of competitive needs while forging a group identity, group norms and selecting leaders;
3   disclosure of individual identity/defining individual goals to be pursued in the group/establishing a work style;
4   exploration of intimacy and closeness;
5   establishment of mutuality and equality;
6   autonomy of members from formal leader;
7   self-confrontation in the context of interdependence;
8   pursuit of independence; and
9   coping with separation and termination.

(Beck *et al.* 1986: 618)

Beck *et al.* emphasise that groups can be expected to move through these phases if they are sufficiently long-term and if membership remains stable. When membership changes, a group may recycle through its earlier stages. Beck's formulations have been based on empirical studies, and she and her colleagues have developed rating scales, questionnaires, and sociometric devices for identifying developmental phases or dynamics associated with developmental phases (see Beck 1977; Eng and Beck 1981; Eng and Beck 1982; Beck 1983; and Brusa *et al.* 1994). They make developmental stages and the processes which occur in them the cornerstone of their thinking about therapeutic and other kinds of groups.

Yalom (1995) sees the formative stage of the group as including an initial stage marked by orientation, hesitant participation, search for meaning, and dependency; a second stage marked by conflict, dominance, and rebellion; and a third (but not final) stage marked by the development of cohesiveness. The achievement of cohesiveness marks the beginning of the 'mature' group. Under conditions of cohesiveness, there is greater mutual trust and self-disclosure. Cohesiveness, once established, allows differentiation and conflict to emerge. After a group reaches maturity, it may return from time to time and for short periods to functioning as in earlier phases.

When comparing theories of development, some points of correspondence can be identified. The early stage tends to be seen as moving from a state of not being a group at all to becoming a unit marked by mutual trust or cohesiveness or readiness to share experiences and express personal feelings in the group. The termination stage is generally seen to involve themes of loss and separation. Apart from this, theories diverge, both with respect to the number of stages posited and what is considered characteristic of each stage. One of the reasons that theories of group development differ has to do with the large number of different variables which can be taken into account when trying to define stages. In particular formulations, some variables are emphasised over others. For instance, the theoriser might focus on or try to accommodate themes, or interactive patterns, or shifting norms, or tasks facing the therapist, or member behaviour such as self-disclosure or conflict, or level of cohesiveness or degree of intimacy, or, of course, a number of these in combination. Some elements may be considered superordinate or subordinate to others.

The kind of population worked with will influence the kinds of themes which emerge within developmental stages. Piper *et al.* (1992) report recurrent preoccupations with 'the empty chair' when a member had dropped out or when there were absences. This theme was fairly obviously related to the group composition, which was made up of people who had suffered personal losses.

One sees different points of view expressed in the literature as to whether integration of diverse theories about development could be achieved. Piper *et al.* (1992: 79) judge that comparabilities are present which are somewhat masked because some theorists subdivide stages more than do others. MacKenzie (1994: 257–60) offers some suggestions for achieving integration, based on the assumption that a larger framework has to be found within which existing theories could be fitted.

CHOOSING FROM AMONG DIFFERENT THEORIES OF DEVELOPMENT

How is one to choose from among the many conceptualisations of development? The answer has to be by comparing what is to be found in the literature against one's own experience. A practitioner can usefully ask: Does what is said here match my own experience? Have I seen these developmental stages in the groups I conduct? Can I translate the terms used in this theory of development into a language more familiar to me, and if I do so, does it help me to understand my own groups? Does this way of looking at development seem to fit some of the groups I work with but not others?

Answers to such questions will incline a practitioner towards accepting some formulations and not others. As is the case with other realms of theory, each practitioner will make personal choices. Each practitioner is his or her own theory selector, theory adapter, and theory user.

Chapter 11

Problems and opportunities

In the course of conducting a group, situations arise from time to time which strike the therapist or one or more of the members as a problem. Something happens which someone is concerned about, thinks is spoiling the group, or considers should be interrupted or dealt with.

Because situations arising in groups are always understood and judged from someone's point of view, a situation might be experienced as a problem by one therapist and not by another, or by one or more group members but not the therapist, or by the therapist but not the members. A therapist might not be worried about a situation but find it intriguing – something to be worked on with pleasure. In the latter case a problem comes close to being an opportunity, which by dictionary definition is 'a time, juncture, or condition of things favourable to an end or purpose' (*Shorter Oxford English Dictionary*). What is regarded as a problem by one therapist could be regarded as an opportunity by another. Many situations which are regarded as problems can be turned into opportunities.

It is evident that neither a problem nor an opportunity is a fact of life – an observable piece of reality like a trolley-car or a pineapple. Perception and judgement are always involved. Even though some situations are likely to be seen as problems by most people, a problem always lies in the eye of the beholder. So does an opportunity.

This chapter is organised as follows:

- Situations which group therapists or workers have regarded as problems.
- Problem situations organised into clusters.
- Some examples of problem situations, with commentaries.
- Two further situations which sometimes worry group therapists, but need not.
- Thinking about problems: questions to ask oneself and try to answer.
- Intractable or nearly intractable problem situations.

SITUATIONS WHICH GROUP THERAPISTS OR
WORKERS HAVE REGARDED AS PROBLEMS

I am about to list quite a large number of situations which have been experienced by therapists or group workers as problems, but first I must explain what this list is based on. For many years I have asked members of courses on therapeutic groups to bring in short written descriptions of situations encountered in their practice which puzzled, intrigued, or concerned them. These accounts become the shared property of the course members and are drawn upon for learning purposes. By now I have a sizeable file of such descriptions. The situations referred to include:

- members dwell on some apparently trivial topic;
- members talk only to the therapist and not to one another;
- a number of members challenge the therapist's competence;
- attendance is irregular;
- one person attends irregularly;
- one person monopolises;
- one person is persistently silent;
- a group member repeatedly asks for advice but always rejects it when it is offered;
- a person becomes upset and runs out of the group;
- a person threatens suicide;
- members take turns at being 'the patient' while the others offer advice;
- a group departs from the structure introduced by the therapist;
- a person announces that he or she does not intend to come back to the group;
- a person declares her- or himself to be upset or harmed by the group;
- one person attacks another;
- two members attack one another;
- one person becomes the concerted target of attack by all or most of the others;
- behaviour on the part of one person irritates the others;
- a member behaves in a bizarre way;
- the therapist is confronted by unanimous support amongst members of a point of view which he or she cannot accept or considers works against the best interests of the group;
- one member is regarded by the others as 'spoiling' the group;
- one or more members complain privately to the therapist about another member, demanding that the therapist take action;
- one or more members break the group's rules, for instance about confidentiality;
- a new member behaves in a way which is unacceptable to the others;
- the group 'explodes' into apparently unmanageable affect or behaviour;
- one person is excluded or disregarded by the others;
- there is a persistent silence in the group;
- someone drops out;
- a number of people drop out in quick succession.

PROBLEM SITUATIONS ORGANISED INTO CLUSTERS

A list with so many diverse items in it has to be tamed by some means so that the forms that problem situations take can be grasped more clearly. This means putting like with like: placing items into clusters and then naming the clusters. Since no two situations are exactly alike, a degree of abstraction is involved. There will of course be more than one way of placing items into clusters. I suggest the following:

1 *Situations in which the problem appears to belong to the group as a whole* Most or all members of the group keep a situation going through their interaction (for instance, all the members talk about some apparently trivial topic, or members talk only to the therapist and not to one another, or members take turns being 'the patient' while the others offer advice, or the members unanimously support some point of view which the therapist considers works against the best interests of the group).

2 *Situations in which one person is seen by the other members or by the therapist as having or being a problem* Instances are: a monopoliser; a persistently silent person; a person who repeatedly asks for advice but then rejects it; a person who exhibits bizarre or conspicuously different behaviour.

3 *Situations in which one person becomes the target or recipient of behaviour on the part of others which leads to disadvantage or harm* For example: one person is the target of a concerted attack by most or all of the others, either through direct attack, or ridicule, or shaming; one person is scapegoated; one person is ignored or disregarded by all or most of the others; one person is cast by the others into an interpersonal position which closes off opportunities for personal gain.

4 *Situations in which one person becomes visibly distressed or declares him- or herself to be distressed* For instance, a person bursts into tears, or runs out of the room, or says that he or she is on the verge of suicide, or says that others are getting him (or her) more and more upset.

5 *Situations in which powerful feelings spread as if by contagion through the group, or else two or three people become involved in an intense, highly charged interaction while others look on* For instance, virtually everyone becomes almost uncontrollably angry or fearful or panicky; two members viciously attack one another; one member attacks or criticises another; one member expresses envy of another; one member reproaches another, who then defends him- or herself.

6 *Situations which have to do with changes in the group* Examples are: one or more members leave the group; a new person enters; someone drops out; there is a change of therapist.

SOME EXAMPLES OF PROBLEM SITUATIONS, WITH COMMENTARIES

The following eight examples have been selected from among many which could have been provided. They show a range of situations and suggest ways in which problem situations can be understood and responded to. I have not included examples which belong in cluster 6, above, because such situations have already been discussed in Chapter 10.

Example I

A woman frequently monopolised the situation, and irritated everyone else (This example belongs in cluster 2: situations in which one person is seen by the others or by the therapist as having or being a problem.)

> In almost every session of an out-patient group, Ruth got into telling some story at considerable length and with many repetitions. Members became restive but no one interrupted. During the ninth session of the group, Ruth talked non-stop for nearly ten minutes and seemed to get more frantic as time went on. The others exchanged resigned glances but said nothing. Ruth finally threw up her hands and said: 'I know I'm boring you', and subsided. The discussion then proceeded, with Ruth not participating.
>
> After this session three group members came to the therapist privately and appealed to him to do something about Ruth, who, they said, was spoiling the group. The therapist said that it was the kind of situation which no one person could control, but that if the members were concerned they could undoubtedly find a way to deal with Ruth's behaviour. All three members protested that they couldn't say anything to Ruth because she would fall to pieces. The therapist said that he was confident that they could find a way, and the members left, dissatisfied.
>
> About ten minutes into the next session Ruth again began to talk in her non-stop way. After a brief exchange of glances with one another, one of the members said: 'Ruth, listen, we all want to listen to you but you go on for so long that it gets harder and harder. It's a real problem for us.' Ruth was visibly relieved and said that she knew she went on for too long but did not know how to stop herself. The therapist asked Ruth: 'How can we help you?' and Ruth said: 'Just say to me, "Stop!"' The other members protested that this would be discourteous in the extreme, but Ruth insisted that she would welcome it. The next time Ruth got out of control, which was later in the same session, one of the group members leaned forward, caught Ruth's eye, and said: 'Stop!' Ruth said: 'Thank you', in a relieved tone, and subsided. In subsequent sessions her monopolising behaviour diminished, but when it occurred, members helped her to control it by responding in the same way.

For whom was this situation a problem? It was a problem for Ruth, who felt out of control of her own behaviour and knew she was alienating others. It was also a problem for the other members, who were irritated and impatient but were unable to express their feelings or deal with Ruth's behaviour. The therapist also considered the situation to be a problem for, if the situation persisted, harm could come to Ruth, who would become more and more entrenched as the rejected or disliked member. Ruth could also fail to gain because she lacked opportunities to examine the functions that talking at such length might be fulfilling for her. Focal conflict theory suggests that talking so much and so uninterruptedly could constitute, for Ruth, a personal solution to some abiding underlying conflict. For instance, her non-stop talking might be distracting her from facing other concerns and feelings. As long as she continued to behave in this way, Ruth would have no access to possible underlying or associated feelings. The other members would be held in a disadvantageous position because much time and energy would continue to be taken up by helpless preoccupation with Ruth's behaviour. The situation was a problem not only because of Ruth's behaviour but because of the helplessness of the others.

Who was responsible for dealing with this problem? It is clear that the three members who approached the therapist privately thought it was the therapist's responsibility. He, on the other hand, placed the responsibility back into their hands. The therapist realised, in retrospect, that he had judged that group members could achieve some gains from confronting Ruth themselves: for instance, they might be able to examine why it was it so hard for them to tell Ruth how they felt.

In this example, the members themselves found a way to respond to Ruth. If they had not, the therapist would have had to take on the task himself. How might he do this? Directly and actively confronting Ruth would not be a desirable course of action because she could feel highly threatened and might resort to some defence which would make her even more inaccessible to help. A better approach would be to ignore the content of Ruth's lengthy comments and focus instead on the interactive pattern in the group. The therapist might simply call attention to what is going on: Ruth behaves in such-and-such a manner; others respond by allowing her to go on despite becoming impatient. The therapist can then enquire into how Ruth feels and how others feel. In response to such interventions, members will most probably begin to explore aspects of the situation themselves, and/or the therapist can assist in this: Why did the others feel so helpless in the face of Ruth's behaviour? What did they fear would happen if they confronted her, or even referred to her behaviour? Were their fears similar to or different from one another? Does Ruth tend to monopolise in other life situations, and if so what are they? Does she gain anything by going on at such length? Does she for instance avoid something worse happening? Ruth's underlying needs or fears might begin to become evident. For instance, it might emerge that she never feels she is being understood and therefore is driven to repeat herself endlessly. In such a case, Ruth could be invited to explore comparable feelings in her current life outside the group or in her past life.

By such interventions, attention ceases to be paid exclusively to Ruth. Explorations move back and forth between focusing on Ruth and focusing on others. Attention is paid to feelings which are important to Ruth *and* to others.

Before leaving this example it should be noted that members do not always respond negatively to a monopoliser. There are times when group members are grateful if one person talks at length, for it protects everyone else from having to participate. If this is the case, the members will not of course experience the situation as a problem but the therapist might, through perceiving that a collusive defence (= restrictive solution) is in operation.

Example 2

Instead of facing a difficult situation which was in everyone's mind, members talked at some length about something quite different   (This example belongs in cluster 2, in which the problem appears to belong to the group as a whole.)

> In the fourth month of an outpatient group which met twice a week, one of the members reported at the beginning of the session that Brigitte would not be coming because she had just had word that her father had been badly injured in a car crash and might not survive. She had gone to the family home in another city to be with her mother and sister. A silence followed this announcement. Then a long discussion followed about how pointless it is to read newspapers or watch the news on television, since one hears nothing but bad news.
>
> Everyone agreed about this. The two therapists exchanged glances, showing one another that they understood that the group was avoiding thinking about Brigitte and her father or anything connected with the event. After about 20 minutes, one of the therapists asked: 'Has anyone been thinking of Brigitte?' One of the members said: 'No! Have you?' in an emphatic tone. The therapist said that he had, and when asked what he had been thinking, said that he had been wondering how Brigitte might be feeling, and what she found when she got home. The members then began to discuss illness in parents. Carl told the group for the first time that his father was suffering from a brain tumour which was likely to be fatal, and Christine talked about her mother's very serious illness a few years ago, and how distressed she had been. The members shared their anxieties around these crises, and wondered how Brigitte's father was and how Brigitte was feeling.

There was ample time to think about this situation, for the lengthy talk about newspapers went on for some 20 minutes or so. For whom was this situation a problem? It was not a problem for the members, whom one could say 'cooperated' in keeping the discussion going. It was not experienced as a problem by the therapists, who expected the focus on news and newspapers to be relatively short-lived. (They would have come to regard it as a problem if it persisted for very long, certainly if it continued for the whole session. If this had happened, the members would be left with the distress stirred up by the news about Brigitte, and the opportunity to explore its implications would have been missed.) Each of the therapists quite quickly formed the view that the members were defending against feelings stirred up by Brigitte's situation, and signalled this to one another through brief eye contact. They each judged that the news about Brigitte had shocked members *and* that no one could bring themselves to talk about the event or any feelings and associations triggered by the event. Both therapists were accustomed to thinking in group focal conflict terms, and regarded the talk about newspapers as a restrictive solution which the members needed at the time to deal with their shock and distress.

One of the two therapists intervened, and at a particular point. Why? The session had been audio-taped. When listening to it afterward, the therapists realised that there had been one small sign that the members might be ready to move away from their talk about newspapers and newscasts. Someone had said that if one never reads newspapers or watches the news one misses out on a great deal. Although neither of the therapists could remember this comment, it was there on the tape. Evidently one of the therapists had registered the comment and was moved to intervene. The question arises as to whether the members would have shifted on their own, without the therapist's intervention. One cannot say for certain, but quite possibly they would have done so, since the shared defence was beginning to crack a bit. It might have taken a little more time.

It is worth noting that the therapist's intervention was spontaneous and unplanned. It was, however, made in the context of his having developed an understanding of the situation. He was also tuned in emotionally to the group, and recognised an opening without realising that he was doing so. The intervention was a very simple one: he asked a question and then shared a feeling.

Example 3

Powerful feelings began to spread contagiously in a group, and panic was imminent (This belongs in cluster 5, which includes episodes in which powerful feelings are expressed, either by virtually everyone or by two or three members while others look on.)

> In a group of psychotic and near-psychotic patients one of them began to talk in a headlong and intense way about his fears of the army. ('They send you out and let you get killed.') One or two joined in, expressing similar anger and fears, and the interaction became more and more intense. One patient who had been silent stood up and began to move towards the door, and several others looked as if they might follow. The therapist said in a clear, loud (but not panicky) voice: 'Stop!' He turned first to those who had been active and said: 'Please stop talking', and then turned to those who had been about to leave and said: 'Just stop for a

moment.' He then turned to the whole group and said: 'We have been talking about things which are important, but we must find a different way to talk about them.' The person who was heading for the door returned to his seat and members began to discuss their feelings in a more measured way.

Who was experiencing this situation as a problem? Certainly the therapist did, for he saw the group virtually disappearing before his eyes. Were the members experiencing it as a problem? This seems too cognitive a way of putting it, but it was clear that anxiety was high and panic was setting in. The situation was triggered by the behaviour of one person, but the anger and fear he was expressing evidently connected with similar feelings held by others. All the members became caught up in the situation. It is hard to judge just what the situation meant to each individual member, but the group dynamic could be seen to consist of emotional and behavioural contagion.

Were negative consequences likely to occur if this situation were not interrupted? Yes, for the group was on the verge of disintegrating and individual members were not able to talk about their feelings. They were able only to express their feelings in behaviour – to act them out. In general, episodes of contagion need to be interrupted fairly early, lest feelings get out of control and lead members to feel overwhelmed, or begin to behave destructively. Unbridled contagion can lead to members fleeing from the group, or destroying property, or threatening one another or the therapist. Even if contagion involves only giddy excitement and is not actually harming anyone, it is undesirable for it to continue because, as long as it goes on, feelings are being expressed only in behaviour, and cannot be acknowledged or examined.

In such a situation the therapist aims to interrupt the contagion *so that* members can acknowledge (rather than merely express) their anger, fears, excitement, and so on, and begin to understand what occasioned them. A simple injunction to 'Stop!' can be effective (as in the example above), providing it is followed up by encouragement to discuss whatever feelings are involved in a more measured way. A therapist might enquire: 'What got this going?' or 'What are we really concerned about?' Or a therapist might get the members' attention and say, in a quiet voice: 'We can calm down and talk about this.' Sometimes displaying contrasting behaviour – measured speech and a quiet tone of voice – breaks into the contagion. Whatever the specific intervention, what needs to be avoided is joining in by expressing strong feelings oneself. The therapist's tone of voice needs to be calm even if emphatic.

For understanding this situation and others like it, the thinking of Fritz Redl on contagion and imitation is relevant, as reported in Chapter 4. Redl would say that one person acted as a trigger by first expressing the fear, but that the fear and panic would not have spread unless others harboured comparable feelings which they usually managed to keep under control. The behaviour of the initiator triggered or released others to behave similarly (Redl 1966b).

Example 4

A member strongly implied that she had been hurt by the group, and fled from the room (This is an example of cluster 4 situations, in which one person becomes visibly distressed or declares him- or herself to be distressed.)

> In the course of the twelfth session of an out-patient group, several members told Wendy that they found her constant complaints difficult to listen to, and in the end lost patience with her even though they were sympathetic at first. Wendy started to cry and ran from the group, snatching her handbag and coat as she went. Kate, another member of the group, followed her out. Neither reappeared.
>
> In the half-hour which remained of the session, the members who remained in the room expressed worries that they had done some terrible damage to Wendy. Some said they felt guilty. The therapist encouraged discussion along the lines of 'who is responsible for what?' The theme of appropriate and inappropriate guilt was explored, and a number of personal stories were told. The worries about Wendy, however, persisted.
>
> Wendy and Kate were both present for the next session. Wendy was met by a mixture of relief and anger. She told the others how angry she had been at their criticism, and others told Wendy and Kate about their discussion the previous time about guilt. In this context Wendy told the group about an earlier suicide attempt, and she and others could see the large component of vengeful anger in it.

For whom was this situation a problem? For everyone, really. Wendy was clearly distressed. The members who remained in the room were worried about the damage they had apparently caused. The therapist saw the situation as a problem which needed to be addressed and also saw opportunities in it. He kept his own worries to himself and supported the members in their explorations of appropriate and inappropriate guilt. He could not respond to Wendy, for she was not there. (Kate could be presumed to be looking after Wendy, though no one knew what was really happening.)

Were there likely to be undesirable consequences, for Wendy or for the others? The immediate consequence was that everyone was upset. If Wendy did not return, negative consequences could persist for her, for she would have removed herself from the arena within which she could come to understand her reactions. Negative consequences would persist for others had they avoided examining their feelings of guilt.

When Wendy and Kate returned to the group for the next session, they and the others shared feelings about the situation and personal experiences which resonated with it. One could say, with confidence, that a problem situation had been turned into an opportunity.

Example 5

One group member exhibited conspicuous, unusual behaviour which others found it difficult to accept (This example belongs in cluster 2, which includes in it people perceived as having or being a problem.)

> Nelson was a member of an in-patient group on a psychiatric ward which met twice a week. He always brought a newspaper with him, and from the very first session and for most of the time, sat with it held up open in front of him. Now and then he would put the newspaper down momentarily and say something, then raise it again. His comments were always in keeping with what was being discussed at the time. No one said anything about this in the group, but after the group had been going on for some time two members approached the therapist outside the group and said that he (the therapist) ought to stop Nelson behaving as he did, because Nelson was being disrespectful of the therapist. The therapist said that, actually, he did not experience Nelson's behaviour as disrespect, but that the two members could bring the matter up in the group if they wished. The members did not do this, and Nelson continued with his typical behaviour.

For whom was this a problem? This situation was experienced as a problem by two of the members, possibly more. The two members who brought up the matter with the therapist did not say explicitly that *they* were bothered by Nelson's behaviour. They made it clear, however, that the therapist *ought* to see it as a problem on the rather thin ground that Nelson was being disrespectful. The therapist judged that these two members were bothered in some unknown way by Nelson's behaviour. The therapist, when telling colleagues about this episode, said that he understood Nelson's use of the newspaper to be a necessary self-protective device, and was pleased that Nelson continued to attend sessions and make comments from time to time which showed that he was in touch with events in the group. On these grounds the therapist did not consider Nelson's behaviour to be a problem, or something which needed to be challenged. Nelson himself showed no sign of anxiety or embarrassment or any other negative feeling.

As in the first example, the therapist *declined* to intervene in a situation regarded as a problem by several members. The outcome was different this time in that the issue disappeared from view. One does not know, therefore, if the two people who approached the therapist became more relaxed about Nelson's behaviour or if it continued to disturb them. One does not know what, exactly, bothered them about Nelson's behaviour and one does not know whether or not others felt similarly. The therapist's response allowed Nelson to go on regulating his exposure to the group – something which was evidently necessary for him and which allowed him to stay in the group.

One could argue that the therapist had behaved appropriately since bringing the matter up for discussion in the group could be unmanageably distressing for Nelson.

On the other hand one could argue that the therapist had missed an opportunity. Perhaps the group members who were bothered by Nelson's behaviour would have profited from examining their feelings overtly. Why, for instance, did they see Nelson's behaviour as disrespect to the therapist? They could have seen it as boredom, or fear, but they did not. Perhaps they felt that Nelson should not go unpunished for (as they assumed) showing disrespect. Perhaps this connected with some of their own feelings and fears. These are all possibilities which were left unexplored.

Perhaps it would have been better had the therapist made an opportunity to raise the issue in the group, since the members did not do so on their own. If the issue were pursued overtly, it would have to be done in a way which protected Nelson's self-protective needs yet opened the possibility for others to discuss why they were bothered. Perhaps Nelson would have become able to give thought to why he needed a shield and what he feared. Whether to intervene actively or not in a situation of this kind is a matter of judgement, based on an estimate of a member's level of vulnerability. Whether the therapist missed an opportunity is also a matter of judgement.

Example 6

A woman who constantly complained about problems facing her, but rejected any offer of help from others (This example, often referred to in the literature as the 'help-rejecting complainer', belongs in cluster 2: situations in which one person is seen by the others or by the therapist as having or being a problem.)

> Mary Ellen, a middle-aged woman in an out-patient group, repeatedly brought personal problems to the group. Sometimes she did not state a problem in words, but sighed and looked dejected. When others asked what was troubling her, she would describe some current problem facing her, usually to do with her son or one of her two daughters ignoring her or her attempts to put them on the right track. Others offered suggestions and advice, but these were always met by: 'That wouldn't work', or 'I tried that already', or 'She just keeps doing it.' Sometimes members suggested explanations for the young people's behaviour – such as 'She is probably jealous of her sister' (for which there was no evidence at all). Members began to show, through non-verbal behaviour, that they were becoming increasingly impatient with Mary Ellen.

Who is experiencing this situation as a problem? The situation, in fact, includes within it several kinds or levels of problem, experienced by one or another of those concerned. First, there are the situations which Mary Ellen presents to the group, which she regards as problems. Second, a problem exists for the other members in that every time Mary Ellen presents a personal problem, they want to help and try to help but all their efforts are in vain, and frustration and anger follow. Third,

Mary Ellen can be seen to have a personal problem which has less to do with the content of her complaints and more to do with the function which help-rejecting complaining is serving for her. Fourth, the therapist experiences these repetitive group situations as a problem, for they prevent other work from getting done in the group.

Is this situation likely to lead to undesirable consequences? The answer is yes, because group members are being deprived of opportunities to pursue matters of importance to them, because Mary Ellen's underlying needs are not being addressed, and because Mary Ellen is becoming increasingly disliked and is in danger of coming under attack or being ostracised.

In the face of this situation, the therapist is likely to be doing a lot of internal thinking, both about the here-and-now situation in the group and about Mary Ellen. The therapist may reflect that the group members, as much as Mary Ellen herself, are holding this situation in place. They *could* interfere or interrupt but they do not. Why not? The therapist might speculate that they are fearful of the damage they could do to Mary Ellen (which means that they are fearful of the consequences of expressing their own anger). Or the therapist might suspect that the current situation resonates with analogous experiences of some of the members outside the group or in their personal pasts. Perhaps they feel as helpless now, in the face of Mary Ellen's powerful cueing behaviour, as they have in the past, in a relationship with some needy person whom they were also unable to help. With reference to Mary Ellen, the explanation might be simple and obvious: she feels frustrated because she never gets the help she asks for. However, there are other possibilities. Mary Ellen is very skilful at cueing others into offering her advice. She then has the opportunity to reject it. Perhaps, at some underlying, unrecognised level, Mary Ellen experiences some personal reward from these repeated situations, or is driven into behaving as she does by powerful unrecognised personal needs. Her behaviour certainly keeps her at the centre of the group's attention, and perhaps it is this which she craves. Perhaps rejecting help and seeing it as useless is a covert way of expressing anger and resentment at those who have failed to help her in the past. Perhaps it is necessary, for some reason, for Mary Ellen to see herself as being in a helpless and hopeless position. Or Mary Ellen's behaviour might be a way of exercising control over others. One or more of these dynamics could be involved. All of this thinking is speculative. The several possibilities are hypotheses to be held in mind provisionally, until such time as indications of the underlying dynamics become clearer.

Whose responsibility is it to do something about this situation? I think it is the therapist's responsibility, because the situation is not yielding through inter-actions within the group. The other members are trapped again and again into taking seriously each problem which Mary Ellen presents, and they seriously try to help her. As she repeatedly rejects their attempts to help, their anger escalates. Mary Ellen remains trapped in repeating the same kind of behaviour over and over again, forever feeling that her needs are unmet. The other members are trapped into being ineffectual helpers. And so it goes.

What actions are available to the therapist? If the therapist joins the group in trying to help Mary Ellen with her problems, he will be colluding in keeping the disadvantageous interactive pattern in place. If he reproves Mary Ellen, however gently, he may be confirming her in her view that no one understands her or can or will help. If he tries to address what he suspects are Mary Ellen's underlying feelings, he may stir up a defensive response from Mary Ellen and at the same time will be ignoring the others.

If the therapist perceives that, whatever else is happening, there is a problem located in the here-and-now dynamics of the group, other intervention possibilities come to mind. It is the *group event* which needs to be addressed, not the content of Mary Ellen's complaints. The therapist might, first of all, summarise the interactive pattern, saying something quite simple and straightforward, such as: 'Mary Ellen has just described a problem, others have tried to help, and Mary Ellen has said that the advice won't work.' This could be followed up by concentrating, initially, on the other members rather than on Mary Ellen. The therapist could invite discussion about how others feel when Mary Ellen presents another problem or yet again rejects their help. Such an intervention interrupts the help-asking, help-rejecting pattern by drawing attention away from Mary Ellen for the time being. Most likely, members will say that they feel frustrated, or angry, or helpless, or want to help but cannot, or are getting impatient. One hopes that group members will express their feelings, and that Mary Ellen will come to see the impact of her behaviour on others. The therapist might then turn sympathetically to Mary Ellen, pointing out that it is not to her advantage to alienate others. The therapist might enquire of Mary Ellen whether she can think of other times in her life when she asked for help and didn't get it. Since this is not such an unusual human experience, the therapist might ask others whether any of them have had such experiences. The therapist might ask the other members how it is that it has been so difficult to tell Mary Ellen how they have been feeling. By such successive interventions, the focus shifts from Mary Ellen as a problem person to a particular kind of interactive situation which needs to be addressed and contains learning for all concerned.

The term 'the help-rejecting complainer' was, as far as I know, introduced by Jerome D. Frank (1952). It has passed into the vocabulary of group therapists. Berger and Rosenbaum (1967) suggest that the help-rejecting complainer is motivated by a need to manipulate and control others, and that many such persons have suffered severe deprivation in early life and feel insignificant and empty. They suggest that it can be useful to offer interpretations to the help-rejecting complainer, pointing out underlying motivations. One of their suggested interventions combines an interpretation, a reference to the resolve not to be trapped by the complainer's behaviour, and support and appreciation of the complainer herself: 'You are trying to defeat me and the group, but we refuse to be defeated. We believe there is more to you than just the failure, the inadequate one, the one who doesn't quite make it' (Berger and Rosenbaum 1967: 368). This kind of intervention seems better to me than an interpretation directed only to the complainer. Bernard (1994) suggests that the person who asks for help and then rejects it is expressing ambivalence about personal change: on the one hand wanting it and on the other hand being fearful of it. He points out that the help-rejecting complainer, like other 'difficult patients', can sustain this interactive pattern only with the participation and cooperation of the other members. In such a situation, Bernard (ibid.: 136) says:

> The therapist wants to get to the point of identifying the paradox in interacting with such patients, as well as what the group can do to be helpful. One way a therapist might put this into words is as follows: 'The dilemma with Lindy is that she says she wants to change, and I am sure she means it at one level, but at another level she seems to have a need to frustrate others' efforts to be of help to her. Our task is to try to describe this conflict rather than continuing to offer suggestions to try this or that. If we keep doing that we will just be repeating what surely happens with Lindy outside the group, and we won't be getting anywhere.'

Nitsun (1996: 86–7) describes an interesting variation on this pattern:

> Another member, Alison, locked the group into double-binding interchanges. She would tantalize the group by saying that she needed to share important information about an extra-marital affair she was having, but feared exposing and humiliating herself. The group was drawn into a game in which they were required to persuade her to share her secrets. She would then open up, only to return the following week and say that she had felt considerably worse after her revelations. She had felt misunderstood and criticized by the group, confirming her belief that she should not trust anyone with her confidences. The group felt perversely used on these occasions, only to rise to the bait the next time the opportunity arose.

In this case, the problem situation was never resolved. The group conductor attempted to interpret the situation to the group (no details are provided) and reports that the group rejected and ridiculed his interpretations. Nitsun emphasises Alison's inability to communicate her feelings to the group, and refers to her behaviour as an example of 'contaminating communication with the group' (ibid: 124), involving projective identification. This omits paying attention to the part played by the other members in maintaining the situation.

In both these examples – Mary Ellen and Alison – one group member repeatedly cues the others into responding to them in some particular way. Mary Ellen cued others into offering help and others could not resist trying to do so. Alison cued others into coaxing her and, again, others could not resist doing so. In both instances, a circular interactive pattern was being maintained in the group which needed to be interrupted. My own inclination would be to avoid interpreting and, instead, first state succinctly what the interactive pattern seemed to be, and then concentrate on enquiring, first, into how the other members felt and then into how the central person felt and now feels, taking care to maintain a sympathetic stance towards all concerned.

Example 7

Members unanimously support some point of view which the group worker considers is against the best interests of the group, and also finds personally unacceptable (This situation belongs in the cluster 1, where the problem seems to reside in the group as a whole.)

> Five of the nine men who were temporary residents in a group home for homeless men attended one of the once-weekly meetings meant to help these men with practical problems. The group worker introduced a different topic each week. On this occasion the topic had to do with how to apply for a single-payment grant from the government's Social Fund to assist in establishing people like themselves in independent accommodation. The worker described the procedure for applying for such money and invited discussion. Tony described his anger and frustration when dealing with the Department of Social Security and told of an incident in which he had lost his temper while in one of their offices, had thrown a chair through the window, assaulted the police officer who came to arrest him, and subsequently was fined and spent some time in prison. Others were sympathetic, and one said that Tony had reached his 'breaking-point'. Several described times when they had reached their own breaking points and had become violent. Alan boasted of fiddles he had perpetrated against the Department of Social Security. Others told similar stories. Alan said that he still owed on an unpaid fine. The group worker asked if it was worth risking going to prison for an unpaid fine, and Alan said proudly that he would never pay it whatever the circumstances. There was more talk about fiddles. The worker was silent until the end of the meeting, when he announced that the topic for the next session would be about job training programmes.

The group worker reported that he was uneasy about this session and especially about how the men seemed unable to stay on the subject or make constructive use of the information provided. He thought he should have intervened but couldn't think how to do so without getting into an argument with the whole group. He wondered what would happen next time and how the men would respond to his planned input.

Who is experiencing this situation as a problem? It is not the members, who seem to be having a good time telling their various tales and enjoying their victories over officialdom. The group worker considered that there was a problem, which he named as the members being unable to stay on the subject or make constructive use of information. Although he did not say so, he may also have felt some concern over the disparity between his own values and those being expressed by the members (as suggested by his one intervention about whether it was worth risking going to prison for an unpaid fine).

This group worker was facing a divide between himself and the members. The members accepted violence, while the worker did not. The members took pride in their 'fiddling', while the worker disapproved (though he did not show this directly). The members were ready to defy the authorities while the worker thought that this would only get them into trouble. This was a cultural divide, in which the members on the one hand and the group worker on the other hand accepted different and incompatible norms, beliefs, and values.

What is a worker or therapist to do in this kind of situation? He cannot join the members in their world view and still hold to his own values. Moreover, he would be supporting members in attitudes and associated behaviours likely to work to their ultimate disadvantage. Trying to persuade the members to change their behaviour or attitudes would almost certainly fail, since their attitudes are held in place by unanimity in the group and are likely also be supported by the outside culture to which they belong. Challenging the members would make the therapist the members' adversary, a position from which it is difficult to offer help. Attempting to get the members to return to the subject is unlikely to succeed, at least not for long.

There is one avenue left, and that is to try to engage with the members at a level where members and worker can join with one another and the cultural divide does not matter. This means focusing on the human need which the members' conversation shows they are concerned about and which the worker also sees as important. There are hints in this episode that these men, like everyone else, are concerned to maintain a sense of self-esteem. Standing up to people in authority, and succeeding in tricking them, appears to be a source of self-esteem and pride for these men. This would in turn suggest that other ways of achieving a sense of self-worth are not available to them, or are not used. If one looks at it in this way, some quite different actions come to mind.

The worker might decide to invite examination of the experiences being reported by the members. He might say: 'I can see that it is satisfying to you to get the better of those people in the Social Security office. How exactly do you feel when that happens?' One does not know what the responses would be, but suppose they showed that members took pride in not being pushed around. The therapist could say: 'It helps you to feel good about yourselves.' Most likely, this would elicit assent, and the worker might follow up by asking: 'What kinds of things do you really like about yourselves?' Whatever followed would be worth pursuing. If the reply is 'nothing', the worker might ask: 'How could that be?' The therapist is aiming to help members name alternative sources of self-pride, other than behaviour likely to get them into trouble. He is also aiming to help the members stand outside themselves and examine the function their behaviours fulfil for them. Whether this strategy would bear fruit or not depends on whether, somewhere within these men and this group composition, there lies some degree of readiness to join in with the therapist in such explorations and to take an observing stance with respect to own behaviours and attitudes.

To even begin to work along these lines, the worker would need to wrench himself away from his previous understanding of the problem ('they don't stay on the subject') and, instead, ask himself what function the members' reported behaviour was possibly fulfilling for them. This would lead to other ways of understanding the situation and suggest different kinds of interventions. He might have to change or adapt the group structure. I think I would keep to the idea of topics, for they provide a taking-off point for discussions, and some of the members might take some of the information on board. It would be necessary, however, to hold less tightly to the topic and be ready to work with the members on other issues, not directly related to the topic, which surface in response to it.

This kind of situation is hard to work with for several reasons: because of the unanimity with which the world-view is being held (which lends it validity in the members' eyes); because of the risk of the therapist slipping into overt conflict with the members and losing his therapist's stance; and not least because the worker would have to tolerate departures from the planned topic.

Example 8

A concerted attack on one person, where the underlying dynamic is that of displacement (This example belongs in cluster 3, where one person becomes the target or recipient of dynamics in the group which lead to harm or disadvantage.)

> The group therapist announced to a group with which she had been working for some time that she expected to be away for a month, starting in two weeks' time. The next contribution was from Madge, who said that she had phoned her mother the night before and asked her to be with her when she had to have minor surgery the next week. Her mother had said that she was very busy, Madge did not really need her, and so on. Madge said she had been really angry and upset. Phoebe said that *her* mother hadn't even been to visit her new baby, saying that she lived too far away, but Phoebe knew she had been into town to shop. The therapist took up each of these topics in turn with the women concerned. After a pause, several members turned to Rhoda, who had frequently been absent, saying that she would never get anywhere if she did not attend regularly. The therapist said: 'Yes, Rhoda, why *are* you absent so much?' Both the therapist and the other members continued to ask questions of Rhoda which contained direct or indirect criticisms. After some ten minutes or so, Rhoda began to cry. One of the members abruptly shifted her tone and asked: 'Why are we all picking on Rhoda?' The therapist said: 'Yes, after all I am the one who is going to be away.' The discussion turned to how the members felt about the therapist's impending absence.

For whom was this situation a problem? The answer is: for different people at different times, since the situation went through several phases. At first, no one experienced the situation as a problem: not the therapist, who apparently did not perceive that her announcement had had an impact on the group. Nor was it a problem for group members, who did not appear to appreciate that the feelings being expressed about mothers might also refer to the therapist. Yet an observer (had there been one) might well have judged that the therapist's announcement had triggered a problem for the members, for why else would they, at just that point, begin to talk about unresponsive, uncaring mothers? Rhoda came under attack from other group members, disguised as 'help'. By joining the group in this, the therapist maintained the situation.

This situation, if it persisted, would lead to undesirable consequences. Rhoda was already upset and likely to become more so. The members were avoiding acknowledging the feelings stirred up in them by the therapist's announcement, when it could be fruitful for them to face them. For some time none of the members grasped that they were really angry with the therapist and were attacking Rhoda in her stead. A turning point came when one member asked: 'Why are we all picking on Rhoda?' This led to a shift: the therapist perceived the likely underlying dynamics, and intervened in a way which made it possible for members to talk directly about their feelings about her forthcoming absence. As they began to do so, the attack on Rhoda ceased.

The underlying dynamic was one of *displacement*. Anger which really belonged to the therapist was displaced on to a member of the group whose behaviour superficially resembled that of the therapist. The members chose, for the target of their attack, someone who really was like, or sufficiently like, the therapist. One can assume that the attackers felt safer in attacking a substitute target because retaliation, abandonment, or other negative consequences were less likely to occur or would not matter so much if they did. In group focal conflict terms a displaced attack is a restrictive solution: it alleviates fears, for instance of retaliation or of permanent abandonment, but it does not provide opportunities to address the real issue.

This example will be referred to again in Chapter 14, which focuses on therapist errors.

TWO FURTHER SITUATIONS WHICH SOMETIMES WORRY GROUP THERAPISTS BUT NEED NOT

Therapists sometimes feel altogether baffled by events which occur in a group. Group members get into a conversation whose point and import eludes the therapist. The therapist has no idea about why the subject came up, what it means to those concerned, or why the members keep it going. Or the members jump from one issue to an apparently unrelated one, and then to something further. Again, the therapist is at a loss to understand what is happening. Not even speculations come to mind. When this happens, and it is bound to happen from time to time, it is best to avoid struggling to understand, but simply to wait and go on listening. One of two things will happen: either the therapist begins to see a pattern in what seemed to be chaos, and gets a cognitive purchase on the situation; or the group leaves the period of apparent chaos behind and moves into expressing a more coherent and perceivable theme. My point is that while it is uncomfortable to feel baffled, it is not necessary to worry about it or see it as a problem. The situation is unlikely to persist for an inordinately prolonged period.

Another situation which can be worrying is one in which a group seems to be going particularly well and then suddenly seems to retreat or regress. Dynamics which account for periods of retreat were described in the previous chapter in the section on a group's established phase (pp. 127–8). It was pointed out that periods of retreat and retrenchment are to be expected in a generally well-functioning group. Members can and do recover from such set-backs. Retreats need not worry a therapist unless they persist.

THINKING ABOUT PROBLEMS: QUESTIONS TO ASK ONESELF AND TRY TO ANSWER

Each of the examples provided above is unique, even though each can be seen to belong to some class of problem situation. It would be possible to present many more examples, each of which would also be unique. However many examples were provided, none would exactly match any situation which a given practitioner will encounter in practice, since each of those will also be unique. What therapists need to have to hand is a way of thinking about problem situations which is likely to assist in understanding any specific situation and hence help them to respond appropriately.

In the course of discussing the eight examples presented above, a number of questions were posed and attempts made to answer them, such as: For whom is this a problem? 'Why is it experienced as a problem? and so on. If these are collected together and ordered, they amount to a framework for useful think-work which a therapist might engage in when faced with a situation which the therapist or someone else in the group experiences as a problem. The following set of questions can be regarded as a supplement to what has already been said in Chapter 8 about think-work and its importance:

- Who is experiencing this as a problem? Is it virtually all the members, or just some of them, or one of them? Do I as group therapist regard this situation as a problem? Do members see the situation as a problem while I do not? Do I regard it as a problem while the members see no problem at all?
- What was my first stab at describing this problem? What words did I first use to name and describe it to myself?
- Did something happen, inside or outside the group, which seemed to instigate or trigger the problem situation?
- Who is participating in this situation? Is everyone involved or are there some onlookers? Who has done or said what, and how have others responded?
- What do I think are the dynamics associated with the observable behaviour? For instance, if one person is being attacked by all the others, what function

does this serve for the members? If one person is 'being a problem' what, inside that person, seems to require him or her to behave in a way which others find unacceptable? What is stopping the members from facing a problem situation and dealing with it?

- What is holding this problem in place? Is it the behaviour of one person (for example the one regarded as being 'a problem')? Are others, through their behaviour, keeping the problem going? Have I, as therapist, done something or failed to do something which is maintaining the situation? Are more than one of these factors, or even all of them, contributing to the problem persisting or failing to be resolved?

- Am I making assumptions about how those participating in this situation feel about it or are being affected by it? Am I making assumptions about how those who remain spectators are feeling or being affected? What evidence do I have for any such assumptions?

- Is this situation likely to lead to undesirable consequences for one person and/or for the group as a whole? How serious are the likely consequences? Might they harm someone or prevent favourable development of the group? (If the situation is unlikely to have undesirable consequences, perhaps it is not a problem at all.)

- Should I restate or reframe this problem to myself because I now see that my first statement of it was a poor fit with what could actually be observed? Did my initial formulation of the problem refer to only part of it? Was it muddled because it mixed up description and interpretation, or ascribed motives to people for which I have no evidence? Did I use jargon or abstract terms which placed a label on the situation but did not help me to understand it? In short, are there different and better words which I could use to capture the nature of the problem more accurately and explicitly?

- Is the problem situation likely to resolve itself through processes within the group without any necessity for me to intervene?

- Can I influence the situation by intervening, or are there forces keeping the problem in place which are too powerful to influence?

- If I judge that I must or could usefully intervene,what actions are open to me? What are the likely consequences of each? Are certain actions likely to exacerbate the problem or lead to some further problem? Are certain actions likely to resolve the problem?

It is not a bad idea to move through this set of questions systematically when first using it. Later, one gets a sense of which questions are most pertinent to particular situations, and can then select from them, emphasising some over others but also trying not to omit any of importance.

The sixth in this list of questions: What is holding this problem in place? is discussed by Bernard. He says that a therapist who realises that difficult behaviour on the part of one person cannot be sustained without the participation and cooperation of the other members (and sometimes also the therapist) will have acquired a new perspective on such situations, and that new intervention possibilities will come to mind:

> Once a group therapist understands and has internalized this perspective, he or she has a greater number of options to choose from in determining how to respond. Although a patient may be addressed directly, the therapist also might talk about others' roles in what is occurring. The therapist can ask the group why it is choosing to respond as it is to the difficult patient. This serves an educative function in helping members appreciate their role in each others' thoughts, feelings, and behavior, and takes the heat off the individual who is manifesting the pattern being addressed. Such an approach might shift a group in a way that frees the individual to interact differently in the group context. While it is often difficult to know how to address an insecurity being manifested by a particular individual in a group, the criterion is easy to state: The therapist should choose the intervention most likely to yield therapeutic movement for both the individual and the group.
>
> (Bernard 1994: 136)

Sometimes there is plenty of time to think about a problem situation because it goes on over a period of time or recurs. Sometimes a problem situation feels like an emergency which requires an immediate response, and there is virtually no time to think. If one is in the habit of asking and answering questions when there is time to do so, a kind of stance towards problem situations becomes established which stands one in good stead when an emergency surfaces unexpectedly.

INTRACTABLE OR NEARLY INTRACTABLE PROBLEM SITUATIONS

Some problem situations feel to the therapist to be intractable or nearly intractable. Are they in fact so? It is hard to be certain, because there is always the possibility that if the therapist were more in touch with group events and more skilful, he or she would find a way. The following are three kinds of conditions which tend towards intractability (there may be more).

First, a behaviour pattern or a world-view regarded by the therapist as a problem is maintained or held unanimously by all the members. The therapist is in a weak position to influence the situation because he or she is the only person who stands against the prevailing behaviour or the prevailing version of reality. Sometimes the behaviour or the world-view is supported by an outside sub-culture to which members belong. If so, the behaviour or the attitude will be well entrenched, regarded as a fact of life not open to examination. There are intervention strategies open to a therapist, as the seventh example above suggests, but whether the therapist's interventions will have the desired effect will depend on whether or not there is *some* receptivity within the membership.

Second, a person who is centrally involved in the problem situation may simply not be there. He or she has fled from the session, leaving everyone else with the aftermath. In the absence of this person, some but not all aspects of the situation can be addressed. No one in the group will have access to the departed person's feelings and reactions, so there is no opportunity to explore them. This is especially unfortunate if the person who has left is likely still to be experiencing distress. If flight can be prevented, or at least deferred long enough for exploration to occur, this is of course desirable. If not, those who remain can be helped to deal with the situation as *they* experience it. If the person returns, the situation can be explored more fully. If, however, the person has departed irrevocably, the situation cannot be used fully as an opportunity.

Third, the problem situation was triggered by the therapist's behaviour and continues to be maintained by errors of commission or omission on the part of the therapist, preventing resolution. In such instances the therapist has the power (in theory) to help to resolve the problem situation but does not use that power because his/her understanding of the situation is incomplete or mistaken. Awareness of how his or her behaviour is contributing to the problem situation is omitted from the therapist's thinking. More will be said about this in Chapter 14, which is devoted to discerning, retrieving, and avoiding therapist errors.

Although some situations experienced as problems tend towards intractability or really are intractable, I believe that many situations which *feel* intractable can in fact be dealt with by the therapist. This usually requires extricating oneself from initial assumptions. One has to find a way to think outside the parameters which one has oneself established. The questions listed above are intended to help in this process.

Chapter 12

Personal gains

Personal gain – what it is and how it occurs in groups – is central to the whole enterprise of using groups to help people. Why have a group at all if individuals cannot gain from participating in it?

The issue of personal benefit or gain was first discussed in Chapter 3. Benefit was defined, and some concepts were presented to assist in thinking out just what gain *is* for different population categories. A list of potential gains was presented, and the point was made that what constitutes significant gain for one population, sub-population, or individual might not be relevant to others. Examples of personal gain appear in some of the earlier chapters in Part III. In Chapter 9 it was shown that gains can begin to occur very early in a group's life. Chapter 11 showed that many situations which are at first regarded as problems can be turned into opportunities for personal gain.

In this chapter, the issue of personal gains and how they may occur in therapeutic groups is examined more fully and systematically than before. This is a very long chapter. To make clear the issues which are addressed and how they connect with and follow from one another, I have divided the chapter into four main sections, the first three of which include sub-sections. They are:

1   Personal gains and how they occur in groups:
    (a   Potential personal gains.
    (b)   Some examples of personal gain, with comments on the processes by which gain occurs.
    (c)   A summary of processes which support personal gain.

2   Looking outside the boundaries of the presenting problem and of the time-frame of the group:
    (a)   Personal gains which transcend the problems which individuals bring with them to a group.
    (b)   How gains may continue to be consolidated and new gains may occur after a group ends.

3   Thinking further about certain issues related to personal gain:

(a)   Forms of insight.
(b)   What is enough gain, or enough gain for the time being?
(c)   The time required for gains to occur.

4   The literature on 'therapeutic factors'.

PERSONAL GAINS AND HOW THEY OCCUR IN GROUPS

I begin by repeating the list of potential personal gains which were first presented in Chapter 3. This is followed by describing episodes in which gain of one kind or another occurred and, in each case, commenting on the processes involved. The examples have been selected to show diverse forms of gain and diverse processes, in different kinds of groups conducted in different settings. A summary of processes which support personal gain is presented at the end of the section.

Potential personal gains

*   Feeling less isolated: that is, reducing the sense of being alone with respect to own feelings or circumstances or history, feeling that no one else experiences anything similar and that no one else can really understand.
*   Getting things 'off one's chest': experiencing catharsis.
*   Feeling more acceptable to others.
*   Feeling more hopeful about the future: developing a sense that things can change for the better, or that it will become possible to cope better with that which will not change.
*   Maintaining a sense of being the person one has always been and still is, even though personal circumstances may have changed drastically; experiencing continuity of the self.
*   Facing what requires facing; facing the previously unfaceable; strengthening one's resolve to acknowledge and deal with difficult real-life circumstances; gaining courage.
*   Revising previously held assumptions about oneself and/or others; thinking differently and more realistically about oneself and about people in one's salient world; revising one's model-of-self-and-surroundings.
*   Developing a more positive view about oneself: feeling better about oneself; appreciating oneself.
*   Developing an understanding, or a fuller and more accurate understanding, of the consequences of one's own behaviours, for oneself and for others.
*   Experiencing fear, guilt or shame when appropriate to circumstances, and not, when not appropriate. For many people this will mean feeling less anxious, less fearful, less guilty, less ashamed. For those who have disregarded the impact of their behaviour on others, it will mean feeling more guilt or shame at times.

- Developing an understanding, or a fuller and more accurate understanding, of how past experiences have, up to now, influenced the present.
- Owning feelings and experiences which have previously been denied or pushed aside. Accepting parts of the self or of past experience which have been felt, previously, to be unacceptable or intolerable.
- Learning new ways and acquiring new skills. Finding better ways to cope with practical tasks and everyday encounters with others.
- Seeing new possibilities: realising that one does not have to go on as one always has; becoming able to relinquish disadvantageous or self-defeating behaviours and life styles; freeing oneself from 'the tyranny of the past': turning oneself around and heading in some other, more advantageous direction.
- Trying out new behaviours more advantageous to self and others and making them a part of one's repertoire.
- Experiencing personal gratification through being helpful to others.

Some examples of personal gain, with comments on the processes by which gain is achieved

Example 1

Members began to experience being accepted by others during the very early stages of a group, during a time when they were seeking to establish a sense of safety in the group:

For an illustration of this one might recall, from Chapter 9 on 'Getting started', the group whose members talked at some length about baseball. Dwelling on this topic protected everyone from revealing anything very personal. In group focal conflict terms this was a restrictive solution: a way of protecting members from whatever fears or reservations followed from the prospect of revealing personal matters in the group. If this persisted, gains would be very limited and perhaps not occur at all. The talk about baseball did not, however, persist beyond the first twenty minutes or so. The members, on their own, moved into a discussion of matters more personally important to them.

The *way* in which the members talked about baseball allowed this movement to occur, and in itself carried some benefit, or the beginnings of benefit. The members showed that each could appreciate and value others' favourite teams, even those which were not doing well. The therapists saw this as an indirect way of showing one another that the members could accept and tolerate, even appreciate, individual differences. Even though the conversation was 'only' about baseball, the emotional message was 'your team is OK, and so are you. You and your preferences will be accepted.'

The point of presenting this example in Chapter 9 was to show how members, through their interaction, can make use of a discussion which has no apparent relevance to personal concerns to reduce fears about the consequences of participating in the group, so making it possible to move on. The point of returning to this example here is to show that personal gains can begin to occur very early in a group, even when members do not as yet feel safe enough to reveal much about themselves, and even when they are operating on a mutually maintained defence. No one, of course, could claim that significant personal gain is achieved by hearing others appreciate one's favourite, though losing, baseball team. Yet it was a beginning, and it paved the way for further gains as members became able to talk more personally about themselves.

Example 2

A member, who was resisting the efforts of others to establish a particular shared belief in the group, became able to shift, just a little, from a previously firmly held view of himself. This example was referred to briefly in Chapter 5, when group focal conflict theory was being described, because it is such a good example of the dynamic of the 'solutional conflict'. It is described here in more detail:

> Four or five members of a relatively new group were developing the point of view that everyone present was alike because everyone has faults. Arnold had been silent, but then broke in to say that, in his case, he had no faults and was perfect. The others protested that this was quite impossible – everyone has some fault or other. Arnold said he knew that it was unusual but the fact was that he was perfect. Others continued to protest that this could not be so. Someone suggested that Arnold was only kidding, but he assured the other members that he was quite serious. As others became more insistent that Arnold could not possibly be perfect, Arnold became more resistant. The other members began to criticise Arnold for his views. The therapist asked: 'Why is it so important that Arnold agree with everyone?' Attention was momentarily diverted from Arnold while others began to discuss their own feelings. A little later, Arnold said: 'If you had a father like mine you would have to be perfect too.' This changed things. The attacks on Arnold did not resume. As the conversation went on, someone said: 'Well, we're all alike because we all *try* to be perfect.' Arnold agreed with this.

This episode, like the previous example, occurred during members' early struggle to establish the group as a safe environment. The theme had to do with faults, and whether everyone had them or not. In group focal conflict terms, members were moving towards the enabling solution 'we all have faults'. If this could be agreed in the group, any 'fault' which was revealed would be taken as an instance of the universal fact that 'no one is perfect'. No one could be blamed or shamed for being like everyone else in the world, and self-revelations and explorations would be more likely to take place. However, Arnold put a stop to this development. He showed that he could not join the emerging consensus. The members became involved in a *solutional conflict*, with Arnold occupying the position of deviant member. Others put pressure on him to change his position. They tried persuasion.

They tried assuming that Arnold did not mean what he said, which Arnold could not countenance. Finally, they began to attack and criticise. Arnold remained firm. In the course of the discussion, Arnold revealed something about his relationship with his father in a very brief comment. After further interaction, the members reached a compromise which satisfied everyone, including Arnold. They agreed that everyone *tries* to be perfect. Implicit in this was the view that having 'faults' is a universal part of the human condition.

The resolution of this solutional conflict within the group facilitated the group's development in that it permitted freer discussion of 'faults'. In group focal conflict terms, the group had established an enabling solution. The members in general benefited because it would now be easier to acknowledge faults. Arnold benefited in a particular way: a firmly fixed but unrealistic view of himself ('I am perfect') yielded to another ('Like others, I try to be perfect'). In among the discussion, Arnold said that 'the kind of father I had' necessitated his having to be perfect.

One can think of this situation as involving a small but nevertheless significant shift in Arnold's assumptive world: an habitual perception or assumption had been dislodged. Arnold began to be able to see that 'I am perfect' was not a fact of life but a point of view which he *had* to adopt in consequence of his relationship with his father. This is an important shift, for he was moving into an observing stance towards himself. For Arnold, this is a good start – not enough, as yet, to make a real or sustained difference, but a good start. In focal conflict terms, the change which has occurred would be thought of as a small but telling shift in Arnold's preferred personal solution. Arnold was likely to be in a better position than before to undertake explorations previously closed off to him. The next step one would like to see would be Arnold explicitly acknowledging that 'It is desperately important to me to regard myself as having no faults, and this has something to do with my relationship with my father'. He has not articulated or examined this as yet, but he is on the way. The episode of course helped the therapists to understand Arnold better, and in consequence to be alert to further opportunities to support his explorations.

Further comments based on examples 1 and 2

These examples show how early struggles to make the group a safe environment not only influence the way the group develops, but can have a positive personal impact on one or even most of those in the group. In both examples, members end up feeling more likely to be accepted, whatever their diverse views and preferences, or whatever their faults. They are now in a better position than before to take personal risks because they feel more assured that they will be accepted sympathetically. The group as a whole can develop in a favourable direction as a context for therapeutic work. In group focal conflict terms, members have abandoned an initially needed restrictive solution. The second example included the further feature of one person being central to the group, occupying the position of (temporary) deviant member. The resolution of the solutional conflict not only allowed the group to move forward, but carried special personal benefit for the deviant member. These two examples show relationships between a *group dynamic* and *personal gains*. In both examples, the members become more ready to share personal feelings and experiences. Is this a shift in the dynamics of the group or is it personal gain? It is both.

Example 3

One person heard from others how his behaviour affected them, and thus learned something new about himself:

> Jerome repeatedly offered advice to others, or instructions as to how they ought to feel about some personal problem. On one occasion, Tom told about the pain and anguish he had felt when his teenaged daughter had run away from home and the family had not known where she was for two weeks. Jerome said that this was not unusual in teenagers ('they get upset about nothing') and that Tom ought not to feel so bad. Tom angrily accused Jerome of being a 'know-it-all'. The therapist said: 'Let's look at exactly what Jerome said and how Tom felt, and at how others felt as well.' In the ensuing discussion Jerome said that he honestly thought he was helping Tom and had no idea it would give offence. Tom said he felt that Jerome was not taking him or his feelings seriously. Others joined in, saying that sometimes they found Jerome's advice helpful but did not like being told how they should feel.

In this situation Tom made very clear how he felt about Jerome's behaviour when he accused Jerome of being a 'know-it-all'. If Jerome could really hear what was being said and take it into account it could be helpful for him, for it was not in Jerome's best interests to alienate others by his behaviour. However, Tom spoke in an angry tone, which would most probably make it difficult for Jerome to take his comments in as useful information. The therapist's comment was an attempt to encourage Tom and others to express their feelings in a form more likely to be heard and used by Jerome. Without saying it in so many words, the therapist was suggesting that the group think in terms of *who said what* and *who then felt what*. By so doing he was in effect *teaching* the members: pointing to a way of thinking and talking about the situation and expressing feelings in a usable rather than an off-putting way.

In this example, Jerome learned that what he regarded as helpful behaviour could hurt someone. This was a useful start, and of course one hopes that more will follow. Most probably, Jerome's behaviour functioned as a defence for him – in focal conflict terms, an habitual personal restrictive solution. He behaved in this way frequently, justifying it to himself as helpful behaviour. In the episode just described, this characteristic behaviour was brought out into the open and discussed. Jerome learned that his behaviour was disliked by others and was experienced by them as intrusive and controlling. This was a new and useful learning for Jerome for, as he said himself, he thought he was being helpful. Jerome was now in a different position from before. As a further step, one would hope that Jerome could come to understand why he so frequently put himself in the position of expert helper. He might for instance begin to realise that his 'helpful' behaviour was in the service of shoring up his own self-esteem (or had some other function). Others besides Jerome might have benefited from this episode. Tom, and others who provided feedback, may have begun to learn that it is possible to express negative feelings in a direct yet non-hostile way.

In this rather complicated episode, the movement was from (a) an interpersonal exchange between two members, to (b) one person learning about his impact on others, and others learning how to offer feedback in acceptable ways, to (c) the therapist's use of the event to point to useful habits of thought for the members in general. Group and interpersonal dynamics, as well as several forms of personal gain, were all involved.

Further comments based on example 3

In groups, 'giving and receiving feedback' is one of the forms of interaction which can lead to personal gain. By 'giving feedback' is meant putting into words what one or several people feel in response to what someone else says or does. By 'receiving feedback' is meant a person hearing and taking into account, as new information, whatever has been offered. There are always two people involved, and often more than two since feedback may be offered by more than one person. Person A will have said or done something which has stirred up a reaction in person B (and possibly also persons B', B'', B''' and so on). If B (and the rest) put their reactions into words, person A (providing he or she hears it) now has information which had not been available before. 'Feedback', however, can be offered with so much associated hostile affect that it stirs up defences which prevent the recipient from hearing and using it. Group members who are familiar with this term sometimes say: 'Let me give you some feedback.' This means: 'Watch out! because something hostile and hurtful is coming your way but I am pretending that it is helpful.' It is up to the therapist to acknowledge the feelings being expressed *and* to assist group members to express their feelings in ways which others can hear and use rather than only defend against.

Example 4

Members observed one person behaving in a way which they themselves would not dare to, and were released to acknowledge and examine similar feelings in themselves:

> When the therapist was five minutes late for a session, most of the members showed no reaction. Mary, however, attacked the therapist fiercely, saying that

he cared nothing for the group and was irresponsible: nothing could be more important than showing respect by coming on time. The therapist apologised, and then asked whether others had felt as Mary had. John and Ken both said that they too had felt angry but would never have dared to express themselves so vehemently. 'Why not?' asked the therapist. 'What would stop you and what do you think would happen if you did?' Ken said that, in his family, he would have been punished had he ever expressed anger towards his parents. John talked about his fears of his father's temper. Others shared similar experiences and expressed similar fears. Hazel said that her father had been dead for twelve years and that she still thought about him and sometimes woke up in the middle of the night feeling afraid of him. The therapist said: 'Then was then, and now is now.' The conversation returned to Mary, who began to speculate about why she had been so ready to assume that the therapist was showing disrespect, and why it was so important to her.

Significant features of this episode are that Mary behaved in a way which others did not dare to, and that other members could observe that Mary did not attract the punishment and retaliation which they themselves feared. This opened the way for others to acknowledge similar feelings and describe analogous personal experiences from their individual past lives. The therapist's comment, that 'Then was then, and now is now', was meant to help members to extricate themselves from assumptions rooted in past personal experiences. One does not know whether this happened or not, or, indeed, whether this somewhat cryptic statement was registered. This episode *could* constitute preparatory work for corrective emotional experiences for several group members. With this as an initial step, they might be able to move towards disconfirming the assumption that expressing angry feelings towards powerful people would certainly be followed by punishment and retaliation. The therapist would be alert to future opportunities for pursuing this. Mary achieved some immediate benefit. By sharing comparable experiences, the others may have gained through catharsis and feeling less isolated. Later follow-up could lead to further benefit.

This episode can be understood in group focal conflict terms. An event occurred in the group (the therapist being late) which stimulated feelings in group members which, later events suggested, resonated for some with earlier experiences in which anger towards parents (a disturbing motive) was in conflict with fears of punishment and retaliation were any such feelings to be expressed (an associated reactive motive). The solution which a number of the group members had adopted was to conceal anger. One person in the group, however, had no such inhibitions. She expressed her anger freely and vociferously. By a process which Redl refers to as 'the infectiousness of the initiatory act', others were released to acknowledge and express their own angry feelings towards the therapist. This led to sharing and comparing within the group.

In this example the movement was from (a) an apparently idiosyncratic expression of anger towards the therapist's lateness, to (b) a response on the part of the therapist which conspicuously did not involve defensiveness or counterattack, to (c) others expressing similar feelings to which the therapist again did not respond punitively, to (d) members sharing personal experiences from their past lives concerning consequences of expressing anger towards parents, and finally to (e) the person who had initiated the episode exploring the reasons for her anger towards the therapist.

Positive consequences followed for the person who was, initially, in a central position *and also* for other members, who were observers at first and then shared resonant personal feelings and experiences. This episode is an example of how interpersonal, group, and individual dynamics can be inextricably associated.

Further comments related to example 4

One of the special opportunities occurring in therapeutic groups is that of observing others' behaviour and its consequences. This is an internal process and may or may not be revealed in what members then say. Whether commented upon or not, a personal learning which can follow is 'disaster did not occur for him/her and might not occur for me'. Direct explorations of own related feelings and assumptions may follow, at the time or later. For those who do not participate overtly, it may be one of the processes by which personal change occurs through 'spectator effects' (see example 12, below).

Example 5

An item in a newspaper triggered a theme of being abandoned by parents:

> A man in an in-patient group opened a session by referring to an item in the morning newspaper which reported that two children were missing and feared abducted. Others talked about what might have happened to the children and how frightened they must be. After some time, the discussion turned to personal experiences. One person told of being taken to hospital as a young child and being left there. Another told of getting lost in a supermarket. Another told about his first day at school, and how he had wanted his mother to stay with him but she did not. Some members described or showed how acutely fearful, or despairing, they had felt at the time. Several expressed anger at the parents who deserted them or did not look after them. One person said his parents had done the best they could.

The news item which triggered this discussion was, of course, only one of many which had appeared in the newspapers that morning. One can assume that one person referred to it because of its emotional meaning for him. This initiated a theme which focused on the likely feelings of the children. Through and around and stimulated by this theme, a number of the members recalled important earlier life events and re-experienced how they had felt at the time. Members were exposed to diverse views about how parents may be understood and regarded. Note that the therapist did not participate at all and did not need to.

Further comments related to example 5

This example shows how members may benefit through exploring, sharing, and comparing within a prevailing theme. It also demonstrates that it is not always necessary, in a group, to concentrate explicitly on one person in order for that person to benefit.

Example 6

A group member told a story about a recent experience with her sister-in-law, and received useful help from another member:

> In a group for mothers of learning-disabled children, the conversation turned to how ordinary people do not understand how demanding it can be to look after such a child. Helen said that her sister-in-law frequently drops in and almost always finds something to criticise about her house-keeping. Helen has come to expect it and always feels remiss: 'I can almost *feel* her noticing the dust under the sofa.' Another group member said: 'I don't suppose your sister-in-law has a hyperactive retarded five-year-old.' Helen paused for a moment, and then said: 'No, she doesn't.'

In this episode the theme had to do with how demanding it is to look after a learning-disabled child and how others often simply do not understand this. In this context, Helen told a story about her critical sister-in-law. She probably experienced some relief simply by relating this event to others who could be expected to understand. Additionally, one person in the group showed that she understood Helen's situation, understood why housekeeping was sometimes neglected, and credited Helen for putting her child first. A consequence for Helen was that she felt better about herself and less vulnerable to her sister-in-law's criticisms. A different meaning was placed on 'dust under the sofa'. Her sister-in-law's meaning was 'you neglect your home'. The meaning which Helen tended to accept was 'I am remiss and worthy of criticism'. An alternative meaning, put forward by a group member, was something like 'you have your priorities right'. The comment made by another group member was not merely a vapid and empty reassurance. It was a plausible interpretation of an observable event (the dust). It could be expected to lead Helen to feel better about herself – a personal gain. The impact on the other members is not known, but it is possible that some of them gained through private, unexpressed reflections, for they too were looking after children who made substantial demands on them.

In this example one person gained through another placing a different meaning on an event brought into the group from current outside life. One person functioned as therapist for another person. This was an *interpersonal interaction* between two group members which occurred within the *group dynamic* of a shared theme. It led to personal benefit for one person, and possibly for others.

Further comments related to example 6

Individual members often bring in stories which refer to what happened yesterday, with a neighbour or a spouse or a child or a shopkeeper. Some therapists consider that such stories are brought in to serve defensive purposes, and therefore discourage members from talking about current outside experiences. That such stories may serve defensive purposes is indeed possible, but this is not always the case and one has to make a judgement each time. A story brought in from everyday life can be like a screen memory in that it may stand for many similar experiences, some of them within the family of origin. A person who is upset by a dismissive shopkeeper may earlier have felt neglected and ignored by a preoccupied mother. In group focal conflict terms, an individual focal conflict, derived from an early nuclear conflict, is being experienced in a contemporary context outside the group, and is then reported in the group. Exploring the emotional content of such stories and hearing the reactions of others to them can be a route towards personal gain. In this case there is no evidence that Helen's experiences with her sister-in-law resonated with anything earlier in life, though it may have done. It appeared to be no more than an irksome, frequently experienced, recurring event in current outside life. By telling the story, and receiving help from another member, Helen experienced relief and was better armed against similar criticisms likely to occur in the future.

Example 7

A theme about others 'playing tricks' recurred over a number of sessions, and was a context for personal explorations:

> In an early session of an in-patient medium-term time-limited group, James said, out of the blue: 'I don't think its clever to play tricks on people.' (The therapist wondered why in the world this had come up, but assumed that it was important for James in some way.) Others agreed that it is bad to play tricks on people, but the point was not pursued.
>
> Several sessions later, the theme re-emerged. James initiated it, telling about how his brother always played tricks on him; for instance, hiding his books just when he had to leave home in order to get to school on time. Another patient told of having had tricks played on him by his father. The therapist tried to encourage members to include in their stories references to feelings experienced at the time, by saying: 'These experiences you've been telling about must have

been quite painful at the time.' No one, however, responded to this cue. Instead, further examples of people playing tricks were reported: one (again) concerned a father; two others concerned teachers. The members dropped the subject and shifted to a different theme.

Several weeks later, the theme of trick-playing re-emerged. This time, members concentrated on how they felt when people played tricks on them and what they did to protect themselves. The therapist pointed out that the members were taking the issue further: 'Last time this came up, we heard a lot of examples of trick-playing. Now we are saying how it feels to have a trick played on you.'

Later, in a further round on this issue, two or three members told of current experiences in their work settings, in which workmates tried to play tricks. One experience had occurred in a pub. The therapist pointed out the similarity with stories told in previous sessions about tricks which had been played on members while they were children. He then said: 'You still don't like trick-playing but maybe you can deal with it better now.' Several individuals responded to this and told stories about how they can recognise people inclined to play tricks, and avoid them. One said he thought of such behaviour as childish, so it no longer bothered him so much.

Of course, during the intervals when this particular theme was not prominent, much else occurred. The episodes in which the theme figured have been extracted from different sessions in order to show recurrences and the sequence in which explorations occurred.

It is worth noting that, in this case, playing tricks did not occur as an interpersonal event in the here-and-now of the group. It could have, but it did not. Instead, group members traded stories and experiences about events in earlier life and in contemporary outside life.

Further comments related to example 7

It is not unusual in middle- or longer-term groups for the same theme to recur a number of times during the life of a group. Members typically take the theme a certain distance each time, exploring it in some particular way. When the theme recurs, some other aspect of it is likely to be explored, or previous explorations are taken 'deeper'. Members often take further personal risks each time the theme recurs.

Example 8

One young woman became important to another through, apparently, representing a part of her ego ideal:

> Early in the first session of a group, Jane said to Barbara: 'What are *you* doing here? You're beautiful!' Barbara replied, feelingly: 'Hah!'

This was a very brief exchange. It consisted of just seven words on the part of Jane and just one on the part of Barbara. It suggested to the two therapists that Jane assumed that beautiful people do not have problems, and that if she herself were beautiful she too would not have problems. One could say that in Jane's model-of-self-and-surroundings (that is, in Jane's assumptive world) being beautiful = being problem-free. Barbara could be said to stand for, or personify, an aspect of Jane's ego ideal.

The therapeutic potential for Jane in this brief exchange was that what she regarded as a fact of life, an obvious truth, might now be exposed as an assumption. In their post-session discussion, the therapists noted that they had learned something important about Jane, and possibly also about Barbara. Neither the therapists nor anyone else followed up on this exchange at the time. For the therapists to have followed up by paying direct attention to Jane would have put Jane in a prominent position and possibly led others to feel that 'she is interesting and important, and I am not'. This would be undesirable from the point of view of the development of the group. It is reasonable to expect that opportunities to explore this issue further would occur in later sessions. Having noted what happened in the first session, the therapists would likely be alert to later opportunities.

Further comments based on example 8

This episode, like the first two examples in this chapter, shows that personal gain can begin to occur very early in the life of a group. It is unlike the first two examples in that it had nothing to do with the dynamics of the group. By an accident of composition, one person was instantly meaningful to another. This example shows a significant, though one-way, pair relationship.

The next two examples also show meaningful pair relationships, each of a somewhat different kind.

Example 9

Two middle-aged women rather suddenly became important to one another: each came to stand for a significant person in the past life of the other. The following event took place in the thirty-first session of a time-limited thirty-six session group:

> In the context of discussing their feelings about the forthcoming end of the group, some of the members recalled earlier separation experiences, going back to childhood. Janice told of having been sent to hospital at the age of three in an ambulance. She was sure that neither parent accompanied her, although she did not remember why. Her parents visited her while she was there, but at one

point she was transferred to a different ward. She was convinced that her parents would never be able to find her again, and was terrified. In later life she was aware that she resented her parents for causing her this distress, but never discussed it with them. She thought that her emigration to another country as a young adult was in some way linked to this experience. Lydia, an older woman in the group, said that Janice's parents' behaviour was understandable. She herself had a son who had to be hospitalised when he was seven. She could not accompany him because of the other children. Janice turned on Lydia and said, in a voice full of scorn and reproach: 'You! You did that to your son! What kind of a mother *are* you?' In the exchange which followed Janice poured out her anger and resentment on to Lydia. Both women were upset and in tears.

The other members fell into silence, and for some fifteen minutes or so the therapist was the only person to engage with Lydia and Janice. He did this by encouraging each to comment on how they had felt during the earlier life experience and on feelings and assumptions in the here-and-now of the group. When others came back into the conversation, several told about separation experiences of their own. Janice was able to recognise that an abiding inability to trust others, which plagues her current relationships, had its roots in this earlier experience. The therapist encouraged her to consider whether, as an adult, she needed to carry feelings of mistrust and expectations of abandonment into every new relationship. Lydia examined feelings of guilt concerning her son, which she had not previously acknowledged.

What had happened was that under the pressure of the approaching termination, a theme of separation and loss surfaced in the group. For Janice, the here-and-now experience of impending separation resonated with important earlier experiences. When Lydia responded to Janice as she did, both women were immediately locked into an intense pair relationship in which Lydia stood for Janice's mother and Janice stood for Lydia's son. The sheer intensity of the situation was such that others withdrew, leaving the therapist to be 'the person of last resort' for dealing with and seeking to make positive use of the situation. As Janice and Lydia became less vehement and upset, and more reflective, others rejoined the conversation, pursuing the theme in their own ways. The therapist perceived that an opportunity was present for Janice to undergo a corrective emotional experience, and tried to support this by his enquiry as to whether Janice needed to continue feeling mistrustful and vulnerable to abandonment in her current relationships.

In this example the movement was from (a) a theme around separation becoming established in reaction to the forthcoming termination of the group, to (b) one member telling about an important past experience which concerned separation from parents. This (c) triggered a pair interaction in which mutual transference occurred, with each person standing for a significant person in the past life of the other. Because of the emotional intensity of the exchange between two members,

(d) others withdrew and the therapist intervened to help both members of the pair learn from the experience. Later, (e) other members related personal experiences related to the theme of separation, and sharing and comparing occurred.

Further comments based on example 9

This example demonstrates how two persons can become transference figures for one another. The person 'selected' to be a transference figure resembled a significant person in an individual's past personal life. The example also shows that a group situation can become so emotionally fraught that other members become immobilised, leaving the therapist as the person of last resort. It furthermore shows how an intense interaction between two people can express a theme which others can explore later for its relevance to themselves.

Example 10

A young woman underwent a corrective emotional experience which constituted a turning-point for her.

Jean was a young woman in her twenties, a member of a long-term mixed-sex out-patient group composed of six people of about the same age, all of whom felt in one way or another that life was passing them by. Jean suffered from such low self-esteem that she expected little of life. If anyone made a positive overture towards her she either did not recognise it as such or else she assumed that the person had bad judgement. She was desperately dissatisfied with her isolated life but did not know what to do about it. In the group she participated actively, but it was always in the service of 'proving' her unworthiness. She once said that she had won a prize for her violin playing in a regional contest, but quickly added that it had been only a second prize. Despite the efforts of other members to reassure her, Jean maintained her low opinion of herself. It was clear to the therapists that it would be a red-letter day for Jean when she could begin to value herself.

A turning-point occurred for Jean when a new member, Martin, joined the group. Martin was a young man of similar age who by all outward appearances was succeeding in life. He was a medical student, doing well, and verbally fluent. In a preliminary interview with one of the therapists he said that he was dissatisfied with his personal relationships, which never seemed to last. He did not mention this in the group until some time after the following episodes had occurred:

> Upon joining the group, Martin was very active immediately. He was very ready to talk about himself, but only in terms of his accomplishments. He never referred to personal problems, and presented as a rather self-satisfied individual, not exactly boasting, but ready to talk about his successes on his medical course and to report compliments paid to him. He offered advice freely to others and behaved in a rather superior manner. In the course of the second session after Martin

joined the group, Jean fell silent, and remained so for two further sessions. This was uncharacteristic of her. When others invited her to speak, she said she had nothing to say. The therapists did not intervene to encourage or press her.

At first the other members did not appear to notice Martin's characteristic way of behaving. However, irritation with him soon began to build up. In the third session after Martin joined the group, one person told him that she found his superior ways off-putting and two others joined in. At this point, Jean expressed her dislike of Martin's behaviour and wondered why the therapists had found it necessary to bring a new person into the group. A few sessions later, Jean told about her intelligent and successful younger brother (also a medical student). She expressed anger and resentment towards her brother for being favoured and towards her parents for bringing an unwanted sibling into the family in the first place and then preferring him over her. Other members sympathised with Jean, and took her resentments to be 'natural'. The therapists gave her credit for being able to express these feelings. It was clear that Jean felt relieved.

A few sessions later, Jean again referred to her parents' preference for her brother and said: 'No wonder I have always felt no good.' Soon after, she began to report small personal successes to the other group members. She puzzled over her life-long low self-esteem and came to the conclusion that it was easier for her to feel unworthy than to express anger towards her parents. If she assumed that the reason for their preference was that she was no good, then this made sense of her parents' behaviour. Their preference for her brother was understandable and justified. It was all her fault, not theirs, and anger towards them was not justified. Jean worked out this understanding herself, over a number of sessions. The therapists participated by commenting from time to time that she seemed to be on the right track. They pointed out that she was beginning to see that her sense of personal unworthiness was an understandable response to earlier experiences and not an incontrovertible 'fact'.

This course of events can be understood in group focal conflict terms. First, with respect to Jean herself, it is possible to invoke the concepts of a nuclear conflict and derived focal conflicts. In diagrammatic form, the conceptualisation is as shown in Figure 12.1.

In this formulation, low self-esteem was a personal solution to an underlying conflict. If she were a worthless person her parents' preference for her brother was understandable. Not getting the love and acceptance she yearned for was her fault, not theirs. There was thus no cause to be angry. She could be 'content' with the amount of love and attention she received, and not expect more. Her feelings of anger and resentment went totally underground and were neither acknowledged nor expressed. That her yearnings for love and acceptance were still present, though unacknowledged, could be inferred from her pervasive dissatisfaction with her isolated life as a young adult. Jean accepted her lack of self-worth as a fact of life and carried this assumption into contemporary life situations including, of course, the group. This personal solution was functional for Jean, but also massively disadvantageous.

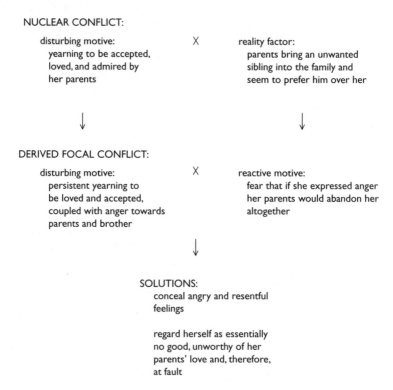

NUCLEAR CONFLICT:

    disturbing motive: X   reality factor:
      yearning to be accepted,   parents bring an unwanted
      loved, and admired by   sibling into the family and
      her parents   seem to prefer him over her

           ↓   ↓

DERIVED FOCAL CONFLICT:

    disturbing motive: X   reactive motive:
      persistent yearning to   fear that if she expressed anger
      be loved and accepted,   her parents would abandon her
      coupled with anger towards   altogether
      parents and brother

                    ↓

    SOLUTIONS:
      conceal angry and resentful
      feelings

      regard herself as essentially
      no good, unworthy of her
      parents' love and, therefore,
      at fault

Figure 12.1 A diagram showing the nuclear/focal conflict of one group member who underwent a corrective emotional experience

Other members repeatedly attempted to reassure Jean and show her that they valued her. This had no impact. When Martin entered the group, the group situation suddenly was transformed into something which corresponded closely with her early experiences. The therapists brought an unwanted 'sibling' into the group just as Jean's parents had brought an unwanted sibling into the family. Martin fitted the role of brother by being rather superior and polished. He was even a medical student. Jean went silent in the face of this.

The turning point was triggered by other members expressing their annoyance with Martin. Jean observed that others expressed anger and were not punished for it. This, it can be hypothesised, reduced Jean's own fears that expressing anger would surely be followed by punishment. Almost at once, Jean began to express her own similar feelings.

Jean's expression of anger towards Martin was soon followed through by expressing and re-experiencing comparable feelings which had been present long ago in her own family, though long repressed. Jean became explicitly aware of the connection between Martin and her brother, and between the therapists and her parents. A sympathetic and non-judgemental response from others in the group supported her explorations. Jean's outburst of anger towards Martin and then her acknowledgement of anger towards her brother and parents were *not* followed by rejection by or criticism from the therapist or other members. The other members accepted her reactions as entirely understandable and 'natural'. A corrective emotional experience occurred for Jean. The feared consequences – that is, total abandonment – of acknowledging angry, resentful feelings did not occur, and the restrictive solution (of regarding herself as no good and as at fault) was no longer needed. It became possible for Jean to give up the habitual personal solution of perceived unworthiness which was causing her so much trouble in her adult life.

In giving this account, I have omitted reference to the consequences for Martin. Martin had received feedback from the other members, who made it plain to him that they were put off by his superior attitude and his tendency to put himself forward as an expert who could advise everyone. Though defensive at first, Martin was able to make good use of this feedback. It constituted useful preparatory work for him, preliminary to his exploring just what personal experiences, in his past life, required him always to display his superiority to others.

Further comments on example 10

This example shows how a corrective emotional experience can occur in a group therapeutic setting. An habitual personal solution, which was functional yet disadvantageous, was revealed in behaviour in the group and in Jean's reports about contemporary outside life. Finding 'transference' figures inside the group facilitated acknowledging feelings which belonged to past events and to significant family members. As in the previous example, the key transference figure – Martin – seemed made-to-order, being so similar to Jean's brother. An important change occurred when previously avoided feelings could be explored and the disadvantageous personal solution became less necessary. Follow-up both inside and outside the group occurred. Group, interpersonal, and personal dynamics were interlinked.

Example 11

A middle-aged man in an in-patient group on a psychiatric ward underwent a corrective emotional experience which enabled him to shift towards becoming more confidently assertive.

George, a middle-aged member of an in-patient group, was plagued by a persistent fear that he was being followed. The group therapist and other members of staff knew about George's fear of being followed, and hoped that he would become able to put this fear behind him, for it was clearly disadvantageous to him. Nothing was known or indeed ever discovered about what had led to this fear becoming established. George was in both group and individual psychotherapy at the same time. After a number of group sessions, the following occurred:

With some difficulty and hesitation, George confessed to the other members that he often feared that he was being followed, and could not stop himself looking back and checking. Sometimes he noticed someone whom he suspected to be following him. This revelation was received matter-of-factly by the others.

In the interval between this session and the next, another member of the group, Bruno, came up behind George in the hospital corridor, tapped him on the shoulder, and said: 'You're being followed.' George was startled and upset. He sought out one of the group therapists, saying that such behaviour should not be allowed and that the therapists should do something about it. The therapist said he could understand George's feelings, but was quite sure that George could find a way to deal with this situation the next time the group met. Though obviously not satisfied, George did not take the matter further.

During the next session, George referred obliquely to the event, addressing the other members in general and asking: 'What would you think of a person who used something he found out in the group against another person?' Several members made it clear that they would regard such behaviour as unacceptable. George then described what had happened in the corridor. Bruno protested that it 'had all been a joke'. George asked Bruno: 'If you saw a man with a broken arm, would you joggle it?' Bruno said: 'Of course not', and George said: 'Well, my broken arm is inside me.' Bruno mumbled something which could have been an apology, and subsided.

George was a rather passive, unassertive, self-effacing person. He made himself inconspicuous on the ward, not interacting much with others and avoiding confrontations. If others confronted him, he tended to withdraw. It was, in other words, quite uncharacteristic of George to stand up for himself. Facing Bruno in the way that he did was a new behaviour and can be assumed to have required considerable courage.

In what way was the group involved? It had developed, on the whole, into being a supportive context for most of its members. George had acquired the courage to reveal his fears to the others. When he did so, others accepted what he had to say without comment at the time. Bruno apparently could not resist using what he had heard to hurt and injure George. This was entirely in character. Bruno was well known on the ward and in the hospital as a person who frequently found ways to frighten and torment others. Bruno did not, however, attack George within the group. He did so outside the group, in the hospital corridor. When George appealed to one of the therapists to deal with Bruno, the therapist declined to do so, placing responsibility in George's hands. The therapist's refusal to intervene on George's behalf was crucial. It meant that if anyone was to deal with Bruno and face him with his behaviour, it would now have to be George.

George's comment that his broken arm was inside him was an interesting one. It struck the therapists at the time as being a rather poetic statement of his feelings.

It was of course a metaphor, and a very apt one. He was sensing that there was something broken and wrong inside him and that Bruno's behaviour had made things worse. A trained psychotherapist would use other language, but could hardly do better in capturing the essence of George's feelings and personal state.

George tackled Bruno himself, which was an astonishing act of personal courage. He had taken the risk of behaving in a way which he ordinarily did not allow himself, and no bad consequences followed. Bruno even half-apologised! The therapists judged that George had undergone a corrective emotional experience. What followed confirmed this:

> George's behaviour began to change. In the group sessions which followed this episode, he began to tell stories of how he had defended people against the intrusions or cruelties of others. He had reprimanded a patient for 'talking dirty in front of the nurses'; he had told off a cafeteria worker for ignoring a patient who was next in the queue, and so on. After a few weeks George became a disc jockey on the hospital's internal radio station. Soon afterwards, he told the therapists that he no longer had time to attend the group because he was so busy with his new job. Besides, he said, there was no point in staying in the group because it had not helped him. After leaving the group, George continued to see his individual psychotherapist.

The therapists judged that by finding diverse opportunities to be assertive outside the group, George was following through on the corrective emotional experience. True, one might note that he protected himself from possible adverse consequences by always being assertive in the service of an underdog or a victim. Still, one can assume that each of these test-outs strengthened his courage and reduced his fears. A month or so later, George was considered ready for discharge, and his individual therapist helped him to prepare for it.

In this case, the therapists knew that it would be a 'red-letter day' for George when he could walk down the street without fearing that he would be followed. They had noticed George's rather passive behaviour, but had not understood that George's fear of being followed was connected with his sense of forever being in a helpless position, at the mercy of others.

The corrective experience was underway before the therapists understood how important it was for George to overcome his sense of helplessness and to become more able to be assertive in his dealings with others. That George faced up to Bruno was a considerable achievement. The therapists' most useful intervention was *declining* to intervene on George's behalf. To have taken on Bruno themselves, as George requested, would have deprived George of the opportunity to do so, and it would have confirmed him in his conviction that he was helpless in the face of such as Bruno.

It was clear to the therapists that George had undergone a corrective emotional experience in the group and that this had been a turning point which made a real difference for him. This, however, was *their* conceptualisation. George dismissed the whole group experience as not having been helpful. He did not perceive that his new behaviours had anything to do with what had happened in the group, or even that his behaviour had changed. He simply considered himself 'too busy' to attend, and indeed he was far busier than before. To acknowledge that the group experience had anything to do with personal changes was not in fact essential to the change which had occurred. George's behaviour showed that he no longer had to be the victim, no longer needed to avoid assertive behaviour. It was this which was important. After all, a vote of thanks to the therapists is not, or ought not to be, requisite evidence of benefit.

In this episode, events within the group provided Bruno with ammunition to use against George, and the group was a context in which George could later try out the new (for him) behaviour of confronting a powerful person. It was an accident of group composition which provided George with the opportunity for a corrective emotional experience. Bruno happened to be in the group, and it was Bruno's behaviour which triggered this crucial event.

Further comments related to examples 10 and 11

In both these examples, a corrective emotional experience occurred for a group member. Jean and George both dared to do something, to face something, which had hitherto been avoided because of their fear of the consequences. Each found that bad consequences did not follow from doing what they had hitherto avoided. This is the essence of a corrective emotional experience. However, the conditions which facilitate the occurrence of a corrective group experience can be different. In example 11, that of George, the group had become a sufficiently supportive environment for him to acknowledge his fear of being followed. What happened next (Bruno's attack) was a consequence of an accident of group composition. Bruno was a member of the group. He took pleasure in tormenting others, and events in the group had provided him with another victim. It was Bruno's behaviour which triggered the crucial episode. The fact that the therapist *declined* to intervene to protect George and solve his problems for him was a significant event. If the therapist *had* been prepared to intervene, the corrective experience would most likely not have occurred. In example 10 – that of Jean, who became able to value herself rather than to regard herself as totally no good – the corrective emotional experience occurred through the operation of group and interpersonal interactions, and Jean's own determination to understand what she was experiencing. The therapist played only a small part in this, mainly underlining what Jean was experiencing and the understandings she was arriving at, and giving her credit for her accomplishments.

Once a corrective emotional experience has occurred one can often, though not always, see that preparatory work has been done which brought the person into a position in which he or she is more ready to use, rather than to flee from, an opportunity for such an experience. Neither example 10 nor 11 in fact illustrate this. After the experience itself has occurred, follow-up work is done, usually both inside and outside the group. New behaviour is tried out in different contexts (as happened for George), or new feelings and self-percepts are experienced in diverse situations (as happened for Jean). The new behaviour or feeling or percept becomes consolidated as part of a person's repertoire and self.

Is 'insight' involved? This depends on what is regarded as insight. Jean was in the habit of articulating her feelings and her understandings. George was not. Yet George 'knew' that there was something broken inside him, which is a form of insight.

Example 12

In an out-patient group, a woman who was virtually silent during the whole group experience nevertheless achieved personal gains. (*Note*: This example was used in the first edition of this book. It is repeated here, verbatim.)

> A woman of about 35 was a member of a mixed-sex out-patient group which met twice a week. She habitually said nothing, and sat with her hands in her lap, relaxed, turned upward, staring at them or at the floor. From time to time someone in the group asked: 'How do you feel about that, Loraine?' or 'What are you thinking?' or 'What are you doing at Christmas?' To all such questions Loraine responded with a sidelong look, a shake of the head, or a muttered 'nothing' or 'nothing much'. This went on for four or five months, when one day Loraine asked if the meeting time of the group could be changed, as she could no longer come on Thursdays. When asked why the time was no longer convenient she said that she had taken a job as a check-out girl in a supermarket and would have to be at work. The members agreed on a different time. Loraine subsequently told the group that for four years she had hardly left the house, keeping house and cooking for her father and brother. Her brother always brought her to group sessions and waited for her. She suddenly felt dissatisfied with this life and sought a job. When asked how it had become possible for her to seek and hold down a job she tried to find an explanation but could not.

Taking a job was an important positive accomplishment for Loraine. It was preceded by another important accomplishment: joining the group in the first place. This must have required considerable personal resolve, considering her circumstances. Sitting in the group, week after week, in close proximity to other people even though she said nothing herself, was probably also an achievement. Since it was four or five months before she took the further step of taking a job, it is reasonable to assume that events in the group had something to do with her being able to manage it, though perhaps the journey back and forth from home, twice a week, helped her to become accustomed to being in the outside world. Just what had made it possible for Loraine actually to apply for and take a job remained a mystery.

Another example of a member who did not participate but nevertheless apparently gained was reported by a colleague. Throughout the life of a short-term time-limited group, one man sat on a broad window-sill, half turned away from the others. When other members invited him to participate he did not respond, and the therapist did not interfere with him 'participating' in what seemed to be his *only* way of being in the group. When the group ended, this group member gave the therapist his sheath-knife, saying that he had no further use for it. The therapist accepted the knife, knowing that giving it away must mean something important. *Something* had changed, but just what it was and by what means it occurred remained unknown.

Further comments related to example 12

'Spectator effects' is an apt phrase for naming a route towards gain for a non-participating member but it is not an explanation. Whatever processes are involved, they take place internally and are not open to observation. One can see that a positive change has occurred and *surmise* its connection with events in the group, but one may never know for certain. Possible dynamics are considered in Chapter 16, where non-participating members are discussed (pp. 260–1).

A summary of processes which support personal gain

The twelve examples provided above point to processes which support gain. They include:

- Members show one another that they can tolerate, accept, and appreciate individual differences.
- An individual may be jolted by events in the group into revising a long-held personal view of him- or herself, perhaps only a little, but enough to gain a bit of distance from previously held assumptions. The individual becomes able to examine assumptions *as* assumptions rather than as incontrovertible and unquestioned truths. Two ways in which this can occur is through not being allowed by other members to maintain an habitually held self-percept (as in example 2), or through being faced with someone else in the group whose very presence disconfirms some habitually held view (as in example 8).
- An individual may learn something new about his or her impact on others through receiving explicit feedback from members in the form of: 'When you do *x*, I (or we) feel *y*.'
- Members may gain courage to face some of their own feelings and experiences through observing the behaviour of others and the consequences which follow. Someone in the group behaves in a way, or acknowledges and expresses some feeling, which others do not allow themselves. By observing that feared

consequences do not follow, members may become more ready to explore similar feelings in themselves, or reveal comparable experiences, or try new behaviours.

- In the course of exploring within some prevailing theme, members share personal experiences related to the theme and describe accompanying feelings. By telling their own stories, individuals may experience catharsis. When they hear others tell similar stories, they may feel less isolated. If others accept the personal stories they hear without criticism, individuals are likely to feel more accepted and may become more accepting of themselves. By hearing about other people's experiences, individuals are exposed to alternative ways of feeling about and responding to comparable situations. They become aware of alternative ways of construing their own experiences, and of behaving.

- An individual who tells a personal story may receive direct help from someone else in the group who shows understanding and empathy, and whose comments suggest a new way of understanding the event, or of arming oneself against pain, or of coping.

- An individual can re-experience significant earlier life events in the here-and-now of the group. This can occur either through exchanges with one other person, where that person stands for someone who is significant in one's personal life, or else by re-experiencing an earlier event while a theme is being explored which is resonant with earlier life experiences. Where the significant event is an exchange with one other person, one can say that the group provided 'raw material' in the form of a person who resembles someone significant in the other's past life.

- Under some group circumstances, a corrective emotional experience can occur: an individual experiences the emotional learning that the feared consequences of acknowledging or expressing some previously censored feeling or behaviour does not occur. Fears or guilts which have been harboured for years and carried into adult life are tested and found to be unjustified by current circumstances (though understandable in terms of the past). The individual becomes freed from having to continue to maintain views of self or characteristic behaviours, which are disadvantageous but up to now experienced as essential to survival. The group provides a context in which these realisations can occur and also an arena within which new, previously censored behaviours can be tried out. Individuals can become freed from 'the tyranny of the past'. Once a new behaviour is tried out successfully in the group – that is, without dire consequences occurring – it is likely to be tried out repeatedly in other situations in current outside life. By such means, the gain becomes consolidated. Corrective emotional experiences occur through several different processes: by finding someone in the group who stands for a significant person in one's own current or past life (as in example 10) or by feeling compelled by some group event to express own feelings even though it feels very risky to do so (as in example 11). Preparatory work often precedes a corrective emotional experience, and follow-up work, needed to consolidate gains, typically follows.

- Behavioral try-outs can occur in groups. Some are associated with a corrective emotional experience. In addition, one sees, for instance, people rehearsing new behaviours which they anticipate new personal circumstances will require of them. Members may make use of a group to practise new practical or interpersonal skills. In general terms one can say that individuals sometimes try out new behaviours in the group which are not a part of their established repertoire but which help them to move advantageously beyond some current frontier. If the individual experiences a personal feeling of satisfaction and reward, and if new behaviour is received well (or well-enough) by others, he or she will be encouraged to try again and the new behaviour becomes established.

Significant personal gains do not usually follow from one event alone, but from a series of interconnected events.

LOOKING OUTSIDE THE BOUNDARIES OF THE PRESENTING PROBLEM AND OF THE TIME-FRAME OF THE GROUP

The gains illustrated and discussed in the first section occurred, for the most part, within the time frame of the group and with reference to presenting problems. Some of the gains which can occur through a group experience go beyond these boundaries. Members can acquire new, internalised ways of thinking which can be taken into further life situations. These are discussed below. The second sub-section discusses processes by which gains may be consolidated after a group ends and further gains may continue to occur.

Personal gains which transcend the problems that individuals bring with them to a group

Entirely apart from gains which may occur with reference to the problem which brought members into the group, they can acquire useful habits of thought that they can take with them into subsequent life experiences.

'Reality-checking' own assumptions

Group members may learn to examine their own assumptions and get into the habit of 'reality-checking' them: considering whether or not they are justified by actual events. Within the group, they are encouraged to check their perceptions and understandings against actual events. Through examining assumptions against evidence, they may arrive at a different point of view. The habit of reality-checking own assumptions and understandings can become internalised and carried into encounters and experiences beyond the life of the group.

'Interpersonal accounting': sorting out 'what belongs to me' from 'what belongs to others'

Members may learn to sort out and disentangle their own feelings and behaviours from assumptions they make about the feelings and behaviours and motivations of others. The therapist may repeatedly show the members that when expressing an opinion about someone else or describing a situation, it is possible and beneficial to factor out: (a) what he or she did or said; (b) how I then felt; (c) what I assumed were the other person's feelings or motivations; and (d) what I then did. This helps people to avoid the confusions and complexities contained in compressed statements which masquerade as explanations, such as 'she is selfish', or 'he always has to be first', or 'he was trying to get away with something'.

Developing an 'observing ego'

Individuals in groups may develop the skill and the habit of observing themselves and their own behaviour, and the consequences of their behaviours for themselves and for others. Rather than behaving impulsively and unthinkingly and paying no attention to their impact on others, they begin to use their *observing* self to understand their *experiencing and behaving* self. In psychodynamic terms, they develop an 'observing ego'. This is a point emphasised by Louis Ormont, who sees it as central to the therapeutic process. He names five steps by which it can be achieved:

> (1) help the members see how they are affecting others when they do not see this themselves, (2) help the members see how they produce this effect, (3) help the members see the self-injurious nature of their behaviour, (4) resolve resistances to seeing any of this, and (5) help the members arrive at new modes of behavior.
>
> (Ormont 1995: 489)

Such gains as these will most likely have been worked out in relation to problems which individuals brought with them to the group and to interactive events within the group. However, once achieved and consolidated, they have a wider and a persisting impact. These are new habits of thought which place people in a better position than before to tackle both ordinary and more serious future life situations.

How gains may continue to be consolidated and new gains occur after a group experience ends

Some of the follow-up work needed to consolidate gains may occur after an individual leaves the group. Evidence for this is sometimes but not always available. One could see it happening in example 11, where George's newly acquired self-assertiveness was consolidated through experiences occurring elsewhere in the hospital after he had left the group. It seems plausible to assume that gains can become more firmly established after a group experience ends, through further experiences outside the therapeutic setting. There is nothing to say that the literal end of the therapeutic experience will coincide with the completion of the consolidation process.

Sometimes a gain is such as to put a person in a position to achieve further gains, beyond those achieved during the life of the group. For instance, the parent who comes to feel less guilty about sometimes resenting the time needed to look after her physically disabled child may become more able to seek out pleasures for herself in day-to-day life. The group experience has led to a beneficial shift in life style.

Personal gains do not have to be momentous to be important and to lead to further gains. I sometimes think of individuals as moving along some path which may be rewarding in some respects but also carries disadvantages. That person enters a therapeutic group. In the course of the group experience something happens which leads to some personal shift, perhaps just a small one, perhaps an important one. The person, one could say, 'rotates in place' and is now heading in a different direction. On this new path, the individual encounters everyday experiences which are not so different from those he or she has encountered before, but the person now experiences and responds to them differently. The new behaviours elicit different responses from others. Changes occur in both self and surroundings which fix the person more firmly in the new path.

THINKING FURTHER ABOUT CERTAIN ISSUES RELATED TO PERSONAL GAIN

There are certain issues related to benefit or gain which need further examination, especially in these days when groups are being utilised with such a wide range of people facing very different personal circumstances. Time-honoured assumptions about the importance of insight, the 'depth' of change to aim for, and the time required for change to occur need to be reconsidered. This section looks at forms of insight, at what constitutes 'enough' gain, and at the time required for gains to occur.

Forms of insight

Practitioners tend to assume that, in order for significant positive change to occur, individuals need to achieve 'insight'. It is certainly the case that some internal change occurs which then shows itself in a shift in how self and others are perceived, or in new and more personally advantageous behaviours. By tradition, this internal change is referred to as 'achieving insight'. It becomes necessary to understand what this term means and the forms it can take.

By dictionary definition, insight is 'discerning the true or underlying nature of something' (*Longman's Dictionary of the English Language*). Although the dictionary does not say so explicitly, the implication is that discernment is a cognitive act.

Psychotherapists often distinguish between intellectual and emotional insight. The phrase 'intellectual insight' is not uncommonly prefaced by the word 'mere', implying that it is not 'real' insight, or at least not the kind that matters. What is considered important is emotional insight: the *experience* of coming upon some new understanding of the self or of one's salient world. I suggest that the term 'cognitive' is preferable to the term 'intellectual', since the latter has pejorative connotations. Important questions are whether insight can occur at an experiential or non-verbal level without being expressed explicitly in words, and whether words necessarily express the emotional experience of having achieved a new insight.

Looking back over some of the examples presented in this chapter, one might compare and contrast George, Loraine, and Jean, all of whom showed some positive change. With respect to George, who faced Bruno with the comment: 'My broken arm is inside me' (example 11), the therapists could see that George became much more courageous in asserting himself and that this worked greatly to his advantage. They understood this change as the consequence of George having undergone a corrective emotional experience within the group. This was the therapists' conceptualisation, not George's. George only knew that he was busier than before and no longer had time for the group, which as far as he was concerned had not helped him. Had 'emotional insight' occurred? One could argue that it had, for George now 'knew' that he could be more assertive than before – at least, he showed this in his behaviour. There was, however, no sign of accompanying cognitive insight.

Loraine was the woman who took a job in a supermarket and evidently gained from her experience in the group although she had not participated actively (example 12). Loraine knew that she had changed for the better, but she had no idea what made the change possible. Nor did the therapists, for whatever had gone on which benefited Loraine remained locked inside her and was not open to observation. As with George, there was no evidence of accompanying cognitive insight.

Jean was the young woman with the much-envied younger brother whom she felt had been favoured in her family (example 10). She showed a striking increase in level of self-esteem. Jean tended to make everything that was happening to her explicit to herself and others – she reflected on connections between the here-and-now of the group, the there-and-then of her earlier family life, and current outside experiences. This was a part of her personal style. The therapists judged that Jean was verbalising what she was experiencing emotionally. For her, cognitive insight went hand-in-hand with emotional insight.

One has to conclude that 'insight' is a complex matter. The emotional experience seems to be the essential part. The emotional experience does not necessarily have to be recognised or expressed in explicit terms for personal gain to occur. An individual may not refer to it at all, or may refer to it in symbolic language. For another individual, stating what has happened and what seems to account for what has happened directly and explicitly seems to strengthen and support the emotional learnings.

It is also possible for someone to say something which *sounds* like insight, but is in fact mere intellectualising. Quite possibly, this functions as a defence. When someone says something like 'I see now that my father's high expectations of me have created problems for me in later life', he or she *may* be putting into words an important new emotional understanding, but on the other hand such a statement *could* amount to a personal defence. The person might merely be parroting the therapist's interpretations, and may be saying, in effect, 'I understand myself, so let me alone'. In such a case what is being said is unconnected to any emotional experience. Words in themselves do not necessarily reflect significant emotional experiences.

It follows that it is important for a therapist to listen carefully to what people say about personal changes, connections with past life, and so on, and to form a judgement as to whether or not what is being stated in words reflects meaningful emotional insight. Some comments made by group members will strike the therapist as unmistakable expressions of 'real' emotional insight. The following verbatim quote from a patient is taken from an earlier article in which I explored the role of insight in personal change. It was made by a patient named Alex, in the course of the twentieth session of a therapeutic group:

> Getting into – not this problem but a problem I face in general – many times the two doctors brought up and I just realized, I mean I had realized it but it never struck me – you know, the idea of approval. I'd ask them something [and they'd say] 'do you want our approval on everything?' That's one of the basic problems I have – I'm trying to get approval from people. I mean I realize this now tremendously – it's a big thing. I mean I'm trying to get – be told that I'm g-o-o-d, good.
>
> (Quoted from Whitaker 1965: 136)

In this comment, the sense of discovery is apparent. This young man was not merely repeating something which had been put to him. He is putting together what is for him a new understanding, expressing it as best he can, in his own language.

What is enough gain, or enough gain for the time being?

Not everyone needs to achieve the same sort of gain. For some people, relief of a sense of isolation is in itself a substantial gain, and enough. For some people, it is a great achievement if they can strengthen their resolve to face and deal with an impending transition, or some other difficult real-life circumstance. This point is made to counter any assumption that, to be worthwhile, a gain has to involve a profound and fundamental change in personality. Sometimes it does, but sometimes it does not.

Sometimes the gains achieved are 'enough for the time being'. The individual leaves therapy with enough to work on and work through for some time to come. Such a person may or may not benefit from a further therapeutic experience later on. To invoke the concept of 'personal frontier', the individual has moved past some personal frontier and is now in a different and more advantageous position than before. The life-space is somewhat different from before. From this new position, further frontiers might become identifiable which it would also be advantageous to cross. Time will tell.

The time required for gains to occur

How long is long enough? Different time-spans are needed for different kinds of personal gain to occur. This point has already been discussed in Chapter 2 on 'Who are groups for?' and in Chapter 6 on 'planning'.

What is a necessary and sufficient time-span depends on the state and needs of those concerned. For instance, if prospective members are relatively sturdy people who are facing some unusual stressor, they may profit from a short-term group which provides opportunities for catharsis and mutual support. If prospective members have engaged in self-defeating behaviours which have gone on for years and years and are rooted in early life experiences, a longer-term experience is likely to be needed. If prospective members are chronically unable to manage work or personal life, they may need long-term support in which a group experience figures from time to time.

This point is made to counter the assumption – still frequently seen – that 'real' gain requires an intensive, long-term group experience. This is not necessarily the case. What constitutes 'real' gain is different for different people. Some kinds of gain, important to those concerned, do not require a vast time span, and not all groups need to be long-term.

THE LITERATURE ON 'THERAPEUTIC FACTORS'

The term 'therapeutic factors' has become common currency amongst group therapists. It is a term and a concept which needs to be examined carefully.

Crouch *et al.* (1994) have produced a comprehensive history of this concept. They evaluate its usefulness and limitations, and describe empirical studies. They define a therapeutic factor as:

> an element of group therapy that contributes to improvement in a patient's condition and can be a function of the actions of the group therapist, the other group members, and the patient himself.

> (Ibid.: 270)

The authors track this concept back to Pratt ([1917] 1975), Burrow (1927), and Wender (1936); go on to Corsini and Rosenberg's (1955) list of ten 'dynamics leading to successful therapy', based on an examination of 300 or so articles on group psychotherapy; thence to Yalom's (1970) list of ten 'curative factors', and to their own classification system (Bloch and Crouch 1985). To these can be added Yalom's most recent formulation, in which ten factors have been increased to eleven and 'curative factors' have been renamed as 'therapeutic factors' (Yalom 1995).

As Crouch *et al.* say, there is as yet no definitive list of therapeutic factors. Early formulations mention fewer factors than do later ones. Those listed earlier have mostly been incorporated into later lists, sometimes in a modified form. There is considerable overlap among later formulations, starting with Corsini and Rosenberg.

Bloch and Crouch offer, as their list: self-understanding, catharsis (release of feelings), self-disclosure (revelation to the group of private material), learning from interpersonal interaction (relating constructively and adaptively by trying new behaviours), universality, acceptance, altruism, guidance, vicarious learning, and the instillation of hope (Bloch and Crouch 1985). They point out that they have made an effort to formulate their therapeutic factors in atheoretical terms.

Crouch *et al.* (1994) point out that some of the therapeutic factors named and discussed in the literature can have adverse as well as positive effects. It is important to emphasise this. They say for instance that catharsis can be too intense for some patients, and create dysfunctional distress. A similar point can be made about self-disclosure, for under some group conditions patients disclose more than they subsequently find that they can tolerate. I have pointed out earlier that very high cohesiveness can serve defensive functions and that some kinds of patients require low cohesiveness in order to tolerate remaining in a group. With reference to cohesion, Rosenbaum (1993) regards a group atmosphere that promotes sharing and mutuality to be a more accurate term than group cohesion. This fits my own view that a group marked by predominantly enabling solutions constitutes an optimum environment for personal gain.

Yalom's most recent list of therapeutic factors is: instillation of hope, universality, imparting information, altruism, the corrective recapitulation of the primary family group, development of socialising techniques, imitative behaviour, interpersonal learning, group cohesiveness, catharsis, and existential factors (Yalom 1995).

Yalom points out that these factors interact, and that this is a mixed list in that some refer to what the patients learn (such as universality); some refer to behavioural change (such as the development of socialising techniques); and some refer to preconditions for change (such as cohesiveness). One can add that some refer to processes which facilitate the acquisition of gains (for example, the imparting of information, the corrective recapitulation of the primary family group, imitative behaviour) and that still others refer *both* to what can be gained and the associated contributing processes (for example, instillation of hope, catharsis, interpersonal learning). Cohesiveness is, perhaps, both a personal gain and a process which facilitates gain.

Crouch *et al.* consider that much more work needs to be done, particularly in devising more precise definitions of some of the usually named therapeutic factors, and in giving thought to whether there might be some altogether different way of categorising therapeutic factors from those which have been provided so far.

My approach to this issue has been to distinguish between the personal gains which group members may achieve and the mechanisms by which gain is generated. It is the latter which, strictly speaking, can be regarded as 'therapeutic factors'. For instance, 'instillation of hope' can be factored out into the personal gain of acquiring or augmenting hope, and 'instillation', which refers to processes whereby hope is instilled or augmented. 'Catharsis' refers to expressing feelings which have hitherto not been acknowledged or expressed. The associated personal gain is *relief*. Cohesiveness, as remarked earlier, is a complex phenomenon. In its sense of members sticking together it is a group phenomenon. It can generate a sense of belonging, which is an individual experience and a form of gain.

This chapter raises a number of issues which need further discussion. First, not everyone who becomes a member of a group gains, and some may be harmed by the experience. This issue is examined in the next chapter. Second, personal gains are sometimes prevented from occurring because of the behaviour of the therapist. Therapist error, and how errors may be avoided, or retrieved if they occur, is the subject of Chapter 14. This chapter also raises a further question about how theory and practice are connected. It is: 'How do therapists use theory in their practice?' This question will be added to those already named in Chapters 5 and 8. It will be discussed, along with the others, in Chapter 17.

Chapter 13

Little or no gain, or actual harm

Not everyone who becomes a member of a therapeutic group gains in personal ways. Some people gain very little from their experience in a group, some seem hardly to gain at all, and some experience actual harm. This chapter considers influences on little or no gain and on harm, and discusses what a therapist can do in the face of them. The chapter is organised into the following sections:

- Definitions of little or no gain and of harm.
- The influence of a group's composition on little or no gain or harm.
- The influence of a group's size: groups which are or become too small.
- The influence of interactions and dynamics within the group.
- The influence of therapist actions or failure to act.
- The influence of the stance and behaviour of individual members, which can either support or limit the gains which they achieve.
- Are individuals in groups neglected or deprived because of the presence of other patients?
- Dynamics associated with little or no gain compared with dynamics associated with harm.
- References in the literature to no-gain or to harm-generating features of groups.
- Can a therapist avoid the occurrence of no-gain and/or of harm?

DEFINITIONS OF LITTLE OR NO GAIN AND OF HARM

One might at first assume that 'little or no gain' must refer to people who emerge from a group experience much the same as when they entered it. No movement, no 'progress' has occurred. Yet for some people it is a considerable achievement to hold their own in the face of stressors in their environment from which they cannot escape, or their own hard-to-manage feelings and impulses. If such people can continue to manage their daily lives, against the odds, without breaking down in some way, this can be regarded as a form of gain. It follows that one cannot be satisfied with a definition of 'little or no gain' which emphasises lack of positive change.

In Chapter 3 it was said that 'benefit' could consist of (a) moving from some current state which works against a person's well-being and effectiveness to something more advantageous for that person; (b) expanding coping skills for dealing with stress-generating circumstances and/or experiencing relief and support through sharing feelings and experiences with others who are similarly placed; or (c) maintaining a current state which, while unsatisfactory, is at risk of becoming worse. With respect to each of these forms of benefit, there is a 'current state' and a 'preferred state'. The preferred state may consist of some change or movement, or it may consist of not losing ground.

'Little or no gain' is the converse of these three forms of benefit. The little-or-no-gain person either (a) remains stuck in some disadvantageous current state, or (b) fails to develop more satisfactory ways of coping with stressful life circumstances or achieving support or relief, or (c) is caught in some downward spiral which draws him or her into a worse state than before.

Actual harm is different from little or no gain. An individual who is untouched by a group experience is different from one who is significantly damaged by it.

The *Shorter Oxford English Dictionary* offers two meanings of harm, as a noun: '1. Evil (physical or otherwise) as done or suffered; hurt, injury, damage, mischief; and 2. Grief, pain, trouble, affliction'. In thinking about the harm which may come to individuals in consequence of their participation in a therapeutic group, the meanings of *injury* or *damage* are the more salient. Experiencing distress or pain is different from experiencing harm. One should not be surprised or unduly alarmed if, in the course of achieving personal gains, individuals sometimes experience pain (though one ought to acknowledge that unbearable pain is unproductive). However, one would be concerned and sorry if a person left the group still in a state of pain, with no opportunity within the therapeutic situation to recover from it or make positive use of it. The outcome would then be damage or injury.

THE INFLUENCE OF A GROUP'S COMPOSITION ON LITTLE OR NO GAIN OR ON HARM

Group composition influences no-gain or harm in at least three ways: by its influence on the norms and shared beliefs which become established; by the consequences of including a very vulnerable person in a group otherwise composed of more sturdy individuals; and by the consequences of including one person who is conspicuously different from all the others in some way. These are considered in turn.

In a group which is composed homogeneously with respect to personally preferred defences, norms and shared beliefs are likely to develop which constrict and limit opportunities for gain for everyone

In such groups, the defensive postures of individuals converge and become mutually supported. Mutually maintained defences take different forms. Norms may develop which influence members' behaviour: everyone denies, or avoids, or intellectualises and so on. Or a mutually maintained defence consists in a shared belief which again influences behaviour: everyone believes that they are victims of society, or of bad luck, or of parents' terrible mistakes when they were young. This constrains areas of exploration within the group.

Unanimity strengthens any norm or shared belief. If everyone denies, then there is nothing within the group composition to challenge this as a behavioural norm. A shared and mutually supported belief that it is bad parenting going back to early childhood which has led to current problems is a barrier to examining whether events in childhood need continue to affect people in their adult lives. It is hard for anyone to think or behave outside strongly mutually maintained norms or beliefs.

In group focal conflict terms such norms and beliefs are restrictive solutions. They buy comfort but curtail or prevent explorations which can lead to gain. As was shown in Chapters 9 and 10, restrictive solutions are frequently seen in groups, especially during the formative phase. However, given a reasonably favourable composition, they need not and usually do not persist. Interactions amongst the members occur which make it possible for initial restrictive solutions to give way to enabling ones which support rather than curtail the therapeutic process. Or the therapist may intervene to support a shift from predominantly restrictive to predominantly enabling solutions. It is when restrictive solutions persist for long periods of time that they have an abiding negative impact.

What can a therapist do about this potential source of little or no gain? First, at the planning stage, a therapist should aim for a group composition which is *heterogeneous* with regard to preferred personal defences (see Chapter 6). Second, when a therapist perceives that a group is operating on a restrictive solution, the members will need the opportunity to work their way out of the situation they are in through their own resources, uninterrupted by the therapist. Group members are often able to do this because, although they harbour fears which hold the restrictive solution in place, they also have hopes of the group which lead them to try to find safe ways to take risks (if that is not a contradiction in terms). As they find that no bad consequences follow, they become able to shift away from the restrictive solution. This, however, does not always occur. Members sometimes get stuck in a restrictive solution, which persists. It follows, third, that if the therapist notes that the members are *not* shifting away from a restrictive solution through their own efforts, or that the particular restrictive solution which is in place is harming someone, the therapist can and should intervene by helping the members to name and face whatever fears they are experiencing about being in the group.

The most difficult situation for a therapist to deal with is a too-homogeneous group composition. Unanimity is powerful. It is known from the study of cults that unanimity in a group can sustain a belief which outsiders regard as bizarre. No one outside the membership can find convincing evidence for it but the members persist in it. In a therapeutic group a norm or a belief which is supported by virtually everyone is very hard to dislodge, because there is nothing and nobody in the group composition to challenge it. The therapist stands alone in opposition to powerful group forces, and his or her power to influence the situation will be limited. No one is likely actually to be harmed, but opportunities for gain will be much constricted for all members.

A group composition in which one person is more personally vulnerable than all the others carries considerable risk of harm coming to that person

Suppose that one member of a group is more vulnerable than any of the others. He or she quickly feels threatened by group events which others take in their stride or at least are able to manage without disabling anxiety. When members are exploring some theme, the more vulnerable person begins to experience anxiety and distress while others are still comfortable enough to continue. The majority of the members move the group into realms which the vulnerable person cannot tolerate, or they move at too fast a pace. If the vulnerable person is unable to bring defences to bear, anxiety and distress escalate intolerably, and the person becomes overwhelmed by unmanageable feelings. Such individuals sometimes drop out of the group. This may in fact be the only course of action open to them. If they drop out, they may experience relief. At the same time, however, lingering feelings of anxiety, of having been injured or of feeling inadequate may persist. Sometimes a vulnerable person finds a way to stay in the group through distancing or insulating him- or herself from whatever is going on. Harm is averted but gain does not occur. The relatively more vulnerable person has merely survived the group experience.

What can a therapist do about this potential source of little or no gain? First, and at the planning stage, a therapist should aim for a group composition in which members are more or less similar with respect to 'level of vulnerability'. This is not always easy to achieve, and if a therapist is faced with one group member who is conspicuously more vulnerable than the others, what then? If there are signs that the individual is moving towards dropping out, the therapist might ease the exit, trying to make it possible for the person to leave with as little anxiety or shame as possible. If the individual remains in the group it will be because, despite being so vulnerable, he or she has found a safe-enough position in the group. Often this is achieved by silence or withdrawal or by only intermittent participation. In my view, it is right for the therapist to support such individuals in their preferred form of participation, rather than try to press them into more than they can tolerate. Usually, other members will put a degree of pressure on the non-participant to join in, and the non-participant's responses will show whether or not s/he can become more active. A person who participates little or even not at all may nevertheless gain through spectator effects, as was shown in Chapter 12 (example 12).

A group composition in which one person is conspicuously different from all the others – the 'odd man out' – may lead to stereotyping and other dynamics which limit opportunities for personal gain

If one person stands out as conspicuously different from everyone else, by virtue of age, race, sex, social status, and so on, he or she may become the recipient of attitudes and assumptions about what 'people like that' are believed to be like – often imported into the group from the wider culture. Such members risk being seen in stereotyped ways by the others. Feelings and motivations may be imputed to them which have little to do with them as individuals and much to do with assumptions held by others. Such individuals may also disadvantage *themselves* by assuming, without evidence, that others harbour negative feelings or stereotypical perceptions.

What can a therapist do about this potential source of little or no gain? Again, this kind of unfavourable composition might be avoided at the planning stage. Therapists are nevertheless sometimes faced with an unbalanced composition, perhaps through some members dropping out. What then? If a therapist sees any sign of stereotyping, from whatever source, he or she should intervene. This can be done directly but not punitively, for instance by saying: 'There seems to be an assumption here that Sara [by far the youngest person in the group] is flighty, but what is this actually based on?'

THE INFLUENCE OF A GROUP'S SIZE: GROUPS WHICH ARE OR BECOME TOO SMALL

How small is 'too small'? Most therapists would, I believe, consider a group with three members to be too small. Probably a group consisting of four members is also too small. Five seems to be a minimum number but six or seven is better, and some therapists are quite happy to work with a few more than that.

Why is a group which consists of four, or three, members usually regarded as too small? In the previous chapter it was shown that under favourable conditions, themes emerge from the interactions of members which are relevant in one way or another to all or most members. These themes then become a context within which fruitful explorations, interpersonal comparison, feedback and so on can occur. *Diversity within commonality* is needed for this to happen. There needs to be enough commonality for a theme to touch all or most of the people in the group, and enough diversity so that members relate to the theme in somewhat different ways. For instance, in a group for mothers of learning-disabled children which included eight people, there was commonality with respect to life circumstances but diversity with respect to feelings about, and responses to, those life circumstances. In a group of young adults which included six people, there was enough commonalty to ensure that the themes which emerged were relevant to virtually everyone (for instance, loneliness, doubts about personal competence) but enough diversity for sharing and comparing to take place.

Groups which are very small may be so diverse as to lack commonality. For instance, a group which had dwindled to three members, having started out with seven, ended up with the following group composition: a middle-aged man with marital problems, a socially isolated woman of about thirty, and an obese, unattached young man of twenty who was still a student. The members did not perceive commonality amongst themselves, so their diversity became a handicap rather than an asset. Interaction amongst them began to take the form of one of them presenting a problem while the others offered suggestions. More often than not, it was the young man who described a problem while the other two tried to help. Possibly, the young man gained something from this, but he was deprived, as were the others, of opportunities to compare and contrast experiences. There was no build-up of shared themes, and little or no interpersonal comparison or feedback.

Bernard (1994) points to the risk of an unbalanced composition when a group shrinks in its membership. He describes a group of five patients – two women and three men – which had been functioning very well. However, when one of the women dropped out, this left a gender balance which was unsatisfactory to the remaining woman patient, who felt that she needed another woman in the group in order to gain. (The three men would have been happy to carry on with a membership of four, with only one woman.) The therapist chose to suspend the group until two new members could be found. This of course is just one example of how a very small group could become unbalanced in its composition.

What can a therapist do about this potential source of little or no gain? The answer seems obvious: if a group becomes too small, bring new members into it. This is a power which therapists should retain. Giving this power away to members may result in their pressing for a small group, which may seem safer and cosier to them, but which is likely to work against their best interests.

THE INFLUENCE OF INTERACTIONS AND DYNAMICS WITHIN THE GROUP

That one person can become stereotyped by the others has already been mentioned. Other dynamics which can affect one person adversely include being locked into a role which restricts opportunities for personal gain; becoming the persistent object of attack; being ignored after having taken some personal risk; being the object of advice, interpretations, or feedback which are not relevant or useful; being drawn by group processes into experiencing unbearable affect; and being psychologically excluded from the group.

Collusive defences (restrictive solutions) which require one person to occupy a position that constricts opportunities for personal gain or that generates actual harm

Certain collusive defences require one person to occupy a role which serves protective functions for the others but at the same time holds that person in a little-or-no-gain position. For instance, it may fulfil the needs of most of the members if one person occupies the position of substitute therapist. The members need not face their anger towards the actual therapist for not helping them as they think he or she should, because they have found a substitute. The person cast into the therapist role may feel gratified and rewarded, and quite ready to occupy the role. He or she is happy enough and is not being actually harmed, but will find it difficult to engage in personal explorations which lie outside the role. Opportunities for personal gain are limited.

Some collusive defences which involve role differentiation do more than restrict opportunities for personal gain. They generate pain and actual harm for one person and at the same time hold the whole group back. In example 8 in Chapter 11, for instance, one group member became the target of a displaced attack. That person became dysfunctionally upset and the whole group, for a time, avoided facing their anger towards the therapist through having found a substitute target for their feelings.

In the face of this kind of situation a therapist can begin by simply asking the group: 'Why does everyone expect John to be the helper in this group?' 'Why is everyone attacking Molly, at just this point?' What happens next, after such interventions, will guide the therapist in judging how to follow up.

Being ignored after having taken some personal risk

In a group, a person may reveal experiences about which he or she feels guilty or ashamed, or to which pain is attached. A person may behave in some new way which carries potential benefit but feels very risky. Suppose that persons who take risks get no response at all from the others. They are likely to feel unsupported and unappreciated, and may also feel they have done something thoroughly unacceptable. Intensified distress follows. They feel themselves to be, and are, well and truly out on a limb. They are worse off than before because they have taken a risk and then not received a supportive and understanding response (or indeed, any response at all).

Why do the members not respond? Unless the group is composed of people incapable of listening and paying attention to one another, the most likely explanation is that they have been stunned and immobilised by what one person has revealed or done. They are fearful, or at the least surprised. The person who has been ignored may well be discouraged from trying again. Actual harm may follow if he or she experiences severe and unmanageable anxiety and/or is confirmed in some adverse self-perception. Sometimes an ignored person drops out. If this happens the damage is compounded: first, harm occurred; and second, the individual is no longer in the situation in which remedial action could take place.

What can the therapist do? At such times, it is the therapist's responsibility to acknowledge and pay attention to whatever is being ignored. Even if the therapist does no more in the first instance than mention what has happened, this would begin to retrieve the situation. If the therapist, too, is immobilised – if the therapist joins with the group in ignoring the event and the person – then the situation will not be retrieved, let alone utilised for anyone's benefit. No one has gathered their wits together in time to respond to the person concerned, and damage will persist.

Being offered by other members advice, interpretations or feedback which is irrelevant, unusable or harmful

When group members offer interpretations, advice or feedback to one another, their comments are often sensitive, apt and well-timed. Sometimes, however, what they say is off the point, tinged with condescension or impatience, or destructive. Sometimes, a proffered interpretation or piece of advice reveals much about the interpreter or the advice-giver and is hardly relevant at all to the person to whom it is directed. Sometimes interpretations and so on mix up own and others' feelings and/or contain assumptions about others' motivations which are not justified. The same can be said about advice and 'feedback'.

Such behaviours can interfere with gain or can lead to actual harm if they are left standing without correction. The therapist's non-interference can be understood to be assent or support. Therefore, the therapist must intervene.

What can a therapist do? The therapist needs to assist members to distinguish between their own feelings and those of others, to see that a comment such as 'you are being uncooperative' is an interpretation (not an observation) which mixes up own feelings, imputations of (unspecified) feelings held by the other, and assumptions about the other's motivations. Furthermore, it does not make clear just what the behaviour is which is being referred to. Essentially, the therapist stops the action and invites members to sort out what one person (let us say it was Bert) actually said, how others felt when they observed his behaviour, what they assumed were Bert's feelings and attitudes, what they then said, and what Bert felt or thought about what they had said to or about him. This sorting out helps members to see the assumptions they make when offering advice, interpretation, or feedback. They are more likely to perceive how their own feelings influence their perceptions and judgements. Sorting out feelings and assumptions also helps the recipient, for he or she can see more clearly the interpersonal consequences of his/her behaviour.

(This kind of intervention figured in example 3 in Chapter 12, where one member applied a derogatory label to another.)

Being drawn by certain group processes into experiencing unbearable feelings which the individual has no resources to cope with.

Sometimes a theme emerges in a group which most people feel able to explore but which one person finds excessively threatening. Or emotional contagion occurs which draws one or several individuals into experiencing feelings which they find overwhelming.

Such individuals are not *generally* more vulnerable than all the others, but there is something about the situation arising in the group which connects with some personal feeling, some preoccupation, some concern, in a way which the individual cannot cope with.

What can a therapist do? Sometimes such a personal reaction remains undetected by the therapist or anyone else because it occurs internally and the first sign of it is that the person breaks into tears or flees from the room. At other times a therapist picks up non-verbal cues which show that someone is reaching the point of being unable to tolerate whatever feelings are being stirred up.

If the therapist acts soon enough, undesirable consequences can usually be averted. Providing that the person is still physically present in the room, the therapist can take action. If the theme appears to be disturbing one person, the therapist could say: 'I think that some people are benefiting from this discussion but some are bothered by it.' Or the therapist could turn directly to the person and ask: 'Is this getting to be too much for you?' Such simple interventions name the event which the therapist thinks is occurring in the here-and-now of the group. Recognition and relief often follow. The person for whom anxiety has been building up sees that the therapist empathises with his/her state. He or she may gain a degree of control over distressing feelings. The therapist can follow up by saying something like: 'I think that what has been happening has some personal meaning for you which you might want to explore, either now or at some later time.' This gives the individual permission either to join the members in their explorations or else withdraw psychologically. The other members will have acquired information about that person's state which they did not have before, and will often reorientate themselves towards the distressed person and show empathy and support.

Episodes of contagion need to be interrupted, because feelings and behaviours may become unmanageable and because potentially useful explorations do not occur. When feelings are being expressed in behaviour (acted out) no one can acknowledge or examine them. An example of contagion, showing how it may be interrupted and used positively, appears in example 3 in Chapter 11.

Being psychologically excluded by all the other members

It sometimes happens that one person comes to be seen by all the others as being beyond the pale, altogether unacceptable. I remember one group member whom no one could stand after he complained that his parents had given him a gift of a Ford rather than the BMW he really wanted. He was regarded as a spoiled brat and became a kind of non-person in the group.

Excluding one person is a form of defence on the part of the other members. If the person is 'not there', not to be taken seriously, then there is no need to face the feelings which his behaviour has stirred up. If such situations persist without resolution everyone suffers. The individual him- or herself is insulated from possible gain-promoting experiences, and the others are deprived of opportunities to face and understand their feelings and behaviours. Both the excluded person and the others need help.

A therapist can often intervene effectively in such situations by naming what has happened. For instance a therapist might say: 'Since Matthew said that he often bullied younger children at school, no one has paid any attention to him or referred to what he said.' If the members do not respond to this, the therapist might try: 'Remember when Matthew said that he often bullied younger children at school? How did others feel at the time?' The therapist may then enquire why others could not tell Matthew how they felt, how Matthew felt, what the event reminded people of, and so on. The intention is to examine the whole situation, with attention to the feelings and reactions of all concerned, and any resonant experiences.

THE INFLUENCE OF THERAPIST ACTIONS OR FAILURE TO ACT

That the therapist, through his or her actions or failure to act, can lead to no gain or to actual harm is already evident from some of what has been said so far. A therapist might fail to intervene with respect to a restrictive solution which is placing one person at risk, or might not deal soon enough with an episode of contagion, or might allow one person to continue to be ignored after having taken some personal risk.

Another way in which a therapist might cause harm is by becoming so intrigued with a problem brought in by one person that he or she attends only to that person and excludes the others. Yet another way of causing harm is by pursuing one person, or the group in general, with interpretations which no one can see the point of or accept, and which lead members to establish some hard-to-dislodge defence. Still another possibility is that the therapist places one person at risk as part of a self-protective manoeuvre. A therapist may find one person hard to like and in consequence miss opportunities for benefiting that person.

All these are, of course, errors on the part of the therapist. No more will be said here because a full discussion of therapist errors is the subject of the next chapter.

THE STANCE AND BEHAVIOUR OF INDIVIDUAL MEMBERS WHICH CAN LIMIT THE GAINS WHICH THEY CAN ACHIEVE

Some individuals do not address their problems or acknowledge their feelings or confront their circumstances. They may participate actively in the group, but they do so in an uninvolved way. For example, in a long-term group for young adults with relationship problems, one young woman was a fairly active participant but was rather bland and serene in her manner throughout. Nothing that happened seemed to reach her. She somehow held the group experience at a distance, and emerged from a relatively lengthy group experience both untouched and unscathed. Yet, from the preliminary interview, the therapist knew that she was dissatisfied with her life and wanted to make some changes.

Some no-gain or little-gain individuals close themselves off from the group in another way. They participate little and seem not even to listen. They differ from those who are mainly spectators but nevertheless participate emotionally in the group. These no-gain individuals do not participate much nor do they 'spectate' in an involved way.

Some individuals persistently participate in ways which repeatedly demonstrate how intractable their problems are. This seems virtually to be their reason for having joined the group. The other members and the therapist function for them as witnesses to this repeated testimony. Group events do not impinge on them.

Some individuals quickly establish themselves in a role position in the group in which they are insulated from anything which might shift them from their preferred view of the world or preferred set of defences. One such role consists in repeatedly showing others how to cope by displaying one's own successes. Many contributions begin with: 'When I had that problem, I . . .' or 'When I have those feelings, I always . . .'. Another position which insulates against being touched by the group experience consists in maintaining a rosy optimism in the face of difficult circumstances. This pattern was displayed by a woman who joined a group for mothers of mentally retarded children. Whatever theme was being pursued in the group, she asserted that all was well in her world, that she was glad to have a learning-disabled child, that she experienced no adverse feelings. She consistently displayed and affirmed this attitude, and held fast to it in the face of others protesting that she must have *some* adverse feelings. She tried to convert others to her point of view and, although she did not succeed in this, neither did the other members succeed in getting her to acknowledge any pain or regret. The therapists judged that her attitude that 'all's well in the world' functioned for her as a necessary defence. It was essential to her and she was expert at maintaining it.

The various stances towards the group just described place the individuals concerned in a position from which gain is unlikely or impossible. They do not experience harm but they remain essentially untouched by the group experience.

It could be argued that, were the therapist more skilful or had the group gone on longer, all of the people just described could, in the end, benefit. I see no way to counter this argument. I can only say that I have seen and have been told about individuals who seem so firmly defended that they insulate themselves successfully from any impact from the group. Indeed, it could be argued that they are right to do so, for they may be protecting themselves from being exposed to more than they can tolerate.

From what has just been said, it is clear that gain or no-gain is not necessarily associated with degree of active participation. A person who participates little or not at all may nevertheless gain, and a person who participates a great deal may be doing so in a way which insulates against anything beneficial occurring.

ARE INDIVIDUALS IN GROUPS NEGLECTED OR DEPRIVED BECAUSE OF THE PRESENCE OF OTHER PATIENTS?

The answer to this question is: 'Possibly, but not necessarily'.

There was a time in the history of group psychotherapy when this question aroused strong passions and was a matter for debate and conflict within the field. S. R. Slavson (1957: 131) said:

> The question whether *group dynamics* in the ordinary sense of the phrase arise in therapy groups of nonpsychotic adults is a pivotal one. Its importance lies in the fact that if such dynamics are operative, much that we understand of group psychotherapy and the intrapersonal therapeutic process would have to be revised, and its practice, which is *clinical therapy* and not a sociological theory or construct, would have to be altered. The question whether we deal in group therapy with the group as a *unitary entity*, or with the individuals, that is, the patients in them, *as individuals*, may well determine the course of its development as a science and as a therapeutic tool.

It is clear that Slavson was very concerned and thought that group psychotherapy was under substantial threat. He states quite directly that taking account of group dynamics in therapeutic groups would mean overturning previous ideas about the therapeutic process and hence lead to new forms of practice – 'dealing with the group as a unitary entity' – in which the group would be emphasised over the individual.

Almost contemporaneous with Slavson was the work of Wolf and Schwartz (1962), who took a similar position. Their book *Psychoanalysis in Groups* was so titled to underline that the therapist's principal concern is with individuals and not with the group. Their position has been re-presented more recently in a book written by Wolf *et al.* (1992) *The Primacy of the Individual in Psychoanalysis in Groups*. Kutash and Wolf (1993: 126) say that:

> Group psychotherapy is a misnomer for a technique that, although conducted in a group, is designed to aid an individual patient; it is a treatment of ailing

individual patients in a group setting, not a treatment of ailing groups, since only individual patients have intrapsychic dynamics.

I do not see how anyone could disagree with the view that the therapeutic group is there for the purpose of benefiting individuals. How, then, could the idea develop that group therapists who acknowledge that group dynamics are present in therapeutic groups thereby treat the group and not the individual? I think that the answer must lie at least in part in the fact that Bion's and Ezriel's thinking came into the field in the 1950s, and both of them emphasised total-group phenomena. Bion directed his interventions and interpretations to group-level phenomena, employing the concepts of the work group and the basic assumption groups of fight–flight, pairing, and dependency. Ezriel used the term 'the common group tension' to refer to affects pertaining to the group as a whole. In his practice, he attended to both individual and group dynamics but his intervention style emphasised the latter in that he named all aspects of the common group tension before turning to its meaning for individuals. Wolf and Schwartz placed Foulkes in the same camp as Bion and Ezriel, which is not quite correct. Although Foulkes coined the term 'the group matrix' and considered group-level phenomena to be crucial, his writings make it clear that he attends to and often directs his comments to individuals. Wolf and Schwartz made it clear that they were reacting against these developments and the threats that they considered were posed by them.

Leonard Horwitz (1977) explored these issues in an article titled 'A group centered approach to group psychotherapy'. He pointed out that, while Bion did indeed focus on the group-as-a-whole and offered only group-wide interpretations (leaving it to individuals to make of it what they could), his method was directed to helping members to understand group processes, not to helping individuals with their personal problems. Horwitz therefore excuses Bion from accusations of neglecting the individual. Ezriel's thinking, and the Tavistock method which stemmed from it, was used as a basis for therapeutic work. It risks over-emphasising the dynamics of the group. Horwitz refers to Malan's research into the Tavistock approach (Malan *et al.* 1976), which showed that members of these groups tended to feel that the therapist had little concern for them as individuals. This was related to long periods of silence on the part of the therapist, which in turn were dictated by Ezriel's insistence that the therapist should not intervene until s/he could provide a formulation of all aspects of the 'common group tension'. Horwitz concludes that Ezriel set serious restrictions on the therapist's role and on the interventions which were and were not permitted, and that this led members to feel that their needs for individualised attention were being ignored. Horwitz makes the further interesting observation that it is hard to disentangle Ezriel's preferred style of intervening from the dictates of his theory.

The debate over whether attending to the dynamics of the group leads to neglecting the individual, though somewhat dimmed nowadays, has not entirely disappeared. Scheidlinger (1997) re-examined this issue in his article 'Group dynamics and group psychotherapy revisited: four decades later'. The issue is further illuminated by comments on Scheidlinger's article provided by Dies (1997), Fuhriman (1997), and MacKenzie (1997). These immediately follow Scheidlinger's article in the same journal issue.

To understand whether attending to the dynamics of the group leads to neglecting individuals, it is useful to distinguish between a therapist's internal thinking and that which he or she then chooses to say in the group; consider how therapists make use of their understandings of group-level dynamics in their practice; and to remember that interventions about and directed to the group can be combined with interventions which focus on individuals.

With reference to the first point, a group therapist can recognise group-level dynamics in the group, such as norms, shared beliefs, degrees of cohesiveness, prevailing themes, shared unconscious fears, and so on, without either assuming uniformity within the group with respect to them or feeling compelled to offer interpretations 'at the group level'. Kibel (1993: 172) has said that 'a clinical focus on group-level processes is not the same as construing the existence of group-as-a-whole dynamics'. There is a distinction, in other words, between what a therapist thinks – the meanings which he or she puts on observed events – and what the therapist then says or does in the group. A group therapist may note group-level dynamics. This does not mean that he or she will necessarily intervene or interpret at the group level, and it does not follow that the therapist is 'treating the group'.

When making use of group focal conflict theory, a therapist pays attention to group-level dynamics in order in part to encourage group conditions which support therapeutic processes likely to benefit individuals, and in part to perceive resonances between group-level and individual dynamics. This does not involve neglecting individuals. It involves acknowledging and making positive use of features of the group with the aim of benefiting individuals.

In their interventions, many group therapists refer to group dynamics *and* to how individuals participate in them or respond to them. This is not necessarily done in a single intervention, as Ezriel advised. In a series of interventions while some issue is being explored, some interventions are likely to refer to particular individuals, some to features of a prevailing group dynamic, and some to both.

The concern that, in a group, individuals may be neglected seems to linger on. I have seen comments in the literature to the effect that one can never get to know a person as well in a group as in individual psychotherapy; that members necessarily compete for the therapist's undivided attention; that therapists are often unable to pursue matters important to one person because of the presence of others. I suggest that such concerns are rooted in the assumption that individual gain derives from the relationship with, and specific attention from, the therapist, and not from any other sources. Such an assumption is most likely carried over from experience of one-to-one psychotherapy, where no one is present *except* the therapist and one patient. It does not take into proper account the benefits deriving from peer interaction and from sharing and comparing personal feelings and experiences within prevailing themes.

To return to the question posed at the beginning of this section: individuals *may* be neglected or deprived because of the presence of other patients, but only if the therapist restricts interventions and interpretations entirely to group-level phenomena, never inviting discussion of their relevance to individuals and altogether avoiding attention to individuals. Slavson and others quoted earlier are, I believe, wrong in assuming that attending to group-level dynamics inevitably means that one is treating the group and neglecting individuals. Slavson was right, however, when he said that taking account of group dynamics in therapeutic groups would mean overturning previous ideas about the therapeutic process and hence lead to new forms of practice. New forms of practice *are* required when making use of a group for therapeutic purposes. This is discussed in detail in Chapter 16.

DYNAMICS ASSOCIATED WITH LITTLE OR NO GAIN COMPARED WITH DYNAMICS ASSOCIATED WITH HARM

Somewhat different dynamics appear to be involved. Little or no gain for particular individuals may follow from a range of factors. Some follow from the individual's own initiatives to insulate him- or herself from the group. Some follow from group and interpersonal interactions which press individuals into positions which limit gain. *Everyone* in a group will be limited with respect to achievable gains if collusive defences not only emerge but persist. A therapist who colludes with the members in some shared defence, or who fails to perceive and make use of opportunities which could lead to gain for particular individuals, is contributing to no-gain experiences.

Harm, when it occurs, seems to follow from a different though overlapping set of dynamics. Personal efforts to avoid involvement do not seem to play such a part. Rather than being skilful at keeping themselves untouched by the group, people who experience harm seem to be in a more helpless position, unable to defend against harm-inducing experiences. They may be caught up by contagion in an irresistible way. They seem helpless when being pilloried or ostracised or deserted by the others. If they are more vulnerable than the others, they may be drawn into more than they can tolerate or handle, and again are helpless. Persons who come to harm seem often to be at the mercy of processes which they cannot resist or cope with.

REFERENCES IN THE LITERATURE TO NO-GAIN OR TO HARM-GENERATING FEATURES OF GROUPS

That destructive processes can occur in groups is well recognised. Heap (1965) and Scheidlinger (1982) have written about scapegoating in groups. Both refer to the original scapegoat as described in the Old Testament (Leviticus 16: 8–34). Heap shows how this dynamic operates in youth groups and Scheidlinger shows how it operates in therapeutic groups. Scheidlinger tracks the use of the concept through the literature on social psychology and group psychotherapy. (Scapegoating is discussed more fully in Chapter 16.)

Bullying is common enough in schools to have become the special object of study (see for instance Olweus 1994).

Dub (1997) describes the 'pivotal group member' whose behaviour dominates, distracts, or controls the group in ways which prevent the group from becoming or remaining an environment in which therapeutic processes can occur. A pivotal group member may express persistent despair and gloom over the possibility that the group could provide any sort of help, or monopolise through long repetitive discourses about personal problems experienced outside the group, or hold the group's attention for long periods by presenting him- or herself as weak and helpless, or repeatedly express an intention to leave the group. Dub says that such behaviours *and the responses they elicit* lead the group into a state of stagnation or hopelessness. She emphasises that it is only by collusion between the pivotal member, the other members, and the therapist that the pivotal member can immobilise the group. By pointing this out she avoids regarding the pivotal group member as the sole 'cause' of the problem situation. Collusive processes within the group, including the response of the therapist, are what give the pivotal member his or her destructive power. Such persons can often be dealt with and their effects on the group undone, providing that the therapist extricates him- or herself from being caught up in collusive processes. From an extricated position, the therapist can work both with the pivotal group member and with the feelings generated by him or her in others. Dub says that, when challenged, pivotal group members often flee from the group. She adds that she questions the advisability of keeping such persons in the group because they absorb so much of the therapist's time and energy. I have taken the view that many such members can be responded to in ways which allow them to remain in the group and which lead to benefit for themselves and others. (See Chapter 11 on 'Problems and Opportunities'.)

Morris Nitsun (1991, 1996) has put forward a concept which he has named 'the anti-group'. This refers to destructive forces in groups. He considers that such forces need to be acknowledged and examined to counter the overly optimistic views about groups held by S.H. Foulkes and other group analysts. I consider Nitsun's use of the definite article in the term 'the anti-group' unfortunate because it conveys that there is an actual entity which opposes the constructive forces in the group. Nitsun says that this is not so, and explains that he is describing 'destructive elements'. Indeed, the subtitle of his book is 'Destructive forces in the group and their creative potential'. Still, his repeated use of the term 'the anti-group' reinforces the impression of 'anti-group as entity'. I shall put this point aside in order to examine Nitsun's views about the 'dissonance' between optimistic views about groups and destructive events which happen in groups. Nitsun (1996: 43) says:

The predominant areas of dissonance I encountered were 1) resistance to participation in groups linked to fear and dislike of groups, 2) hostility and anger arising in the group that could not only threaten interpersonal cohesion in the group but be directed destructively at the group itself, and 3) spirally destructive processes in the group that could not be contained by the usual clinical management. . . . I have seen groups flounder badly in training and clinical practice, groups break down, end abruptly, or linger on in states of tense, negativistic impasse.

The fear and dislike of groups which Nitsun refers to in his first point is frequently seen in groups, especially but not exclusively at the beginning. In Chapter 9, out of a total of eleven examples of members' responses to the therapist's opening comment, all but three showed forms of resistance to becoming involved in the group experience. These were rooted in members' fears of what might happen in the group. However, as I emphasised earlier, members often work themselves out of initially established resistances (which I prefer to conceptualise as restrictive solutions). They experience fears but they also have hopes of the group. Influenced by both hopes and fears, members often begin to interact in fear-alleviating ways. If they do not, there are interventions available to the therapist which help to resolve fears and reduce the need to resort to restrictive solutions.

Nitsun's second point is that hostility and anger can be directed destructively at the group itself. This can occur. I suggest that when it occurs, it tends to express and at the same time mask fears. In group focal conflict terms such hostility and anger directed at the group is a restrictive solution. It is maintained by unanimity or near-unanimity of opinion, feelings, and behaviour amongst the members, and it functions to protect members from becoming involved in the group. If thought of in this way, Nitsun's second point merges with his first, and similar points can be made.

I am puzzled by Nitsun's third dynamic – that 'spirally destructive processes [occur] in the group that could not be contained by the usual clinical management'. What puzzles me is not that such dynamics can arise in therapeutic groups, but Nitsun's assertion that they arise so frequently and are so intractable. Perhaps the explanation lies in part in the fact that Nitsun describes work groups and staff support groups as well as therapeutic groups. In staff groups, dynamics located in the larger organisation affect group functioning. Some group members may have more real power than others, in the form of fate control. It is easy for members to get into competitive positions with respect to scarce resources, such as monetary support for favourite projects or office space. There will be many opportunities for group members to meet in variously formed sub-groups, both formally and informally, and for alliances to form and conflict to occur. Norms may be in operation which preclude openly acknowledging interpersonal problems and by this route finding ways to resolve conflict. All these extra- and intra-group phenomena increase the likelihood that destructive processes will occur and will persist.

I have certainly observed therapeutic groups which failed to develop favourably. In my experience, when this occurs it is for one of three reasons. Either (a) the group was unfortunately composed, in that individually held defences were so similar to one another that they quickly became established as collusive defences in the group; or (b) a structure was imposed which the members were incapable of making use of, and the therapist failed to recognise this and change the structure; or (c) the therapist persistently intervened in ways which forced the members into a defensive posture and kept them there.

Edelson and Berg (1999) devote one of the seven sections of their book to 'pernicious processes in groups', emphasising scapegoating; blaming; stereotyping individuals on the basis, for instance, of gender; a leader protecting him- herself by 'throwing someone to the wolves' (that is, offering someone to the members as a substitute target for himself); and a group 'electing' one of its members to take all the risks. Of these, scapegoating, blaming, and 'electing' one person to take all the risks are understood in group focal conflict terms as restrictive solutions which involve role differentiation. The members 'need' a scapegoat or someone to blame or someone to take the risks. To put this the other way around, the scapegoat or other serves a function for the other members. The therapist who 'throws a member to the wolves' is of course committing an error, for this is a self-protective manoeuvre which causes harm to someone. It functions as a personal solution for the therapist which causes damage to one group member. The risk of one person being stereotyped by the others is increased in certain group compositions.

CAN A THERAPIST AVOID THE OCCURRENCE OF NO-GAIN AND/OR OF HARM?

My answer to this question is: 'Often, but not always.' In each of the sub-sections above, which refer to influences on no-gain and on harm, I have posed the question: 'What can a therapist do?' and suggested intervention possibilities. I shall sum up briefly.

Some circumstances which generate either little or no gain or harm are extremely difficult if not impossible for a therapist to deal with effectively. One such circumstance consists of shared defences which are mutually maintained by group members over long periods of time. Everyone except the therapist supports the defence and keeps it in operation. It is hard for the therapist to find an effective way to intervene because of the power of unanimity. Mutually maintained shared defences *which persist* are usually the product of a group composition which is too homogeneous, or else of therapist behaviour which has driven the members into an intractable defensive position. They form a group culture which is antithetical to favourable development of the group and to it being a favourable environment in which personal gain can occur.

It is also very difficult to help individuals who are both highly defended and vulnerable. Indeed, there are arguments against trying to do so, since such persons are likely to be very brittle and inclined to break under what they experience as confrontation. However gentle a therapist tries to be, his or her interventions are experienced as unbearably harsh and threatening.

Most other group situations which *could* lead to little or no gain or to harm can be dealt with by a combination of therapist interventions and interactions amongst members. Sometimes group members work their own way out of gain-limiting dynamics for, as I have said, they harbour hopes as well as fears. A whole range of interventions is available to a therapist for overcoming bad starts, helping a group to recover from a period in the doldrums, averting destructive processes, turning problems into opportunities, avoiding adversarial relationships with members, and establishing a therapeutic alliance. Many of these have been referred to already, and they will be discussed more systematically in Chapter 15.

Certain forms of internal think-work are a helpful foundation for seeing how to intervene. Drawing from group focal conflict theory, it will be helpful to keep in mind the concepts of restrictive and enabling solutions, and the forms which restrictive solutions can take (that is, those which involve role differentiation and those which do not). It will be helpful to form hypotheses about each member's preferred defences and the particular functions these serve. As part of one's internal think-work, it will be helpful to try constantly to be in touch with levels of anxiety, either for the group as a whole or for particular members. It will be helpful to keep an observer's eye on one's own interventions and their consequences, in order to avoid colluding with the members in maintaining unproductive or destructive processes, or triggering them oneself.

This last point is a reminder that sometimes the therapist could intervene to prevent harm occurring or to forestall no-gain but does not do so, either out of fear and a need to protect the self, or simply through failures of skill or courage. Sometimes a therapist behaves in ways which in themselves lead to harm or constrict opportunities for personal gain. These are of course therapist errors. A full discussion is reserved for the next chapter.

Chapter 14

Discerning, retrieving and avoiding making errors

A therapist error is an action or a failure to act which has undesirable or harmful consequences for one or more members or for the group as a whole as a medium for personal gain.

Errors may occur in planning or in the course of conducting a group. They may be of commission or of omission. Some errors are very serious in their consequences; others less so. Some errors affect the group as a whole; some affect individuals. The consequences of some errors are retrievable; the consequences of others are not.

Examples of therapist errors have already been referred to from time to time in earlier chapters in the context of some other issue which was in focus at the time. I shall refer back to some of these examples and provide some new ones.

This chapter is organised as follows:

- Some examples of therapist errors.
- Further kinds of error not illustrated by these examples.
- Consequences of errors. Errors of commission and errors of omission. Behaviours which may or may not be errors, depending on context.
- Differing opinions as to what constitutes an error.
- Conditions under which therapist errors occur.
- How an error may be discerned (that is, noticed and recognised as an error).
- Retrievable and irretrievable consequences of errors.
- Reducing the frequency of errors.
- Two more questions concerning theory and its connections with practice, arising from this chapter.

SOME EXAMPLES OF THERAPIST ERRORS

Example 1

An error which a therapist repeated, in the course of the first four sessions of a group, that was serious in its consequences because it led to three members dropping out

During the first session of a newly formed, seven-member group, one member, Margaret, offered a personal problem for discussion. The other members and the therapist showed interest, asking questions and offering suggestions. This continued into the second session. After a time most of the other group members who had been active subsided, and it was mainly the therapist who carried on interacting with Margaret. A member who had not participated actively during the second session did not appear for the third session. In this session only Margaret and the therapist participated. Two further members failed to appear for the fourth session. Early in this session Margaret said she was tired of being the only one who talked, and that 'it's someone else's turn'. A silence followed, and then one of the other members, Frank, began to speak about a personal concern. The therapist and the members turned their attention to him. The three absent people did not return, and the group continued with four members. Each of these in turn received the attention of the therapist and of the other members.

In this example the therapist committed several errors. It was an error in the first place to concentrate so exclusively on one person so early in the group's life. It was an error not to invite discussion of how others might be feeling as this was happening. The therapist failed to appreciate that the first drop-out and the succeeding two might possibly have been in response to her behaviour. This deficiency in understanding led to persisting in the original error. The therapist continued to concentrate on one person (even when no one else was participating) until that person herself said 'it's someone else's turn'. This led to another person becoming 'the patient'. It was, in my view, a further error to allow the pattern of turn-taking to continue, for within this pattern there was room for only two role positions: the patient and the therapist. Sharing and comparing amongst members could not occur.

One does not know for certain how the other members felt while the therapist was concentrating on one person. What *is* known is that three members dropped out. It is reasonable to infer that, in consequence of the therapist concentrating so much on one person, others felt there was nothing in the group for them. Sometimes members feel relieved and protected if someone else is in the centre of attention. However, as time goes on, they are likely to begin to feel deprived, envious, or resentful of the therapist for showing favouritism. One possible consequence is loss of interest in the group. Once people have actually dropped out, it is too late to retrieve the consequences of the error. The lost members are no longer accessible to the therapist or to the group.

This kind of error is easily avoided, provided that the therapist recognises that it *is* an error. Even if one person is eager to occupy the therapist's time and attention, the therapist does not have to respond consistently to such cues. Without being curt or dismissive, he or she can show interest in the others by looking round the circle of participants, silently inviting their participation. Or, more actively, a therapist could refer to the issue being raised by one person and invite others to say whether and how it connects with their own experiences.

Example 2

An error of commission which was not very serious in its consequences, and where retrieval was not necessary because the group was able to proceed in a constructive way

> A group therapist opened a new group by offering a lengthy introduction which went on for some twenty-five minutes. He dwelt on the history of group psychotherapy and mentioned a number of benefits which members were likely to experience. When he stopped, members took it in turn to mention their names. Two people added information about the jobs they did. The fourth person to speak said something about the problems which had brought her to the group, and after that, each subsequent speaker did the same.

Afterwards, the therapist said he realised that such a lengthy introduction was unnecessary and a mistake. He understood that it was a product of his own fears that he might be unable to handle whatever would happen after he stopped speaking.

The consequence of this error was to delay the start of the group by twenty minutes or so. No doubt it would have been better if this delay had not occurred, but losing twenty minutes was not such a serious matter. As soon as there was an opportunity for them to speak, the group members got off to a reasonable start.

Example 3

An error of commission whose consequences could have been retrieved but were not, and which had a serious negative impact on the development of the group

> An experiential group was being conducted for professionals who wanted to improve their understanding of groups. The first session was being held on a very warm day in early autumn. One of the members asked for a window to be opened, and several others supported him. The therapist said that the members evidently wanted to escape from the group. Several protested, saying that they simply felt too hot. The therapist said that his first interpretation must have been correct or they would not be protesting. Further protests brought only a smile from the therapist. The members fell into a silence which prevailed for the rest of this session and all of the next. In the session after that, they brought the matter up again, but met with the same response. Someone said, in a resigned tone, 'Well, we tried.' The members lapsed into silence again, which persisted for the remaining life of the group.

In this example the therapist introduced an interpretation which the members could not accept, and then followed with a further interpretation which asserted that the members' protests were proof that his first interpretation had been correct. This placed the group members in a difficult position. One can surmise that they began to feel that anything they said, short of accepting the therapist's version of events, would be taken by the therapist as evidence for the correctness of his interpretations. I suggest that the prolonged silence was a response to recognising that saying anything at all would be met with a condescending interpretation of their feelings and motives. They could not resort to dropping out, since the group was a part of their training course and they had to attend or else forfeit the qualification they were aiming for.

A solidly maintained silence on the part of group members is very hard for a therapist to deal with, since, after all, no one can force people to speak if they choose not to do so. Thinking in group focal conflict terms, the therapist's behaviour had driven the members into adopting a particularly intractable restrictive solution.

The therapist could have avoided this situation by refraining from his first interpretation, or by refraining from following it up with the second one. Even after the second interpretation he could have retrieved the situation by naming the sequence of events and asking members to say something about how they felt at the time and were now feeling. During the third session, when the members brought the matter up again, the therapist had a further opportunity to correct for the consequences of his errors. He did not take advantage of it.

Even if the therapist's first interpretation had been technically correct, it would still be an error to persist with it. The members' response showed that there was such a wide gulf between the therapist's understanding of the situation and their understanding of it that the members were most unlikely to accept the interpretation. Repeating the interpretation could not be expected to help. It is also an error, in my view, to convey to a group that 'I, the therapist, know what the real reality is, while, you, the members, do not'. Such a message makes it very hard to establish a working alliance between the therapist and the members. I think that this error stemmed from the therapist clinging too rigidly to a perspective on groups which asserts that virtually any manifest content has underlying personal meanings which are unrecognised by those concerned.

Example 4

An error of omission which led to one member dropping out, the harmful consequences of which were impossible to retrieve

> Seven ten-year-old boys met regularly in an activity group. On one occasion the therapist provided each of the boys with a large sheet of paper and felt pens, and asked them to draw anything they liked. The idea was to follow this by everyone commenting on the drawings. Most of the boys drew cartoons or space-ships, but Dave filled his sheet of paper with many repetitions of the word 'SHIT' (in capital letters). When it came time to comment, everyone's drawing was discussed

except Dave's. Neither the other members, nor the therapist, nor Dave himself mentioned his drawing. When the time was up, everyone left. Dave did not return to the group.

Everyone must have noticed Dave's drawing. Perhaps the other boys simply did not know what to say, or found the situation worrying, or were triggered into feelings which they did not want to face. It is not clear just what Dave's drawing meant to him. Perhaps he had strong feelings of some kind which he was expressing in this somewhat mysterious way, or he was displaying defiance, or his drawing was a cry for help of some kind, or he was drawing attention to himself.

Whatever was going on in Dave and in the other members, the therapist's failure to draw attention to Dave's production was an error of omission. By saying nothing he was defining Dave's behaviour as undiscussable, and showing himself incapable of facing this unexpected situation.

Saying 'No one has said anything yet about Dave's sheet of paper' would have changed the situation. Perhaps the boys, including Dave, could begin to comment. Or perhaps Dave would show embarrassment, or others start to ridicule or tease him. If either of these responses were to occur, the therapist could follow up with something like: 'Wait a minute. This must be important to Dave in some way or another . . .'. Such an intervention would cast a different light on the situation: instead of Dave's behaviour being seen as unacceptable or funny, it would be redefined as important. Dave might have been able to say something further. Even if he did not, he would not have to carry away with him the experience of having been ignored.

This was a serious error because Dave was now lost to the group. There would be no opportunity to turn this situation into an opportunity to benefit Dave, because he was no longer there. Moreover, Dave took with him, we can assume, some feelings of distress – perhaps a sense that he had done something totally unacceptable, or that his feelings really *were* unfaceable, by him or anyone.

Example 5

An error of omission which allowed one group member to remain in the role of 'expert', limiting his opportunities for personal gain

In an in-patient group one man, Don, was both older than any of the others and had more status, having been a lawyer in outside life. Early in the group, members presented personal problems and turned to the two therapists for advice. The therapists did not offer guidance but encouraged the members to explore their problems further. The members turned to Don for advice. He was very ready to provide it.

This pattern recurred over the life of the group. Don continued to occupy the role of 'expert'. He said little about himself, but always responded when the other members asked for his advice. Apart from his readiness to be an expert, Don remained unknown in the group.

The persistence of this interactive pattern had disadvantageous consequences for Don and also for the other members. Don's opportunities for personal gain were limited, for he did not join discussions as a member, and the others did not invite or press him to do so. The others lost the opportunity to explore how it was that they expected the therapists to provide the answers. They did not examine feelings stimulated by the therapists' non-response, or possible connections with experiences outside the group or earlier in life. The therapists' error lay in allowing this situation to continue. A useful intervention strategy would be to draw attention to the situation as an interactive *event*, for instance by saying: 'I remember that it was after we two therapists did not respond to requests for advice that members began to turn to Don.' The aim would be to interrupt the pattern and to examine the function which Don's advice-giving was fulfilling for the members, including, possibly, Don. Another way of responding would be to try to extricate Don from the position he so consistently occupied by, for instance, pointing out that members repeatedly turned to Don for advice, and then saying something like: 'There must be more to Don than just being a good advice-giver.'

Don's position in the group is an example of what Bogdanoff and Elbaum (1978) call 'role lock'. These authors describe, as examples of roles in which members may become trapped: the mistruster, the professional patient, the monopoliser, the performer, helpful Hannah, war lover, misfortune hunter, and isolate.

Example 6

An error of commission which led to members being more cautious in their participation than they otherwise would have been and to a generally depressed mood

> In the first session of an in-patient group, one member noticed that there was a crack in one of the windows. Others mentioned further examples of poor maintenance within the hospital – for instance, one of the lifts was not working, and a stopped-up wash basin had not been repaired. Someone said that the 'top doctor' must be responsible, but he probably had other things on his mind, or didn't care about the convenience of the patients. The therapist said: 'Perhaps you are worried that I am not interested in you and don't care.' There was a pause, which lengthened. When the discussion resumed, it focused on the unlikelihood that any of them would be helped by being in the hospital or ever recover. A depressed mood spread in the group.

In this example, the therapist judged that the members were making use of a metaphor to express their feelings about the therapist and their fears about being in the group. He introduced an interpretation in the expectation that the members would then speak more directly about their feelings. However, instead of opening up, the members first fell into a silence and then expressed hopelessness. Judged by its consequences, the therapist's intervention was an error: not because it was technically incorrect but because it was introduced too soon and, possibly, unnecessarily.

One might consider that this interpretation was 'premature' or that the members were 'not ready' for it. This would not be incorrect but it does not get to the heart of the matter. In trying to think out *why* the members responded as they did, one might hypothesise that the members felt caught out and exposed by the therapist, that it suddenly felt risky to go on talking, and that in the members' eyes the therapist had become a source of threat rather than of help.

In group focal conflict terms, one would say that the members moved from one form of restrictive solution (which was speaking in terms of a metaphor) to another restrictive solution (which was silence) and then to no solution at all, but rather to an intensified expression of fears of receiving no help. The therapist's intervention led to an intensification of the members' fears. It would have been preferable for the members to be allowed to continue with the metaphor, since they were after all expressing and communicating their fears, though in a disguised way.

Four alternative ways to respond to member-constructed metaphors are described in Chapter 16. Of these, I consider interpreting the metaphor to be the most risky, in terms of likely consequences. In this example, the therapist made a single leap from the metaphoric content to its implications for members' here-and-now feelings towards himself and the group. In the face of this, the members retreated.

Example 7

An error of commission which had temporarily damaging consequences for one person, but was retrieved by the therapist with the help of a group member before more abiding damage was done

This example was originally presented as example 8 in Chapter 11. It was stated there as 'a concerted attack on one person, where the underlying dynamic is that of displacement'. As a reminder, one of the members, Rhoda, was attacked by other members for being frequently absent from the group. This occurred soon after the therapist had announced her forthcoming temporary absence from the group. I suggested that the anger felt by the members towards the therapist was displaced on to Rhoda, who was a safer target.

In this situation the therapist's error consisted of joining in the attack, pointing out that Rhoda would not gain if she did not attend. The therapist retrieved the error only after another member eventually asked: 'Why are we attacking Rhoda?' This apparently reminded the therapist of the context in which reproaching Rhoda had surfaced, and she said: 'Yes, I am the one who is going to be away.' In response to this, members ceased their attack on Rhoda and began to talk about their feelings about the therapist's impending absence.

Had this situation continued, real harm could have come to Rhoda, who was already in considerable distress. The other members would have been deprived of opportunities to explore their feelings about the therapist who was 'deserting' them. They would furthermore have been deprived of opportunities to explore whatever personal experiences this event resonated with. Perhaps the members themselves would eventually have made the necessary shift away from attacking Rhoda, without the therapist's tardy intervention. One person had, after all, already asked: 'Why are we attacking Rhoda?' Even so, it was almost certainly helpful that the therapist recognised that she had made an error and took steps to retrieve it by giving explicit permission to the members to explore their feelings towards her.

FURTHER KINDS OF ERROR NOT ILLUSTRATED BY THESE EXAMPLES

Other errors include:

- A therapist makes rules at the very beginning of a group which he or she does not have the power to enforce.
- Soon after the start of a group, members show that they cannot or are not prepared to work to the planned structure, and the therapist persists with the structure for too long or gives up on it too soon.
- The therapist fails to intervene when one member is becoming increasingly upset and shows signs of fleeing from the group.
- The therapist allows a group to become too small by not replacing members who leave.
- The therapist unnecessarily gets into an antagonistic or adversarial relationship with the members of the group; for instance, as members insist more and more strongly that the group cannot be of any use, the therapist insists more and more strongly that it can.
- The therapist fails to respond satisfactorily to one or another of the problem situations discussed in Chapter 11.

CONSEQUENCES OF ERRORS; ERRORS OF COMMISSION AND ERRORS OF OMISSION; BEHAVIOURS WHICH MAY OR MAY NOT BE ERRORS, DEPENDING ON CONTEXT

Consequences of errors

Some therapist errors affect the group as a whole. The therapist behaves in some way which erodes the sense of safety in the group. Anxiety shoots up to dysfunctional levels, or else the members resort to some shared defence which is hard to dislodge. The group becomes a less favourable environment for therapeutic work, and all the members suffer limitations on what can be achieved.

Some therapist errors affect individuals. The therapist fails to rescue an individual from a situation within the group which is causing harm, or persistently fails to recognise and support opportunities for therapeutic gain, or behaves in a way which drives an individual out of the group, or supports a collusive defence which is harming one person.

Errors of commission and errors of omission

In terms of group focal conflict theory, errors of commission include cooperating with members in maintaining some restrictive solution, or behaving in a way which generates or exacerbates fears and leads members to construct some relatively more intractable restrictive solution.

Errors of omission include allowing some restrictive solution to go on for longer than necessary, failing to intervene in a restrictive solution which involves role differentiation and which is harming some one individual, or failing to take advantage of opportunities cast up by periods of resonance between individual and group focal conflicts or by episodes in which two people become especially important to one another.

An error of omission involves, almost by definition, missing an opportunity. This may or may not have abiding negative consequences. In example 5, above, where the ten-year old dropped out, the consequences of missing an opportunity were serious, for the boy dropped out of the group. The opportunity was not only missed, but a similar opportunity cannot recur. Some missed opportunities are not as serious in their consequences because a similar opportunity will almost certainly arise again. For instance, a therapist might miss an opportunity to assist a group to shift from some restrictive solution to a more enabling one, or to encourage wider participation, or to invite one person to elaborate on some elliptical comment. Providing that the therapist, on reflection, realises that an opportunity has occurred and been missed, he or she will be alert to a similar opportunity the next time it arises.

Behaviours which may or may not be errors, depending on context

Many behaviours may or may not be errors, depending on the context in which they occur. For instance, asking a question or offering a personal opinion or sharing a personal feeling might be an error, but might on the other hand be entirely appropriate. Therapist behaviours have to be judged in context.

DIFFERING OPINIONS AS TO WHAT CONSTITUTES AN ERROR

It is probably safe to say that group therapists generally agree that an error is anything which works against the positive development of a group or the best interests of individual members. However, therapists differ in their views about which behaviours and decisions are likely to support the therapeutic effort and which are likely to undermine it.

For instance, I consider it an error to encourage turn-taking or to fail to try to move a group away from a turn-taking pattern. Yet I know that some group therapists see positive advantages in concentrating at length on one person at a time. They may, for instance, encourage members to 'ask for the group's time'. I consider certain short cuts risky and to be avoided on those grounds, though others recommend them (see discussion in Chapter 9). I consider intrusive or confrontational interventions to be counter-productive, while some therapists see them as necessary to the therapeutic process. Some group therapists consider it appropriate and proper to persist with interpretations in the face of protests from members. As the third example in this chapter shows, I consider this to be an error.

Some group therapists consider it not only appropriate but part of the therapist's proper role to press silent members to participate. My own view is that one should be very careful about this. Some individuals manage to stay in a group only if they are allowed to be mainly silent. They may gain from their non-participant position and could be driven out by too much pressure on them to participate overtly. Of course a group is no use if *no one* participates. However, a group can tolerate one or even two people who participate little or even not at all.

Some therapists make rules for themselves, such as 'never answer a personal question' or 'never express a personal feeling'. Such rules are sensible most of the time but it can be counter-productive to adhere to them rigidly, under all circumstances. I have come to the view that one may have a general rule in mind but take circumstances into account when deciding whether and when to make an exception to it.

Sometimes it is hard to judge whether or not an action is, or would be, an error. Suppose that someone flees in apparent distress from a group. Is it an error to follow that person out, leaving the other members to themselves? Or is it an error to remain in the group, leaving the departed member alone with his/her distress? Is it appropriate to encourage or allow another group member to follow the departed person? It seems best to make a decision in the light of the actual circumstances, since no two such episodes will be exactly alike. One has to make a quick judgement about the meaning of the event and the best response to it.

CONDITIONS UNDER WHICH THERAPIST ERRORS OCCUR

1 *Events may be so fast-moving or so unexpected that it is hard for a therapist to grasp their import quickly* It can be hard to muster all one's sensitivities and skills when members abruptly shift from one theme to another, when everything seems confused, when a situation is particularly intense and fraught, when members seem particularly resistant, when members behave entirely out of line with one's expectations, or when one suddenly comes under attack oneself from a number of the members all at once.

2 *The therapist may be experiencing some worry about the group and then shows it in behaviour which distracts or alarms the members or slows the group down* For instance, suppose that, early in a group's life, the therapist is worried that the group will flounder and prove useless or that members will leave if they do not see quick results. In response to these half-recognised concerns, the therapist reassures the members that groups do indeed help people, that many have benefited, that there is a need to be patient, and so on and so forth. The error does not lie in having the worries, but in expressing them, and in expressing them in a way which interferes with the movement of the group. Members may wonder why the therapist is going on about such matters. Doubts may be aroused in them which were not there before. At the very least, the therapist is preventing the members from getting on with what concerns *them.*

3 *The therapist may be engaging in self-protective manoeuvres* For instance, a therapist sees signs of, or senses, a build-up of angry feelings towards him or her. Without exactly realising it, the therapist wants to avoid becoming the target of attack or criticism. He or she ignores the build-up of anger, or makes a joke, or offers a cryptic comment, or joins in with and supports the members in aiming their attack elsewhere. Such responses either distract the members or support them in behaviours which avoid having to acknowledge their angry feelings towards the therapist.

4 *The therapist may be immobilised in the face of a particularly tense and fraught situation arising in the group* Perhaps two members suddenly become involved in an angry confrontation, or the group is moving towards panic and flight, or one person becomes grossly upset. The therapist needs to intervene but does not do so. He or she is at least momentarily stunned and immobilised.

5 *The therapist may lose interest in a particular group member, or feel angry or disappointed or dismissive of him or her* If this happens, that group member ceases to receive sympathetic attention from the therapist, or possibly much attention at all. The therapist is less likely to notice and act upon opportunities for benefiting the person.

6 *The therapist may behave in a way which serves some unrecognised and abiding personal need* As examples: a therapist may intervene too frequently or intrusively out of a need to be in control of events. Or a therapist may introduce fancy interpretations in order to demonstrate cleverness. Or a

therapist does not confront some difficult situation because he or she is excessively concerned to be 'friends' with the members. Such behaviours are likely to be part of a therapist's style. They are not situation-specific but, rather, are responses to personal needs which therapists carry around with them from situation to situation.

7   *A shared theme which emerges in the group may resonate with some personal concern of the therapist. The therapist loses his/her therapeutic stance and so is more prone to make errors*   This point can be expressed in group focal conflict terms: a prevailing group focal conflict involves impulses or fears which resonate with impulses and fears held by the therapist. He or she is drawn into participating, at least emotionally, in the theme. It then becomes difficult to maintain an appropriate therapeutic stance – that is, of being close enough to the affective experiences of members to understand them, but at the same time far enough out to monitor events. If a therapist departs from an appropriate therapeutic stance errors are more likely to occur. The therapist will be responding more to his or her own stirred-up feelings than to members' feelings and behaviours.

8   *The therapist may be preoccupied with fears that colleagues will form negative judgements about him/her or the group*   Preoccupations of this kind distract the therapist from paying attention to what is going on in the group, or lead him or her to understand events in ways which are coloured by the preoccupation. The therapist may become impatient with what seems to be slow progress, and in consequence push the members too hard.

9   *The therapist under-appreciates the special opportunities afforded by a group as a medium for help*   If this is the case, a therapist may operate in the group in ways which are more suited to individual psychotherapy. He or she may, for instance, fall into conducting individual therapy with an audience, either concentrating on particular group members in turn, or engaging with one person for a long time without taking into account the impact on others. While some benefit can follow from this, a whole range of gain-promoting experiences are precluded. Interventions which make use of the *group* as medium for help remain outside the therapist's repertoire.

10   *The therapist adheres too rigidly to some theoretical framework*   A therapist who is very firmly attached to a particular theory may understand events arising in the group in stereotypic ways, in line with the theory. Alternatives do not come to mind. This in turn leads to the therapist making use of a limited range of interventions. There is a risk that both understandings and interventions are more driven by theory than by attention to group events. Rigid adherence to a particular theory places the therapist in an inflexible position.

Some of these sources of error might be regarded as instances of counter-transference. However, I would be cautious about declaring them to be 'counter-transference' without considering the specifics of the dynamics involved. What the literature has to say about counter-transference was reported in Chapter 8 in the context of discussing how a therapist can keep in touch with own behaviour in a group and its consequences. Without repeating that extended discussion, I shall summarise by pointing out that counter-transference proper refers to reactions on the part of the therapist which are rooted in unresolved intrapsychic conflicts. Not all personal responses to members can be explained in these terms. For instance, a therapist may feel anger towards a member who frequently interrupts productive discussions, or causes another member to feel seriously distressed. A therapist may feel disappointed when a group which has been going well suddenly loses momentum. These are understandable responses to what has occurred, not necessarily rooted in personal unresolved conflicts. As Ormont (1991) reminds us, a distinction can be made between 'objective' counter-transference, which refers to a therapist responding as most others would, and 'subjective' transference, which is individual and idiosyncratic and derives from experiences in a therapist's individual past life. This cautions against considering any affective reaction on the part of a therapist as being a form of counter-transference.

Of the ten situations described above, 2–7 have to do with therapist feelings stirred up by events occurring in the group. Of these, probably 6 and 7 come closest to fitting counter-transference, if properly defined. The fifth point could be an instance of what Ormont refers to as objective counter-transference. The second point describes concerns which are not unusual in a therapist when a group first starts. This leaves points 3 and 4. These *could* involve counter-transference as strictly defined but could, in contrast, be regarded as understandable responses to particularly difficult situations which almost anyone might experience. One needs to look for evidence on which to base a judgement.

The eighth source of error involves a therapist's personal feelings but they are stimulated by events (or presumed events) occurring outside the group rather than inside it.

Points 9 and 10 are somewhat related, for both have to do with the boundaries within which a therapist thinks and consequently operates. It would be stretching it to regard either of these as manifestations of counter-transference, since so many other influencing factors could be present. For instance, regarding effective therapeutic work as primarily involving interactions between therapist and patient (involved in point 9) is understandable in historic terms. Becoming overly attached to some theoretical perspective (point 10) is understandable if the therapist is closely associated with a group of colleagues who support the same point of view. Group dynamics within that colleagueship become a powerful influencing factor.

Point 1 is different from all the others in that it refers to group situations which face all group therapists from time to time. The realities of such situations make it difficult for any therapist to form views about the meaning of events which he or she can have confidence in and which suggest appropriate interventions.

HOW AN ERROR MAY BE DISCERNED (THAT IS, NOTICED AND IDENTIFIED TO ONESELF AS AN ERROR)

In the title of this chapter, 'discerning' comes first because if one does not notice errors one cannot attempt to correct for their consequences; and if one lacks experience in discerning and attempting to correct for the consequences of errors, one is in a weak position to avoid making errors in the future. Being able to discern errors is crucial, and 'discerning' requires think-work.

Retrieving errors, or attempting to retrieve them, depends on their being recognised as errors. If recognised, much depends on *how soon* they are recognised.

One may begin to suspect that an error has occurred if there is an unexpected reaction to what one has said or done in the group. For instance, suppose that one has introduced a structure and the members do not follow it. Suppose that one makes an interpretation and it is not used by members, but is ignored or met by protest. Suppose that the members respond to a therapist's intervention by clamming up or shifting the topic. If any of this happens, it may or may not be in response to a therapist error. How is one to judge?

In Chapter 11, some questions were put forward which, it was suggested, would be useful for a therapist to have in mind when faced with some event experienced as a problem. Similarly, it is useful to ask certain questions of oneself when trying to puzzle out whether one has made an error and, if so, what to do about it. For instance:

* Has a set-back occurred in the group or has there been a rise in the level of anxiety? Is one person suddenly in a more disadvantageous position than before?
* If so, did my own behaviour play some part in this, or is the situation understandable in other terms?
* As a test as to whether my own behaviour played a part, did I intervene in this situation and, if so, what followed from my interventions? Did whatever I said open things up, or close them down?
* Did I persist with a form of intervening which, on reflection, made things worse? Did I, for instance, continue to ask challenging questions, or persist with an interpretation which members showed they could not accept?
* Were there times when I let a situation go on when I ought to have intervened?
* Was I drawn into the dynamics of the group? Did I lose my 'therapist's stance' and did this lead me into some error of commission or omission? For instance, did I take sides, or join in a collusive defence, or become upset by something to the point of being immobilised? Did I become intrigued by one person and spend excessive time with him/her?

There is one further question which is in a sense more fundamental, in that it could underlie a tendency to make particular kinds of errors. It requires standing back from oneself and reflecting on a run of sessions rather than just one. It is:

- Do I tend to make unjustified assumptions, either about the meaning of particular kinds of events arising in a group or about what therapists ought always (or never) to do?

By asking and answering such questions a therapist may become convinced that he or she has made an error or, alternatively, judge that the situation can be understood in other terms. Perhaps the therapist suspects that he or she has made an error but is not certain. Further actions will be based on the therapist's conclusions or provisional hypothesis.

RETRIEVABLE AND IRRETRIEVABLE CONSEQUENCES

If the therapist sees or suspects that an error has been made, the next step will be to try to retrieve its consequences.

If the error has been one of commission – something said or done which leads to undesirable consequences – then the error itself cannot be retrieved. It has been made and cannot be unmade. However, the *consequences* of having made the error can be ameliorated, or corrected for, or retrieved.

If the error has been one of omission, then its consequences can be retrieved by watching for the next opportunity to intervene as one thinks one ought to have done in the first place, or by reminding members of the event and so creating an opportunity to retrieve the error.

Some consequences of therapist errors are much harder to retrieve than others. If the error has led to someone dropping out there is no corrective or restorative action which a therapist can take with respect to that person, though a therapist can deal constructively with the aftermath for others. Some consequences are very difficult to deal with, or take a long time to deal with. For instance, it will not be easy to undo the consequences of an error which has forced the members into adopting some relatively intractable restrictive solution, or which has generated feelings of mistrust or fear of the therapist, or which has led one person to establish a firm and persisting defence against becoming emotionally involved in the group.

Errors which are made repeatedly are hard to make up for because repetition tends to fix the group or one member in the response which the error has stimulated.

Under some circumstances it is a mistake to try to retrieve the consequences of an error. It is not unusual for a therapist to realise that an error has been made only after a session finishes and he or she has time to reflect on events. Before the next session begins, the therapist will need to make a preliminary judgement about whether or not to make an active retrieval attempt. It is then best to wait to see how events unfold in the group before deciding whether or not to take action. Sometimes events show that the group has moved on and the error has apparently had no lingering effect. If so, it may be best to let it go. To refer back to the error would amount to imposing something on the group which is no longer relevant to its operations. One would be responding to one's own guilty or uneasy feelings rather than to the needs of the members.

If one decides that it is important to try to correct for consequences, one will have to decide how to go about it. Some ways of attempting to retrieve consequences create further problems. For instance, confessing to the members in some abject way is a further error, likely to make matters worse. It is better to refer straightforwardly to the error and invite discussion of it. This, incidentally, has the further positive consequence of demonstrating to members that errors can be acknowledged without guilt or shame.

REDUCING THE FREQUENCY OF ERRORS

It is not possible to avoid making errors altogether. If one scans the reasons put forward above as to why therapists make errors (pp. 225–6), one can see that the first, at least, cannot be avoided, and probably certain of the others cannot be avoided altogether. Because of the complexity of the group situation, any therapist will make errors from time to time. It is unrealistic to expect always to do or to say just the right thing at the right time.

It is, however, possible to learn to reduce the number of errors one makes, on the basis of experience. It is possible to become more skilful in correcting promptly for the consequences of errors. This chapter is intended to be helpful in this respect.

TWO MORE QUESTIONS CONCERNING THEORY AND ITS CONNECTIONS WITH PRACTICE THAT ARISE FROM THIS CHAPTER

Examples presented in this chapter show that theory can be misused (example 3); that an intervention based on sound-enough theory could nevertheless be an error (example 6); that therapist error can follow from a therapist's need to protect him- or herself (example 7).

From this, two further questions concerning theory and its uses arise. The first is: What, besides theory, influences how therapists practice? I shall attach this to the question raised at the end of Chapter 12, making it into: How do therapists use theory in their practice? What, besides theory, influences how therapists practice?

The second question is: How can or might theory be misused, or lead one astray? Does all theory carry risks of being misused?

These two further questions will be added to those already raised in Chapters 5, 8 and 12. They constitute questions 8 and 10 in the series, and will be carried forward into Chapter 17 for discussion.

Chapter 15

Intervening in groups

Why, how and when

Practitioners are constantly faced with decisions about whether and how to intervene in their therapeutic groups. If, as is surely the case, only a fraction of what a therapist *thinks* while conducting a group is expressed in the form of a spoken intervention, issues immediately arise about why, how and when to intervene, and reasons for choosing whether or not to intervene.

This chapter draws together what can be said about intervening, based on what has been said in Chapters 9–14. Virtually all the examples presented in Chapters 9, 11, 12 and 14 bear on the issue of why, how and when a therapist may usefully intervene in a group or refrain from intervening. Commentaries attached to examples sometimes pointed to further possible interventions. The discussions of successive stages in group development, the goings and comings of members, and the dynamics associated with little or no gain also feed into this chapter, which is organised as follows:

* Why intervene?
* How a therapist might intervene: the choices available.
* When and when not to intervene.
* High-risk and low-risk interventions, and sequences of interventions.
* The issue of whether and when to concentrate on one person.
* Offering interpretations in groups.
* Spontaneity, flexibility, rules and guidelines.

WHY INTERVENE?

It is obvious enough that a therapist intervenes in order to pursue his or her purposes on behalf of the members of a group. In Chapter 1, an overall purpose and a number of sub- or instrumental purposes were set out to serve as guides to a therapist when planning and conducting a group. At that point, however, purposes were necessarily stated in general terms. It is only when a group comes into being that a therapist can formulate purposes in terms which are attached to actual, concrete situations.

There is a level of conceptualisation of purposes which lies somewhere between, on the one hand, the purposes as stated in Chapter 1, which pertain to any group, and, on the other hand, situation-specific purposes attached to actual concrete and unique events, no two of which are alike. At this middle level, purposes are attached to classes of situations. The following is an attempt to formulate purposes at this middle level. I have chosen to avoid language specific to group focal conflict theory or any other theoretical approach:

- If members show that they feel unsafe in the group situation, the therapist's purpose will be to assist them to feel sufficiently safe that they need not respond to their fears by fleeing from the group or by remaining in it but insulating themselves from its potential emotional impact.
- If members maintain a sense of safety by establishing some collusive defence which constricts the therapeutic potential of the group, the therapist's purpose will be to monitor the situation and, if members do not move beyond the collusive defence through their own interactions, intervene to assist such movement to occur.
- If a collusive defence involves role differentiation in which one person is being kept in a position which puts him or her at risk, the therapist's purpose is two-fold: to extricate the individual from the position he or she is in, and to assist the group to yield up the defence.
- If a person is coming to harm or is at risk of being harmed through a concerted attack on him or her on the part of other members, a therapist's purpose will be to understand why the attack is occurring and what function it is serving, and to interrupt it in order to curtail harm and turn the situation into something potentially helpful for all concerned.
- If intense affect is building up in a group to the point where the situation is becoming overwhelming for one or more individuals, or even everyone, the therapist's purpose will be to interrupt the process, calm things down, and assist members to explore their feelings and their related experiences in words rather than expressing them through excitement or panic or by literally fleeing from the group.
- If one person is regarded as a 'problem' by the others, the therapist's purposes will be *both* to protect the 'problem person', who is at risk of becoming ostracised or becoming the target of attack, *and* to encourage all concerned to give thought to their own feelings and behaviours – including why the person is seen as a problem and how it is that the other members are able to do nothing about the situation.
- If a situation (not centred around one person) arises which is regarded as a 'problem' by group members or by the therapist, the therapist's purpose will be to encourage members to look squarely at it, face and examine their own feelings, and thus begin to resolve the situation and make positive use of it.
- When some particular theme emerges in a group, the therapist's purpose will be to encourage members to explore their own position *vis-à-vis* the theme;

share and compare personal feelings, experiences, and assumptions; give and receive interpersonal feedback; and observe the consequences of own and others' behaviour.

- If a therapist perceives that a special opportunity is present for one person to experience a significant personal gain, the therapist's purpose will be to assist him or her to make maximum use of the opportunity. This may include supporting someone who is experiencing, or is on the verge of experiencing, a 'corrective emotional experience'. At the same time, the therapist will be alert to the impact on others, and look for opportunities to benefit them as well. This point also applies to situations in which two people are engaged in some mutually meaningful interaction.
- If a group which has been going well seems to regress or seize up, the therapist's purpose will be, first, to try to think out why this is happening, and then to take action on the basis of whatever hypothesis comes to mind, both to test the hypothesis and to see if acting on it enables constructive work to resume.

A purpose which underlies all else will be to carry out the kind of think-work described in Chapter 8.

It will be clear that, although I have avoided using the specialised language of group focal conflict theory, my comments have been influenced by having that theoretical framework in mind. Making use of plain language will, I hope, assist therapists of different theoretical persuasions to test these ideas against their own experience and translate them into their own preferred terminology.

HOW A THERAPIST MIGHT INTERVENE: THE CHOICES AVAILABLE

Interventions differ in their (a) form; (b) target; (c) choice of language; and (d) the tone of voice and body postures which accompany spoken words.

Forms of interventions

The range of possible interventions is very wide. It includes:

- Showing interest: for example, by brief comments such as 'This is an issue worth exploring', or by non-verbal behaviour which conveys attentiveness.
- Offering a read-out of events, or naming a situation: for example, 'When we first started today, there was a fairly lengthy silence and then people started to talk about a murder which was reported in this morning's newspapers.'
- Building into one's read-out a reference to something which has *not* happened: for example, 'At the start of this session, we probably all noticed that Alice was absent. So far, no one has mentioned this.'

- Inviting members to say how they have been feeling during the past few minutes while a discussion has been going on or some particular event has occurred: 'How did others feel, just now, when Anna criticised Ellen so directly?' or 'I can see that people were startled by what I just said, but can you say what you were feeling or thinking?'
- Inviting members to think back over a run of interactions and reflect on how each thought or felt at different times: for example, 'What happened just now was rather complicated: first James said he thought we are not getting any- where. Then some agreed with him and some disagreed. The subject changed to medications different people are on and whether they are helping or not. Then there was a silence. Let's think back on this, step by step.' This combines a read-out of events with invitations to members to reflect on how they were thinking and feeling. I think of this as a slow-motion action replay.
- Inviting wider participation: for instance by looking around the group, or by asking others to express or share their views about some group event or issue under discussion – for example, 'What do others think?' or 'Who else has something to say about this?', or 'Is it only James who feels this way, or does it ring bells with others?'
- Asking one person or the members in general to elaborate on what has just been said: for example, 'Can anyone say more about this?' or 'Ann, I am not sure that we understand yet what you are wanting to say'.
- Emphasising events which have just occurred by 'underlining' certain events, or by summarising or extracting from a longish run of events the kernel of what has happened: for example, 'What we've really been exploring is how hurt a parent can be when people stare at their handicapped child or act as if he were an object and not a person' or 'We have spent quite a bit of time discussing mixed feelings people can have about parents. This is important to practically everyone, though in different ways.'
- Naming what appears to be a shared concern: for example, 'So the main concern seems to be around what you'll be facing after you leave this hospital' or 'The gist of this discussion seems to be that people who haven't faced it themselves just don't know what it is like to see a relative gradually deteriorate through having Alzheimer's.'
- Giving a direct instruction to a group or to an individual about how to proceed, or what to stop doing: for example, 'Decide for yourself what you are going to say or not say' or (if contagion is building up) 'Stop! Let's sit down and talk about what is happening.'
- Giving direct advice to an individual who has presented a personal problem: for example, to someone who reports that he has just been told he is to lose his job and asks what he should do: 'I reckon the first things will be to figure out just how you feel about this and what your choices are.' (Note that the advice is not about what to do but about how to begin to think about the situation.)
- Referring a problem back to one or more of the members, after having been asked for help or advice: for example, 'I think this is something that members

of the group can tackle' or 'I think you will find a way to tell Ray how you feel when he says something you find hurtful.'

- Providing information: for example, 'I know that there have been a lot of rumours, but what really happened was. . . .'
- Offering choices, to the group in general or to particular individuals, in response to a specific request: for instance, if someone asks: 'How should we get started?', the therapist says 'Well, there are different possibilities: mentioning your name and saying something about yourself, or saying what brought you to the group, or saying how you are feeling now. . . .'
- Teaching, especially as to what constitutes useful feedback: for example, that it is useful for members to speak in terms of 'When you say (or do) that, I feel . . .' rather than to make judgements or offer interpretations of others' feelings or motives.
- Inviting members to reflect on the interpersonal consequences of their behaviour: for example, 'Ralph, what followed just now from you offering advice to Betty?' or 'No one was exactly criticising Frank just now, but they were criticising his favourite composer. What happened after that?'
- Offering credit to an individual or to the group: for example, 'That's something new that you haven't been able to do before' or 'The group could have avoided talking about this awful event which took place yesterday in this hostel but, instead, people have faced it and said how they feel about it.'
- Recognising that some one person has achieved something of particular importance to him or her: for example, 'This sounds like a turning point: you've allowed yourself a pleasant evening out instead of feeling compelled to study every minute' or 'Gerry, this is the first time I've heard you say you have felt really envious of your sister.' Such an intervention combines offering credit with underlining an event.
- Working within metaphors or other symbolic material: for example, if the members have been talking rather anxiously about cracks which have been appearing in the walls of the building, asking: 'How can we find out if this building is safe or not, and what can we do about it?'
- Assisting members to talk directly about an issue which is first expressed in terms of a metaphor, but doing so step by step: first, by extracting the emotional meaning from the metaphor and expressing it in general terms (for example, if the members have been talking about how indifferent and uncaring the women are who work in the hospital canteen, the therapist first extracts the emotional meaning from the metaphor by saying something like: 'It is worrying to feel that people you hope will be interested in you don't seem to care'). Then, depending on the members' response, the therapist might encourage the members to consider connections with personal experiences (for example, 'When else has this kind of thing happened to you?'). This in turn might be followed up by enquiring into possible relevance to the here-and-now situation (for example, 'What about here? Have you had such feelings right here in the group?')

- Turning something which looks like a problem held by one individual into a problem held by the group: for example, 'People have been trying to persuade Graham to change his mind but we haven't discussed yet why it is so important to everyone that he do so.'
- 'Naming the unnameable' or 'mentioning the unmentionable' – that is, putting into words something which is going on in the group or its environment, which everyone has noticed but no one is mentioning: for example,: 'We are tiptoeing around and not mentioning something we all know has happened – there has been a suicide on the ward' or 'Violet is saying how awful it is of her mother to say that she is getting fat, but I expect that we have all noticed that [turning to Violet] you *have* been gaining weight.'
- Sharing a personal opinion or feeling, in the context of a prevailing theme ('joining the group'): for example, when members of a group on a hospital ward are discussing forthcoming staff changes, saying: 'I've been thinking about this too, especially about how it might affect us and how we might handle things'; or, when people hear that one of the group members has been involved in a car crash, participating in the discussion as a member and saying, for instance: 'I would like to know whether she is hurt, and how badly.'
- Remaining silent. During a period when one is not sure what is going on, waiting until events begin to reveal what members are concerned about or wish to pursue. Or, when members have shown what their concerns are, giving them time to sort out the issue or work on the problem situation themselves.
- Casting a new light on a situation or placing meanings on events which are not evident to the members (interpreting). This can be done at the level of the group ('We seem to be getting more and more bothered by the break in group sessions which is about to occur'); or at the level of an individual ('You're saying that you never feel that anything you do is good enough'; 'Far from neglecting your child, you seem to be facing how important it is to find sources of satisfaction for yourself, and to keep everything in balance'); or at the level of interpersonal interactions between two people ('It looks like Ann and Frieda are getting into the same kind of quarrel that each of them used to have with their sisters'); or with respect to sub-group relationships ('New members seem to feel that they don't know their way around this group yet, and old members are not so sure they like a number of new people coming into the group all at once').

Any or all of these forms of intervention could be appropriate or the intervention of choice, depending on circumstances. They can also occur in combination, or in sequences.

The above list is not of course the only way to put names to therapist interventions. Pollack and Slan (1995) suggest that therapist interventions fall into five basic types: A: 'Return to sender' (the therapist asks for elaboration); B: 'Pass it along' (encouraging more members to participate and to respond to one another's comments and behaviours); C: Group level intervention – 'Look for the whole' (pointing to commonalities in issue or theme); D: Confrontation – 'Taking a hard look' (confronting individuals with the consequences of their behaviour; showing them their impact on others); and E: No leader intervention – 'the silent type' (choosing not to respond, but instead letting the group sort out its current problem).

The target of interventions

The 'how' of intervening includes the target of interventions. A therapist can address the group in general, or an individual, or two or more people in interaction one with another, or a sub-group, or (apparently) 'nothing' – that is, 'the air'.

At times, a therapist may address one person directly, especially to ensure that he or she has registered and noted some event which the therapist judges to be of particular importance to him or her. This does not require dwelling at length on one person. It can consist of offering a quick comment in a discussion in which many are participating. For instance, in a discussion about parents who make heavy demands on their children, the therapist might say: 'In your case, Philip, it was your father who expected such high things of you.' In a discussion of feeling depressed and no good, the therapist might say: 'Sarah, you are starting to see that it is not that you are no good, but that you tend always to *think* that you are no good.'

Choice of language

Choice of language may convey emotional closeness or distance. Using technical or professional language rather than everyday speech is likely to convey that there is a substantial gap between the therapist and the group members. Professional jargon may baffle members. Anything one has to say ought to be expressible in plain language. If this proves to be difficult, it indicates that one needs to think further about the meaning of a specialised term.

Tone of voice and body posture

The 'how' of intervening also includes the tone of voice and body posture which accompanies the content of the intervention. Interventions often have a kind of affective 'shimmer' which is part of the intervention itself. The accompanying 'affective message' may be as important as the content – sometimes, more important.

An accompanying tone of voice may convey blame, boredom, interest, support, superciliousness, or reproach. It may be excessively matey or excessively distant.

Kinseth (1982) points out that non-verbal behaviour – the therapist's own or that of members – can be used deliberately as a form of intervention or a focus for an intervention. He includes in his discussion 'non-verbal reinforcement' (head nods, smiles, leaning back or leaning forward) which can be used to emphasise something or to draw attention away from something; and 'non-interpretive feedback' (verbal references to members' tone of voice, body posture, hand gestures, and so on) which are ways of showing people what they are doing without offering an interpretation.

WHEN AND WHEN NOT TO INTERVENE

The following are some guidelines which can usefully be kept in mind when considering the timing of interventions, and when deciding whether to intervene at all.

Intervene when there is a need or an opportunity to pursue some purpose. Members might, for instance, need rescuing from a rapidly escalating sense that the group is an unsafe place. They might need assistance in moving away from some interactive pattern which is harming someone. There may be a need to intervene if some dynamic in the group as a whole is preventing the development of the group in gain-promoting ways. If the therapist realises that he or she has made an error there may be a need for an intervention directed towards retrieving the consequences of the error.

Special opportunities occur which may be supported or developed through a therapist's intervention(s). Opportunities to benefit more than one person at the same time occur when a theme connects with significant personal concerns of a number of the members. An event which has occurred in the group's environment may have special though somewhat different meanings for more than one person. Sometimes, two people become important to one another, with each 'standing for' someone important in the personal life of the other. In all these circumstances, exploration can be encouraged.

Don't intervene if pursuing one purpose interferes with achieving another which is, for the moment, more important. For example, a therapist might see an opportunity for benefiting one person in the very first session of a group. The therapist might also judge that to do so directly and explicitly at that time would undermine the sense of safety for others by conveying to them that the therapist now has a favourite. In such a case one instrumental purpose (directly pursuing benefit for one person) should temporarily be put aside in order to support another instrumental purpose (assisting the members to feel safe enough to take personal risks). Nothing is lost, because another opportunity to pursue benefit for one person will surely recur in another context which does not threaten the viability of the group and often carries the potential of benefit for others as well.

Don't intervene when the intervention is unlikely to be effective, or even heard. For example, there is no point in interrupting if a restrictive solution in the form of an off-target discussion is being supported unanimously through rapid-fire interactions amongst members. The time is not right and whatever the therapist says will not be heard or else will be received as a reproach.

Don't intervene when the members are doing good, effective work themselves, without the help of the therapist. Group members can often deal effectively with difficult situations arising in the group. It is good practice to preserve opportunities for them to do so. Dealing with a difficult situation on their own shows members that they have useful skills, and also provides an opportunity for them to gain experience in using skills. It follows that a therapist needs to monitor a difficult situation but may delay intervening so that group members have the opportunity to deal with the situation themselves.

This point also applies to situations in which members are interacting with one person sensitively and effectively. Group members are often in close emotional touch with one another's feelings. When their comments are closely in tune with other members' needs there is no point in interrupting or taking over the task oneself. One might decide to underline and emphasise, but doing more than this may very well not be needed.

If, on the other hand, one judges that a problem situation is not being addressed or that comments directed by members to one person are driven by defensive needs and are doing harm, it will be necessary to intervene. Therefore:

Intervene if damage is being done or about to be done to some individual. It is best not to do this by obvious direct attempts to protect, but rather by seeking to understand the dynamics – both group and interpersonal – which have led to the harm-doing and which are now holding it in place. It will be these dynamics which need addressing, in such a way as to render the harm-doing unnecessary.

Intervene when there are opportunities to 'pave the way' for effective work. Many situations arise in groups where the therapist can see a theme or issue beginning to emerge which it would be useful for group members to explore. However, the therapist might also note that the members are defending against exploring the theme. In other words, there is a gap between where the group is *now* and what the therapist considers would be more beneficial. The same point can be made about individuals: a therapist might have ideas about what would constitute a 'red-letter day' for a group member, yet perceive that much preparatory work needs to be done before that person can get to the nub of the problem. Simple interventions, such as summarising events, or showing interest in an issue under discussion, or putting a name to a prevailing theme, can help the group or one person to move closer towards potentially helpful explorations. 'Paving the way' involves moving a step at a time, starting in simple ways, with the intention of making opportunities for members to use their own skills and undertake their own explorations.

When considering directing a comment to an individual, keep in mind the state of the group. Members of a well-established group can tolerate the therapist paying sustained attention to one individual, especially if they perceive that person to be in crisis. If the group is still in its formative phase, attention to one individual can lead others to feel deprived. If one judges that a comment or a series of comments should be made to an individual and also that doing so could cause problems for others, it is possible to attend to one person but also to make room to pick up on the consequences later: for example, 'I talked with Denise at some length just now. How did others feel while that was going on?'

Intervene when something needs dealing with and the members run out of their own resources. This can happen when some external event impinges powerfully on the group, or one person behaves in a bizarre, frightening way, or two people engage in an intense mutual attack. Such events can generate almost unbearable tension in members whether or not they are directly involved. Withdrawal and immobilisation may follow, leaving no one but the therapist to deal with the situation. He or she must then do so. The therapist becomes, and must operate as, the members' last resort.

If confused by events, wait a bit before intervening. Sometimes a therapist is confused by group events, and has no idea of the meaning of what he or she is hearing and seeing. By deferring intervening, and meanwhile listening to and watching a group, a therapist can gain further information on which to base an hypothesis about what is going on, and why. Remaining silent for a time (meanwhile showing interest through non-verbal behaviour) can be the best course of action.

The guidelines just described may not be a complete set, even from my own point of view. I might be accepting some guidelines implicitly or taking them so much for granted that it does not occur to me to set them down. These points about when and when not to intervene should be regarded as being open to adjustment and augmentation.

HIGH-RISK AND LOW-RISK INTERVENTIONS AND SEQUENCES OF INTERVENTIONS

Some interventions are low-risk in the sense that, if ill-timed or unusable by the members, no really bad consequences follow. Amongst low-risk interpretations are offering a read-out of events, emphasising events by 'underlining' them, or asking for clarification or elaboration.

Some interventions are high-risk in the sense that, if ill-timed or unusable by the group, undesirable consequences are likely to ensue. I consider interpretations to be high-risk, with 'deep' interpretations carrying the highest risk of all. If members are baffled by a therapist's interpretation, or consider it far-fetched, or feel forced into acknowledging something they are not yet ready to face, then increased defensiveness is likely to follow. An interpretation addressed to the group as a whole which declares or implies that everyone is feeling the same way is likely to lead individuals to believe that their uniqueness is being overlooked or unappreciated. The therapist appears to be regarding each of them as just part of a mass, and each feels neglected. Asking probing questions of individuals is also high-risk, for the person concerned may feel pursued, and pushed by the behaviour and status of the therapist to move into realms which feel to be very hazardous. Offering prescriptive advice (which an individual may or may not see the sense of, or be able to follow) is a relatively high-risk intervention.

Referring to some interventions as high-risk and some as low-risk calls attention to trying to forecast the likely consequence of an intervention before actually making it. A therapist will wish to intervene in order to further the interests of individuals and to support the group as a gain-promoting environment. A therapist will wish to avoid intervening in ways which cause harm to individuals or set the group back. It is therefore well to keep in mind that different forms of intervention carry different likely consequences and different risks.

A further point is that not everything has to be done or can be done all at once. Explorations occur and understandings are achieved over a period of time. A therapist's interventions, too, are usually made over a time span, in a sequence which relates to some particular theme or pursues some particular purpose.

Interventions can be made in chains. I suggest that it is advantageous to begin with a low-risk intervention. Even something so simple as *giving a read-out* (summarising what has happened so far) can encourage members to explore an issue in a more direct way. If so, a read-out is all that is necessary for the time being. If the therapist sees that the members do not take the exploration forward on their own, he or she might introduce a further intervention along the same track or line, such as *inviting members to say how they had been feeling* while the events referred to in the read-out were going on.

As an example, suppose that three or four people are discussing recent experiences which involved friends or family members breaking promises, and are expressing anger and disappointment. The therapist may judge (in his internal think-track) that a theme is being explored which is likely to be relevant to everyone, and may decide that for the time being s/he need do nothing, since some of the members are already exploring the theme. The therapist might subsequently decide to support explorations by emphasising the feelings being expressed and sanctioning members' having them. He might say something like: 'It is understandable to feel really angry when someone disappoints you.' Later he might wish to encourage members to connect current with past experiences, and might ask the group in general: 'What other experiences of this kind have you had – perhaps earlier in your life?' As the discussion continues, the therapist may note that one of the members has been referring to earlier experiences but has not articulated his or her feelings in succinct terms. The therapist might decide to address the member directly and underline for him/her what in the therapist's judgement s/he is experiencing, saying something like: 'Mary, you seem to be saying that you've learned never to count on anyone because, that way, you won't be disappointed.' This comment can be regarded as a summary or else as an interpretation. If it is an interpretation it is very close to what Mary has been saying and is probably making use of the language which she herself has used. Suppose that the therapist thinks or suspects that group members feel angry or disappointed with him or her. If so, the therapist might enquire, at some point: 'Has that happened here? Have I broken a promise?' Still later the therapist might think that some of the members have been spectators for long enough and decide to ask, in a deliberately vague manner: 'What have others been thinking while this has been going on?'

Proceeding by chains of interventions, starting with low-risk ones, often makes offering an interpretation unnecessary, because individuals arrive at their own interpretations – by which I mean they arrive at new understandings of themselves, or of their impact on others, or of earlier experiences which keep some disadvantageous self-percept or behaviour pattern in place. The therapist often makes a substantial contribution to this by 'paving the way' through a series of lower-risk interventions. He or she may be able to stop short of offering an interpretation because the individual has become able to arrive at some new insight by him- or herself.

Proceeding by chains of interventions also enables the therapist to judge the impact of his or her initial interventions, and to take this into account when deciding what to do next. Sometimes a therapist follows through on the first intervention. Sometimes he or she changes tack because of the way in which member(s) have responded to an intervention. The therapist is engaging in 'continuous purposeful planning': each decision about when and how and why to intervene is made on the basis of reformulated understandings and reformulated purposes tied to successive events. 'Successive events' include but are not restricted to members' responses to therapist interventions.

THE ISSUE OF WHETHER AND WHEN TO CONCENTRATE ON ONE PERSON

I have already made the point that a therapist sometimes addresses one person directly, in and among a group discussion of some theme, in order to emphasise the meaning of the theme for that person. This is different from concentrating on one person at length.

Concentrating on one person at length is a group event. It is not merely an exchange between the therapist and one group member. It is an event which consists in the therapist dwelling on one person for a shorter or longer period of time, with the others as audience. Consequences follow. The person being concentrated on may become uneasy at being in the limelight for so long, and other members may feel left out, ignored, or deprived. They may feel that 'the therapist has a favourite, who is not me'. Feelings of envy, disappointment, anger, or despair may be stirred up. If this happens, something further has occurred in the group and the therapist has an additional task, which is to deal with the emotional residues for others. Another possibility is that the other members feel quite happy, even relieved, when the therapist engages with one person. As a group event, it functions as a defence for them because they are protected from having to reveal themselves. A quite different possibility is that the members of a group appreciate and accept an individual's need for special attention from the therapist. If others perceive that someone is experiencing a personal crisis, empathy and altruism are often activated, and no one interferes or feels angry or envious or deprived. In other words, different feelings and responses may be stirred up in group members when the therapist concentrates on one person. Which of them is present is not always immediately obvious. A therapist needs to watch and listen carefully to form an hypothesis, and sometimes will need to enquire of the group in order to get further clues on which to base a judgement.

If the therapist suspects that others feel relieved and protected because one person is the focus of the therapist's attention, he or she will need to decide whether to continue with the interaction or interrupt it. Continuing is, in effect, colluding with a shared defence in the group. Interrupting may leave one person high and dry. If the therapist judges that a person needs individual attention, s/he may provide it for a period of time but then enquire how others have been feeling. If the therapist thinks that others may be feeling envious or resentful, he or she will need to make opportunities for such feelings to be revealed and discussed. Whatever the therapist's internal hypothesis, a careful decision will have to be made about when to shift away from concentrating on one person, and how to help others to make use of the situation-as-event.

OFFERING INTERPRETATIONS IN GROUPS

Earlier I made it plain that I consider interpretations to be a high-risk form of intervention, especially if they impute unconscious motives or feelings to one person or to the members in general. In my own groups, I make infrequent use of interpretations. If I offer an interpretation I try to keep it close to the language used by the members themselves.

The issue of offering interpretations in groups deserves special attention for several reasons. First, many group therapists believe that it is their special task and responsibility to offer interpretations. Second, many options exist with respect to what an interpretation can be about, who or what may be its target, and possible consequences for those to whom an interpretation is and is not being directed. Third, interpretations occur first of all in the therapist's mind. A separate decision is then made as to whether and how to express them in words in the group.

An interpretation held in a therapist's mind could be about an individual, two people in interaction, sub-groups, the group as a whole, or some combination of these. As examples of combinations, a therapist might have ideas about a group-level theme and about the meaning of the theme for certain of the members. A therapist could have ideas about what an interaction between two people means to each of them, and about the impact of that interaction on other members.

An interpretation, if verbalised, could be directed towards an individual, a pair, a sub-group (or two sub-groups in interaction), the group as a whole, or to no one in particular – 'the air'.

In a group, a distinction can be made between the explicit target of an interpretation, the intended target, and the actual or effective target. The explicit target is not necessarily the same as the therapist's intended target, since a therapist might, for instance, hope that an interpretation addressed to one person is heard and used by certain others. A therapist might hope that an interpretation addressed to 'the air' is particularly registered by a particular group member, to whom he/she thinks it likely to be pertinent but does not, for the moment, want to single out. The actual or effective target of an interpretation may be different from either the explicit or the intended target. This happens when an interpretation meant for one person turns out to be meaningful to others, or when an interpretation directed to the group generally has a particular meaning for certain group members. An interpretation might mean something to someone who the therapist did not have in mind at all.

In a group, as in individual psychotherapy, an interpretation directed to one person may assist him or her to arrive at some new and useful personal understanding. In a group, as in individual psychotherapy, a possible undesirable consequence is that the person will feel overfaced and overwhelmed by what is being imputed by the interpretation, and in consequence become dysfunctionally anxious and disturbed. In both therapeutic settings, an individual to whom an interpretation is addressed may accept or reject it, make good use of it, find it irrelevant, or find it unbearably threatening.

There are some forms of interpretation which are never a good idea. These include 'plunging' interpretations; interpretations which declare or imply that everyone present has the same opinions or attitudes or motivations; and interpretations tinged with superiority, condescension, or any implication that 'I, the therapist, know the real truth'.

It was S.H. Foulkes who used the term 'plunging' interpretations to refer to interpretations which are so 'deep' that they are virtually out of sight from the patient's point of view. Foulkes offers the following example of an interpretation which plunges too far:

> Another example of what I consider an unwarranted type of interpretation is the following. The patient reported that when he was about sixteen, he had one day had an intuitive feeling that his house was being burgled and he telephoned home. When he got home, he found that the house had indeed been robbed, and he thought that his telephoning must have disturbed the burglars because they had been through his own and his sister's room and had been halfway through his parents' room when they broke off. The idea that he had interrupted the burglars made him feel omnipotent. After this he made his father put bars on all the windows and was so frightened that for two weeks he slept in the parents' bedroom. His therapist interpreted: 'The burglar whom you felt you must keep out is the bad father breaking in to have intercourse with mother. You feel that he will come and kill you for omnipotently and from a distance disturbing them in their room. Later you actually sleep in their room to make sure they don't have intercourse.'

(Foulkes 1968: 442–3)

This was an interpretation directed at one person while a group was in session. Equally plunging interpretations are sometimes directed towards the group as a whole, or to a person the therapist assumes is speaking for others.

Interpretations which declare or imply that everyone present has the same opinions or attitudes or motivations are inappropriate because such uniformity simply does not occur. Each person is unique and not exactly like any other. There are times when a mood or a feeling is shared across the group, or a theme surfaces which has meaning for everyone. Naming a theme which is important to all or most members is different from imputing the same motivation or feeling to everyone. Members can share in a theme while at the same time relating to it in different ways. The issue of what is shared and what is not is taken further in the next chapter, in the context of discussing situations and events which can arise in groups and not in individual psychotherapy.

Interpretations tinged with superiority, condescension, or any implication that the therapist knows the 'real truth' while others do not are a bad idea. Such interpretations are based on the assumption that the therapist is the custodian of 'the truth'. This is an indefensible assumption. Anyone's version of events, including that of the therapist, is from one person's perspective. Perspectives differ from person to person, and so do versions of events. Each will feel that he or she has grasped something true and real about the situation.

The meaning which a therapist imputes to some run of events could be skewed in some way, or just plain wrong. An interpretation which is offered in a superior or condescending manner places the therapist on a different plane from the patients, creating a distance between them which makes it more difficult for all concerned to see themselves as working together in a therapeutic or working alliance. An interpretation which is offered with total certainty leaves the group members with only two choices: accept it as given, or reject it. Opportunities to explore it tend to be closed off. I consider it better to offer an interpretation as an hypothesis to be discussed and investigated, rather than as 'the real truth'.

I do not mean to imply by this discussion that any point of view is as good as any other, for some are a better fit with observable events than others. There are times when the therapist's training, combined with his or her special therapist's position and stance in the group, places him or her in a better position than the group members to perceive meanings which underlie the manifest content of a patient's productions or a group discussion. There also are times when members see and understand things that the therapist does not see, or when members see things before the therapist does.

I have found the following quotations from the literature particularly interesting. Foulkes (ibid.: 443) said:

> Interpretation is only one of the analyst's functions. It is a slow process which, in a sense, goes on unceasingly and which only from time to time culminates in the actual act of making an interpretation in the strict psychoanalytic sense of the term. It is important not to add new elements without sufficient evidence

and instead, to develop slowly a new interpretation of what the patient is, says, or does from his own communications. These communications are originally disconnected by being expressed on different levels of language, as it were, and they are also separated in time by being dispersed over different sessions. Using to the full our psychoanalytic experiences, we must continuously be guided by the patient's own clues and avoid forcing our own schemata upon him.

Pines (1993a: 101) takes the view that interpretative work with individuals is essential in a long, ongoing analytic group. He comments:

My belief is that the therapist has always to earn the right to make any interpretation. Truths are always personal. There is no objective, impersonal truth given by a therapist who is pronouncing objective truth about the patient. To speak out what you believe to be true about another person's life is to engage with them in a shared encounter. Any interpretation is an intervention, an entry into the private space of the other, and it is not sufficient to say that the client has come to ask for such intervention. The therapist should act from a sophisticated compound of empathy and of informed understanding. We feel with and for the other and at the same time draw on all our knowledge of the human condition to give form to our understanding so that the other can listen, take in and make use of our words.

Much of my work in supervision has been to get therapists to put aside their interesting and often clever interpretation and instead begin to show the patient in a group their acceptance and their understanding of them. This is done by very simple non-verbal and unverbal gestures. As Foulkes said it is not what the therapist does but what the therapist is that is important in his or her work.

Yvonne Agazarian (1997: 56) has pointed out that in her Systems Centered Therapy (SCT) there is a relative absence of interpretations, and that:

Interpretations are actually a sophisticated way of indicating that you can read another's mind. Moreover, they often give the impression that you think you know something about others that they do not know themselves. One SCT substitute for making an interpretation is to reframe the interpretation as a hypothesis and to disclose the data that led you to your opinion. This invites the other person to see his or her situation through your eyes and to then decide about the fit between the hypothesis you offered and his or her own experience.

From these quotations I extract the following points:

• that offering an interpretation is just one option and that other forms of intervention can be appropriate;

- that it can take time for a therapist to formulate an internally held understanding of a person or a situation and that he or she then makes a separate decision about whether or not to express it in the group;
- that therapists need to be very, very careful and sensitive when formulating and then offering interpretations;
- that fancy, glib, or 'clever' interpretations are to be avoided;
- that an interpretation is best offered as an hypothesis (which of course it is); and
- that as important, or even more important, than offering interpretations is showing group members that one accepts and understands them.

There cannot be said to be consensus amongst group therapists about the nature and place of interpretations. Differences of opinion exist as to whether or not to offer interpretations, the forms which interpretations may usefully take, their 'depth', to whom they may be directed, and so on. These differing views are well displayed if one examines, in combination, an article by Scheidlinger (1987a), brief comments on this article by three discussants, and Scheidlinger's rejoinder (1987b).

Scheidlinger provides an historical account of 'interpretation', as used in therapeutic work, beginning with Freud. He argues that 'insight-promoting interventions' in group psychotherapy include explanation and facilitation, clarification, and confrontation, as well as interpretation. Interpreting the unconscious motivations which underlie behaviour is seen as crucial and as the particular province of the group therapist, who has been trained for the task. Comments on his paper, provided by Horwitz, Graham, and Napolitani, show convergent and divergent points of view. Differences of opinion have to do with whether or not it is necessary for a therapist to offer interpretations; whether offering interpretations should be relegated to the therapist or is (inevitably and desirably) a process in which everyone participates; and how other forms of intervention connect with interpretations – especially whether they are themselves forms of interpretation or whether they are distinctive forms of intervention which can be valuable in themselves, or else lead up to therapist-provided interpretations, or else obviate the need for interpretations.

In examining such differences of opinion it should be pointed out that Scheidlinger had in mind *psychodynamic psychotherapy*, in which emphasis is placed on the development of self-awareness and insight. If one looks more broadly at populations of people who might benefit from some form of group experience, it becomes clear that self-awareness and insight is important for some populations and not for others. This is a reminder that therapists need always keep in mind the population they are working with and what they hope that members of that population will achieve. Again, one returns to the point that groups can serve diverse populations – as discussed in Chapter 2 – and that both the structure and the conduct of the group need to be adjusted accordingly.

SPONTANEITY, FLEXIBILITY, RULES AND GUIDELINES

I have been emphasising in this chapter that interventions ought to be made on the basis of internal think-work and a therapist's best prediction as to the likely consequences of an intervention, both for individuals and for the group.

What of spontaneity? By dictionary definition, 'spontaneous' means 'springing from a sudden impulse; unpremeditated' (*Longman's Dictionary of the English Language*). There are times when a therapist responds instantaneously, even impulsively, to some group event. Spontaneous interventions may be triggered by a therapist registering some group event without realising that he or she is doing so. This is what happened in example 2 in Chapter 11, where one of the therapists suddenly and without thinking it out beforehand asked the members: 'Has anyone been thinking about Brigitte?' (As a reminder, this was the situation in which group members, after hearing that Brigitte's father had been seriously injured in a car accident, spent twenty minutes discussing how pointless it is to read newspapers or watch the news on television, since one hears nothing but bad news.) The therapist intervened quite spontaneously. It was only afterwards, when listening to the audio-tape of the session, that he and his co-therapist realised that a group member had just said that if one never reads newspapers or watches the news one misses out on a great deal. This comment was not registered by the therapists at the time but nevertheless was the trigger for the spontaneous intervention. As this example showed, spontaneous interventions can be appropriate and effective – just exactly right – if the therapist is sufficiently in tune affectively with the group members. In contrast, a spontaneous intervention could be made in response to some suddenly intensified sense of personal threat. In such a case, the intervention is less likely to fit the situation or the needs of the members. These points lead to a somewhat odd conclusion: 'Be spontaneous, but be careful about it.' What this means is that spontaneous interventions are most likely to be effective if the therapist has been attending closely to what group members have been saying and doing, and is emotionally in tune with their feelings.

It may be worth pointing out that there is a distinction between 'spontaneity' and 'intuition'. It is possible to say that a therapist 'responded intuitively' but this is, strictly speaking, incorrect, for intuition refers to grasping the meaning of a situation while spontaneity refers to taking some action. (See the dictionary definition of 'intuition' provided towards the end of Chapter 8.) Intuition and spontaneity have different meanings but are related in practice, in that a therapist's spontaneous intervention may be based on his or her intuitive grasp of the meaning of contemporary events.

Therapists sometimes make rules for themselves, such as 'never answer personal questions'; 'never share personal feelings'; 'never provide personal information about oneself'. The problem with such rules is the word 'never'. One ought to substitute 'hardly ever'. In most circumstances these rules make sense, for the group is not there for the therapist to make use of as if he or she were another member.

However, as was discussed in the preceding chapter, there are times when rigid adherence to a rule can be an error. There are times when rules ought to be broken.

Guidelines are different from rules in that rules tend to be prescriptive while guidelines function to support order and consistency without being prescriptive. By dictionary definition, a guideline is 'an indication or outline of policy or conduct'; 'a principle or model on which a course of action may be based' (*Longman Dictionary of the English Language*). The term derives from engineering drawing, where guidelines are the parallel lines which aid in keeping one's printing consistent and in line. I have offered guidelines of several kinds earlier in this chapter, for instance by listing a range of interventions from which choices can be made, and by suggesting what can usefully be kept in mind when choosing when and when not to intervene. None of these are rules or prescriptions, for the good reason that a therapist needs to choose from amongst interventions in the face of unique, ever-changing situations. Judgement is always required.

Chapter 16

The therapist in the group

The previous chapter focused on why, how and when a therapist might intervene in the course of a group session or over a series of sessions. In this chapter I shall take a longer view of the therapist in the group, examining some broader issues which stem from there being five to seven or eight or so patients or clients in a group rather than just one. The discussion will include attention to situations that face group therapists which do not arise in one-to-one therapy; the therapist's position in the group; and implications for how a therapist may make use of a *group* in order to benefit individual group members. The chapter is organised as follows:

- Similarities between individual and group psychotherapy.
- Some obvious differences between the group as a medium for therapeutic work and one-to-one-psychotherapy, and some not-so-obvious consequences.
- Situations and events which can arise in groups which do not occur in individual psychotherapy, and how a therapist may respond to them.
- Some complexities concerning transference dynamics in groups.
- The position of the therapist in the group: purpose and task, power, responsibility, and information; closeness, distance, and neutrality.
- How may a therapist make use of a *group* in order to benefit individual members?
- The group therapist as a person.

SIMILARITIES BETWEEN INDIVIDUAL AND GROUP PSYCHOTHERAPY

Group and individual psychotherapy have in common their purpose, which is to benefit the individual patient or client. If working from a psychodynamic perspective (broadly defined), a therapist expects the patient(s) to reveal personal experiences and feelings, and to reflect on them. The therapist expects to facilitate patients' explorations and reflections, and help them to make sense of them and learn from them. In both contexts, patients (or group members) reveal themselves in what they say, the stories they tell, how they think about their current and past experiences and about the connections between them, and how they interact with whoever else is present, whether a therapist only, or one or two therapists and a number of fellow group-members.

In both settings, individuals bring particular expectations, fears, and hopes to the therapeutic situation. They have feelings about and expectations of the therapist, seeing him or her as a potential source of help and sometimes also as a source of disappointment or a target of deserved anger or resentment. In both settings, individuals are likely to want to change and yet be loath to give up habitual ways of thinking, feeling, and viewing themselves and others in their salient worlds. In both settings, therapists strive constantly to improve their understanding of the patient(s), to perceive the import of successive events, to intervene in helpful ways, and to be alert to their personal reactions to the patient(s) and to ongoing events.

Many therapist interventions are appropriate in either group or individual psychotherapy. These include, for instance, inviting elaboration, 'underlining' certain events, extracting from an extended run of events the kernel of what has been expressed or has happened, and offering credit. A therapist can offer interpretations in both settings but, as has been discussed in the preceding chapter, interpretations can take more and different forms in group psychotherapy as compared with individual psychotherapy.

SOME OBVIOUS DIFFERENCES BETWEEN THE GROUP AS A MEDIUM FOR THERAPEUTIC WORK AND ONE-TO-ONE-PSYCHOTHERAPY, AND SOME NOT-SO-OBVIOUS CONSEQUENCES

In a group, there are five or six or seven patients or clients rather than just one, and there may be co-therapists. This is so obvious that it may seem hardly worth mentioning. However, though it is an obvious difference it is not a *simple* one, for much follows from it.

Group members interact with one another and not just with the therapist. These interactions can be seen and heard by the therapist and by all the members. In one-to-one psychotherapy, here-and-now interactions are necessarily between the patient and the therapist. Interpersonal interactions with others may be reported to the therapist but none of them is directly observable in the therapeutic setting. In a group, it is not only the therapist who forms views about a patient, and it is not only the therapist who sometimes comments about or imputes meaning to what someone has said or done. In a group, how members respond to one another and what they say about one another become part of the material available to the therapist and to the group. Group members will sometimes support one another, sometimes oppose one another; sometimes function as helpful therapists, sometimes threaten or undermine others.

In a group there is the possibility that individual expectations, fears, and hopes will converge or diverge. Members sometimes join together to support the emergence of some theme. Sometimes individual members interfere with the emergence of a theme, or give it a particular twist. Members may collude in maintaining some defence in the group. Attacks on the therapist may of course occur in both group and individual therapeutic settings, but in the group there may be concerted attacks on the therapist, which tend to have a greater emotional impact because of the power of unanimity. In a group, contagion of affect or of behaviour can occur. Norms, shared beliefs, degrees of cohesiveness, and other group-level phenomena emerge from interactions and communications amongst members. These phenomena do not occur in one-to-one psychotherapy.

Certain consequences follow for the therapist. In individual psychotherapy, the therapist attends exclusively to the patient or client, who is of course the only person present besides him- or herself. In group psychotherapy, the therapist attends to each group member as an individual *and* to the ways in which members interact and respond to one another *and* to group-level phenomena generated by their communications and interactions, *and* to him- or herself as a participant in the group, *and* to connections amongst all these.

A broader range of interventions is available to a group therapist compared with an individual therapist. For instance, a group therapist might invite interpersonal comparisons, or invite members who have been silent to say something about how they felt during some dramatic event in the group, such as two members quarrelling.

SITUATIONS AND EVENTS WHICH CAN ARISE IN GROUPS WHICH DO NOT OCCUR IN INDIVIDUAL PSYCHOTHERAPY, AND HOW A THERAPIST MAY RESPOND TO THEM

Such situations include:

1 shared themes;
2 collusive defences;
3 member-constructed metaphors;
4 behaviour on the part of one member which is regarded as a problem by other members;
5 concerted attacks on one person by most or all of the others;
6 interpretations, advice, and feedback offered by members to one another;
7 non-participating members; and
8 emotional or behavioural contagion.

All of these situations have been referred to and discussed in previous chapters, often in connection with concrete examples. I am bringing them together here to emphasise the special character of the group as a medium for psychotherapy.

Shared themes

In therapeutic groups, shared themes emerge from the interactions of members, or are 'given' to the group by the therapist in the form of a topic, or are given to the group by the therapist and then transformed by the members into something which may be a little different, or a good deal different.

In a group, one of the ways in which a therapist can increase his or her understanding of each group member is to observe how individual members contribute to or react to an emerging theme or an introduced topic. An important route towards personal gain consists in members exploring within shared themes, and comparing and contrasting own experiences and feelings and assumptions with those of others. It follows that it is important that a therapist keeps in touch with how a theme is developing, how it is being shaped and transformed through the interactions of the members, and how members are participating in it or reacting to it.

Therapeutic processes are supported if the therapist allows themes to emerge through the members' interactions, or gives scope to members to respond to a therapist-introduced theme in their own ways. This often simply means not directing or interrupting the group too much. If members are free to develop or shape themes, they will either influence themes towards something meaningful to them, or else conspicuously avoid some theme, or prevent a theme which is present at a covert level from surfacing more explicitly. Consider the first possibility: while a particular theme, meaningful to some or to most of the members, prevails, a therapist may invite wider and fuller participation, in order to encourage more people to explore within the theme and make explicit their position *vis-à-vis* the theme. A therapist may sometimes explicitly invite members to compare and contrast individual feelings and experiences related to the theme. A therapist may refer to the convergence or divergence of individuals' feelings, attitudes, and stance towards a prevailing theme, with the same end in mind. If members deviate from a theme, or abandon a theme abruptly, the therapist will try to understand the reasons for this, and will need to decide whether to draw the members back to the theme or to let it go. If the therapist decides to let a theme go, he or she will still hold it somewhere in mind as a piece of unfinished business in the group, and will be alert to signs of it re-emerging. Consider the second possibility: that members are conspicuously avoiding some theme. The therapist will pick up indications of this from the context or from disguised references to the theme. He or she will then be alert to any indication that members are ready to acknowledge and work within the theme, or may see how to 'pave the way' for them to do so.

One sometimes hears it said that one member may 'speak for' the group. This phrase can be a little misleading. I believe that what happens is that one person says something which resonates with the concerns, fears, or hopes of others. Others then allow or encourage the speaker to continue, or may join in. The speaker does not *intend* to 'speak for' anyone else, and may not realise that he or she is expressing something which connects with the feelings or views of others. 'Speaking for the group', when it occurs, could be a part of theme-building. It could initiate a new theme, as would occur when one person is the first to acknowledge a feeling or respond to some significant outside event.

Collusive defences

In a group, collusive defences can take several different forms. Sometimes, preferred personal defences held by different group members are similar enough to lead members to support one another in maintaining them. Everyone, or at least everyone who speaks, supports denial, or avoidance, or intellectualising, and so on. This lends power to the defence, for 'unanimity lends validity'. Another form of collusive defence involves role differentiation, in which one member is pressed or cued into behaving in a way which serves the needs of the others.

Such collusive defences are functional in that they protect members from certain fears. They also disallow exploration of whatever feelings or impulses or wishes are associated with the fears. If maintained, collusive defences interfere with therapeutic processes or may cause harm to the person who is being held in a particular role. It behoves the therapist to be alert to the possibility that collusive defences could become established. The therapist may note whether and in what context they arise, and whether members through their own efforts become able to relinquish the defence, or, in contrast, require help from the therapist. I have emphasised in previous chapters that challenging a collusive defence directly is less effective than striving to alleviate the fears which are holding it in place.

Member-constructed metaphors

Members of groups sometimes get into a conversation which the therapist understands to be a metaphor that refers to feelings about the group or being in the group. Examples of metaphors appeared in some of the previous chapters: group members discussed recordings which are compilations of different pieces of music, and wondered whether they were worthwhile or not; members had noticed cracks in the walls of the building, and wondered whether it was safe or not; members talked about how uncaring the women were who worked in the hospital canteen. These can justifiably be regarded as metaphors which refer to how the patients are feeling about the therapist or the group. Otherwise, why would such topics, amongst all the possible ones which might come up in conversation, just happen to happen? Metaphors both express and conceal feelings – that is, feelings are being expressed, but in a way which allows members to avoid recognising or acknowledging them.

When faced with a member-constructed metaphor, a therapist has four choices: to ignore it and let it run on; to join the members in the metaphor and work within it; to move step by step towards discussing the feelings contained in the metaphor more explicitly; or to interpret the metaphor to the members.

I suggest that in the first instance it is best to do nothing, in case the members can work their own way out of needing to operate in terms of a metaphor. As an example, suppose that members have been discussing whether the architect who designed the building was competent or not. It is a tall building and sometimes it sways in the wind. Is it sound? Are the foundations strong enough? Did the architect know what he was doing? The therapist understands this to be a metaphor which expresses shared concerns about the group and the competence of the therapist. He or she also realises that the members are not aware of the meanings contained in and concealed by the metaphor. The therapist first of all listens and waits to see how the members develop this metaphor. Suppose that the members eventually decide that the architect must have been competent after all since the building has already stood for some years without collapsing. If they move on to some other theme related to personal experiences, the therapist may judge that there is no reason to intervene. The therapist will, however, hold in mind that concerns about the reliability of the therapist (and of whoever the therapist stands for in the personal lives of the patients) may surface again, probably in a more accessible form.

A second option is to work *with* the group members within the metaphor. Gil Katz (1983) provided the following example, which occurred in the course of a hospital ward meeting. These meetings were held in the dayroom, in which there happened to be a large fish tank. A major turnover of therapists was announced and, immediately afterwards, the patients began to talk about the fish. A patient whose job it was to feed the fish suddenly remembered that he was soon to be discharged. Who would feed the fish? Others began to worry about the fish. Who would look after them? Would they starve? Would they just be forgotten? The staff responded entirely within the terms of the metaphor, taking the matter seriously, helping the patients to make sure that the fish continued to be well looked after and encouraging the patients to see to it that the fish were fed immediately, while the meeting was still in session. Everyone was relieved. The imminent change in therapists was not discussed in this meeting, and the relevance of the discussion about the fish to the forthcoming change was not made explicit, either then or later. During the next ward meeting the members talked directly about the changeover. Katz, in his discussion of this episode, makes the point that these were psychotic patients, and that an interpretation risked generating intense and intolerable anxiety and could lead to the mobilisation of massive defences or else to an upsurge in psychotic symptoms. On these grounds, Katz argued against interpreting the metaphor. An interpretation would have been technically correct. It was the likely consequences which would have been undesirable.

A third option when faced with a member-constructed metaphor is to work gradually towards the members' being able to leave the metaphor behind. Suppose that, in the example about the architect, events unfolded in another way. Suppose that the members get stuck inside the metaphor, and there is no sign of movement. The therapist, judging that there would be advantages in discussing the feelings directly, wants to help the members to move towards more explicit discussion of their feelings. He or she might begin by using the language of the metaphor: 'You're not sure whether you can trust this architect or not.' Members are likely to agree, for this, after all, is what they have been saying. The therapist might then

decide to emphasise the feelings contained within the metaphor without immediately attaching them to dynamics in the group: for example, 'It's hard to feel you
may not be able to trust a person you ought to be able to rely on.' Depending on
how this intervention is received, the therapist might go on to ask: 'When else has
this sort of thing happened?', and then, perhaps: 'How about here?' Each successive
intervention depends on how the members responded to the previous one. By such
a series of interventions, members may become able to move beyond needing to
speak in metaphoric terms, and begin to discuss their feelings about the therapist
and the group more directly. The therapist has not offered an explicit interpretation,
though he or she is moving towards one. Sometimes members arrive at their own
interpretation. For instance, someone might say: 'I see now why we were talking
about the architect.' Seeing the connection between the metaphor and here-and-now
feelings is not, however, essential to movement. Members can move away from
speaking in terms of a metaphor to more direct explorations of their feelings without
realising that they *have* been utilising a metaphor, and without understanding it as
a vehicle for expressing their own feelings. In some groups, the therapist might
want to make the meaning of the metaphor explicit for educational purposes. For
instance, in groups for people who are training to become therapists or professional
helpers (category 9 in Chapter 2) the therapist will want members to become alert
to member-constructed metaphors as a group phenomenon, and to their possible
underlying meanings.

The fourth option is to interpret the metaphor. I suggest that this carries
considerable risks. An interpretation, especially if offered early, can lead members
to feel that they have been detected in holding feelings for which they might
be punished (for instance, that they have been harbouring critical feelings toward
the therapist and that the therapist will reproach them or lose interest in them).
Or members might privately conclude that the therapist has far-fetched ideas
(for instance, that what is said about an architect could have anything to do with the
group). Such reactions could lead members to mistrust the therapist, or become
more wary of expressing themselves than before; neither of which, of course, the
therapist wants to see happen.

Behaviour on the part of one member which is regarded as a problem by other members

As discussed in Chapter 11, situations sometimes arise in groups in which one
person is seen by the other members or by the therapist as *having* or *being* a problem.
For instance, one member may monopolise the group, or elicit advice and then
reject it, or conspicuously refuse to conform to some norm or belief which others
want to institute or maintain. Such individuals tend to become central in the group,
for a time. Even if others suffer in silence, they are preoccupied by the 'problem
person'. Other members may try to persuade, advise, or coax the person into
changing his or her behaviour or attitudes. In the end, members may attack the
person, out of exasperation. A 'problem person' needs help, and so do the other

members. The problem person needs help with the problem behaviour itself, and may need to be protected from harm generated by how others respond. The others need help too, for they have become increasingly frustrated and angry and are losing opportunities for personal benefit. Such situations typically contain opportunities for the other members to gain by examining their responses to the problem person, which can include the inability to express anger and resentment through fears of becoming destructive.

A useful intervention is to point out that the situation is a problem for the group as a whole and is not located solely in one person. Possible interventions are: 'Why is it so important for everybody that John sees things the way everyone else does?' or 'I wonder why people are behaving in ways which keep John's behaviour going, even though they seem not to like it.' Such interventions direct the attention of the other members to their own needs and feelings, tend to give John a breathing space, and often pave the way for some change advantageous to all.

Concerted attacks on one person by most or all of the others

Four distinguishable dynamics can underlie concerted attacks on one person. They are: (a) scapegoating; (b) displaced attacks; (c) attacks on individuals who deviate from an existing or an emerging norm or shared belief; and (d) attacks on individuals who behave in a way which others regard as spoiling the group.

The dynamic of scapegoating is described in the Bible (Leviticus 16: 8–34). The crucial points are made in verses 10, 21 and 22 (quoted from the Authorised King James Version):

> But the goat on which the lot fell to be the scapegoat, shall be presented alive before the Lord, to make an atonement with him, *and* to let him go for a scapegoat into the wilderness.

> • • •

> And Aaron shall lay both his hands upon the head of the live goat, and confess over him all the iniquities of the children of Israel, and all their transgressions in all their sins, putting them upon the head of the goat, and shall send *him* away by the hand of a fit man into the wilderness:
>
> And the goat shall bear upon him all their iniquities unto a land not inhabited: and he shall let go the goat in the wilderness.

If one reads the fuller account one sees that there are two goats, one sacrificed to the Lord and the other, as just described, laden with the sins of the Jewish people and banished to the wilderness. In the Leviticus account, the scapegoat was banished, not killed. However, Scheidlinger (1982) points out: that in later days the goat was killed by being pushed over a cliff near Jerusalem; that the magical belief that exculpation could be achieved by sacrificing an animal figured in primitive rites in other cultures; and that Roman priests sacrificed goats and dogs as embodiments of citizens' evils.

The magical belief that guilt can be done away with by such means persists. In contemporary language one might say that the sins of the many are 'projected' on to one person, who is banished, ostracised, reviled, or otherwise punished. This is the precise meaning of the term 'scapegoat'. Heap (1965) discusses the operation of this dynamic in youth groups, and Scheidlinger (1982) discusses its relevance to therapeutic groups.

A displaced attack is different. One person is attacked in lieu of another, against whom anger is really felt. Usually, a group member is chosen as a target of attack when the anger is really being felt towards the therapist. A direct attack on the therapist is experienced as being risky, so the members find a safer target.

Attacks on a person who deviates from an existing or emerging norm or shared belief are usually rooted in fear. The norm or the belief is experienced by the other members as essential to a sense of safety in the group. The person who cannot accept the norm or belief threatens this sense of safety. As an initial response, members often try to coax and persuade the deviant member to join them in supporting the norm or the belief. If this fails, anger and attack may follow, or the deviant may be dismissed as not worth bothering about.

Group members do not always attack individuals regarded as spoiling the group (monopolisers, help-rejecting complainers, and so on), at least not at first. As is the case with norm-violators, members may try persuasion, usually with no effect. Frustration and anger build up. Sometimes anger is expressed directly, sometimes in indirect ways. Sometimes members are unable to express their anger directly because they fear becoming unacceptably destructive.

Concerted attacks tend to look alike in that everyone gangs up on one person, but the underlying dynamics differ, as just described. Here and there, in the literature, one sees scapegoating equated with any form of concerted attack. This is an error, since scapegoating is a very specific dynamic, and just one of several possible underlying mechanisms. A therapist who has some idea of the particular dynamic underlying an attack is more likely to intervene appropriately. When a person is being scapegoated, a useful intervention is: 'Is it really only Jack who has ever done [felt] thus-and-such?' In response to a displaced attack, a useful intervention is: 'Wait a minute! I think it is really me who has behaved in a way that Phyllis is being attacked for.' An attack on a deviant member is best responded to by asking the group: 'Why is it so important that Eugene believes [behaves] in line with everyone else?' In response to a situation in which one person is seen as spoiling the group, a useful intervention is to ask the group in general: 'How have people been feeling while Anita has been complaining at some length [interrupting, asking for advice and then saying it won't work, repeatedly returning to her problems with her daughter, not participating, and so on]?'

It should be noted that in individual psychotherapy, concerted attacks cannot arise, so the therapist is not faced with any of the underlying dynamics described here. These underlying dynamics need to be recognised and dealt with, first, to maintain the group as a context for therapeutic help *and*, second, to make positive use of the situation for personal gain.

Interpretations, advice, and feedback offered by members to one another

Interpretations impute meanings to what someone has just said or done. Advice consists of how someone thinks someone else should feel about some situation or what they should do about it. Feedback provides information about how one or several people feel about what someone else has just said or done. All three are offered by one or several group members to another group member: there is always a target person.

Sometimes, interpretations, advice, and feedback fit the person to whom they are directed and are expressed in usable terms. However, this is not always the case. An interpretation may be inaccurate, and a piece of advice may miss the point of an individual's actual concerns and feelings. Or what is said may be heavily loaded with negative affect which makes it difficult for the target person to hear it and use it. Feedback, in particular, can be a vehicle for attack or destructive criticism, taking the aggressive form of 'Let me tell you what I really think of you'. Listening carefully to what is being offered in the way of interpretations, advice, or feedback often reveals much about the person offering the interpretation, and so on. Sometimes what is being said is hardly relevant at all to the target person.

If the therapist judges that what is being said fits the person concerned and is expressed in a usable way, he or she may say nothing, or may support what has been said by underlining it. If the therapist thinks that a comment directed to one person is inaccurate or off the point or is a disguised form of attack, it will be appropriate to encourage the members to review the exchange which has just occurred, looking to what was said and how each person felt as the situation developed. The person offering the interpretation, advice, or feedback can find out how his or her comments were received, and may realise that something from his or her own current or past experience has prompted his/her comment. The target of the comment can say how he or she felt, elaborate on what he or she felt or said, and/or offer modifications or corrections. The 'help' which was offered was not really help, but it was nevertheless an opportunity for learning. All can learn from the situation.

The general point being made here is that feedback, advice, and proffered interpretations can be influenced by personal needs and heavily loaded with unrecognised projections. Members' own feelings and assumptions get tangled up in the feedback and the interpretations which they offer. Comments addressed by one person to another may mix up, in one big bundle, own feelings, judgements about others, assumptions about others' motivations which are not accurate or justified, and assumptions about what others ought to feel or do. This kind of thing happens in everyday life. People offer 'advice' to one another in the form of 'You ought not to feel like that' or 'Why don't you try ignoring him'. They express such opinions as 'You're being uncooperative' or offer interpretations and explanations such as 'You're probably just depressed'. People may bring with them, into the group, habits of thinking and speaking which do not further the therapeutic process. If this happens, no one gains: the person to whom comments are directed does not gain, for the comments are off the point or destructive; the senders do not gain, for they are unaware that personal needs and assumptions are influencing their perceptions and opinions.

It follows that teaching, of a particular kind, is often useful. Group members sometimes need to learn to sort out their own feelings from what they presume are the feelings of others. They profit from seeing how their own feelings and assumptions influence what they think about others and what they say to them. It can be useful to call to the attention of members that it is possible to distinguish between (a) what someone else actually has done or said; (b) one's own internal responses to this – the feelings and opinions stirred up by the other's behaviour; (c) what one thinks or assumes that the other feels, needs, is denying, and so on, and/or should do or think; and (d) what one then actually says or does. This of course is always done in context. The teaching does not have to be done in a 'teachy' way, and can be done in a series of comments rather than in one big one.

I have emphasised that the teaching is 'of a particular kind' because I want to make it clear that I am not thinking of didactic forms of teaching.

Non-participating members

It is relatively easy for one person to remain silent in a group, if he or she prefers to do so, because in a group the silent person is shielded by the active participation of others.

Most therapists and group workers take the view that persons who participate actively are more likely to achieve benefit than those who remain in a spectator position. On the whole this opinion is justified. A person who remains a spectator cannot influence the group in directions which are particularly relevant to his or her own concerns. Interpersonal comparisons occur covertly and there is therefore no way for others to offer explicit support or commentary. Opportunities to test out in action the consequences of particular ways of behaving and expressing oneself are precluded.

Although some important opportunities for personal gain are lost if a group member remains silent, other opportunities remain, always providing the silent person is participating emotionally in the events of the group and is not altogether tuned out. What may go on inside a mostly non-participating group member which makes gain possible? One possibility is that, in the context of some prevailing group theme, the non-participating person may be reflecting internally on personal feelings and experiences related to the theme. Another possibility is that the non-participant may be comparing own feelings and experiences with those being recounted by others, internally and privately. Still another possibility is that the person achieves emotional learning through observing that others behave in ways which seem risky *and* are not criticised or ridiculed by others and do not experience undue distress. Through observing this, a non-participating member may feel freer to shift his or her own behaviour. Example 12 in Chapter 12 showed a gain made by a non-participating member. It also showed that whatever has influenced the change may remain unknown.

Bernard (1994) has described three approaches to encouraging a silent person to participate: asking the person to say something about his or her experience of being in the group and about feelings connected with revealing the self; asking others how they feel and think about the silent person; and talking about the therapist's own feelings when struggling to help the silent person to participate. Note that none of these involves putting direct pressure on the silent person to talk. In addition to reflecting on the impact of the group on a silent person, one may reflect on the impact of the silent person on the other members. A person who is silent may or may not influence the group. A silent person will have no discernible impact on the course of the group if others accept his or her silence as no more than the expression of a personal preference for how to behave. However, it is also possible for one person's silence to become the repository for fantasies on the part of the others. If so, the impact on the group is substantial. It is not the silence itself, but the meanings which others put on it, and how they respond to it, which makes the difference.

Escalations of anxiety or uneasiness fuelled by member interactions

Sometimes emotional or behavioural contagion occurs in a therapeutic group, or something happens which is so unexpected, so disturbing, that the members are immobilised and can do nothing in the face of it. Yet whatever triggered the contagion is regarded by the therapist as important and not to be ignored. Ignoring it would not only lose an opportunity for therapeutic work, but would collude in the members' belief that the issue or situation is too difficult, too highly charged to be faced.

If contagion occurs, simple commands may be appropriate, starting with a simple but emphatic 'STOP!' This tends to interrupt the contagion, and the therapist can follow through by inviting members to say what they have been feeling during and just prior to the episode of contagion (see example 3 in Chapter 11).

A situation may fall short of contagion, yet the therapist notes mounting tension or uneasiness, or may realise that the end of the session is approaching and judge that it is important that the members do not carry an unresolved issue away with them. It is then the therapist's responsibility to do something. It is up to the therapist to 'name the unnameable' or 'mention the unmentionable'. An episode of contagion, or of mounting tension, is one of the circumstances in which the therapist may have to function as the members' 'last resort'. I am thinking of quite simple comments which do no more (and no less) than name what is happening. In line with Fritz Redl's thinking, the therapist performs the 'initiatory act', thus taking responsibility for opening up the issue for discussion, and demonstrating to the members that it is possible to examine a fraught situation without bad consequences following.

SOME COMPLEXITIES CONCERNING TRANSFERENCE DYNAMICS IN GROUPS

I have not included a discussion of transference in the preceding section because transference can occur in both individual and group psychotherapy, though it takes different forms in each.

Tutman (1993: 98–9) describes Freud's definition of transference thus:

> the patient directs toward the therapist intense feelings that are based on no real relationship between them but that can be traced back to old wishful conflict-laden fantasies and impulses that are often repressed.

This definition refers to a dynamic which sometimes occurs in individual psychoanalysis. In the early days of group psychotherapy, some theorists saw no need to modify this view of transference. Wolf and Schwartz (1962), in their book *Psychoanalysis in Groups*, emphasised that they focused on each individual in the group, exploring each person's transference relationships with the therapist. For them, Freud's definition was both applicable and sufficient. Others expanded the concept, but in a particular way. The group as a whole was regarded as an entity which formed transference relationships with the therapist. Still other group therapists recognised that members could become transference figures for one another. Nowadays it is generally understood that the concept of transference, if applied to groups, has to be expanded.

This still leaves the question of the specific forms which transference can take in groups. A review of the many examples provided in previous chapters. with this question in mind, reveals the following.

With reference to transference dynamics amongst group members, sometimes one person becomes important to one other person through 'standing for' a parent or sibling or some other significant person in earlier life. In such case, the transference is 'one-way'. Transference between two group members may also be 'two-way' and complementary, with each being a transference figure for the other. Is projection involved, or not? This is complicated. The members of a group are not neutral figures. One member may actually behave in ways very similar to that of another's father, mother, or brother. Projection in the usual sense is not involved, or else plays a small part. However, an individual can be said to be predisposed to re-experience certain important past relationships in contemporary situations, and so can be said to be seeking transference relationships. Tendencies to re-experience early relationships in contemporary contexts are brought into the group situation, as they are brought into other situations outside the group.

In addition to one person standing for someone important in an individual's past, one person can personify another's ego ideal, or a feared aspect of the self, or a threat presumed to be lurking in the environment. Again, there is something about that person, or the person's behaviour, which makes him or her a suitable candidate for being experienced in such ways.

Sometimes more than one of those present function as transference figures for one group member. In example 10 in Chapter 12, one group member stood for Jean's brother while, at the same time, the two therapists stood for her parents. This occurred when the therapists brought a new and unwanted 'sibling' into the group.

Individuals may experience transference reactions to the therapist, as in individual psychotherapy. Several, even most, group members may harbour comparable feelings towards the therapist. It would be surprising if only one person expected the therapist to have magical powers to cure, or desperately wanted to have the therapist's exclusive attention, or felt disappointed or angry when a therapist failed to meet all expectations. Thus a number of the people in a group may experience a transference relationship with the therapist at the same time. The specifics of the feelings and the specific links with past experience will be different, person to person, but there is nevertheless something common or shared about their feelings.

The group as a whole can become a kind of transference figure for members if, for instance, they experience the group as a source of nurturance, or a secure base, or a source of threat.

Reliving earlier experiences can occur in a group through other processes which are not exactly transference. For instance, one person may feel overcome by the presence of so many 'siblings' in the group. A group member who becomes the target of a concerted attack on the part of the others may re-experience earlier events within his sibship or at school. In group focal conflict theory, it is postulated that conflicts shared across the group can sometimes resonate with individual nuclear and focal conflicts. This is not exactly transference, but it is a situation in which significant re-experiencing can occur.

Taking all this into account, one can see that transference is an umbrella term which can refer to a number of different kinds of relationships and dynamics. If one makes use of the term transference it seems important to explicate further, to make clear just exactly what form of transference one has in mind, and how it connects with observable events in the group.

De Maré et al. (1991: 103–4) make use of the term 'transposition' rather than 'transference'. They say:

We have coined the term 'transposition' for the introduction of matters from previous contexts into the group, similar but distinct from the manifestations of transferred relationships in psychoanalysis (i.e. transference). Transposition is an extension of Foulkes's constructs of group matrix and location, itself an extension of Gestalt thinking of foreground figures against the background of the total communication network as a slowly evolving specifically group phenomenon; it consists of the pattern of an individual neurotic response mapped out against its social context . . . Whilst in psychoanalysis it is the transference that constitutes the cornerstone of therapy, in group analysis it is transposition.

'Transposition' is a better term than 'transference', which is too narrow. The term 'transference', however, continues in common use.

A separable issue concerning transference is its 'depth'. Horwitz (1994) has explored this issue in his article, 'Depth of transference in groups'. After reviewing the thinking of a number of authors, Horwitz (ibid.: 275) summarises by saying that:

there are at least three clear levels of functioning which have been delineated: a conscious, reality-oriented, mature, adaptive level; an oedipal transference level that emphasizes earlier relationships with paternal and maternal figures; and a pre-oedipal transference level in which the split good and bad mother images predominate.

He says that the more rational levels are associated with transference dilution and the more primitive levels with transference intensification, and then goes on to discuss factors in groups which promote either dilution or intensification. He concludes that neither dilution nor intensification is intrinsic to group psychotherapy, but that one or the other may be dominant in particular groups, or in the same group at different times. Important determining factors are the patients' pathology and the therapist's practice approach.

In the examples of practice presented in earlier chapters, I believe that I have emphasised Horwitz's middle level, including relationships with siblings and peers as well as relationships with parental figures. As Horwitz points out, his first level is not transference. Rather, it refers to patients' capacities to think rationally about their problems, which exist alongside transference proper. Many of the examples demonstrate this, also.

THE POSITION OF THE THERAPIST IN THE GROUP: PURPOSE AND TASK, POWER, RESPONSIBILITY, AND INFORMATION; CLOSENESS, DISTANCE, AND NEUTRALITY

Purpose and task, power, responsibility, information

Purpose and task are related. A therapist undertakes certain tasks in order to pursue certain purposes. In previous chapters, I have identified purposes and described tasks at different levels of specificity. In the most general terms, a group therapist's purpose is to benefit the persons in the group, and the associated tasks are two-fold: (a) to monitor the state of the group-as-a-whole and encourage it to become (and remain for as much of the time as possible) an environment in which potentially beneficial experiences can occur for members; and (b) to understand individual members as thoroughly as possible in order to recognise and utilise opportunities arising in the group for the benefit of particular individuals, either singly or for more than one person at the same time.

Two further purposes and tasks can be named which support the accomplishment of the two-fold core task: to avoid harmful consequences for the members of the group, and to avoid making errors as much as possible and seek to retrieve the consequences of errors, if they are made.

Purpose and task have so far been stated in general terms. They can be, and need to be, elaborated much more specifically with reference to the many actual, specific situations which arise in groups. At this more specific level, purposes and tasks continually need to be reformulated, to fit closely with the ever-shifting and unique situations which follow one upon the other in the course of a group session. More specifically formulated purposes and tasks will pertain in one way or another to the two core tasks, which often need to be pursued simultaneously.

The *power* of a group therapist derives from his or her real power over members in the form of fate control; from his or her capacity to influence the course of events in groups; and from members' assumptions about the therapist's power and about how he or she is likely to use it.

A therapist has certain direct powers over the group and its members. He or she will have made choices which determine the structure and the membership of the group. A patient or client can be removed from a group if the therapist chooses to do so, though I have argued earlier that this power should be used rarely. A therapist should retain the power to introduce new members into the group.

A therapist's powers include deciding whether to retain certain powers or give them away to members or to share them with members.

In many situations a therapist has influence, but not direct power. A therapist, for instance, can support a sense of safety in a group and members' capacities to take personal risks. A therapist can support facilitative norms in a group, or help members to perceive that they are operating on a non-facilitative norm and invite them to reflect on its functions for them. A therapist may try to reduce the level of threat in a group. A therapist can create opportunities and openings for individuals to benefit. A therapist can invite wider participation. A therapist can do all these things, and more. They are *attempts to influence*. A therapist cannot guarantee the results of his or her efforts.

Group members not infrequently assume that the therapist has more or different powers than he or she actually has. They harbour assumptions and fantasies about the therapist's power and how he or she will use it. For instance, members may assume that the therapist has magical powers to help or to destroy. They might assume that once the therapist knows the 'facts' about them he or she will be able to give advice which will make them feel better or 'cure' them. They might assume that because the therapist has the power to expel members, he or she will in fact do so. By such assumptions and expectations, power is imputed to the therapist which the latter does not in fact have or else does not intend to use. Examining assumptions or fantasies about a therapist's power is of course a potential source of personal gain.

While a therapist has real powers, they are also limited, as the comments about influence already illustrate. For instance, a therapist cannot make people get better or require them to use the group constructively. A therapist cannot impose norms which members are not prepared to accept. A therapist can declare rules, for example about confidentiality or regular attendance, but cannot enforce them. A therapist *does* have power over his or her own behaviour in the group. A therapist can, for instance, decide to respond or avoid responding to pressures to behave in certain ways – for instance, to provide advice. A therapist can decide when to share personal feelings and experiences and when not to. He or she can decide when to intervene and when to be silent. In short, the therapist has power over his or her own behaviour inside the group. This is the limit of his or her *direct* power.

Therapists hold attitudes about their own power. They may think that they have more power than they actually have. They may prefer not to exercise the power they do in fact have. Therapists may decide to make explicit to group members the powers they do and do not have, or else not refer to power at all. Either could be appropriate, according to circumstances. They may decide to give some of their powers away to group members, or hold on to them.

The term *responsibility* takes on a somewhat different meaning depending on the preposition which follows it: responsibility *to*; responsibility *in*; responsibility *for*.

The therapist's responsibility *to* the group and its members can be stated in general terms as an obligation or duty to do everything possible to work towards the overall purpose of utilising the group for the benefit of the members, with all that this implies. A therapist's responsibility *in* the group is to be clear in his or her own mind about purposes and tasks, to be attentive to events as they unfold, to choose interventions carefully in the light of their likely consequences, and to note the actual consequences of own behaviour and regulate future behaviour accordingly.

What is a therapist responsible *for*? For instance, is a therapist responsible for outcomes, for whether or not individuals benefit from their group experience, for what actually happens in sessions? The answer to these questions must be 'yes and no'. The therapist cannot altogether control or determine outcomes, since factors other than his or her behaviour operate. On the other hand, the therapist can influence them. Through decisions made when planning, and through the interventions a therapist makes or does not make, he or she can increase or decrease the likelihood of a positive outcome for the members in general or for particular members. Is the therapist responsible for what happens during sessions? Again, the therapist cannot be entirely or exclusively responsible because too much else besides his or her own behaviour influences group events. On the other hand, there is no doubt that the therapist's own behaviour has consequences in the group and sometimes influences events crucially.

A therapist may feel guilty if things do not go well. Sometimes that is appropriate, if he or she has made avoidable errors. Sometimes it is inappropriate, since unwished-for outcomes may come about for reasons which are outside the therapist's control.

With regard to *information*, a group therapist typically has more information than the members have about some matters and less information about others. A therapist will have acquired information about individual members through referral notes and information provided by individuals in the course of preliminary individual interviews, if these have been held. Some of this information will be available to the persons concerned and some of it will not, and none of it will be available to other members. Therapists also hold information about the organisational setting in which the group is operating, and about prospective changes in it (such as forthcoming changes in staff) which group members may not know.

On the other hand, some information is held by individual members which is not available to the therapist. Individuals do not always reveal everything that is important to them, either in preliminary interviews or in the group itself. They may feel that they could not tolerate the pain or embarrassment or guilt which they anticipate would follow from certain self-revelations. Most therapists can recall group members who have waited for months to reveal certain crucial life experiences.

I have discussed purposes and tasks, power, responsibility, and information separately, but it is clear that they interact. If one accepts responsibility for something, one also accepts certain tasks, and one will need to have, acquire, or retain certain forms of power in order to discharge one's responsibilities. Without certain forms of information, tasks cannot be undertaken and responsibilities met.

This discussion has been limited to its relevance to the therapist's position in a therapeutic group. These concepts can also be applied to a therapist's other roles: for example, as a member of staff in a service-providing organisation, and as a person operating within a wider network of other organisations and referrers (for example, the police, schools, hospitals, and so on).

Closeness, distance, and neutrality

It is obvious that the therapist participates in the group and observes what occurs in it. So do all the members. The therapist, however, observes from a somewhat different vantage point than do the members. In terms of closeness to or distance from members, the therapist needs to be close enough, emotionally, to empathise with their feelings and experiences, but at the same time far enough away to avoid getting caught up personally in powerful feelings and being inappropriately influenced by them.

The group therapist maintains a monitoring and an observing stance, whilst also participating in the group. Monitoring and observing does *not* mean that the therapist places him- or herself outside the group, participates little, or takes a cold and distant perspective on the group. An appropriate therapist stance is entirely compatible with warmth, sympathy, and a conversational style of participating. It is compatible with the view that the therapist and the members are participating in a common enterprise with the same overall purpose in mind: that of achieving benefit for individual members. It is in some sense true that it is part of the therapist's task to work *on* the group. However, if the therapist works *on* the group it is from the position of working *in* the group and of being a part of it. Reid and Reid (1993: 247) put this well when they said that 'therapists are not objective observers of group behaviour; they are part of a problem-solving field. As such, the stance is one of being in mutual dialogue with the members, not speaking from a remote vantage point.'

It is often said that the behaviours of group members and of the therapist become more like one another over time. From very early in a group's life, members may ask someone for clarification or elaboration, encourage someone to participate, and so on. As the group moves along, members often learn to operate more as the therapist does, in further ways. By taking the therapist as a model, group members often become better able to monitor their own interactions, and to perceive consequences of their own and others' behaviours. They may begin to reflect on their own behaviours and feelings without needing the therapist to encourage them to do so. They may intervene in group events in the style which the therapist has displayed. The other side of this coin is that as a therapist becomes more comfortable in a group, he or she may become more flexible in sharing opinions or feelings in the group, in this sense becoming more like the members, at least some of the time.

It would, however, be an oversimplification, and untrue, to say that the therapist becomes a member of the group in the same sense as the members themselves. The members on the one hand and the therapist on the other hand are in the group for different reasons. They hold different purposes and responsibilities, and the ways in which they expect to participate are different. The therapist has responsibilities to and for the group which require him or her to maintain self-discipline, and to make careful choices about what to say and what not to say, and when. There is a further, overriding reason for the therapist to remain in a special position throughout the life of the group: group members are supported in feeling safe enough to take risks if they can hold on to the sense that there is one person in the group who retains sufficient understanding, strength, courage and even-handedness to handle difficult situations and emergencies if they arise. Even though such situations may occur rarely, the members need to know that, when they do, the therapist can be relied upon to carry out his or her special responsibilities and tasks from his or her special position.

Therapists do of course differ from one another with respect to both stance and style. I refer to this again in the last section in this chapter.

HOW MAY A THERAPIST MAKE USE OF A *GROUP* IN ORDER TO BENEFIT INDIVIDUAL MEMBERS?

Dictionaries offer a number of definitions of the verb 'to use'. The sense which best fits 'using groups to help people' is 'to put into action; employ' (*Longman*); 'to employ for a purpose' (*Shorter Oxford English Dictionary*).

A group offers routes towards personal gain which are different from those available in one-to-one psychotherapy. In a group, no single patient or client can have the exclusive attention of the therapist throughout. On the other hand, interactions with other members and the character of the group itself significantly affect the gains which can occur. It follows that a group therapist needs to have in mind the specific opportunities which a group affords, as well as its limitations. The following points can be made about using a group to benefit individuals.

Planning

A therapist tries to create the kind of group which has a high probability of generating benefit for individuals. This begins at the planning stage, where a composition is sought in which there is commonality of certain kinds and diversity of certain kinds, as described in Chapter 6. Certain individuals may need to be selected out, because they are in a state of severe crisis or because their fears of being in a group are gross and primitive. A structure needs to be devised which is likely to be usable by the members. Preparation of individual members is useful for some populations but not necessary for others. Through careful attention to planning, a therapist can increase the likelihood that the group will be a fruitful experience for its members.

The therapist's introductory comments

In his or her introductory statement to the group when it first assembles, the therapist will try to make the structure clear and to support members in beginning to participate.

Recognising and respecting initial fears, and aiming to alleviate them

A therapist needs to be aware that most people in most groups have reservations and fears about what may happen in groups, and to themselves when in a group. Members may fear negative reactions from others if they reveal themselves, or fear becoming overwhelmed by their own feelings, if they are too much acknowledged. In many groups, these fears dominate the early sessions. A therapist therefore aims to alleviate such fears as arise. A therapist does not need to take on this task single-handedly, for members' hopes lead them, despite their fears, to work towards making positive use of the group. Members themselves often interact in ways which lead to the alleviation of fears, and when they do so, the therapist need not intervene, except perhaps to underline and emphasise, and to credit the members for the progress they are making.

The therapist will of course have been monitoring the group, and if events show that fears persist, or that a sense of safety is being achieved for most at the expense of one or two people, the therapist will have to intervene with the intention of alleviating fears. During this early phase of the group, the therapist's role is to monitor the group, note the fears which surface and observe how the members themselves strive to deal with them, intervening if the members need help. The aim at this early stage is to work towards establishing an environment in which members feel safe enough to take risks. In group focal conflict terms, the therapist hopes to see a shift from predominantly restrictive solutions to predominantly enabling solutions.

Working within themes

During times when a group is working within some enabling solution, themes evolve through processes of association which are pertinent to many, and sometimes to all, of the members. At such times, benefit can occur through members comparing themselves with others, hearing how others deal with problems and feelings similar to those they have experienced, giving and receiving feedback, noticing the consequences of their own and others' behaviours, and the like.

Explorations can occur which profit more than one person at the same time, for each can examine the personal meaning of the theme, and relate to it and explore it in individual unique ways. Exploring within themes which are meaningful to a number of the group members, though in different ways, is one of the principal sources of gain in a group. While such gain-promoting explorations are going on, a therapist often does not need to intervene because the members are doing constructive work themselves. Or a therapist may intervene from time to time to underline, emphasise, lend support, give credit to what members are achieving, bring other members into the discussion, and point to commonalities and differences amongst members.

Dealing with problem persons and situations

Sometimes one or another member becomes prominent in a group and is regarded as a 'problem person' by the therapist or by others. Sometimes a problem resides in the group as a whole, as occurs when members establish some collusive defence. Situations which present as problems can, more often than not, be turned into opportunities for gain. Although the way in which this may be accomplished will be different in its detail in each situation, there is a general point to be made. The therapist needs to understand the function the behaviour is fulfilling for the members in general, or for particular members. Usually, fears are present which keep the behaviour in place. If the therapist can find ways to alleviate fears, members can be unlocked from the problem situation. Exploring its many facets can lead to gain.

Noticing opportunities for corrective emotional experiences, and the forms these take in a group

As in individual psychotherapy, significant early experiences can be re-experienced within the group. Advantageous consequences follow if individuals achieve the emotional learning that the feared consequences of harbouring or expressing certain feelings do not in fact occur. If the feared consequences do not occur, the individual no longer needs to cling to disadvantageous personal defences or assumptions or behaviours. This is what is meant by the term 'corrective emotional experience'. The therapist can help, first of all, by developing a sufficiently good understanding of each individual to recognise what would constitute a beneficial change; and second, by coming to understand the fears – always unique to each person – which are holding the disadvantageous defence or assumption or behaviour in place. Armed with such understandings, a therapist is more likely to recognise opportunities for preparatory work, perceive that a corrective experience is occurring, and note subsequent follow-up work. A therapist can assist the process, sometimes simply by being attentive, and sometimes by a variety of interventions which name, underline, or emphasise what is happening, encourage further exploration, or give credit. Other group members often play a part: by being figures who stand for significant persons in an individual's past life, by responding in ways which disconfirm fears, and by making the same kinds of comments as might the therapist. In a group, the therapist is not the only helper.

Choosing from among a range of possible interventions, and having sequences of interventions in mind

Many different kinds of interventions are available to a therapist. A therapist may address him- or herself to an individual, to several individuals, to the group as a whole, or to 'no one in particular'. Offering an interpretation is only one option among many, and is best used sparingly. A therapist profits from having a repertoire of interventions in mind, selecting from them to suit the circumstances.

Thinking in terms of *sequences* of interventions is a good policy, beginning with low-risk interventions and moving towards stronger and more insistent ones if necessary, and taking care not to push members into defensive positions which work against the therapeutic process. It is good practice to try to anticipate the likely consequences of an intervention before making it, and to take into account the actual consequences of one intervention before saying anything further.

Knowing when not to intervene

There will be many times when it is unnecessary to intervene because members are engaging in productive therapeutic work themselves. Making good use of a group includes getting out of the members' way and allowing constructive processes and interactions to have their effect.

Tolerating and understanding periods of retreat

All does not go smoothly all of the time, even in a generally well-functioning group. There will be periods of stagnation, times when members retreat because their explorations have taken them into realms which carry threat. A therapist will need to monitor such periods, try to figure out what triggered them, and sometimes ride them out until members recover enough through their own efforts to resume their work. It is often best not to hurry the group too much or to try too hard. Having said this, whilst *not* putting excessive pressure on group members (which only exacerbates anxiety) a therapist sometimes see ways of intervening which alleviate the fears which led to the retreat, thus assisting the members to resume their work.

Making sure that the group does not become too small

As a group moves along, some members may leave. A therapist needs to take care that the group does not become so small that useful heterogeneity is lost, or the group becomes unbalanced, for instance with regard to gender, race, or age distribution. To this end, a therapist should retain the power to add new members. If existing members protest that the group is big enough and no new members are needed, the therapist should help them to investigate their feelings.

Making use of the special opportunities offered by the termination phase

The termination phase of a group tends to stimulate particular themes, especially to do with separation and loss, and with time running out. A therapist needs to be alert to these in order to see and use them as opportunities. (This is not to say that such themes are necessarily restricted to the termination phase.)

Being alert to the possibility of destructive processes occurring, and nipping them in the bud

Destructive processes can occur in groups. Some of these damage the group itself as a context in which personal gain can occur. Some harm particular individuals. In group focal conflict terms, destructive processes often have to do with the nature of the solutions which group members construct in order to deal with their fears. Some forms of restrictive solutions constrain the explorations which can occur and hold the whole group back from being as useful and productive as it could be. Other forms of restrictive solution damage or hold back one individual, by placing him or her in some position from which gain cannot occur or which causes damage and persistent pain. A therapist can influence many such situations by encouraging the examination of underlying fears, with the aim of understanding and alleviating them.

Being aware of one's own potential for creating problems for group members or setting a group back

Therapists can, through their own behaviour, create problems in groups and cause damage. Such behaviours are, of course, errors. They may be of commission or omission. Some have serious consequences. Others have less serious consequences. Some errors have their principal impact on individuals, while others affect the whole group, setting it back as a constructive environment for therapeutic work. While errors cannot be eliminated altogether, because of the complex and fastmoving character of group events, therapists can become more sensitive to the kinds of errors they are prone to make. They can then engage in what could be called 'preventive maintenance', by knowing when to take it gently or to remain silent, waiting for clarification and/or giving themselves time to sort out and gain control over feelings and alarms which can lead to errors. Therapists can usefully have in mind interventions which help to curtail the consequences of errors, choosing when and how to intervene in the light of circumstances. Counter-transference reactions are one source of errors, but not the only source.

Recognising the need for ongoing 'think-work'

The therapist's internal 'think-work' is important when conducting a group, as it would be in any form of psychotherapy. What a therapist directs his or her thinking *to*, however, is different in a group. In a group, the therapist tries continually to develop a fuller understanding of each individual in that group, whilst also paying attention to the character and development of the group as a whole, and to his or her own feelings. Therapists need constantly to make decisions about what, from amongst all that they are thinking and feeling, to express overtly in the group. Such decisions are best made by keeping purposes in mind (both general purposes and purposes attached to the current group situation), and by doing one's best to predict the likely consequences of an intervention. In predicting the latter, I find it useful to remember that certain interventions are high-risk, as judged by their likely consequences, while others carry lower risks.

In the preceding paragraphs, certain points have recurred. They can be thought of as requisites if a therapist is to work effectively towards benefiting individuals when using a group as a medium for help. When planning for a group, selecting members, and conducting sessions, therapists' choices influence the probabilities of a group becoming, or failing to become, a positive environment for personal benefit. While a group is in session, continuous monitoring is essential – keeping in touch with events as they evolve and develop, and perceiving as best one can their import for the development of the group as a whole and for the experience of individuals. It is necessary to formulate purposes connected with the specific, always shifting, and often unexpected situations which arise in a group. Some purposes have to do with maintaining the group as a supportive and facilitative environment. Others have to do with pursuing opportunities for benefiting individuals: often, for benefiting more than one person at the same time. It is particularly important to realise that other members, as well as the therapist, contribute to benefit through their interactions. For this to happen, the therapist needs be careful not to intervene too much or too often or too soon, so that group processes may have their effect. At the same time, a therapist needs to be ready to intervene if members run out of their own resources and need special help from the therapist, or if destructive processes take hold.

A general strategy is to support constructive interactions and to interrupt destructive ones, and to try to correct for the unwanted consequences of the latter. To work effectively in a group a therapist needs to be aware of the great diversity of potential interventions from which it is possible to select, and of the diverse possible targets of interventions. Monitoring needs to include attention to the impact of one's interventions on the group as a whole and on individuals other than those who were their intended target. A group therapist needs to be sufficiently in touch with own feelings to maintain control over how those feelings are expressed and to reduce the likelihood of making errors. This is also the case in individual psychotherapy, of course, but it is well to recognise the power of group events to stimulate strong feelings in a therapist, especially when resonances occur between group-level dynamics and a therapist's personal concerns and vulnerabilities.

Certain assumptions and attitudes towards groups are associated with, or underlie, these requisites. It is sometimes said that a therapist can 'trust the group'. This needs to be examined, for how can one 'trust the group' when one knows that destructive processes can occur in groups? How frightened need one be of groups and of what might happen in them? These are in fact related points. It is prudent to be aware of the destructive processes which can occur in groups. There is evidence for this all around us. At the same time it is well to recognise that a group can be a supportive, 'cradling' environment, and that individual members can be ingenious, sensitive, and constructive in their interactions with one another. One can trust a group – by which I now mean the members collectively – without losing sight of a group's capacity to do harm. A therapist who is over-trusting may assume that all will come right in the end and that there is no need to monitor or to be ready to intervene when a group stagnates or when harmful behaviours occur. A therapist can also be under-trusting – that is, preoccupied with the harm-doing capacity of a group and under-appreciative of the constructive potentials of a group and the interpersonal sensitivities and skills of members. A therapist who is fearful of a group much of the time, and who does not face his or her fears, will not be in a good position to be helpful. A therapist who is blandly optimistic and does not face the real risks is also in a position from which it is difficult to be helpful.

Göran Ahlin (2000) has offered three metaphors for the group: the cradle, the cage, and the climbing frame. These are rich metaphors for understanding the group's capacity to contain and to comfort, to imprison and to do harm, and to be an environment in which profitable personal 'climbing' can occur. A therapist who recognises all these aspects and potentials of a group, and makes them a part of his or her attitudes towards, and assumptions about, groups, will be a more effective helper.

THE GROUP THERAPIST AS A PERSON

The therapist's personal stance and style have implications for the experiences of group members. A warm, attentive, respectful therapist will support the development of trust in the group, and of a working alliance between therapist and members. Wariness on the part of members is likely to be reduced and members will find it easier to reveal themselves and explore matters of importance to them.

The kind of person a therapist *is*, in the group, influences the experiences which members can have. Consider a therapist who is interested in each person in the group, warmly human, has a certain humility, and sees him- or herself as on a par with group members as a human being, even though occupying a special role. Such a therapist will be a different person in the group from a therapist who is cold and distant, or defensive, or challenging, or fearful, or ingratiating, or controlling, or forever displaying superiority.

I am not recommending chumminess. A warm and respectful personal style does not preclude differences of opinion between therapist and members. It does not stop members from sometimes attacking or challenging the therapist. It will not prevent a group from getting stuck in some unproductive way of going on. It will, however, make it more likely that when any such events occur they become matters for mutual exploration.

Other stances and styles have quite different consequences. A therapist who observes the group as though from a great height, or conveys that he or she is the expert who is in touch with 'the truth', will create a distance between him- or herself and the members, almost as if they were of two different species. Such a stance, such a set of attitudes, can generate a defensive response in members, or adversarial stand-offs between therapist and members. An ingratiating style, or a keenness to be 'friends', can lead members to feel that they must protect and gratify the therapist. A frightened therapist will find it very difficult to help members to face what has to be faced, and will almost certainly convey that the group is full of dangers which cannot be managed. An over-controlling therapist makes it less likely that members' own concerns will surface.

A quotation from Malcolm Pines which appeared in the previous chapter referred to Foulkes's comment that it is not what the therapist does, but what the therapist is, that is important in his or her work. This can be amended slightly by inserting the phrase 'in the group'. The comment becomes 'it is not what the therapist does, but who the therapist is in the group, that is important in his or her work'. The reason for this amendment is that it emphasises that 'what the therapist is' is the product not only of abiding features of personality (which suggests immutability) but of how the therapist experiences being in the group and how he or she chooses to behave in the group. A therapist's behaviour is open to change. Thus, a therapist who fears that the group could become unmanageable can learn through experience to be less frightened. A therapist who maintains a great distance between him- or herself and the members may be using excessive distance defensively, and may come to have less need of this defence. A therapist who feels helpless and confused (and who does not, from time to time?) may learn to be more tolerant of such feelings and in consequence be less inclined to communicate confusion in his/her behaviour.

I am being as clear as I can about the stance and style which I consider to be preferable in a therapist. I hope that it is evident that I am not being moralistic about being a 'good' person, or a 'good' therapist. I am concerned with the consequences which follow in practice from various attitudes and courses of action. Who the therapist is, as a person in the group, is of great practical importance. It is therefore enormously useful for a therapist to be aware of own personal stance and style, and of their consequences, so as to be able to exercise some choice in the matter.

Chapter 17

Theory and its connections with practice

I shall begin by referring back to where the questions treated in this chapter have come from. Groundwork for this chapter has been laid in earlier ones. In Chapter 5, dictionary definitions of 'theory' were provided. Processes whereby theory is built and developed were discussed, and it was pointed out that most theories have antecedents in the thinking of others or in the *Zeitgeist* of the times. Theory always pertains to some particular set of observable phenomena. It is made up of propositions which explain and account for the observations made to date with respect to the phenomena. If experience shows that a theory as originally formulated does not account for all of the observable phenomena to which it was meant to pertain, the theory sometimes has to be developed further, or additional concepts have to be brought in. If new information comes to light which shows that a previously established explanation is inapplicable, a theory may be abandoned. It is not unusual for a new theory to be resisted because it threatens to overturn some previous way of understanding a phenomenon and/or some already established way of operating. This pertains to any theory, related to any universe of events.

Chapter 5 went on to discuss theory pertaining specifically to therapeutic groups. Group focal conflict theory was described and a number of other theories were referred to. Evidence was put forward to support the view that therapists can subscribe to the same or to closely related theories, yet practise quite differently. At the end of Chapter 5, four questions about theory and its connections with practice were posed but not discussed. They are reproduced below, as questions 1–4.

The content of later chapters stimulated further questions concerning theory and its connections with practice. Chapter 8, which was about the internal 'think-work' which practitioners engage in while conducting a group, suggested three more questions, which are shown as numbers 5–7, below. The many examples provided in Chapter 12, on personal gain, showed theory being used in different ways in the face of diverse situations which occur in groups. A further question was posed, namely: How do therapists use theory in their practice? Chapter 14, on therapists' errors, made it clear that theory was just one of a range of factors which influence practice. This raised the question: What, besides theory, influences how therapists practise? I decided to combine this with the question raised by Chapter 12, and the two questions when combined now appear as question 8, namely: How do therapists use theory in their practice? What, besides theory, influences how therapists' practice? Chapter 14 also showed that some errors derive from misuses of theory. This led to the question: How can or might theory be misused or lead one astray? Does all theory carry risks of being misused? (see 10, below). I have inserted another question, which appears as question 9, which does not derive from any single chapter. It has to do with influences from the wider culture on both theory and practice. Finally, a question about implications for the appropriate use of theory has been added, appearing as question 11.

The questions concerning theory and its connections with practice which form the framework for this chapter are as follows:

1   What is theory *for*? What functions does it fulfil for the practitioner?
2   How is it that some theories are closely connected with a particular practice approach while others are not?
3   Which comes first: theory or practice? Does a therapist's preferred theory influence how he or she operates in a group? Does practice experience influence theory development? Or do theory and practice influence one another?
4   Why are there so many theories? Can they be reconciled? What function is served by seeking to reconcile theories?
5   How do practitioners acquire theory? Where do they start from?
6   How can practitioners make explicit to themselves the ideas or set of concepts which they actually use in their practice? Why is it useful to do this?
7   By what criteria may a therapist judge the merits and demerits of a theory, and its usefulness and applicability?
8   How do therapists use theory in their practice? What, besides theory, influences how therapists practise?
9   How do habits of thought or assumptions, common in the wider culture, influence both theory and practice?
10 How can or might theory be misused or lead one astray? Does all theory carry risks of being misused?
11 What, then, is the 'appropriate' use of theory?

This is not a definitive set of questions, nor is what I have to say a complete set of responses. I am aware that the final question, in particular, would be answered differently by different practitioners. I nevertheless think it worthwhile to pose and to address questions about theory and how it is used in practice.

I turn now to each of the individual questions.

I WHAT IS THEORY *FOR*? WHAT FUNCTIONS DOES IT FULFIL FOR THE PRACTITIONER?

A theory can be useful to practitioners in that it can be used to make sense of the complex events which arise in therapeutic groups. Rather than being faced with a confusing mass (or mess) of events, the therapist gains an understanding about what is going on. He or she then has a sense of being in cognitive control of the situation, and can avoid a sense of inner confusion, helplessness, or even panic. Instead of being faced with chaos, the therapist is faced with something which can be seen to have order and sense to it.

With respect to the functions of theory, Lonergan (1994: 189) has said:

> Theories are relevant to group leaders in three ways: (1) they help organize data that otherwise would be overwhelming, (2) they generate new ideas for group interventions, (3) having a theory increases confidence that therapists know what they are doing; patients pick up on this and increase their engagement in the therapeutic process. (Lonergan 1994:189)

This statement needs to be somewhat reformulated to make it clear that it is not the theory which helps (a theory not being a person) but that theory can be used by therapists to organise their thinking, identify new possible ways of intervening, and increase their self-confidence when working with a group.

Lonergan's first point is the same as the one I have just made, that is, a therapist can use theory to make sense of complex events in a group. Her second point is that a therapist, having a theory in mind when looking at a situation in a group, might think of possible interventions which would not otherwise occur to him or to her. The therapist is then in a position to make choices about how, when, and why to intervene from a wider range of possibilities than before.

I have not seen Lonergan's third point made elsewhere. It certainly is important. A therapist who feels confident that he or she understands what is going on most likely does communicate this to patients, with positive consequences, as Lonergan says. On the other hand, a therapist might have confidence in a faulty or incomplete theory. Over-confidence can lead a therapist to cling to an unsatisfactory theory, or use it in circumstances where it does not apply.

A little later in the same article Lonergan (ibid.: 190) makes the point that:

> Theory helps to organize these data and simplify them, so that the information can be grasped better. This does not mean theory equals the truth. A theory is simply an idea that gives the feeling of understanding (which is different from actual understanding).

This is a reminder that it is well to pay attention to both the dictionary definitions of theory provided at the beginning of Chapter 5 (theory as a coherent, plausible, and internally consistent set of ideas for understanding some phenomenon; and theory as 'mere speculation'). It is a reminder that to feel one possesses 'the truth' about a situation does not mean that one actually possesses it. In fact, it is a mistake to believe that there is a truth. A theory is not 'truth'. It consists of a set of propositions or hypotheses which need to be tested constantly for their fit with observable events and new information.

2 HOW IS IT THAT SOME THEORIES ARE CLOSELY CONNECTED WITH A PARTICULAR PRACTICE APPROACH WHILE OTHERS ARE NOT?

Some theories are closely associated with, and even prescribe, particular forms of practice. Bion (1959), for instance, made it very clear that therapists should offer interpretations which pertain to group-level dynamics. Ezriel (1950a, 1950b, 1956) took the view that the common group tension should be interpreted to the members as soon as the therapist grasps all three aspects of it (the required, the avoided, and the calamitous relationships), and that a group-level interpretation should be followed by showing how individuals relate to the common group tension. For Bion and for Ezriel, the theory and the associated model of practice are close. Other theories, amongst them that of Foulkes and of group focal conflict theory, suggest ways of understanding situations arising in groups but their proponents do not point specifically or directly to forms of practice. Choices about how to intervene are left rather more in the hands of the practitioner.

Ezriel had strong views about the proper way to make use of his theory in practice. This, however, does not mean that there is only one way to make use of Ezriel's theory when working with a group. Horwitz accepted much of Ezriel's thinking but arrived at different conclusions about appropriate forms of practice. That part of group focal conflict theory which applies to group-level phenomena corresponds point for point with Ezriel's three-part formulation of the common group tension. Group focal conflict theory nevertheless allows for a wider range of interventions. (See the discussion in Chapter 5, pp. 62–3).

I am making an argument that some theory-builders point explicitly to a particular way of making use of their theory when conducting a group. The theory-builder regards a particular form of practice as integral to the theory. Others then make the same assumption. The fact, however, is that people have the theory and look at phenomena. They then decide how to make use of the theory in practice. They may change their minds about how best to make use of theory in practice, by observing the consequences of initially favoured intervention strategies. This is what Horwitz did: he observed the consequences of Ezriel's preferred intervention style, came to the conclusion that individuals tended to feel neglected, and arrived at an alternative way of using theory in practice.

3 WHICH COMES FIRST: THEORY OR PRACTICE? DOES A THERAPIST'S PREFERRED THEORY INFLUENCE HOW S/HE OPERATES IN A GROUP? DOES PRACTICE EXPERIENCE INFLUENCE THEORY DEVELOPMENT? OR DO THEORY AND PRACTICE INFLUENCE ONE ANOTHER?

A therapist can turn to theory for ideas about what to be alert to and what to aim for. Sometimes turning to theory can alert a therapist to what to expect next. On the basis of theory, a therapist may predict the likely consequences of one form of intervention over another. In this sense, theory influences practice.

Practice also influences theory. It does so through the intermediate step of influencing the events which occur or prevail in a group. Events occur in consequence of a therapist's decisions and actions. Theory is then devised or invoked to explain those events. Kibel and Stein (1981) point out that Bion recognised that his practice of basing interpretations on group responses to himself as leader resulted in members being preoccupied with him as leader. In consequence, his theory had to include propositions which describe and account for those preoccupations.

As another example, those who participated in developing group focal conflict theory were already in the habit of conducting groups in a way which allowed associational processes to occur. This practice predated theory-building. When associational processes are allowed free rein, themes emerge which are shaped by members' interactions. Therapists then need theory addressed to understanding the nature of themes and how members relate to them. Group focal conflict theory includes propositions which meet this need, though it is not the only theory which can be brought to bear. Many therapists, though by no means all, espouse a form of practice which encourages associational processes, and they devise and adopt theory to account for what then happens. They do not necessarily devise or use the same theory or comparable ones. Forms of practice which restrict the operation of associational processes do not need an associated theory to account for the products of such processes.

Sometimes it is hard to see whether theory or practice comes first. Ezriel's practice of restricting himself to interpretations and deferring intervention until he could understand and name all aspects of the common group tension led to a relatively inactive intervention pattern which held him in a rather cold and distant position *vis-à-vis* the members and kept his groups therapist-centred. His theory emphasises the therapist as a transference figure for the members. Did the theory come first and point Ezriel towards certain ways of practising, or did his practice preferences come first and require theory to account for the consequences of the way in which he practised?

Theory may come first for those practitioners who have been schooled in a particular theory and then apply it to their practice. Practice may come first for those practitioners who develop a characteristic way of working with groups, without recourse at first to an established or an articulated theory. These latter practitioners observe events which are consequent upon their intervention style, and then seek an explanation for what they observe. Theory, events in the group, and practice constantly interact. The sequence could be: a preferred form of practice generates certain events in a group which requires theory to make sense of them (practice comes first). Or the sequence could be: a particular theory is accepted which, when translated into practice in particular ways, influences the events which occur in the group, which in turn tend to be understood in terms of the theory (theory comes first). A therapist's established way of practising within a group is likely to lead to concomitant and compatible theory. Conversely, a therapist's preferred theory is likely to lead to practice consistent with, and hence likely to reinforce, the theory. It seems likely that therapists move back and forth between theory and practice, and that theory and practice influence one another.

4 WHY ARE THERE SO MANY THEORIES? CAN THEY BE RECONCILED? WHAT FUNCTION IS SERVED BY SEEKING TO RECONCILE THEORIES?

It is an observable fact that there is no single way to understand events occurring in groups. There is no theory which everyone accepts, which everyone uses. This is understandable when one considers that a theory-builder is likely to have had experience with certain patient or client populations and not others, has in mind certain forms of hoped-for gains and not others, and has most probably been exposed to different antecedent influences.

Some theories pertain to different populations of people, with different capacities and personal resources. Hoped-for gains are also different. There is nothing to say that a theory which fits, say, people who repeatedly become involved in disadvantageous or destructive relationships will fit people who are facing a real-life crisis or people who need to develop basic communication skills. It is unlikely that a single theory will fit all these disparate people and circumstances. Different theories are required and useful. It is best to keep such theories separate and not try to reconcile them. A therapist is better off selecting from amongst available theories according to what needs to be understood about different populations of people, and the tasks cast up by working with each.

Some theories pertain to the same population of people but to different aspects of the work. For instance, there may be theory which points to the dynamics to be expected when the group is in session, or which a therapist can make use of when composing a group, or which focuses on group development. There may be theory to account for how it is that some individuals gain while others do not. Such theories have been devised to serve different purposes. Rather than trying to reconcile them, which is not really possible, one might well use them in combination. One would then wish to make sure that the theories are compatible and complementary even if different. One does not want to adopt theories which lead in different and contradictory directions.

Some theories are alternative explanations for the same phenomena. Consider the theory which Harwood and her associates (Harwood and Pines 1998) are building, based on Kohut's self psychology (Kohut 1971, 1977). It is different from Foulkes's group analytic theory (Foulkes 1964) but potentially compatible with it. Ahlin's theory of the matrix representation grid (1996) owes something to Foulkes's thinking about group analysis and the matrix, and something to group focal conflict theory, yet it is distinct from either. Comparing such theories will reveal compatibilities and divergences and show whether they are potentially reconcilable or not. I can think of three ways in which theories could be reconcilable. First, careful examination may show that they share similar underlying assumptions and that the terms they use, though different, are translatable into one another. They are then closely comparable. Second, compatible but different theories could be fitted together – that is, inserted into one another. The theories are not closely comparable, as in the first case. However, they complement, fit, and enrich one another, and are reconcilable in that sense. Third, it may be possible to construct some meta-theory which is capable of containing two or more theories.

Different theories pertaining to the same phenomena may turn out to be strict alternatives to one another with no overlap or comparabilities. Conversely they may be compatible or convergent. Theories can be compatible or convergent without being entirely reconcilable. Theories may be partially reconcilable: they are comparable in some ways but not in others. For instance, a number of different theories make use of the concepts of the corrective emotional experience, transference, counter-transference, and resistance. That these terms are component parts of a number of theories does not mean that the theories are fully reconcilable. Theories may be reconcilable with respect to how they explain phenomena but they may be used differently by their proponents in practice.

In order to test the reconcilability of theories it is necessary to compare them. Comparing theories which purport to explain the same phenomena is always a profitable exercise, whether one is aiming for reconcilability or not. Suppose that one compares one's favoured theory with another which appears to be an alternative to it. This may reveal that one's favoured theory has gaps in it, or that there are nuances in observable events which one theory addresses while the other does not. As a kind of 'thought experiment', one can imagine what it would be like to adopt a different theory and make use of it in practice. Perhaps a theory other than one's own suggests group structures, or a practice stance, or forms of interventions which one judges would be useful to add to one's repertoire. Perhaps another theory suggests a way of conceptualising events which seems a closer fit with those events or a fuller explanation of them. Comparing theories can unfreeze one from being stuck in a set of beliefs and assumptions which does not entirely fit the phenomena one is seeking to understand. Comparing theories forces reflectiveness. It could help one to realise that one is accepting beliefs and assumptions as if they were the indisputable real world rather than one possible way of construing observable events.

I come to the point of view that while there are great advantages in comparing theories, there could be disadvantages in trying to reconcile them, especially across the board. There is no ground for believing that somewhere (if one could only find it) there is a theory which is 'right' and will fit all circumstances. It can be valuable to preserve diversity, because this also preserves choice. This is not meant to imply that all theories are equally acceptable. This is a point taken up later in this chapter, under section 7, where criteria for evaluating theories are discussed.

5 HOW DO PRACTITIONERS ACQUIRE THEORY? WHERE DO THEY START FROM?

A therapist might: (a) adopt a theory already available from the literature; (b) be eclectic, drawing from different theories and concepts available in the literature; or (c) seek to be atheoretical.

There are advantages and potential hazards connected with each of these routes towards acquiring theory. A theory already worked out by others provides a set of ideas for understanding complex events, but one risks falling into the trap of believing that everything that comes along can be understood in terms of that theory. If one tries to be eclectic, drawing from a wide range of theories, one has the advantage of being able to select that which makes most sense in terms of own experience, but one risks accumulating a hodge-podge of ideas, some of which may contradict each other. Some people who say they are atheoretical claim not to use theory at all. This is in fact impossible, for everyone uses *some* set of ideas to explain the observable phenomena they encounter. Being atheoretical in this sense almost certainly means that the ideas being used to understand events remain unarticulated. Others who say they are atheoretical mean that they express their ideas in plain language which is unassociated with any established theory. I consider this to be laudable, because the theorist is not hiding behind specialised terms and jargon, and using plain language reduces the risk of being misunderstood. Using plain language is not, however, the same thing as being atheoretical, for theory *can* be expressed in plain language.

Working out a theory of one's own is a further alternative. A practitioner may start from any one of the three positions just described and then constantly question, test, and modify theory in the light of experience. Unless a therapist is thoroughly trapped inside his or her own theory, and is inclined to fit every observable event into it, I believe that this is what most therapists do. Each therapist, as I have said before, is his or her own theory-builder, theory-adjuster, and theory-adapter.

6 HOW CAN PRACTITIONERS MAKE EXPLICIT TO THEMSELVES THE IDEAS AND SET OF CONCEPTS WHICH THEY ACTUALLY USE IN THEIR PRACTICE? WHY IS IT USEFUL TO DO THIS?

The concepts, assumptions, theory, or pieces of theory which therapists actually hold and operate on are often a mix of the explicit and the implicit. Furthermore, the theory which a therapist *considers* him- or herself to be using may not exactly or entirely coincide with the theory which the therapist is *actually* using.

It is advantageous to become explicitly aware of the ideas which one holds in mind when planning and conducting groups because it then becomes possible to take a good hard look at them and evaluate their usefulness, their completeness as a set, areas of application, and limitations.

One can become clearer in the mind about the ideas one actually uses by paying attention to one's own 'think-work' and by examining one's own behaviours in a group and their consequences. One can ask oneself: In what terms did I understand the problems and needs of each person in the group? On what evidence did I base my formulations? When noting what one actually says or does in response to situations arising, one can ask oneself such questions as: What did I think was going on? What do I think precipitated this event? What did I fear/expect/hope would follow, and why? Why did I intervene as I did? In what directions did I hope to influence certain individuals, or the group in general, and why did I think these were desirable directions? What was I trying to forestall or correct for, and why? What followed from my interventions? Did I see benefits occurring for one or more persons in the group? What were these benefits, and what do I think accounted for them?

It will be useful to ask some further questions: If I want to subscribe to some particular theory, does that theory offer plausible explanations for all that I observe happening? If not, what does the theory not cover? When trying to understand certain situations do I bring additional concepts to bear which lie outside my preferred theory? Under what circumstances do I deviate from my preferred theory and why do I do so? If I regard myself as eclectic, what concepts do I draw upon, and from what sources? Do I rely quite a bit on intuition and, if so, on what are my intuitions based? (See the discussion of intuition on p. 108.)

Asking oneself these sorts of questions and attempting to answer them is hard work and takes time, but it pays off. If one can get into closer touch with the ideas, assumptions, and expectations which one actually holds in mind when seeking to understand complex events, one is in a better position to evaluate the usefulness of one's ideas and to modify or reach outside them if this seems indicated.

7 BY WHAT CRITERIA MAY A THERAPIST JUDGE THE MERITS AND DEMERITS OF A THEORY AND ITS USEFULNESS AND APPLICABILITY?

I suggest the following as criteria by which a theory may be judged. The theory one is examining may be one encountered in the literature, or it may be one's own theory, once one has made it explicit to oneself.

(a) *A satisfactory theory ought to help one understand*: (a) the current state of individuals, how these manifest in group contexts, and how a preferred state might best be described and defined; (b) communication processes, interaction patterns, and interpersonal relationships within groups; (c) group-level phenomena, conditions, and processes; (d) oneself as therapist in the group; and (e) interconnections amongst these.

(b) *A satisfactory theory ought plausibly to fit actual, concrete, observable, describable events.* This seems an obvious point. However, as the dictionary definitions show and, as Lonergan (1994) points out, a theory is not necessarily 'truth'. For this reason, it is appropriate to consider every theory as provisional. One keeps in mind that it fits the events I have observed *so far*, and is the best explanation I have found *so far*.

(c) *A satisfactory theory ought to be expressed or expressible in clear, unambiguous language.* Most theories include at least some specialised terms, specific to it. These may be (as it were) either nouns or verbs, referring to both states and processes. If specialised terms are used, they should be defined clearly, and be capable of being defined clearly. Specialised terms are usually introduced for the sake of convenience, because the idea one has in mind would otherwise require many words to describe it. The specialised term is functional in the sense of being economical: it offers a condensed way of referring to some complex phenomenon. The terms 'restrictive solution' and 'enabling solution' in group focal conflict theory are examples of this. Both can be defined in plain language, but many words are required to do so, and it would be cumbersome to have to repeat lengthy phrases every time one wanted to refer to the phenomenon. Once defined, specialised terms can be used as short-cut references to particular events or processes. Sometimes specialised terms are introduced into a theory unnecessarily. This places a burden on those who are trying to understand the theory because they have to master a new language which serves no real function. Using plain language wherever possible is desirable for other reasons: it minimises the risk that abstract terms will be accepted as if they were observable realities and it minimises the risk that a theory will be misunderstood, or understood differently by different people. It minimises the risk that a theory will be taken as a set of phenomena, or 'facts', instead of a putative explanation – which is what theories are.

Some terms are not sufficiently explicated that someone coming upon them for the first time can be sure of their meaning. Some terms are portmanteaux, containing multiple meanings. If the intended meaning is not made clear, the term is open to misunderstanding.

(d) *A satisfactory theory can be used by a therapist to predict events.* This statement needs to be elaborated, for some forms of prediction are possible and others are not. On the basis of group focal conflict theory, for example, one might predict that group members will seek to protect themselves from the presumed dangers of being in a group (in group focal conflict terms, members are likely to establish restrictive solutions). One could not, however, predict the form of the protective device nor how long they will be maintained. On the basis of group focal conflict theory one might predict that, at some point in its development, a group which is going well will shift from operating predominantly on restrictive solutions to operating predominantly on enabling solutions, but one cannot predict just when this shift will take place. The general point is one can make use of theory to predict likely future events but that there are limits to the detail which can be predicted. An important form of prediction fits into the 'if this, then that' format. For instance, one might predict that 'if there is homogeneity amongst group members with respect to preferred defence, then the likelihood is increased that individually preferred defences will become established and maintained in the group as a collusive defence'. One can have confidence in this prediction but still not be able to predict exactly how long a collusive defence will prevail. One might predict that 'if a group is working particularly well, there may then follow a period of retreat because the members have over-reached themselves and have become more anxious'. One might not, however, be able to predict who will reach their limit of tolerance first and be the one to spearhead a retreat. Again, there are limits to the specificity of predictions.

(e) *A satisfactory theory will be more than description, but not so remote from observable events as to have little discernible connection with them.* Some theory is more speculative than others. If one cannot see a plausible connection between the theory and observable events, the theory is either unserviceable or something is missing from it which would show connections.

(f) *A satisfactory theory is one which a therapist can use for practical decision-making.* Kurt Lewin is widely quoted as having said that 'there is nothing so practical as a good theory' (see Marrow 1969). With reference to theory which pertains to therapeutic groups, a theory which is of practical use will assist in planning a group to maximise opportunities for personal gain, and it will assist in seeing how and whether to intervene while a group is in operation in order to utilise situations for the benefit of individuals and to avoid harm occurring.

Certain of these criteria are based on underlying assumptions which not everyone accepts. My first point, for instance, includes the assertion that a satisfactory theory ought to include attention to 'group-level phenomena, conditions, and processes'. This is based on the assumption that dynamics pertaining to the group-as-a-whole are not only inevitably present in groups but need to be understood in order for a therapist to make the fullest possible use of their positive potentials for therapeutic work. Those who do not accept this point of view will not make this one of their criteria for judging theory. It follows that practitioners may accept the criteria I have just set out, or may want to modify or expand or discard some of them. All practitioners, however, need some set of criteria for evaluating theory, for otherwise they are in the untenable position of assuming that any theory, any set of explanatory ideas, is as good as any other.

8 HOW DO THERAPISTS USE THEORY IN THEIR PRACTICE? WHAT, BESIDES THEORY, INFLUENCES HOW THERAPISTS PRACTISE?

When faced with a complicated situation in a group, a therapist will try to understand it by using his or her existing theory or theories, which is to say his or her repertoire of ideas. The therapist's next actions will be influenced in part by his or her understanding of the situation, in part by the feelings stimulated by it, in part by what the therapist hopes will happen next, and in part by assumptions about the likely consequence of different forms of intervention. Whatever the therapist does (or decides not to do) will lead to further events which provide new information. The therapist should then take that new information into account.

This sequence may happen in a flash, or the therapist may have time to give considered thought to the steps involved. If one could slow the process down, one would find something like the following:

1 Before a specific event occurs, a therapist will 'hold a theory' – that is, have in mind a set or pool of ideas regarded as potentially useful for understanding whatever may arise. These ideas are best thought of as being like tools, to be selected for use according to which of them seem to suit a particular situation or task. This is a fundamental point.

2 When a group session begins, events occur. The therapist notices what actually happens: who says what, what happens next, and next, and next. The therapist, however, will not notice everything that happens. He or she cannot take in everything, and furthermore will judge that some things are not important, or not as important as others, and will let them fade into the background of attention. A therapist will not notice whether or not it is raining outside, unless the rain has influenced interaction in the group.

3 The therapist draws upon his/her theory to try to understand what he or she has observed. He/she chooses, from among the set of ideas which comprise the theory, those which seem to fit the events. He creates a model, for use in the current situation, which makes use of some aspects of the theory but not all of it. For instance, if I were faced with a group situation in which members were talking about something in metaphoric terms, I would draw from group focal conflict theory the concept of the restrictive solution, and assume that the metaphor is functioning to express feelings which are important to the members but which they are not, for the moment, able to express directly. This would point me towards trying to understand underlying feelings in the group, both wishes and fears, and towards whether some precipitating event can be identified. The concept of the 'restrictive solution' is just one of a number of concepts which are a part of group focal conflict theory. It would come to mind because it seems to fit the current situation. Other concepts – for instance, solutional conflicts, or the corrective emotional experience – would not come to mind and would not be drawn upon, because they do not fit the *current* situation in the group.

Sometimes it is easy to move from observing a situation to extracting concepts from theory which fit it. Ideas from theory come to mind immediately and the therapist feels confident that his/her conceptualisation of the situation fits the event. This is by no means always the case. Sometimes the situation seems utterly confusing. No part of the theory seems to fit the event. No hypotheses come to mind, or else two or more possibly contradictory hypotheses about the meaning of the events come to mind. The therapist will probably then wait for events to unfold further, and may cast about for concepts which lie outside his or her usual theoretical framework. At some point, the therapist will judge that he or she has arrived at an understanding which seems to fit the events. There is no logical rule to apply which will tell one which piece of theory will fit which event. The therapist needs to recognise that he or she has arrived at an hypothesis, not at an ultimate truth. It is important that an initial understanding be held provisionally, for it might have to be abandoned or changed in the light of subsequent events.

4 As a further internal act, the therapist develops a point of view about what it would be desirable to have happen next. If, for instance, members evolve a theme which it seems reasonable to suppose is important to most of them, the therapist will want to see this theme explored by many, rather than by just a few members. If one person comes under attack by most of the others, then the therapist will want to see the attack cease, and to see all concerned examine their own feelings and related experiences.

5 On the basis of both theory and practice experience, the therapist makes a prediction as to what could happen and is likely to happen if he or she takes certain actions. What are the possible consequences and the most likely consequences if the therapist does nothing, or decides to wait before doing something, or chooses to begin with one kind of intervention rather than another? In other words, the therapist gives thought to the *possible* consequences and the *most likely* consequences of possible actions which come to mind.

6 The therapist's own affective concerns also influence his or her actions. Some of these are transient; some are abiding. Transient affective concerns tend to be situation-specific and are likely to be experienced by every group therapist from time to time. For instance, virtually any therapist is likely to be dismayed by a suddenly erupting situation which places someone at risk, or to be pleased when a group is going well, or confused when everything seems chaotic. Some affective concerns are more abiding, taken into many interactive situations. Some of these more abiding affective concerns are widespread amongst therapists. Virtually all therapists, for instance, are concerned to maintain a sense of effectiveness, to avoid feeling helpless, and to avoid looking foolish. This, of course, is true of group members as well. Some abiding concerns are more idiosyncratic. These might include, for instance, a need to be seen to be helpful, or to demonstrate own cleverness, or to maintain control over events. Some affective concerns can be understood as being manifestations of counter-transference, but this is not true of all of them. For a discussion of the complexity of the concept of counter-transference, see pp. 226–7.

Whether a therapist's affective concerns help or hinder a group depends on whether and how they are expressed in action. For instance, suppose that a therapist feels guilty when a member fails to attend a session, assuming that something the therapist said the previous time has kept the member away. To express this guilt in the group would be to impose own concerns on the group and pre-empt members' expressing their own feelings about the absence. Depending on the course of the discussion, it might be appropriate later to refer to one's previous actions. It could be helpful to members to acknowledge one's own behaviour and its possible consequences because this offers the model of accepting responsibility for the consequences of own actions. In contrast, expressing guilt by abjectly confessing it offers an undesirable model of self-flagellation.

A therapist may or may not be explicitly aware of his or her own affective concerns. If unaware of them, they are more likely to leak out uncontrolled in behaviour, possibly in ways which work against the interests of the members and which interfere with the therapeutic process. On these grounds, it is advantageous to be aware of one's own affective concerns, for one is then more likely to be able to make decisions about whether and how they should be expressed in the group.

7 A therapist takes action (which includes deciding not to act) on the basis of a combination of the therapist's understanding of the situation, point of view about desirable next events, internal predictions about the consequences of alternative actions, and affective concerns. Whatever the therapist does is a new event which has consequences in the group.

8 Group members respond in one way or another to the new event. What happens next will therefore be different in some way from what happened before. Even if 'nothing' happens – that is, the members do not respond to what the therapist has said or done – this too is a new event, to be taken into account. The therapist notices what happens and will form up-dated ideas about these new events.

The process is repeated, but in its detail it is never the same because events in the group are always new. It follows that the aspects of theory drawn upon, the practice experience regarded as relevant, the therapist's hopes and expectations, and the therapist's particular affective concerns, ought likewise to be different.

To check this proposed account of the sequence of events, I examined all the examples of therapist interventions which were provided in Kennard et al.'s (1993) book, A Work Book of Group-analytic Interventions. The authors had presented a large number of group analysts – all associated with the Institute of Group Analysis based in London – with brief descriptions of eight group situations. With respect to each of these, the authors asked their respondents to answer three questions: '1. Write down your understanding of the situation, i.e., what's going on? How did things get to be like this? 2. What intervention, if any, would you make? and 3. Finally write briefly your reasons for making this intervention.'

Selective attention to the described situation was evident. Different aspects of the presenting situation were understood to be important. I do not mean that each respondent differed from every other, but that respondents fell into clusters with respect to what they emphasised. All the respondents were group analysts and were inclined to look for underlying meanings for observable events, and underlying motivations. There was a widely shared interest in getting things out in the open where they could be examined. Opinions as to how this might best be done differed considerably. Some respondents showed that they were choosing interventions on the basis of their likely consequences. Few mentioned their own personal affective concerns although sometimes these could be inferred. (The three questions did not, in fact, direct attention to a therapist's likely personal feelings.) Some respondents commented on how they would be influenced by members' responses to their initial intervention.

Was there a reasonable match, or not, between the eight points which I have made above, about theory and how it and other factors influence practice, and the results of this interesting investigation? I cannot answer with a simple yes or no. The three questions posed by the authors, which each respondent was asked to answer, fit within the model but omit mention of respondents' personal feelings, as stirred up by the event. The responses also fit within the model, though none match all aspects of it. The diversity of responses shows that, in practice, therapists differ in what they emphasise when working out an understanding of a situation, when formulating to themselves what they hope will happen, and when predicting the likely consequences of their actions. It is reasonable to expect that such diversity will always be the case.

In referring to diversity, I do not mean to support the view that any point of view, any response, is as good as any other. Errors, as discussed in Chapter 14, and the misuse of theory, as discussed in Chapter 17, can also contribute to diversity.

I believe that the value of thinking in terms of the eight points which I have set out above lies in their being used to alert practitioners to connections between actions taken, and internal thoughts and feelings. It spells out factors which influence therapists' responses to specific situations. A practitioner's preferred theory is located within an array of other influences on behaviour.

9 HOW DO HABITS OF THOUGHT OR ASSUMPTIONS, COMMON IN THE WIDER CULTURE, INFLUENCE BOTH THEORY AND PRACTICE?

This issue is hard to think about since, if certain assumptions and habits of thought *are* pervasive in the wider culture, they are likely to be accepted as givens and therefore will not be easy to recognise.

Consider nevertheless that in society generally, at least in western society, it tends to be assumed that when people need help they seek out some individual who is an expert and who can be expected to provide it. Thus people, when feeling unwell, seek out a medical doctor. When faced with a legal problem, they seek out a lawyer, and so on. When faced with an emotional problem, especially given the prevalence of the term and concept of 'mental illness', most people seek out an expert practitioner. It is not a part of the wider culture to assume that help with emotional problems can be achieved through interacting with other people who are grappling with emotional problems of their own, and in fact to do so can seem downright strange. Hence one frequently observes that potential group members are wary of groups, and hears them ask: 'How can other sick people help *me*?' Such assumptions are embedded in the culture. They are peculiarities of the culture, accepted as 'truths'.

Within the wider culture there are sub-cultures. One is that of professional helpers who espouse psychodynamic theory. A widely held assumption within this sub-culture is that it is the one-to-one relationship between mother and infant or small child which is crucial to later development. Indeed, there is considerable research and clinical evidence to support this view. This assumption is beginning to give way, or at least to be augmented. Kohut (1971, 1977) has pointed out that concentrating on the mother–child dyad ignores the observable fact that infants are born into a social group, which soon begins to influence development. It is well known that in some cultures the extended family is the 'nest' into which children are born, and the biological mother is just one part of that nest. Harwood and others are applying Kohut's thinking to therapeutic groups (see the contributions in Harwood and Pines 1998). It is still the case generally, however, that the mother–child dyad is emphasised as crucial; some of those who accept this make the further assumption that problems arising from relationships within this dyad are resolvable through relationships within another dyad – that is, that of patient and therapist. Some group therapists, accepting these assumptions, try to turn the group situation into a set of dyadic relationships, either treating each group member in turn, or thinking of the group as an entity and working with the 'dyad' of the therapist and the group-as-a-whole.

Within the world of individual and group psychotherapy there are a number of schools of thought which can be considered as sub-cultures. Each makes different assumptions about what will facilitate personal gain and what a therapist can best do to encourage gain to occur. Carl Rogers, for instance, considered it important to enter into the world of the client and see things as he or she does. One of the ways in which he attempted to do this was to 'reflect' back to the client what the client was attempting to express, concentrating on the emotional quality of his or her communications. This improved Rogers's own understanding of the client and also created in the client a sense of being understood (Rogers 1961: 52–3). Rose (1993) describes how, in cognitive-behavioural group therapy, the therapist makes use of reinforcement, modelling, cognitive restructuring, training in coping skills, systematic problem-solving and other strategies rooted ultimately in learning theory. Rutan (1993: 141), when speaking of psychoanalytic group psychotherapy, says that the goal of therapy is to help the patients learn about the previously unexamined assumptions – in other words, to make the unconscious conscious – and that to accomplish this the therapist, as his or her main task, must analyse the transference.

Historically, the practice of psychoanalysis and psychotherapy with individuals, and psychodynamic theory pertaining to individuals, preceded group dynamics and group psychotherapy. Many current-day practitioners have worked with individuals before moving into working with groups. Assumptions rooted in theory and practice concerning individuals are, not surprisingly, often imported into group psychotherapy. For example, it may be assumed that what matters most is the relationship between each group member and the therapist; that offering interpretations is the therapist's principal task; that acquiring insight is essential to achieving personal gain. These assumptions have the force of tradition behind them. They need to be re-examined to check whether and how they apply when a therapist is working with six or eight people in a group, rather than with just one person.

It is without doubt extremely difficult to question the assumptions of a culture of which one is a member. It is difficult to, as it were, stand aside from widely held assumptions sufficiently to recognise them *as* assumptions. It is nevertheless important to try to do so, because failing to recognise one's assumptions *as* assumptions keeps one trapped in taken-for-granted ways of thinking and behaving.

10 HOW CAN OR MIGHT THEORY BE MISUSED OR LEAD ONE ASTRAY? DOES ALL THEORY CARRY RISKS OF BEING MISUSED?

The following are some of the ways in which a practitioner can misuse theory. There may be more.

A theory can be applied to a population of people to which it is not suited. If for instance one is working with patients on long-stay chronic psychiatric wards who are stable and who now need to learn practical skills, a theory which includes the idea that current behaviours in the group are linked with early experiences will be of little help. A theory which directs attention to internalised conflicts will only be relevant secondarily, if at all, to adolescent offenders for whom peer-group relationships are centrally important. A theory which 'instructs' one to examine childhood experiences will not be immediately relevant to people deep in some current crisis or disturbed by some enforced life transition. Failing to select from amongst available theories that which fits the population one is working with is one way to misuse theory.

A theory can fit the population one is working with in general terms but nevertheless be applied inappropriately to specific events arising in a group. For instance, a therapist may offer an interpretation which is in line with a favoured theory, but does not in fact fit the situation into which it is introduced. The interpretation owes more to the theory than to the events actually occurring in the group. Influenced by assumptions embedded in theory, a therapist may intervene prematurely. If, for instance, theory says that an important route towards personal gain is to make the unconscious become conscious, the therapist may attempt to do so at the earliest possible moment: before sufficient evidence has emerged on which to form an hypothesis, or before people are ready to hear what the therapist has to say, or when some alternative and more straightforward explanation fits the circumstances better. If a premise within a theory is that surface behaviour almost always refers to and conceals underlying feelings or motivations, a therapist may probe for underlying feelings in the face of increasing anxiety on the part of the person being probed and regardless of the impact on others. In all such instances, the therapist's understanding and behaviour is being driven by the theory. The theory is not necessarily faulty, nor is it necessarily irrelevant to the group being worked with. However, it is being applied unthinkingly. It is imposed on events which could be understood in other, usually simpler, terms, or it is expressed in action without adequately anticipating the consequences of doing so.

The terms of a theory may be assumed to be explanations when they are in fact only names or labels. A therapist may observe to him- or herself that a transference reaction, or projective identification, or a restrictive solution is in place and, without realising it, think that he or she has explained what is happening. The name or label stops further thinking, for the therapist thinks that he or she has an explanation and therefore does not need to go on trying to understand the situation. This does not mean that theoretical terms are to be avoided. It only means that when they are applied to a specific concrete situation they should be regarded as a reasonable first approximation, to be amplified by further thinking.

A therapist can become, as it were, hermetically sealed inside his or her own preferred theory. This is manifested by seeing every situation in terms of one's preferred theory, insisting to oneself and to others (including group members) that a situation or an interaction or a person is to be understood in *this* way, and in no other. If this happens the therapist has become a slave to his or her favoured theory. Instead of making discriminating use of theory, the therapist then allows theory to make use of him or her. Faith outweighs evidence, and the therapist has yielded up choice. 'True believers' are at a disadvantage when working with a group. The preferred theory has become a kind of secular religion which constrains and channels how events are to be understood, and prescribes certain forms of interventions and proscribes others.

A therapist may draw concepts from here and there without attending to whether and how they fit together. One bit of theory may suggest one kind of intervention while another suggests another. A consequence can be that the therapist behaves in contradictory ways. Eclecticism tends to be highly regarded, and for good reasons, since by definition it means being open to ideas drawn from different sources. However, it carries its own risks, which are that the practitioner may end up with unintegrated ideas which push him or her first in one direction and then in another.

Does all theory carry risks of being misused?

Fuhriman (1997: 170) makes the following point:

> our adopted perspective guides the way we look at things and how we interpret

their meaning. This is not a negation of the use of theory or theoretical models, but an illustration of the risks we take. Regrettably, we are at risk of seeing only what we know or what we bring, rather than knowing what it is that is actually taking place. In essence, we see what we know, rather than *know* what we see. The 'reality' that is tapped runs the risk of only being a confirmation of our antecedent expectation.

This is a reminder that *any* theory can be misused or misapplied. It is easy to become trapped in one's own theory-linked assumptions, and difficult to stand far enough outside them to consider alternative explanations.

11 WHAT, THEN, IS THE APPROPRIATE USE OF THEORY?

A therapist who uses theory appropriately appreciates its applications and limitations. For instance, a theory may be applicable to some populations and not to others. A theory could assist in understanding events which occur during a group session, but not be a satisfactory foundation for making planning decisions. There may be limitations with respect to the range of events occurring in a group which the theory is capable of explaining. For instance, I consider group focal conflict theory very useful for understanding collusive defences in groups – how they arise and the functions they serve – but I know that the theory does not help me to understand episodes of contagion. For this, I find it necessary to go outside the theory and I rely instead on the thinking of Fritz Redl.

A therapist who is using theory appropriately will draw selectively from it those parts of the theory which fit or illuminate the specific situation currently being faced. A theory can be thought of as a set of cognitive tools, akin to actual tools found in a kitchen or a workshop. Each of these workplaces has in it a wide range of tools, some used frequently, some rarely, but all available to the craftsman or the cook, according to need. When selecting from group focal conflict theory, I find that I use the concepts of restrictive and enabling solutions frequently, and the concept of solutional conflict rarely. This does not mean that the concept of solutional conflict is of no use. It means that situations to which it applies do not arise so very often in groups. Depending on the situation itself, and one's purposes and intentions, one chooses from amongst the available tools. They are not all used at the same time but they are there, as resources. Which conceptual tools a therapist draws upon will depend on the specific situation being faced, and the therapist's purposes and intentions with respect to it.

Conceptual tools are essential to a therapist's operations, but whether they assist the therapeutic process or not depends on how and when they are used in practice. At the mad tea-party in *Alice in Wonderland*, the Mad Hatter, when trying to get his watch to tell him the day of the month, complains angrily to the March Hare, 'I told you butter wouldn't suit the works', to which the March Hare replies, 'But it was the best butter', and then gloomily repeats, 'It was the *best* butter, you know' (Carroll 1865). The moral is that a theory may be a 'good' theory, but if it is not pertinent to the situation or task to which it is being applied, it is of no use.

The appropriate use of theory includes being ready to draw from sources outside one's favoured theory if events occur for which the theory offers no explanation.

Using theory appropriately requires regarding any meaning placed on events as provisional – that is, as an hypothesis to be tested against further information. As has been emphasised, neither a theory nor hypotheses based on a theory are 'the truth'. They are possible, tentative explanations. A theory logically contains possible explanations and an hypothesis is a tentative explanation, derived from theory, of some observable event. It follows that if a therapist has an idea, based on theory, about how a specific concrete event may be understood, the idea needs to be held provisionally. The value of the hypothesis, which means its usefulness as a basis for action, can be tested by acquiring further information which will either support the hypothesis or show that it needs to be amended. Such information may become available through the interactions of members without the therapist's specific intervention, or may become available in consequence of a therapist's deliberate attempts to elicit it. One way to acquire further information is to act on an hypothesis and observe the consequences of doing so.

One can have confidence in a theory and in that sense 'believe' in it. Confidence in a theory will be based on having observed regularities in the observable world which the theory explains to one's satisfaction. This does not alter the need to hold theory provisionally, for it is always possible for new events to occur or new information to become available which requires one to modify hypotheses based on theory, or the theory itself.

The points made in this chapter lead to a point of view about the appropriate use of theory. It can be stated succinctly: a theory is a set of ideas from which one draws, selectively, in order to understand particular observable situations. A therapist needs a sufficient body of ideas to select from – enough to understand the phenomenon in question. Ideas may be drawn from a single theory or from a range of theories and concepts. Therapists form hypotheses by drawing from theory while observing the events which they want to understand. These hypotheses need to be held tentatively and provisionally. Subsequent observable events, including those which occur in consequence of a therapist's hypothesis-based actions, will show whether the hypothesis needs to be modified.

The thinking put forward in this chapter has had a long incubation period. In 1994 I wrote a paper titled 'Intervening in therapeutic groups: connections with theory'. It was to have appeared in a book of collected papers but this project collapsed and what I had written never appeared in print. In 1998 I prepared a shorter, re-worked version of this paper, titled 'Theory-building, theory-use and practice in group psychotherapy'. This was published just recently in *Group Analysis* (Whitaker 2000). The present chapter is my most recent thinking about theory and it's connections with practice.

Part IV

How therapists can continue to learn

Chapter 18

Learning from one's own practice experience

This chapter and the two which follow it concentrate on what a therapist can do to develop and enhance own understandings and skills, thereby also increasing the likelihood that group members will gain and that harm will be avoided. The focus will move from learning from one's own practice experiences (this chapter), to learning from the experiences of others (Chapter 19), to enhancing understandings by planning and conducting small-scale research on one's own groups and/or on groups conducted in one's workplace (Chapter 20).

Learning from own experience requires careful examination and reflection on one's own groups: on the planning decisions which were made, on events arising in a group and how they were (or could be) understood, and on one's own contributions and their consequences. Such reflections can usefully be undertaken at a number of points in the course of one's work with groups.

This chapter is organised into the following sections:

- Reflecting on events in a group while they are occurring.
- Post-session reviews.
- Medium-range reviews undertaken from time to time in the course of long-term groups.
- Reflecting on a group which has just ended.
- The need to plan in advance.

REFLECTING ON EVENTS IN A GROUP WHILE THEY ARE OCCURRING

While a group is in session, the group therapist will be paying attention to what members do and say as a session moves along, to sequences of events, and to own interventions and their consequences. He or she will form hypotheses about the meaning of these events, and will have certain purposes in mind with respect to them. A therapist will intervene or choose not to intervene on the basis of these hypotheses and purposes. The events shift, and so do the purposes, even though the overall purpose – that of benefiting each individual member – remains the same.

This is the basis for continuous purposeful planning while a group is in session, as discussed in Chapter 15.

All this is necessarily done on the therapist's own, and there is no escaping it. It is obvious enough that a therapist cannot stop the action and take time out to give considered thought to events occurring in the group. For better or for worse, he or she necessarily relies on immediately available sensitivities and understandings.

Co-therapists can learn from each other while the session is going on. Each may pick up cues from the other about how a situation may be understood. By noting how the co-therapist intervenes and how members respond, one sometimes adjusts one's own behaviour and shifts one's purposes.

POST-SESSION REVIEWS

Reviewing each session soon after it has ended not only contributes to one's own learning, but the learning occurs when it can be taken into account in the next and subsequent sessions of the group. Reviewing a session on one's own is not nearly as useful as having someone to talk *with* – a co-therapist or a colleague or a supervisor. The person with whom one discusses a session will bring a perspective different from one's own. This helps to avoid getting stuck in some unproductive or mistaken way of thinking. Reviewing a session with a co-therapist has the added advantage of revealing convergences and divergences in point of view and intervention strategies.

Reflecting on each group session soon after the session has ended is aided by having certain questions in mind which one intends to discuss.

With respect to developing, refining and expanding one's understanding of each person in the group, one can think about each person in turn and ask oneself such questions as: What is my current understanding of this person? In what ways has it changed from my initial understanding? Has this session had any particular importance for this person and if so, what was it, and is the person now in a better or a worse position than before? Did anyone become notably upset? or come to any harm? or benefit crucially during this session? Was anyone conspicuously ignored? or attacked?

With respect to keeping in touch with the dynamics of the group as a whole, one can ask oneself such questions as: Was the group working productively and if so what seemed to assist with this? Did the group seem to get stuck? Did the members seem to feel safe or unsafe, or safe up to some point in the session and then unsafe, or vice versa? Were members protecting themselves to the point of rendering the group so comfortable that little useful work was done? Were there shifts in topic or theme, when did this happen, and what seemed to account for it?

With respect to interactions between individuals, and between individual and group dynamics, one can ask: What part did different members play in generating a group theme, or in obstructing or reshaping it? Did one person become central in the group and, if so, what dynamics supported or maintained this, and what were the consequences for that person and for others? Was one person particularly important to another, or did two people become important to one another? If one person seemed to benefit crucially, by what group or interpersonal processes did this occur?

With respect to keeping in touch with one's own feelings and noting one's own behaviour and its consequences, one can ask oneself such questions as: Did I feel I understood what was going on or was I confused? Was I comfortable or uneasy? Did I feel angry with or critical of a group member or the group in general and, if so, why? Was I especially pleased with the group or with some one member and, if so, why? On reflection, did any of my interventions seem particularly apt and useful, or a mistake, or unnecessary? What kinds of interventions did I seem to favour and, taking into account what followed in the group, were these useful or not?

There is a further form of post-session review – other than discussing the session with someone else – which I particularly recommend since it has multiple pay-offs. It consists in examining very closely one or a few brief episodes extracted from the session. One might, for instance, have made a spontaneous intervention and want to understand better what triggered it and what the consequences were. Or one might realise that one person became very upset, or that one person seemed to achieve a sudden insight. Again, one might want to understand better what led up to the event and what followed it. One chooses a nodal point and then works backwards and forwards to decide when the episode began and ended. This is not a difficult task and one does not have to be precise. One wants to start far enough back to see what led up to the nodal event and continue for long enough to be able to see the consequences or the follow-through.

Closely examining one episode – comment by comment as it unfolds – often generates new understandings. One can examine the successive events, and also one's own intentions, feelings, and expectations. The material of the episode stimulates recall, and one can often understand more explicitly the meaning one placed on the events at the time, and what one drew upon from one's repertoire of theory and concepts for understanding the episode, and how one's own feelings at the time entered in. Looking at what happened after a therapist intervention helps one to understand its impact and judge its aptness.

It is a good idea, for any and all review purposes, to make written notes of a session as soon as possible after it finishes. The simplest form of written record is a personal diary in which events are recorded in the sequence in which they occurred. Straight description may be accompanied by notes on the therapist's thoughts and feelings at the time. I have noticed that the main deficiencies in written records are that (a) they condense too much, so that afterward not even the therapist, who was present at the time, can reconstruct what actually happened; and (b) they do not distinguish between description and interpretation. By the latter I mean that an interpretation is offered as if it were the event itself. For instance, the therapist notes down that the group was resistant. This is an interpretation. It may be justified, but one cannot judge because there is no information about the event itself. To keep description separate from interpretation, I often suggest that a page be divided vertically down the middle, so that straight descriptions can be entered on the left ('he said and then she said and then I said'), and directly opposite, notes made as to what the therapist thinks a run of events means, implies, portends, and how he or she felt at the time. Although keeping such notes takes time, it carries great pay-offs for learning.

If there are co-therapists, do they each take notes, or do they reconstruct the events of the session together? I think that this depends on how well they know one another and how compatible they feel they are. If working together is new to them, much could be learned by each writing down what they remember of a session prior to discussing it. Comparing views can help in getting to know one another better, and in facing differences and working out how to make positive use of them.

MacKenzie suggests that therapists keep a brief one-page record of each session, and provides a form for that purpose. He recommends organising notes into major themes, critical incidents, therapist issues, supervision comments (that is, anything emerging from a post-group session with a supervisor), and 'for next session' (anything the therapist wants to have in mind when the group next meets) (MacKenzie 1990: 263, 276). MacKenzie recommends including examples, naming events that were critical to each member, providing evidence of transference and counter-transference reactions, and so on. It is hard to do all this briefly or quickly, but there is much to be gained from taking the time.

If sessions, or some of them, are audio-taped, this of course supports the review effort. (An audio-tape is nearly as good as a video-tape, when one considers that it is for the therapist's own use and that the therapist will probably remember postures and non-verbal behaviour well enough.) It can be very illuminating to listen to a complete session but it is time-consuming to do so routinely. A tape provides the option of re-listening to a session or to part of it. It is particularly useful to re-listen if events have occurred which one regards as crucial, or which were puzzling. One can track events in order to understand them better, and check out whether one missed anything of importance at the time. The reasons for wishing to tape sessions of course need to be explained to the members, and their permission gained. Sometimes one also has to get the permission of the head of the service-providing organisation.

MEDIUM-RANGE REVIEWS UNDERTAKEN FROM TIME TO TIME IN THE COURSE OF LONG-TERM GROUPS

If a group is very long-term, it is prudent to review it at intervals. One will most probably decide to undertake a review at some fixed interval: perhaps every six months, or else when there are changes in membership. The following are questions one may wish to ask and try to answer at periodic reviews.

I Are the members of the group benefiting from the experience in the ways in which I hoped? Is anyone failing to gain, and is anyone being harmed?

One will have had certain hopes for personal benefits before the group began, based on one's understanding of the population and its needs. To conceptualise benefit, one may have made use of the ideas put forward in Chapter 3, about current and preferred state, life space, frontier, and preoccupying concern. By this means, or some other means, one will have formed ideas about the likely start-state of people drawn from the population, and what would constitute benefit. One will have been expanding one's understanding of each individual as the group moves along, and will have become clearer and more specific about what would constitute benefit for each. One will have been intervening in ways aimed at increasing individual gain. When reviewing a group at intervals, attention can be directed to whether or not individuals are gaining.

Most likely, some members are gaining and others are not, or some are gaining more than others. One can then try to think out what is contributing to benefit when it occurs, and what is stopping it when it does not. People who are gaining often create their own opportunities, or take initiatives in introducing themes important to themselves. Therapists support gain by having clearly in mind what would constitute a positive experience for an individual, and in consequence being alert to special opportunities arising in the group. A therapist might have recognised that a corrective emotional experience was occurring, or had occurred, and assisted the process by underlining, encouraging follow-up, and offering credit.

It was pointed out earlier that sometimes members fail to benefit because, in consequence of some group dynamic, they become locked into some role or position in the group which constricts opportunities for gain. If someone seems not to be gaining, this dynamic might account for it. Sometimes failure to benefit follows from consistent errors on the part of the therapist, or from a single gross error. Sometimes a group member avoids engaging with the group, and so fails to gain. When a review reveals lack of gain a therapist can usefully ask: What have been the gain-limiting circumstances for particular members and have they been inside or outside my control? Did I make errors or miss opportunities for benefiting members? A review may show that there are actions which a therapist can take to extricate an individual from a no-gain position.

2 Did the members negotiate their formative phase successfully, or did they get stuck and fail to move beyond it?

In many groups, individual members experience fears of the consequences of being in a therapeutic group and in many groups members build up and operate on shared defences which protect them from the presumed dangers of participating in the group. As described in Chapters 9 and 10, a group's formative phase is marked by efforts to become established as a group. A group which has become viable has shifted from operating on predominantly restrictive solutions to operating on predominantly enabling solutions.

Most groups achieve viability within the first five or six sessions, but some do not. They get stuck in some unsatisfactory way of functioning, or seem forever to be restarting. The problem could lie in characteristics of the population from which members are drawn – for instance, if members are unable to listen to and converse with one another. Or the composition may have been at fault in that the members are too similar to one another with respect to personally preferred defence (such as denial or projection). Or the therapist may have behaved in ways which intensified anxieties and drove the members into some particularly intractable restrictive solution, and kept them there.

If the group did not develop as the therapist hoped, the reasons for it need to be understood. It may still be possible to assist the group to develop favourably. Or one may conclude that, when planning the next group, different selection principles may need to be employed, or members may need to be differently or more thoroughly prepared for the experience, or another structure might be more suitable, or the therapist might need to change his or her intervention style.

3 Have there been drop-outs and how can these be explained?

It can be very instructive to review the events leading up to someone dropping out. Often, one sees prodromal signs which were not obvious at the time. The issue of dropping out was discussed at some length in Chapter 10. In general, it is possible that a person who drops out (a) has been misplaced in the group in the first place, being more vulnerable compared with the others and in consequence more threatened by group events; or (b) has been pressed by group processes into an intolerable position, from which he or she can escape only by dropping out; or (c) has been driven out of the group by errors on the part of the therapist. A therapist may judge that, for some members, dropping out was unfortunate and carried penalties. Understanding the reasons may help to forestall dropping out in the future. Sometimes a therapist judges that it was appropriate for a particular member to drop out. In such a case, a review of the circumstances may suggest ways of easing a future departure when it appears to be the best course of action.

4 Have there been fallow periods in the life of the group so far? Has anything occurred which has set the whole group back?

That processes can occur which hold a group back was discussed under point 2, above, in connection with a group failing to move beyond its formative stage. They are referred to again here as a reminder that non-facilitative processes can occur at any stage in a group's life. They can be triggered by changes in membership, or by a therapist leaving and being replaced, or by a therapist's temporary absence, or by some outside event which impinges on the members and intensifies anxieties. Sometimes a group retreats in consequence of the members' over-reaching themselves – moving into some realm which they find particularly threatening. When fears become intensified, for whatever reason, old defences can be reinvoked. In a review, any such episodes can be re-examined, especially to see whether the therapist could have anticipated set-backs, taken steps to avert them, or intervened to shorten them.

5 If there is a co-therapist, is this working out well or are there problems? What do I look for in a co-therapist?

Co-therapists can feel comfortable or distinctly uncomfortable with one another. They can be compatible or incompatible. They can be mutually supportive or they can undermine one another's efforts. Whatever has been the case, it is useful to examine the relationship. As with some of the other points being made here, one hopes that co-therapist relationships will have been examined in post-session discussions as the group went on. Reviewing sequences of sessions, at intervals, offers a further opportunity.

Sometimes junior members of staff rotate through a group as co-therapists, each staying perhaps six months, or four months. A good time to think over how the co-therapist relationship has worked out is when a co-therapist is about to depart. The senior therapist will develop a better idea of what he or she is looking for in a co-therapist, and see better ways to prepare a co-therapist for joining a group.

Sometimes there are obvious incompatibilities: one therapist may consider that the other has created problems which would not otherwise have existed, or frequently behaved in ways which undid his or her own efforts. Post-session discussions can sometimes deal with such problems but on occasion they persist. The two therapists may prove to have been intractably incompatible.

It is especially useful to examine assumptions which the two therapists hold in common, since some may prove to be helpful and some not. Co-therapists will get on better with one another and be less likely to get in one another's way if they hold in common assumptions about suitable forms of interventions and about how soon within any episode it is helpful to intervene and, conversely, how long it is best to wait before intervening. They will also get on better if they hold in common certain assumptions about the probable meaning of situations, since they will be less likely to intervene in ways which undo one another's efforts. However, commonality can also work against the effectiveness of a group if it is, for instance, based on a too-strict adherence to some theory, or if one therapist holds more power than the other, or if there are destructive features in the workplace culture. Problems arising from too much unanimity of outlook are not likely to come to light except through the help of third, neutral person.

In my experience, most problems arising between co-therapists can be resolved providing they are recognised and discussed. I can remember just one co-therapist relationship in which incompatibilities proved to be unresolvable. This occurred when my co-therapist repeatedly followed certain of my interventions with another intervention which tried to 'soften' what I had said. In my view she was undoing my efforts. Discussion revealed that what I regarded as a necessary and rather mild confrontation, my co-therapist regarded as a harsh attack. No amount of discussion resolved this: we simply had a different sense of what marked the border between 'attack' (her word) and 'saying what is' (my term).

6 Am I satisfied with the devices I have adopted for monitoring the group as it goes along?

When reviewing the notes one has taken of a series of group sessions one sometimes finds them too elliptical or abstract to be useful for recapturing the actual events. For instance, if one has said 'John was scapegoated' or 'a transference reaction occurred between Sarah and Michael', one does not in fact know what actually happened. Or one might find that one has listed themes but not shown how they emerged and how the group moved from one to the next. Whether or not notes are adequate in the sense of being full enough, or detailed enough, or satisfactorily organised depends of course on the purposes one has in mind. In general, it seems best to avoid abstract terms and, instead, to set down straightforward descriptions of what followed what, and to separate description from interpretation, as recommended above under the heading 'Post-session reviews'.

If any post-session paper-and-pencil devices were used, for instance check-lists or rating scales of members' degree of satisfaction with a session, these will need to be reviewed. One will particularly need to evaluate whether they are providing the information needed, or are proving to be an empty exercise, or are providing information about some aspects of the group experience and not others.

7 If the group is part of a wider programme, how are the parts of the programme fitting together? If the group is being conducted on its own, are there other avenues for help which should be used in conjunction with the group?

In some settings, individuals belong to several groups, or the same members may meet sometimes as a therapeutic group and at other times as an occupational therapy group, or a task group charged with making plans for a social programme, for instance in a day centre. There are many opportunities for informal contact outside the group sessions. One may judge that the parts of a wider programme fit well together and complement one another. For instance, one might note that gains made in the therapeutic group are being consolidated by being taken into other group and interpersonal settings which are part of an overall programme. Or one might note that problems arising in one kind of group are worked on constructively in another group setting and then brought back into the therapeutic group for further discussion.

Conversely, one may judge that the different parts of the programme, and/or the ways in which people participate in them, interfere with overall effectiveness. If the latter appears to be the case, it needs investigating. For instance, have members exported problems from one group setting to another whose purposes and norms protect members from confronting the problem? Have antagonisms between two people which have arisen in a therapeutic group been 'acted out' in a task group? Has there been friction with colleagues and, if so, with respect to what issues, and why? Have problems arisen through members having informal contact with one another outside the group sessions? With respect to any of these situations, action needs to be taken. In the first instance, this will consist of discussions with colleagues.

Sometimes reviewing a programme reveals gaps in it. For instance, staff may realise that a relatives' group could be set up which would complement a therapeutic group for those attending a day centre.

REFLECTING ON A GROUP WHICH HAS JUST ENDED

The questions listed above can be asked again when reviewing a time-limited group which has just ended, or a longer-term group which the therapist has decided to terminate. Most of them will have to be rephrased slightly, but they are essentially the same questions. There are some additional questions which can usefully be asked. (I am continuing the numbering from above.)

8 Was the planning right?

With reference to this, one can ask: (a) Did the structure suit the needs of the membership? (b) Was anyone included as a member who could not make use of the group or who created problems for others? Was the group composition well balanced, or faulty in some way? (c) Were members adequately prepared for the group experience? and (d) In retrospect, did I arrange for adequate communication with colleagues before the group started and while the group was going on?

9 If I were to conduct a group again with persons drawn from the same population as before, would I open the group in the same way or in a different way?

In retrospect, one sometimes sees that one promised more than one could deliver in an opening statement, or placed requirements on members which they could not comply with, or made rules which one could not enforce. One might see that the opening comment simply went on for too long. Such errors can easily be avoided another time, if they are recognised. If one chose to say nothing at all, how did the members respond? Did they get started reasonably well, or did anxiety rise to a dysfunctional level?

10 If the group was time-limited, what use was made of the group's termination phase? If the group was open-ended, at what point did particular members leave the group and was I satisfied or not with how this occurred/was handled?

After a group finishes, one might judge that the termination phase was not as fully utilised as it might have been. One might decide to make more explicit use of the impending end of a group in the future, by reminding members of the number of sessions remaining and encouraging them to take stock of what they have and have not achieved, bring up matters of importance while there is still time, and explore possible feelings of loss. If it is just one person who is about to leave the group, one might decide to be sure that enough notice is given for that person and for other group members to examine what the departure means for them.

11 What do individual members have to say about their group experience and whether they have gained or not? Does what they say correspond to or deviate from my own judgements as therapist?

It is an illuminating exercise to set members' perceptions of gain and of what has been important or difficult for them during the course of a group's life against one's own views. There is no reason to expect that members' and therapists' views will always be the same, although each should be understandable in the light of the other. Sometimes a group member reports gains which the therapist was not aware of, or refers to events regarded as significant which the therapist had not seen as such or does not even remember. Sometimes a member of a group declares him- or herself to have gained when the therapist judged that nothing of real value had occurred. Occasionally a member declares that he or she has not benefited although the therapist considers that there is clear evidence that benefit has occurred. Sometimes, of course, members' and therapist's perceptions and judgements coincide.

These possibilities are a reminder that there is no such thing as an 'objective' evaluation. Every judgement is necessarily from someone's point of view. Therapists need to accept both their own and the members' perspectives (and an observer's perspective, if there has been one). They need to try to understand differences between perspectives when they occur, and form an overall judgement about the value of the group for individuals which can be named and supported by evidence.

Access to group members' judgements about the group may come to a therapist through ordinary interaction in the course of the group, especially towards the end of the group or of a member's stay in the group. It is at such points that thoughts rather naturally turn to 'was it worthwhile?' Sometimes a therapist may wish to augment information gained in such ways by making time in the final sessions for members to reflect back on their experience. Group members can be asked such questions as: 'Has the group made a difference to you? If so, in what ways?' 'What do you think you will remember about this group?' 'What was most difficult? distressing? pleasing?' Those who participate in groups usually have something to say in response to such questions. A therapist might want to conduct individual post-group interviews to ascertain what each person thinks about the group experience. Such interviews can also assist each person to see how he or she could follow up on the group experience.

Therapists sometimes use, or are required by their managers to use, paper and pencil evaluation forms. People are asked to tick 'yes' or 'no' in response to a list of questions, or else to place a tick somewhere along a five- or a seven-point rating scale in which the extremes are (as examples) 'did not gain at all' and 'gained a great deal'; 'felt a member of the group' and 'did not feel I belonged'; and so on. Such forms may be used at the end of each session, or at the end of a series of sessions or a whole group experience. Forms filled out by individuals are attractive because they can be combined and summarised in statistical terms. Used on their own, however, such scales tend to have limited value. It is not unusual to find that respondents tend to make use of only part of the scale. For instance, on a scale of 1 to 5, with 5 at the positive end, one finds ticks against 3 or 4 most of the time. Mean scores tend to cluster around the middle or just above the middle, reducing the information yielded by the form and leading different groups to look more alike than they in fact were. If used after each session, sometimes one session is given a notably higher or lower rating than others. This *is* potentially useful information, for a session which stands out from the others can be checked against one's record of the content of the session, in an effort to understand the reasons for an atypical rating. It is useful to add an open-ended 'catch-all' question to such forms, such as: 'What else do you want to say about this session (or this group)?' Paper and pencil tests can be used in conjunction with other ways of gathering information. What one learns from them is best combined with what can be learned from what individual members have said during the termination phase or in post-group individual interviews, plus the therapist's and, if available, an observer's judgements. Combined sources are always better than single sources.

12 Were there further outcomes from conducting the group, apart from the group's impact on individual members?

One often hopes for certain further outcomes beyond benefits for individual members. For instance, one might hope that groups of the kind just conducted will be more favourably viewed by colleagues, or that junior colleagues associated with the effort will have learnt from the experience, or that one will have expanded one's own skills and understandings through trying out an unfamiliar structure or working with a new population. After a group has ended one can refer back to such additional hoped-for outcomes and judge whether or not they have been achieved.

13 What have I learned about my own style of conducting a group? Am I satisfied with my style or do I wish to change it in some way?

To assist in this, one can look to one's level of participation and judge whether it was suited to the group's structure and to the needs of the members. One can look at the closeness or distance which one has maintained, and at the level and kind of self-disclosure. One might notice a certain monotony of style: for instance, addressing the group as a whole to the exclusion of addressing individuals (or vice versa), or tending to ask questions, or tending to offer interpretations to the exclusion of other forms of interventions, or restricting oneself to providing summaries. One might notice a tendency to use elaborate or technical language, rather than plain speaking. One might realise that one tends to make long, complicated interventions with so many points in them that members find them hard to follow.

The most general question one can ask is whether one's style suited the needs of the group members, or whether it was, for instance, too cold and remote, intrusive, matey, demanding, or controlling.

14 What about my use of theory? Was there any way in which I misused theory?

This is one of the more difficult questions to address, yet it is quite important if one wishes to learn from experience, be more sure of making *appropriate* use of theory, and perhaps adjust the ways in which one makes use of theory when conducting groups.

Possible ways to misuse theory were discussed in the preceding chapter. With these in mind, one can think back over a group and reflect on whether any misuses have occurred. Avoiding or reducing the misuse of theory is assisted if, first, one maintains a critical stance towards the theory one is in the habit of using when judging its relevance to particular situations, and second, if one is prepared to look outside one's own preferred theory for relevant ideas. This is not an argument against holding a preferred theory for understanding events. It is an argument in favour of a flexible stance towards theory which makes it less likely that events will be understood in stereotypic ways.

The question: Am I misusing theory? is very hard to examine on one's own. One tends to take a favoured theory for granted. It is so much a part of one's thinking that assumptions based on it are likely to be accepted without realising that they *are* assumptions. One needs to observe oneself from a little distance, and this is best done with a helper who understands one's preferred theory and preferred practice approach, but is also aware of alternatives.

15 What kinds of people do I prefer to work with in groups? What structures do I prefer to use in my work with groups, and what is my preferred therapist style?

These questions cannot be answered on the basis of one or a few experiences with groups. One needs to conduct a number of groups of different types and with different populations before getting a sense of one's special skills and interests. One may then find that one's skills fit some populations and some group structures better than others, or that one feels more rewarded when working with some populations or sub-populations than with others. It is unreasonable to expect to be equally good, or equally pleased, with all forms of therapeutic group work. It is reasonable to take personal preferences and special skills into account when planning future work.

16 Should I continue to work with groups, or do I prefer some other mode for helping people?

Some therapists simply do not take to working with small groups and prefer one-to-one psychotherapy or working with the milieu. If this is the case it is as well to recognise it, for there is no way to do one's best work if the route chosen for helping people seems beset with difficulties or second-best.

If a therapist is uncomfortable or anxious when working with groups, some possible reasons are that he or she feels unable to maintain adequate control over the course of group events, or fears being ganged up on by members, or fears becoming confused and getting out of control, or feels to be short-changing individuals by not being able to concentrate on each one at length.

Some of these concerns stem from not understanding how a small group can be a medium for help. They can often be dealt with through consultation or supervision. If such concerns persist, it is probably better to put one's efforts into some other mode of helping people.

THE NEED TO PLAN IN ADVANCE

Virtually all these routes towards improving and extending one's own under-standings and skills require advance planning. One cannot undertake any of these activities unless one has provided time for them, and reached agreements with whoever is to function as one's helper. Creating *structures* for monitoring and evaluating a group was referred to in Chapter 6 as one of the steps in planning. However, what can and should be attended to *within* a structure was deferred until now, in order to take into account what has been said in the Part III chapters about what therapists are likely to encounter in the course of their practice.

Chapter 19

Learning from the experiences of others

The recommendations made in the previous chapter involve making use of a co-therapist, colleague, or supervisor. In doing so, one is of course making use of the experience of someone other than oneself. However, in Chapter 18 the focus was on one's own groups and on one's own behaviour and its consequences. In this chapter I move to making use of the experiences of others when that experience is independent of one's own therapeutic efforts. This chapter is organised in four sections:

- Learning through reading about what others have to say about their work with groups or their thinking about groups.
- Attending courses.
- Learning through regular discussions with colleagues who are also conducting groups.
- Responding actively to what one reads and hears.

LEARNING THROUGH READING ABOUT WHAT OTHERS HAVE TO SAY ABOUT THEIR WORK WITH GROUPS OR THEIR THINKING ABOUT GROUPS

Every author writes from his or her own perspective, which is always at least somewhat different from one's own. One is exposed, through reading, to different ways of thinking about groups and the people in them. One may gain new insights and information about the populations one works with, become aware of alternative ways of structuring and composing groups or of preparing people for participating. One may acquire a different slant on situations encountered in groups and ways of responding to them. In short, one often finds ideas and practices which are congenial with one's own, yet somewhat different, and which seem worth adding to one's existing set of understandings or customary way of practising.

Some of what is available in the literature will be outside one's core interests. Some of it may seem baffling – not wrong, necessarily, but hard to understand. If so, it will of course be difficult to make use of it. When the latter happens, the reason may be that one's mental capacity is not up to the task, but it is also the case that some writing really is obscure. The author uses undefined abstract terms (sometimes, whole chains of abstract terms), or presents conclusions without reference to the evidence on which they are based. Some authors assume that readers have background knowledge which makes it unnecessary to define terms. If so, there will be nothing in the writing which helps the reader to decode or translate.

Many practitioners have very limited time for reading. 'Keeping up with the literature' is virtually impossible if one means by this *all* the literature. There is no choice but to select.

On what basis is one to select? Some practitioners may choose to concentrate on particular patient or client groups, such as people with eating disorders, or HIV patients, or alcoholics, or people who have suffered a bereavement, or borderline patients, and so on. Some may wish to focus on the setting in which the work occurs, such as an in-patient facility for psychiatric patients, or an out-patient clinic, or a hostel. Some will be particularly interested in types of group psychotherapy, such as short-term time-limited groups, or group psychotherapy combined with other forms of help. Some will be interested in particular issues, such as selection and preparation, or composition, or the role of the therapist. Some will want to pursue particular theoretical perspectives, or compare different perspectives. Some practitioners come across authors who seem to them to be particularly wise in the ways of groups, and whose writing they find accessible. They will then be inclined to read anything written by those authors.

Many practitioners will want to expand their reading beyond therapeutic groups as such, into background reading on, for instance, group dynamics, or particular psychiatric disorders, or on theory which is not about therapeutic groups but which bears on them, such as attachment theory, or stress and coping, or developmental life stages, or the impact of transitions. They might want to understand or become informed about matters which pertain specifically to the populations they work with, for instance, particular medical conditions, or characteristics of particular ethnic cultures.

If one is interested in comparative theory, a useful kind of article or book is that which shows how different theories bear on particular situations encountered in groups. An example of this is Rabin and Rosenbaum's (1976) edited book, *How to Begin a Psychotherapy Group: Six Approaches*. They invited six contributors, who subscribed to different theories/practice approaches, to describe how they began their groups, and why. Another approach was taken by Lonergan (1994), who compared seven theoretical approaches by applying each of them to the same group episode. Lonergan first described an episode which occurred in a group therapy session in some detail, then discussed how it would be understood in terms of Freud's group psychology, basic assumption theory, group focal conflict theory, living systems theory, Foulkes's psychoanalysis in groups; Yalom's here-and-now approach; and the cognitive/behavioural approach. In undertaking this exercise Lonergan drew upon her own understanding of these approaches.

Apart from pursuing particular interests, there is value in reading randomly, outside one's own readily specifiable interests, for one often finds treasures by doing so.

I am coming perilously close to saying 'read everything', which I know is impossible. How is a therapist to find a way to begin? The literature on groups is vast and getting vaster. To state the obvious, practitioners will most likely scan the tables of contents of journals and read what strikes them as potentially interesting. Book reviews help one to decide what is likely to be pertinent to one's own interests. However, these routes into the literature direct attention only to contemporary writing. It is a mistake to fall into believing that what is recent is necessarily better. At least, I would not want to do without the insights of Fritz Redl, who wrote in the 1960s, or Kurt Lewin, who wrote earlier still, or Helen Durkin, who wrote perceptively about group dynamics and its relation to group psychotherapy, or Erik Erikson, who shed such useful light on developmental stages through the life cycle. Historical accounts of the development of group psychotherapy can be 'mined' for references to seminal earlier writing (see Scheidlinger 1993; Rutan and Stone 1993; Ettin 1992; and MacKenzie 1990).

With respect to both earlier and more contemporary writing, one has to use one's own judgement in extracting what seems useful and discarding what does not. When evaluating the work of others, everyone makes judgements on the basis of criteria which seem important to them. It is interesting and instructive to think out just what these are. If I ask myself what impresses me and what puts me off, I find that I respect careful scholarship and thoroughness; clear definitions of concepts and of their use in practice; innovative ideas and new forms of practice (providing that a clear rationale is presented for the innovation); and evidence that an author can think outside conventionally accepted assumptions or 'received wisdom'. I am put off by books or articles which use abstract, undefined terms, and by writers whose theory seems to float around in mid-air, unanchored to events. I am suspicious of those who appear to follow some theory uncritically. I am impatient with those who seem still to be in thrall to what I consider to be outdated assumptions, such as that group treatment is necessarily inferior to individual treatment, or that it is only long-term treatment which can be 'deep' and therefore useful, or that if one pays attention to group level phenomena one necessarily neglects or loses the individual.

A number of articles and books have been referred to in the course of earlier chapters, and I will allow these to stand as guides to the literature. They are not an exhaustive list, but many of them are good starting points. Review articles are especially helpful, though I emphasise that they should be used as an initial way into the literature and not accepted as the final word. Many readers will wish to consult textbooks and general guides to practice, such as MacKenzie (1990), Ettin (1992), Rutan and Stone (1993), Yalom (1995), and, indeed, this book.

ATTENDING COURSES

Attending courses is another way to learn from the experience of others – both the course tutors and fellow course members.

It is stating the obvious that choosing a course is influenced by what is available, what is convenient, what sounds promising, and what has achieved a good reputation. Some courses yield a professional qualification, which is important for some people and less important for others. A course will include a series of lectures in which substantive ideas are presented. Most courses nowadays also include experiential learning through small groups, akin to therapeutic groups. The course structure may or may not include time specifically reserved for discussion, or for reading and sharing views about what has been read. My only piece of advice is to choose in favour of courses which provide plenty of time for discussion amongst the members and between members and lecturers, so that opportunities are present for clarifying, comparing, sharing, and testing against own experience. 'Teaching' which is mainly one-way ('I teach; you learn') misunderstands how learning occurs.

LEARNING THROUGH REGULAR DISCUSSIONS WITH COLLEAGUES WHO ARE ALSO CONDUCTING GROUPS

A congenial group of colleagues can learn a great deal from one another, as I know from personal experience. Therapists can gain much from creating peer groups for learning purposes. This is one of the best (and most enjoyable) ways of learning. Points of view and practice preferences are compared and contrasted, and one's own direct experience is augmented by the experiences of others.

I once joined with a group of colleagues in examining the first sessions of therapeutic groups. Each of us in turn brought detailed notes of a first session, or sometimes an audio-tape. The discussions which followed – of the sessions themselves and of issues cast up by them – generated learning for everyone. Such discussions can expand experience by showing how others respond to situations comparable to those one has faced oneself. They help one to realise that one has been operating on unrecognised or untested assumptions, if such is the case. They often illuminate how theory is applied to understanding events.

RESPONDING ACTIVELY TO WHAT ONE READS AND HEARS

Learners are not inert sponges, mopping up what they read and hear indiscriminately. They are likely to be struck by some bits of what they read or hear and not others. They may respond with curiosity: How did this person arrive at this point of view, at these conclusions, at this form of practice? How does what X says connect with the way I look at things? A reader or listener may respond affectively, by thinking: That's a nice idea; I like/admire that way of thinking; What a brilliant way of looking at that; or, alternatively, He's just plain wrong; This doesn't feel right; or, sometimes: That's plausible, but I prefer. . . .

Noting how one feels about some new idea or practice is not a bad first step, but it is of course not enough. The next step, which is essential and takes longer, is to think out the grounds for having had the feeling and whether it can be justified by reasoned argument. For instance, I found myself really liking Harwood's (1998b: 110) point (following from Kohut's thinking) that an infant is born into a social and cultural world and not just to a dyadic pair. Why was this appealing? It struck me as corresponding to what actually is the case, and a necessary corrective to any tradition-sanctioned tendency to account for everything in terms of mother–child pair interactions. It also provides a rationale for working in groups by suggesting the importance of replicating experiences with social groupings. Harwood's thinking also extends how one might think about transference reactions, for it suggests that the term transference ought to include within it the possibility of re-experiencing sibship or peer relationships within a therapeutic group.

I also liked Ormont's (1995) idea of making use of a group to assist members to develop an observing ego. The idea of an observing ego is not new, of course, but Ormont identified five successive steps to help people achieve this (see the discussion on p. 189). I found valuable his orderly discussion of how group members can be helped to acquire an observing ego.

I was struck by a brief comment made by Lonergan in the same article referred to a bit earlier in this chapter. She reports Marmor's finding that 'therapists who were zealous about a theory and explained it to their patients got better results than those who did not. It did not matter what the theory was' (Lonergan 1994, referring to Marmor 1988). My first thought was that it *must* matter what the theory is, for I believe that some theories are preferable to others on the grounds that they are more clearly and closely connected to observable events occurring in groups – in other words, less speculative. However, it then occurred to me that the important part of this statement might be 'and explained it to their patients'. Is it the case that explaining the theory one operates on is beneficial to patients? Why would this be? Does it communicate to the patients that the therapist knows what he/she is doing? Does it fulfil the same function for patients as it does for the therapist: namely, providing a way to understand complicated events? I have never explained group focal conflict theory to patients, though I sometimes refer to it in non-technical language, for instance by pointing to a norm which is in operation and its conse-quences for the group, or by naming a conflict which seems to me to be present in the group. Is this what Marmor meant by 'explaining'? For me, Lonergan's (or Marmor's) point raised further questions about how and when and in what contexts therapists might explain their theory, or parts of it, to their patients, and for what reasons. This provided much food for thought.

One does not have to agree with what one reads or hears in order to learn from it. Sometimes one reads something or hears something which seems wrong, or remote from one's own experience. This too is a stimulus for learning, for one can ask oneself such questions as: What is it, exactly, that I find hard to accept? What do I think this author is omitting or overlooking when he/she examines x, y, or z? In what ways has my own experience been different, such that these formulations or recommendations seem inappropriate? Would I feel uncomfortable with the intervention style being recommended or implied as helpful and, if so, why? What assumptions are being made here about the nature of therapeutic groups or the position of the therapist which are incompatible with my own? And, from the latter: What assumptions do I hold which underpin my own work with groups? Posing and seeking to answer such questions sharpens one's understanding of one's own point of view and practice preferences.

It seems to me unlikely that anyone reads, or listen to lectures or to discussions, entirely passively. People respond to and interact with what they read or hear. Learning proceeds by testing unfamiliar ideas against one's own experiences and formulating new questions which deserve exploration.

Chapter 20

Conducting research on one's own groups and in one's own workplace

Through planning and conducting research, a group therapist can generate new information and enhance understandings related to self-chosen special interests.

The prospect of engaging in research may seem daunting if one has in mind large-scale survey research, experiments (or 'quasi-experiments'), or large-scale clinical studies. It is, however, possible and not so excessively demanding on a practitioner's time to carry out small-scale pieces of research which focus on particular issues. Many of the skills needed for engaging in research are not so different from clinical skills. Practitioners after all become skilful in observing groups and individuals in groups, in noting their own behaviour and its consequences, in keeping observations separate from inferences, and so on. There is not a big gap between reflecting on own experience, by means suggested in Chapter 18, and taking the further step of planning and conducting small-scale research. One does, however, need to take care to be systematic and consistent.

This chapter is organised as follows:

- Sequential steps in planning and conducting a piece of research.
- Increasing the likelihood that research findings will be taken into account by those responsible for policy-making within service-providing organisations.
- Practitioner-conducted research contrasted with other forms of research.
- Using the literature to support one's research efforts.

SEQUENTIAL STEPS IN PLANNING AND CONDUCTING A PIECE OF RESEARCH

To conduct a small-scale piece of research, one needs to move through a series of steps:

1 identifying a 'node of curiosity';
2 defining one's research purposes;
3 examining relevant literature;
4 working out a plan and procedure which will allow one to pursue one's purposes;

5 carrying out the research plan;
6 analysing the data and drawing conclusions;
7 thinking out the implications for further research;
8 thinking out the implications of the research for practice or policy;
9 writing up; and
10 making opportunities for others to gain from one's research efforts.

Each of these will be discussed in turn.

I Identifying a 'node of curiosity'

Research has to be *about* something. It has to have a focus and a subject matter. The focus will be chosen by the practitioner-researcher and will relate to his or her own special interests and curiosities. A group therapist might for instance become interested in how it is that some members gain and some do not; or in certain kinds of 'problem persons' in groups; or in how it is that particular individuals become, for periods of time, the centre of attention in their groups; or in drop-outs; or in understanding better his or her own style of intervening and its consequences. Being curious about something comes first, for without curiosity there is no potential focus for one's efforts, and no energy for the task.

2 Defining one's research purposes

From a written statement of what one is curious about, an overall research purpose can be framed. This is best expressed as a question – for example: Under what circumstances do people drop out?, or What accounts for one person being attacked in a group?, or What accounts for failure to gain in a group?

Having written down one's overall purpose, it is necessary to name further purposes which lie within the generally stated purpose. For instance, if one has become interested in concerted attacks on one individual in a group, one might formulate one's overall purpose as: What accounts for one person becoming the target of a concerted attack on the part or all or most of the others? One will then need to 'unpack' this statement of overall purpose by setting out further, more specific and detailed questions which are included within it. These might include, for instance: What kinds of events precede an attack on one person? What has the person him- or herself said or done? What form does the attack take? What keeps an attack going, or interrupts it? Does everyone join in, or only some? Do those doing the attacking behave in much the same way or in different ways? What seems to motivate the attacker(s)? How does the attacked person react to the attack? What were my own feelings at the time? Did I judge it necessary to intervene and if so, why? Did I intervene and if so, how? What were the consequences of my intervention: did it help or hinder? What were the consequences of an episode of concerted attack on the target person? on the others? on how the group then moved or developed? And so on.

It is best, at first, to follow the dictum 'Don't get it right, get it down'. One can be quite spontaneous in the first instance. This gets one in touch quickly with the issues one wants to address. Subsequently, it will be necessary to review the list of questions with a critical eye: spotting repetitions, eliminating obscure terms, noting omissions and adding further questions, and eliminating questions which do not really belong within the overall purpose.

This step – of defining an overall research purpose and a set of sub-purposes – can be quickly stated. In practice, however, it takes time and should not be skimped. Usually, one has to reframe questions repeatedly before one is satisfied that they represent one's interests and are sufficiently clear and precise. It is helpful to keep in mind that one is seeking to be explicit about *research* purposes – what one wants to find out about or understand better. To say 'my purpose is to conduct post-group interviews with members' is not a research purpose: it refers to a method of data collection. To say 'my purpose is to provide convincing evidence that group psycho-therapy is an effective form of help' is not a research purpose: it refers to an outcome which one hopes will follow from the research.

Having worked out a set of research purposes as well as one can, it is helpful to discuss them with a colleague since someone who stands at a little distance from the research effort can often spot omissions or ambiguities.

3 Examining relevant literature

It is advantageous to familiarise oneself with how others have thought about the issue one is interested in, and/or have addressed it through research. I have placed this task third in the sequence of tasks (rather than earlier) because I think it best to work out one's own purposes first, as fully as one can, on the basis of own experience. One will then have made explicit to oneself just what one's 'node of curiosity or interest' is, and what lies inside it and outside it. This avoids being influenced too soon by the thinking of others, and ending up pursuing someone else's curiosities rather than one's own, or making use of some scale or question-naire or check-list because it is there and convenient, rather than because it fits well with one's own purposes. A researcher wants to make use of the literature but not be diverted or dominated by it.

After research purposes have been worked out, but before a research plan has been made, is a good time to review the related literature. One will want to know what has already been done and thought about the issue. The work of others may suggest further sub-purposes one hadn't thought of, or research procedures or data-collection devices which one could make use of or adapt.

4 Working out a plan and procedure which will allow one to pursue one's purposes

Once the overall purpose and the sub-purposes have been spelled out to one's satisfaction, it becomes possible to attend to what sort of research design will be appropriate and what kind of data collection and data analysis will be needed. Returning to the example of people who become the target of concerted attacks: one would have to decide what the research unit will be: most likely, an episode during which an attack occurred. One would surely need to have some criteria for deciding what constitutes an attack, and what marks the beginning and the end of an episode which involved an attack. When thinking out what constitutes an attack, one will no doubt wish to include indirect as well as direct attacks, subtle as well as blatant attacks. Because indirect or subtle attacks are less easy to recognise, one will have to think out how to recognise an indirect attack when it occurs.

How many episodes will need to be examined, and from how many groups? One will need enough episodes and enough groups to avoid basing conclusions on so small a number of episodes that the full range of circumstances does not come to light, and on so small a number of groups that one is mainly learning about the idiosyncracies of just one or two groups. The judgement of how many can be made on the basis of clinical experience. An experienced practitioner will have a sense of how many episodes are enough, and how many are more than is needed because the dynamics are likely to begin to repeat themselves. For instance, one would surely think that three episodes, from each of two groups, will not be enough. On the other hand, one is unlikely to think it necessary to study eight episodes from each of fifty groups. The judgement is made on the basis of 'how many is likely to be enough to meet my research purposes?'. One might settle on, say, four episodes drawn from each of five groups, making twenty episodes in all. This is likely to be about right.

Having got this far in planning, one will have to devise procedures for identifying the episodes to be included in one's research sample. Could one rely on therapists' notes (one's own and those of colleagues)? Might one ask permission of colleagues to sit in on their groups as an observer? Would a paper-and-pencil questionnaire which group therapists fill out after each group session provide the information needed? Might one need to interview colleagues (or oneself)? One often has to try several procedures in order to decide which will work best.

One will have to devise systematic procedures for gathering and recording information about each episode, to be sure that one does not miss out anything, or end up describing some episodes in less detail than others. The information which one gathers and records should match the sub-purposes previously identified. One might devise a proforma of some kind, to be sure that everything which needs to be included is included, and to be sure that comparable information is recorded for each data unit.

When choosing data-collection procedures, whatever one's research purposes, three considerations are: (a) whether to make use of data-collection devices and procedures already available in the literature or, alternatively, devise one's own; (b) whether to use 'objective' measures such as rating scales and check-lists, or else open-ended devices such as interviews and observation schedules or projective tests which generate qualitative data, or both; and (c) the time likely to be required for data collection and data analysis.

might examine whether the impact on the person being attacked is influenced by the degree of unanimity of the attack: the number of persons joining in. One might examine the effect of an individual's responses to an attack on whether the attack continues or not. One might examine different ways in which therapists react to or intervene in attacks, and the consequences of different forms of interventions.

Suppose that one has reasons to believe, at this late stage in the research, that an insufficient number of episodes has been studied. It is not too late to add more episodes to the sample. One will have decided on a certain number of episodes at the planning stage. However, having analysed that number of episodes, one may find such diversity, episode to episode, that one suspects that if one were to analyse additional episodes there would be greater diversity still – in other words, more to be learned. This would be an argument for increasing the size of the sample. One must of course place a limit on how much data one collects, for practical reasons. In the unlikely event that much more data should be collected and analysed, and one has run out of time, it is possible to analyse what one has and report the results as 'preliminary findings'.

7 Thinking out the implications for further research

Virtually all research findings point to further possible lines of investigation in the future. One chooses for oneself whether to pursue further research or not, but it is always worth thinking out what further work is indicated by what one has learned. If one thinks of research as pushing out the frontiers of knowledge, having reached one frontier one is, more often than not, in a position to see still more frontiers ahead. This is part of the learning which can be achieved, and it is worth noting down and sharing with others.

8 Thinking out the implications of the research for practice or policy

What is learned from research usually has implications for future actions. A study of concerted attacks on one person, for instance, will help practitioners to detect precipitating events, or to perceive that many attacks are more than a matter of villains and victims, but, more subtly, are a matter of some individuals inviting attacks and others responding to their cues. The practitioner-researcher may understand better the functions which attacks may fulfil for those doing the attacking. Is the attack, for instance, a way of protecting oneself from being attacked? Is the person being attacked a substitute target for someone else who is the real object of anger? The practitioner-researcher arrives at a better understanding of *when* an intervention is helpful or necessary, which forms of intervention are more or less helpful, and to whom an intervention is best directed – the attackers or the attacked.

There will also be implications for policy, especially in settings in which a group is only one form of help, or where responsibility for certain individuals is shared, or where there is a key worker. For instance, should other members of staff be informed when an attack takes place within a group? Does a person who is prone to attracting attacks need special one-to-one help? Does the research reveal dynamics which other members of staff should know about: for instance, anxieties about an imminent change in key worker? Research often suggests forms of communication among staff that are likely to support achieving goals and avoiding problems, or that raise questions related to confidentiality which a whole staff group needs to discuss.

9 Writing up

Research reports usually are presented in a series of sections which correspond to the steps followed in the research itself. Details will depend on the nature of the research, but successive sections usually focus on:

- the purposes of the research;
- why the researcher considered the issue an important one;
- background information about the issue as found in the literature;
- the research plan;
- data-collecting procedures;
- data-analysis procedures;
- what was learned ('findings' and conclusions); and
- implications for practice or policy.

10 Making opportunities for others to gain from one's research efforts

The great advantage of conducting research on one's own groups lies in what one learns for oneself. However, one usually also wants to share what one has learned with others. As was said under 7, above, what is learned through research often has a bearing on practice and policy in the workplace, so it is particularly important that findings become known to others and that they have opportunities to think through any implications for action.

It is usual to disseminate research results through the written word, through reports or articles. This is fine, but I would regard it as only a start, especially when the research has been conducted in one's own workplace. Sending out a written report is like sending an arrow into the air: it falls one knows not where. Researchers often do not find out how their research was received by others, and those who read a report or article have no opportunity to share their reactions with the researcher or anyone else. It is therefore useful to make use of dissemination procedures which include opportunities for others to become informed about the research and its findings, *and also* to think over how the research connects or does not connect with own experience, and whether and how it suggests adjustments in practice or in policy. This is best done through workshop formats designed to include plenty of time for discussion and exchanges and comparisons of views. If those attending such workshops are members of staff in the same service-providing facility, they can examine together implications for policy. If the researcher is also a member of staff, then those participating will be one's own colleagues. Disseminating research findings to staff groups has potential pay-offs but also carries risks. I believe that the pay-offs outweigh the risks but it is well to be aware of possible risks in order to be prepared for them. For instance, previously concealed or unrecognised incompatibilities among members of staff may be exposed, or conflict may arise over whether policy can or should be changed. It is counterproductive for a researcher, keen to defend his or her research and its findings and implications, to get into adversarial confrontations with colleagues or managers. It is often useful to make use of some person external to the organisation who has enough distance from the organisational dynamics to help all concerned to address any issue arising as a problem or task which all need to address.

INCREASING THE LIKELIHOOD THAT RESEARCH FINDINGS WILL BE TAKEN INTO ACCOUNT BY THOSE RESPONSIBLE FOR POLICY-MAKING WITHIN SERVICE-PROVIDING ORGANISATIONS

A colleague, Lesley Archer, and I conducted a number of 'learning groups' in which practitioners as well as managers of social services departments were helped to devise and conduct pieces of research on issues arising out of their own work experience. We were subsequently joined in this effort by Dr Leslie Hicks. Those who participated in these learning groups were successful in their research efforts and clearly benefited from undertaking research. Some research findings were relevant to the service-providing organisations within which our course members worked. It was with respect to these that problems sometimes arose. Policy-makers, though they were provided with research reports, did not always take them into account when considering or revising organisational policy. Sometimes the research seemed to sink without trace as far as the organisation was concerned. This of course was frustrating for those who carried out the research as well as for ourselves as teachers and guides.

Such experiences led us to develop a new structure within which research was carried out, which we referred to as 'research partnerships' with service-providing organisations. The heart of the activity remained working with small groups of practitioners and managers, helping each to design and conduct research. However, we also built in, from the beginning, structures which assisted those higher up in the organisation to keep in touch with the research which was being done as it went along. We scheduled thrice-yearly workshop meetings for programme participants and managers at different levels within the organisation. We also built into our overall plan a follow-up dissemination phase, which from the start was understood by everyone to be an integral part of the research programme. A full-day workshop was always planned to follow the completion of the research. In it, there were opportunities for all agency or departmental staff (practitioners and managers) not only to hear the research projects summarised but to exchange views about its implications for policy. This did not lead to research findings being automatically or quickly turned into policy, but it meant that policy implications were examined by people occupying different positions within the organisation, including those with responsibility for policy and power to shape it. Sometimes workshop discussions made clear what would need to be done to make implementation possible, or it brought to light factors which would make implementation difficult, or revealed problems which implementation would most likely bring in its wake, and which would also have to be addressed.

One does not necessarily have to adopt the dissemination and research-utilisation structures just described, but *some* structure or procedure is needed to maintain communication with others in the organisation. This will be important when preparing a piece of research, while undertaking it, and in the follow-up period.

PRACTITIONER-CONDUCTED RESEARCH CONTRASTED WITH OTHER FORMS OF RESEARCH

In outlining the steps which need to be taken when planning and conducting research, I have emphasised the importance of identifying a 'node of curiosity' *emerging from one's own practice experience*, and then spelling it out as an overall research purpose and a set of sub-purposes. Some examples were provided of possible nodes of curiosity when discussing step 2, above, and one research purpose – that of understanding the dynamics associated with a concerted attack on one person – was used as an example when discussing further steps.

Many, many issues can be investigated through practitioner-conducted research but there are some research-worthy issues which are difficult or impossible to investigate from a practice base. For instance, it will be difficult or impracticable to conduct experiments, with control groups and the like, or survey research, or large-scale clinical studies, or large-scale outcome studies. A practitioner is not in a position, for instance, to compare one part of the country with another for the kinds of personal problems which people bring to an out-patient service, or to compare the adequacy of service-provision for different populations of people, or to examine and compare therapist styles associated with different theoretical approaches to groups.

These exclusions, however, leave a large number of issues which could be investigated, and they are the ones most likely to interest practitioners. I have already mentioned, as possible 'nodes of curiosity': how it is that some members gain and some appear not to have gained; certain kinds of 'problem persons'; how it is that particular individuals become, for periods of time, the centre of attention in their groups; drop-outs; and understanding better one's own style of intervening and its consequences. Many more could be added.

Research issues of the kind likely to be undertaken by practitioners on their own groups are often best investigated through multiple-case studies, or sometimes through single-case studies. In a multiple-case study, a number of individuals or situations with characteristics in common are examined and compared. For instance, a number of early drop-outs could be identified and studied from the point of view of the circumstances which preceded dropping-out, the drop-out's position in the composition of the group, the drop-out's participation in the group prior to dropping out, and other factors regarded as potentially relevant. Or a number of similar situations could be examined and compared, for instance episodes of contagion or of members retreating into some defensive position, or responses to bringing a new member into a group. Another form of multiple-case study consists in comparing two contrasting kinds of individuals or situations. For example, comparing high-gain and low-gain group members, or different ways of preparing prospective members for participating in a group.

Single-case studies can also be valuable. Many situations are so complex that much can be learned through following the course of development of a single group, or a single person's group experience. For instance, one person could be followed through his or her group experience, looking also at impact on, or changes in, the person's family and social/interpersonal environment. The concept of 'life space', introduced in Chapter 3, could be utilised. One would probably proceed by examining a run of episodes in which the person figured prominently, or by ascertaining through interviews what the person him- or herself regarded as important about the group experience, or by enquiring of the therapist (who might be oneself) what were regarded as critical incidents, turning points, and 'red-letter days'. Preferably, such methods would be used in combination.

I have, in this chapter, emphasised finding a 'node of curiosity' and defining research purposes explicitly. It is also possible to engage in 'fishing'. For instance, without exactly defining what one is after, one might decide to tape and analyse three group sessions: one towards the beginning, one in the middle, and one towards the end of a group, just to see what can be learned from a close examination of sequences of contributions. This too is a form of research, highly exploratory in character. Such research can be valuable in itself and it almost always points to more focused research which might then be undertaken.

Multiple-case or single-case studies are particularly suited to practitioner-conducted research because of their close connections with practice. The skills required are already likely to be within the practitioner's repertoire. As was said at the beginning of this chapter and is now to be repeated: practitioners are already accustomed to observing events in groups as they occur, and to thinking about the implications of what has occurred in a group session or for particular individuals within a group. They will often be in the habit of keeping case notes, on individuals or of group sessions. Many research skills are extensions of these practice skills. When doing research, special care needs to be taken to devise and make consistent use of a framework for collecting information pertaining to similarly situated research subjects or similar situations. Special care needs to be taken to separate description from interpretations and conclusions. Time needs to be reserved for thinking out and stating explicitly the implications of what has been learned for practice or for policy.

Research of the kind described here is open to the criticism that it will have been conducted on a small number of units, whether those units be groups, episodes within groups, therapist interventions, individuals who fit into a particular category, or whatever. This criticism is sometimes justified, sometimes not. Much depends on whether it is reasonable to suppose that the small number of units has skewed the results. This possibility can be guarded against at the planning stage. Suppose, for example, that one is interested in studying drop-outs, and judges that the personal style of the therapist is likely to influence whether, when, and how dropping out occurs. One would need to be sure to draw instances of dropping out from groups conducted by three or four different therapists and not just one.

When conducting small-scale qualitative research it is important to be careful about how one generalises from the data. Some generalisations are likely to be justified and others, not. For instance, Strauss and Glaser (1977) followed a single cancer patient through her illness. Much that they reported was specific to this particular patient and the treatment facility responsible for her care. One could not assume that the same details would be relevant to other patients and other facilities. Yet the research pointed to what needs to be attended to when seeking to understand the course of anyone's 'dying trajectory'. Small-scale research – even a single-case study – can often examine subtleties which can be missed in a larger-scale study. Large-scale studies are often enriched if they are conducted in parallel with small-scale studies which examine the same issue in depth.

USING THE LITERATURE TO SUPPORT ONE'S RESEARCH EFFORTS

There is a large literature on qualitative research procedures. One might, for instance, consult Strauss and Corbin (1990), who describe a wide range of qualitative methods; Walker (1985), an edited book particularly useful for understanding such data-collection methods as in-depth interviewing and participant observation; and Patton (1980), which offers practical help in designing interview schedules and observation schemes. In Bryman and Burgess (1994), another edited book, one finds examples of moving from practice or fieldwork notes (which practitioners are likely to keep in any case) to systematic research. MacKenzie (1990: 261–78) has described a number of procedures for keeping records, monitoring group processes, and assessing change, in the final chapter of his book on time-limited group therapy. A number of data-collection methods used by Beck and her associates, in the course of their investigations into stages of group development, were referred to in Chapter 10.

Everitt *et al.* (1992), wrote a book titled *Applied Research for Better Practice*, intended for practising social workers. They point out that good practice is 'research-minded' in that effective practitioners hold purposes in mind, approach their work with a spirit of enquiry, take into account the information (= data) they acquire in the course of their work, and take care that any formulations or interpretations they arrive at fit with what they have observed. They go on to show forms of research which social workers may engage in, supported by research-minded attitudes and skills already established through practice.

Guidance with respect to ethical considerations are available from most professional organisations.

Of the articles which describe my own experiences with practice-related research, I will mention four: one written specifically for social workers as a guide to conducting research (Whitaker and Archer 1989); one specifically addressed to how group therapists may conduct small-scale pieces of research (Whitaker 1992a); and two which describe partnership arrangements with service-providing organisations (Whitaker and Archer 1994); and Whitaker *et al.* (1996).

This chapter is obviously meant to encourage practitioners to undertake research. Although there are restrictions on the kinds of research which practitioners can easily engage in, there is much that *can* be done, as I hope this chapter has demonstrated. Many of the necessary skills are already available, and, as Everitt *et al.* (1992) point out, can usefully be enlisted when moving into conducting research. Obviously, time has to be allocated for doing research, and a run of protected days for writing up is extremely helpful. However, I do not think it is a good idea to take substantial periods of time out from practice in order to do research. One learns most when practice and research go hand in hand, for practice tells one what to examine through research, and what one learns through conducting research feeds into practice. Planning and conducting research places the therapist in a proactive and creative position. It is a way of taking initiatives and creating new experiences for oneself, tends to be a satisfying and rewarding activity, and is, of course, another way to learn from experience.

Bibliography

Abbey, S. and Farrow, S. (1998) 'Group Therapy and Organ Transplantation', *International Journal of Group Psychotherapy* 48(2): 163–85.

Agazarian, Y. M. (1992a) 'Contemporary Theories of Group Psychotherapy: a Systems Approach to the Group-as-a-Whole', *International Journal of Group Psychotherapy* 42(2): 177–203.

—— (1992b) 'Systems Theory and Small Groups', in H.I. Kaplan and B.J. Sadock (eds) *Comprehensive Group Psychotherapy*, 3rd edn, Baltimore, MD: Williams & Wilkins.

—— (1997) *Systems-centered Therapy for Groups*, New York: Guilford Press.

Agazarian, Y.M. and Janoff, S. (1993) 'Systems Theory and Small Groups', in H.I. Kaplan and B.J. Sadock (eds) *Comprehensive Group Psychotherapy*, 3rd edn, Baltimore, MD: Williams & Wilkins.

Ahlin, G. (1996) *Exploring Psychotherapy Group Cultures*, Stockholm: Department for Neuroscience, Karolinska Hospital.

—— (2000) 'Cradle, Cage and Climbing Frame: the Use of the Group in Psychotherapy – Today and Tomorrow', paper presented at the Millennium Conference, European Federation for Psychoanalytic Psychotherapy in the Public Sector, Oxford, England, April.

Alexander, F. (1956) *Psychoanalysis and Psychotherapy: Developments in Theory, Technique and Training*, New York: Norton.

Alexander, F. and French, T.M. (1946) *Psychoanalytic Therapy: Principles and Application*, New York: Ronald Press.

Allan, R. and Scheidt, S. (1998) 'Group Psychotherapy for Patients with Coronary Heart Disease', *International Journal of Group Psychotherapy* 48(2): 187–214.

Aronson, S. (1995) 'Five Girls in Search of a Group: a Group Experience for Adolescents of Parents with Aids', *International Journal of Group Psychotherapy* 45(2): 233–5.

Azima, F. (1993) 'Group Psychotherapy with Personality Disorders', In H.I. Kaplan and B.J. Sadock (eds) *Comprehensive Group Psychothrapy*, Baltimore, MD: Williams & Wilkins, pp. 393–407.

Bacal, H.A. (1990) 'The Elements of a Corrective Selfobject Experience', *Psychoanalytic Quarterly* 10(3): 347–72.

Baker, M.N. (1993) 'Self Psychology and Group Psychotherapy', in H.I. Kaplan and B.J. Sadock (eds) *Comprehensive Group Psychotherapy*, 3rd edn, Baltimore, MD: Williams & Wilkins, pp. 176–85.

Bales, R.F. and Strodtbeck, F.L. (1951) 'Phases in Group Problem Solving', *Journal of Abnormal and Social Psychology* 46(4): 485–95. Reprinted in D. Cartwright and A.

Zander (eds) *Group Dynamics: Reseach and Theory*, 2nd edn, Evanston, IL: Row, Peterson.

Bavelas, A. (1950) 'Communication Patterns in Task-oriented Groups', *Journal of the Accoustical Society of America*, 22: 725–30. Reprinted in D. Cartwright and A. Zander (eds) *Group Dynamics: Reseach and Theory*, 2nd edn, Evanston, IL: Row, Peterson.

Beck, A.P. (1977) 'On the Development of a Rating System for the Identification of Group Phase Boundaries', paper presented at the Society for Psychotherapy Research, Madison, Wisconsin.

—— (1983) 'A Process Analysis of Group Development', *Group* 7(1): 19–26.

Belfer, P.L., Munoz, L.S., Schachter, J. and Levendusky, P.G. (1995) 'Cognitive-behavioral Group Psychotherapy for Agoraphobia and Panic Disorder', *International Journal of Group Psychotherapy* 45(2): 185–206.

Benjamin, L.R. and Benjamin, R. (1995) 'A Therapy Group for Mothers with Dissociative Disorders', *International Journal of Group Psychotherapy* 45(3): 381–403.

Bennis, W.G. and Shepard, H.A. (1956) 'A Theory of Group Development', *Human Relations* 9(4): 415–37.

Berger, M.M. and Rosenbaum, M. (1967) 'Notes on Help-rejecting Complainers', *International Journal of Group Psychotherapy* 17(3): 357–70.

Bernard, H.S. (1994) 'Difficult patients and challenging situations', in H.S. Bernard and K.R. MacKenzie (eds) *Basics of Group Psychotherapy*, New York: Guilford Press.

—— and MacKenzie, K.R. (eds) (1994) *Basics of Group Psychotherapy*, New York: Guilford Press.

Berry, C.E. (1991) 'Self Psychology and its Relationship to the Practice of Group Psychotherapy', *International Journal of Group Psychotherapy* 41(4): 523–32.

Bion, W.R. (1961) *Experiences in Groups, and Other Papers*, London: Tavistock Publications, and New York: Basic Books.

Bloch, S. and Crouch, E. (1985) *Therapeutic Factors in Group Psychotherapy*, London: Oxford University Press.

Bogdanoff, M. and Elbaum, P. L. (1978) 'Role Lock: Dealing with Monopolizers, Mistrusters, Isolates, Helpful Hannahs, and Other Assorted Characters in Group Psychotherapy', *International Journal of Group Psychotherapy* 28(2): 247–62.

Bowlby, J. (1969, 1973, 1980) *Attachment and Loss*, vols 1–3, New York: Basic Books.

Brabender, V. and Fallon, A. (1996) 'Termination in Inpatient Groups', *International Journal of Group Psychotherapy* 46(1): 81–98.

Brook, D.W. (1993) 'Group Psychotherapy with Anxiety and Mood Disorders', in H.I. Kaplan and B.J. Sadock (eds) *Comprehensive Group Psychothrapy*, Baltimore, MD: Williams & Wilkins.

Brown, S.R. (1997) 'The History and Principles of Q Methodology in Psychology and the Social Sciences', paper read at a conference on 'A Celebration of the Life and Work of William Stephenson (1902–1989)' at the University of Durham (England), 12–14 December.

Brusa, J., Stone, H., Beck, A.P., Dugo, J.M. and Peters, L.N. (1994) 'A Sociometric Test to Identify Emergent Leader and Member Roles: Phase 1', *International Journal of Group Psychotherapy* 44(1): 79–100.

Bryman, A. and Burgess, R.G. (eds) (1994) *Analysing Qualitative Data*, London: Routledge.

Budman, S.H. (1996) 'Introduction to Special Section on Group Therapy and Managed Care', *International Journal of Group Psychotherapy* 46(3): 293–5.

—— and Gurman, A.S. (1988) *Theory and Practice of Brief Therapy*, New York: Guilford Press.

——, Cooley, S., Demby, A., Koppenaal, G., Koslof, J. and Powers, T. (1996a) 'A Model of Time-effective Group Psychotherapy for Patients with Personality Disorders: the Clinical Model', *International Journal of Group Psychotherapy* 46(3): 329–55.

——, Demby, A., Soldz, S. and Merry, J. (1996b) 'Time-limited Group Psychotherapy for Patients with Personality Disorders: Outcomes and Dropouts', *International Journal of Group Psychotherapy* 46(3): 357–77.

Burrow, T. (1927) 'The Group Method of Analysis', *Psychoanalytic Review* 14: 268–80.

Carbonell, D.M. and Parteleno-Barehmi, C. (1999) 'Psychodrama Groups for Girls Coping with Trauma', *International Journal of Group Psychothrapy* 49(3): 285–306.

Carroll, L. (1865) *Alice's Adventures in Wonderland*, London: Macmillan.

Cartwright, D. and Zander, A. (eds) (1960) *Group dynamics: Research and Theory*, 2nd edn, Evanston, Ill: Row, Peterson.

Casement, P.J. (1990) 'The Meeting of Needs in Psychoanalysis', *Psychoanalytic Quarterly* 10(3): 325–46.

Cohn, R.C. (1971) 'Living–Learning Encounters: the Theme-centered Interactional Method', in G. Gottsegen and L. Blank (eds) *Confrontation: Encounters in Self and Personal Awareness*, New York: Macmillan.

Corsini, R. and Rosenberg, B. (1955) 'Mechanisms of Group Psychotherapy', *Journal of Abnormal and Social Psychology* 51: 406–11.

Crouch, E. D., Bloch, S. and Wanlass, J. (1994) 'Therapeutic Factors: Interpersonal and Intrapersonal Mechanisms', in A. Fuhriman and G.M. Burlingame (eds) *Handbook of Group Psychotherapy: An Empirical and Clinical Synthesis*, New York: John Wiley.

Dalal, F. (1995) 'Conductor Interventions: To "Do: or To "Be"?', *Group Analysis* 8(4): 379–93.

—— (1998) *Taking the Group Seriously: Towards a Post-Foulkesian Group Analytic Theory*, London: Jessica Kingsley.

Davidsen-Nielsen, M. and Leick, N. (1989–90) 'Open Grief Groups: the Resolution of Complicated Loss', *Groupwork* 2: 187–201.

Day, M. (1981) 'Process in Classical Psychodynamic Groups', *International Journal of Group Psychotherapy* 31(2): 153–74.

de Maré, P, Piper, R. and Thompson, S. (1991) *Koinonia: From Hate, Through Dialogue, to Culture in the Large Group*, London: Karnac Books (original publishers).

Dies, R.R. (1992) 'Models of Group Psychotherapy: Sifting through Confusion', *International Journal of Group Psychotherapy* 42(1): 1–17.

—— (1997) 'Comments on Issues Raised by Slavson, Durkin, and Scheidlinger', *International Journal of Group Psychotherapy* 47(2): 161–8.

Dub, F.S. (1997) 'The Pivotal Group Member: a Study of Treatment-destructive Resistance in Group Therapy', *International Journal of Group Psychotherapy* 47(3): 333–53.

Durkin, H. (1964) *The Group in Depth*, New York: International Universities Press.

Edelson, M. and Berg, D.N. (1999) *Rediscovering Groups: A Psychoanalyst's Journey Beyond Individual Psychology*, London: Jessica Kingsley.

Eliasoph, E. and Donnellan, A.M. (1995) 'Group Psychotherapy for Individuals Identified as Autistic Who Are Without Speech and Use Facilitated Communication', *International Journal of Group Psychotherapy* 45(4): 549–60.

Ellis, A. (1992) 'Group Rational-emotive and Cognitive-behavior Therapy', *International Journal of Group Psychotherapy* 42(1): 63–80.

Eng, A.M. and Beck, A.P. (1981) 'Use of Verbal Participation Measures and Pronoun Counts in the Analysis of Group Development', paper presented at the Society for Psychotherapy Research, Aspen, Colorado.

—— and —— (1982) 'Speech Behaviour Measures of Group Psychotherapy Process', *Group* 6: 37–48.

Engebrigsten, G.K. and Heap, K. (1988) 'Short Term Groupwork in the Treatment of Chronic Sorrow: a Norwegian Experience', *Groupwork* 1: 193–214.

Erikson, E.H. (1950) *Childhood and Society*, New York: W.W. Norton.

Ettin, M.F. (1992) *Foundations and Applications of Group Psychotherapy*, Boston, MA: Allyn & Bacon.

Everitt, A., Hardiker, P., Littlewood, J. and Mullender, A. (1992) *Applied Research for Better Practice*, London: Macmillan.

Ezriel, H. (1950a) 'A Psychoanalytic Approach to Group Treatment', *British Journal of Medical Psychology* 23: 59–74.

—— (1950b) 'A Psychoanalytic Approach to the Treatment of Patients in Groups', *Journal of Mental Science* XCVI: 774–9.

—— (1956) 'Experimentation within the Psycho-analytic Session', *British Journal for the Philosophy of Science* VII: 29–48.

Ezriel, H. (1959) 'The Role of Transference in Psycho-Analytic and Other Approaches to Group Treatment' *Acta Psychotherapeutica* Supplementum ad vol. 7: 101–16.

Fenster, A. (1996) 'Group Therapy as an Effective Treatment Modality for People of Color', *International Journal of Group Psychotherapy*, 46(3): 399–416.

Fieldsteel, N.D. (1996) 'The Process of Termination in Long-term Psychoanalytic Group Therapy', *International Journal of Group Psychotherapy*, 46(1): 25–39.

Foulkes, S.H. (1964) *Therapeutic Group Analysis*, London: George Allen & Unwin.

—— (1968) 'On Interpretation in Group Analysis', *International Journal of Group Psychotherapy* 18(4): 432–44.

Foulkes, S.H. and Anthony, E.J. (1957, 1965) *Group Psychotherapy: The Psychoanalytic Approach*, Harmondsworth, Middx: Penguin Books.

Frank, J.D. and Ascher, E. (1951) 'Corrective Emotional Experiences in Group Therapy', *American Journal of Psychiatry* 108: 771–8.

——, Ascher, E., Margolin, J.B., Nash, H., Stone, A.R. and Varon, E.J. (1952) 'Behavioural Patterns in Early Meetings of Therapeutic Groups', *American Journal of Psychiatry* 108: 126–31.

Frankel, B. (1993) 'Groups for the Chronic Mental Patient and the Legacy of Failure', *International Journal of Group Psychotherapy* 43(2): 157–72.

French, T.M. (1952) *The Integration of Behavior*, vols 1 and 2, Chicago, IL: University of Chicago Press.

Fuhriman, A. (1997) 'Comments on Issues Raised by Slavson, Durkin, and Scheidlinger', *International Journal of Group Psychotherapy* 47(2): 169–74.

—— and Burlingame, G.M. (eds) (1994) *Handbook of Group Psychotherapy: An Empirical and Clinical Synthesis*, New York: John Wiley.

Ganzarain, R. (1992) 'Introduction to Object Relations Group Psychotherapy', *International Journal of Group Psychotherapy* 42(2): 205–23.

Gartner, R.B. (1997) 'An Analytic Group for Sexually Abused Men', *International Journal of Group Psychotherapy* 47(3): 373–83.

Geczy, B. and Sultenfuss, J. (1995) 'Group Psychotherapy on State Hospital Admission Wards', *International Journal of Group Psychotherapy* 45(1): 1–15.

Gibbard, G.S., Hartman, J.J. and Mann, R.D. (eds) (1974) *Analysis of Groups*, San Francisco, CA: Jossey-Bass.

Gladfelter, J. (1992) 'Redecision Therapy', *International Journal of Group Psychotherapy* 42(3): 319–34.

Goodman, G. and Jacobs, M.K. (1994) 'The Self-help, Mutual-support Group', in A. Fuhriman and G.M. Burlingame (eds) *Handbook of Group Psychotherapy: An Empirical and Clinical Synthesis*, New York: John Wiley.

Goodman, M. and Weiss, D. (1998) 'Double Trauma: a Group Therapy Approach for Vietnam Veterans Suffering from War and Childhood Trauma', *International Journal of Group Psychotherapy* 48(1): 39–54.

Graham, F. (1987) 'Critique of "Interpretation in Group Psychotherapy"', *International Journal of Group Psychotherapy* 37(3): 357–60. [Refers to Scheidlinger 1987]

Greve, D.W. (1993) 'Gestalt Group Psychotherapy', in H.I. Kaplan and B.J. Sadock (eds) *Comprehensive Group Psychotherapy*, 3rd edn, Baltimore, MD: Williams & Wilkins.

Gross, J. M. (1995) 'Group Psychotherapy in the Managed-care Marketplace: Further Comments following Helfmann', *International Journal of Group Psychotherapy* 45(4): 561–6.

Hahn, W.K. (1995) 'Therapist Anger in Group Psychotherapy', *International Journal of Group Psychotherapy* 45(3): 339–47.

Harper-Giuffre, H. and MacKenzie, K.R. (eds) (1992) *Group Psychotherapy for Eating Disorders*, Washington, D.C.: American Psychiatric Press.

Harwood, I.N.H. (1983) 'The Application of Self-psychology Concepts to Group Psychotherapy', *International Journal of Group Psychotherapy* 33(4): 469–87.

—— (1998a) 'Advances in Group Psychotherapy and Self Psychology: An Intersubjective Approach', in I.N.H. Harwood and M. Pines (eds) *Self Experiences in Group: Intersubjective and Self Psychological Pathways to Human Understanding*, London: Jessica Kingsley.

—— (1998b) 'Examining Early Childhood Multiple Cross-cultural Extended Selfobject and Traumatic Experiences and Creating Optimum Treatment Environments', in I.N.H. Harwood and M. Pines (eds) *Self Experiences in Group: Intersubjective and Self Psychological Pathways to Human Understanding*, London: Jessica Kingsley.

—— and Pines, M. (eds) (1998) *Self Experiences in Group: Intersubjective and Self Psychological Pathways to Human Understanding*, London: Jessica Kingsley.

Hayes, J.A. (1995) 'Countertransference in Group Psychotherapy: Waking a Sleeping Dog', *International Journal of Group Psychotherapy* 45(4): 521–35.

Heap, K. (1965) 'The Scapegoat Role in Youth Groups', *Case Conference* 12: 215–21.

—— (1977) *Group Theory for Social Workers: An Introduction*, Oxford: Pergamon Press.

—— (1988) 'The Worker and the Group Process: a Dilemma Revisited', Groupwork 1: 17–29.

Helfmann, B. (1994) 'Here is Now', *International Journal of Group Psychotherapy* 44(4): 429–36.

Hinshelwood, R.D. (1999) 'How Foulkesian was Bion?', 23rd S.H. Foulkes Annual Lecture, *Group Analysis* 32(4): 469–88.

Horwitz, L. (1977) 'A Group Centered Approach to Group Psychotherapy', *International Journal of Group Psychotherapy* 27(4): 423–39. Reprinted in K.R. MacKenzie (ed.) *Classics in Group Psychotherapy*, New York: Guilford Press, 1992.

—— (1987) 'Discussion of Scheidlinger's Paper on Interpretation in Group

Psychotherapy', *International Journal of Group Psychotherapy* 37(3): 353–6. [Refers to Scheidlinger 1987]

—— (1993) 'Group-centered Models of Group Psychotherapy', in H.I. Kaplan and B.J. Sadock (eds) *Comprehensive Group Psychotherapy*, Baltimore, MD: Williams & Wilkins.

—— (1994) 'Depth of Transference in Groups', *International Journal of Group Psychotherapy* 44(3): 271–99.

Jamieson, R. (no date) *A Practical and Explanatory Commentary on the Old Testament*, London: James S. Virtue.

Johnson, D.R. (1997) 'An Existential Model of Group Therapy for Chronic Mental Conditions', *International Journal of Group Psychotherapy* 47(2): 227–50.

Joyce, A.S., Duncan, S.C., Duncan, A., Kipnes, D. and Piper, W.E. (1996) 'Limiting Time-unlimited Group Psychotherapy', *International Journal of Group Psychotherapy* 46(1): 61–79.

Kanas, N. (1993) 'Group Psychotherapy with Schizophrenia', in H.I. Kaplan and B.J. Sadock (eds) *Comprehensive Group Psychotherapy*, Baltimore, MD: Williams & Wilkins.

Kaplan, H.I. and Sadock, B.J. (eds) (1993) *Comprehensive Group Psychotherapy*, 3rd edn, Baltimore, MD: Williams & Wilkins.

Katz, G.A. (1983) 'The Noninterpretation of Metaphors in Psychiatric Hospital Groups', *International Journal of Group Psychotherapy* 26(2):163–72.

Kelly, J.A. (1998) 'Group Psychotherapy for Persons with HIV and AIDS-related Illnesses', *International Journal of Group Psychotherapy* 48(2): 143–62.

Kennard, D., Roberts, J. and Winter, D.S. (1993) *A Work Book of Group-analytic Interventions*, London: Routledge.

Kibel, H.D. (1993) 'Object Relations Theory and Group Psychotherapy', in H.I. Kaplan and B.J. Sadock (eds) *Comprehensive Group Psychotherapy*, 3rd edn, Baltimore, MD: Williams & Wilkins.

—— and Stein, A. (1981) 'The Group-as-a-Whole Approach: a Reappraisal', *International Journal of Group Psychotherapy* 31(4): 409–27.

Kinseth, L.M. (1982) 'Spontaneous Nonverbal Intervention in Group Therapy', *International Journal of Group Psychotherapy* 32(3): 327–38.

Kipper, D.A. (1992) 'Psychodrama: Group Psychotherapy through Role Playing', *International Journal of Group Psychotherapy* 42(4): 495–521.

Klein, R.H. (1993) 'Short-term Group Psychotherapy', in H.I. Kaplan and B.J. Sadock (eds) *Comprehensive Group Psychotherapy*, 3rd edn, Baltimore, MD: Williams & Wilkins.

Kleinberg, J.L. (1995) 'Group Treatment of Adults in Midlife', *International Journal of Group Psychotherapy* 45(2): 207–22.

Kohut, H. (1971) *The Analysis of the Self*, Madison, CT: International Universities Press.

—— (1977) *The Restoration of the Self*, Madison, CT: International Universities Press.

Kutash, I.L. and Wolf, A. (1993) 'Psychoanalysis in Groups', in H.I. Kaplan and B.J. Sadock (eds) *Comprehensive Group Psychotherapy*, 3rd edn, Baltimore, MD: Williams & Wilkins .

Leszcz, M. (1992) 'The Interpersonal Approach to Group Psychotherapy', *International Journal of Group Psychotherapy* 42(1): 37–62.

—— and Goodwin, P. (1998) 'The Rationale and Foundations of Group Psychotherapy for Women with Metastatic Breast Cancer', *International Journal of Group Psychotherapy* 48(2): 245–73.

Lewin, K. (1948) *Resolving Social Conflicts: Selected Papers on Group Dynamics*, New York: Harper & Row.

—— (1951) *Field Theory in Social Science*, New York: Harper.

—— Lippitt, R. and White, R.K. (1939) 'Patterns of Aggressive Behaviour in Experimentally Created "Social Climates"', *Journal of Social Psychology* 10: 271–99.

Lieberman, M.A. (1967) 'The Implications of Total Group Phenomena Analysis for Patients and Therapists', *International Journal of Group Psychotherapy* 17: 71–81.

—— (1993) 'Self-help Groups', in H.I. Kaplan and B.J. Sadock (eds) *Comprehensive Group Psychotherapy*, 3rd edn, Baltimore, MD: Williams & Wilkins.

——, Lakin, M. and Whitaker, D.S. (1968) 'The Group as a Unique Context for Therapy', *Psychotherapy: Theory, Research and Practice* 5: 29–36.

——, —— and —— (1969) 'Problems and Potentials of Psychoanalytic and Group Dynamics Theory for Group Therapy', *International Journal of Group Psychotherapy* 19(2): 131–41.

Lonergan, E.C. (1994) 'Using Theories of Group Therapy', in H.S. Bernard and K.R. MacKenzie (eds) *Basics of Group Psychotherapy*, New York: Guilford Press.

Longstreth, G.F., Mason, C., Schreiber, S.G.M. and Tsao-Wei, D. (1998) 'Group Psychotherapy for Women Molested in Childhood: Psychological and Somatic Symptoms and Medical Visits', *International Journal of Group Psychotherapy* 48(4): 533–41.

Lothstein, L.M. (1993) 'Termination Processes in Group Psychotherapy', in H.I. Kaplan and B. Saddock (eds) *Comprehensive Group Psychotherapy*, 3rd edn, Baltimore, MD: Williams & Wilkins.

Lubin, H. and Johnson, D.R. (1997) 'Interactive Psychoeducational Group Therapy for Traumatized Women', *International Journal of Group Psychotherapy* 47(3): 271–90.

MacKenzie, K.R. (1990) *Introduction to Time-limited Group Psychotherapy*, Washington, DC: American Psychiatric Press.

—— (ed.) (1992) *Classics in Group Psychotherapy*, New York: Guilford Press.

—— (1994a) 'Group Development', in A. Fuhriman and G.M. Burlingame (eds) *Handbook of Group Psychotherapy: An Empirical and Clinical Synthesis*, New York: John Wiley.

—— (1994b) 'Where is Here and When is Now? The Adaptational Challenge of Mental Health Reform for Group Psychotherapy', *International Journal of Group Psychotherapy* 44(4): 407–28.

—— (ed.) (1995) *The Effective use of Group Therapy in Managed Care*, Washington, DC: American Psychiatric Press.

—— (1996) 'Time-limited Group Psycotherapy', *International Journal of Group Psychotherapy* 46(1): 41–60.

—— (1997) 'Comments on Issues Raised by Slavson, Durkin, and Scheidlinger', *International Journal of Group Psychotherapy* 47(2): 75–181.

—— (1998) *Time-managed Group Pychotherapy*, Washington, DC: American Psychiatric Press.

Malan, D.H., Balfour, F.H.G., Hood, V.G. and Shooter, A. (1976) 'Group Psychotherapy: a long-term follow-up Study', *Archives of General Psychiatry* 33: 1303–15.

Marmor, J. (1988) 'Psychiatry in a Troubled World: the Relation of Clinical Practice and Social Reality', *American Journal of Orthopsychiatry* 58(4): 484–91.

Marrow, A.J. (1969) *The Practical Theorist: The Life and Work of Kurt Lewin*, New York: Basic Books.

Miller, A. (1986) *Thou Shalt Not Be Aware: Society's Betrayal of the Child*, London: Pluto.

—— (1987) *The Drama of Being a Child and the Search for the True Self, For Your Own Good: Hidden Cruelty in Child-rearing and the Roots of Violence*, London: Virago.

Miller, J.P. (1990) 'The Corrective Emotional Experience: Reflections in Retrospect', *Psychoanalytic Quarterly* 10(3): 373–88.

Mone, L.C. (1994) 'Managed Care Cost Effectiveness: Fantasy or Reality', *International Journal of Group Psychotherapy* 44(4): 437–48.

Mullen, H. (1992) '"Existential" Therapists and their Group Therapy Practice', *International Journal of Group Psychotherapy* 42(4): 453–68.

Müller, U. and Barash-Kishon, R. (1998) 'Psychodynamic-supportive Group Therapy Model for Elderly Holocaust Survivors', *International Journal of Group Psychotherapy* 48(4): 461–75.

Munich, R.L. (1993) 'Group Dynamics', in H.I. Kaplan and B.J. Sadock (eds) *Comprehensive Group Psychotherapy*. 3rd edn, Baltimore, MD: Williams & Wilkins.

Napolitani, F. (1987) 'Commentary on Scheidlinger's Paper on Interpretation', *International Journal of Group Psychotherapy* 37(3): 361–5. [Refers to Scheidlinger 1987]

Nightingale, L.C. and McQueeny, D.A. (1996) 'Group Therapy for Schizophrenia: Combining and Expanding the Psychoeducational Model with Supportive Psychotherapy', *International Journal of Group Psychotherapy* 46(4): 517–33.

Nitsun, M. (1991) 'The Anti-group: Destructive Forces in the Group and Their Therapeutic Potential', *Group Analysis* 24(1): 7–20.

—— (1996) *The Anti-group: Destructive Forces in the Group and their Creative Potential*, London: Routledge.

O'Hearne, J.J. (1993) 'Transactional Analysis in Groups', In H.I. Kaplan and B.J. Sadock (eds) *Comprehensive Group Psychotherapy*, 3rd edn, Baltimore, MD: Williams & Wilkins.

Olweus, D. (1994) 'Bullying at School', *Promotion and Education* 1(1): 27–31.

Ormont, L.R. (1991) 'Use of the Group in Resolving the Subjective Countertransference', *International Journal of Group Psychotherapy* 41(4): 433–47.

—— (1994) 'Developing Emotional Insulation', *International Journal of Group Psychotherapy* 44(3): 361–75.

—— (1995) 'Cultivating the Observing Ego in the Group Setting', *International Journal of Group Psychotherapy* 45(4): 489–506.

Parkes, C.M. (1972) *Bereavement: Studies of Grief in Adult Life*, London: Tavistock Press.

Patton, M.Q. (1980) *Qualitative Evaluation Methods*, London: Sage.

Pines, M. (1990) 'Group Analysis and the Corrective Emotional Experience: Is it Relevant?', *Psychoanalytic Quarterly* 10(3): 389–408.

—— (1993) 'Interpretation: Why, for Whom and When', in D. Kennard, J. Roberts and D.S. Winter (eds) *A Work Book of Group-analytic Interventions*, London: Routledge.

—— and Hearst, L.E. (1993) 'Group Analysis', in H.I. Kaplan and B.J. Sadock (eds) *Comprehensive Group Psychotherapy*, 3rd edn, Baltimore, MD: Williams & Wilkins.

Piper, W.E. (1995) 'Discussion of "Group as a Whole"', *International Journal of Group Psychotherapy* 45(2): 157–62.

—— (1996) 'Editor's Note #3', *International Journal of Group Psychotherapy* 46(3): 291–5.

—— and Joyce, A.S. (1996) 'A Consideration of Factors Influencing the Utilisation of

Time-limited Short-term Group Therapy', *International Journal of Group Psychotherapy* 46(3): 311–28.

——, McCallum, M. and Azim, H.F.A. (1992) *Adaptation to Loss Through Short-term Group Psychotherapy*, New York: Guilford Press.

Pollack, H.B. and Slan, J.B. (1995) 'Reflections and Suggestions on Leadership of Psychotherapy Groups', *International Journal of Group Psychotherapy* 45(4): 507–19.

Powdermaker, F. and Frank, J.D. (1953) *Group Psychotherapy*, Cambridge, MA: Harvard University Press.

Pratt, J.H. ([1917] 1975) 'The Tuberculosis Class: an Experiment in Home Treatment', in M. Rosenbaum and M. Berger (eds) *Group Psychotherapy and Group Function*, New York: Basic Books.

Pressman, M.A. and Brook, D.W. (1999) 'A Multiple Group Psychotherapy Approach to Adolescents with Psychiatric and Substance Abuse Comorbidity', *International Journal of Group Psychotherapy* 49(4): 486–512.

Rabin, H.M. and Rosenbaum, M. (eds) (1976) *How to Begin a Psychotherapy Group: Six Approaches*, London: Gordon & Breach.

Redl, F. (1966a) *When We Deal with Children: Selected Writings*, New York: Free Press.

—— (1966b) 'The Phenomenon of Contagion and "Shock Effect"', in F. Redl, *When We Deal with Children: Selected Writings*, New York: Free Press.

—— (1966c) 'Group Emotion and Leadership', in F. Redl, *When we Deal with Children: Selected Writings*, New York: Free Press.

Reid, F.T. Jr and Reid, D.E. (1993) 'Integration and Nonintegration of Innovative Group Methods', in H.I. Kaplan and B.J. Sadock (eds) *Comprehensive Group Psychotherapy*, 3rd edn, Baltimore, MD: Williams & Wilkins.

Rice, C.A. (1996) 'Premature Termination of Group Therapy: a Clinical Perspective', *International Journal of Group Psychotherapy* 46(1): 5–23.

Roberts, J. and Pines, M. (1992) 'Group-analytic Psychotherapy', *International Journal of Group Psychotherapy* 42(2): 469–94.

Rogers, C.R. (1961) *On Becoming a Person*, London: Constable.

Roller, B. and Nelson, V. (1993) 'Cotherapy', in H.I. Kaplan and B.J. Sadock (eds) *Comprehensive Group Psychotherapy*, 3rd edn, Baltimore, MD: Williams & Wilkins.

—— and —— (1999) 'Group Psychotherapy Treatment of Borderline Personalities', *International Journal of Group Psychotherapy*, 49(3): 369–85.

Rose, S.D. (1993) 'Cognitive-behavioral Group Psychotherapy', in H.I. Kaplan and B.J. Sadock (eds) *Comprehensive Group Psychotherapy*, 3rd edn, Baltimore, MD: Williams & Wilkins.

Rosenbaum, M. (1993) 'Existential-humanistic Approach to Group Psychotherapy', in H.I. Kaplan and B.J. Sadock (eds) *Comprehensive Group Psychotherapy*, 3rd edn, Baltimore, MD: Williams & Wilkins.

Rosenbaum, M. and Berger, M. (eds) (1963) *Group Therapy and Group Function*, New York: Basic Books.

Rosenberg, S.A. and Zimet, C.M. (1995) 'Brief Group Treatment and Managed Mental Health Care', *International Journal of Group Psychotherapy* 43(3): 367–79.

Roth, B.E. (1982) 'Six Types of Borderline and Narcissistic Patients: an Initial Typology', *International Journal of Group Psychotherapy* 32(1): 9–27.

Rutan, J.S. (1992) 'Psychodynamic Group Psychotherapy', *International Journal of Group Psychotherapy* 42(1): 19–35.

—— (1993) 'Psychoanalytic Group Psychotherapy', in H.I. Kaplan and B.J. Sadock (eds) *Comprehensive Group Psychotherapy*, 3rd edn, Baltimore, MD: Williams & Wilkins.

—— and Stone, W.N. (1993) *Psychodynamic Group Psychotherapy*, 2nd edn, New York: Guilford Press.

Sacks, J.M. (1993) 'Psychodrama', in H.I. Kaplan and B.J. Sadock (eds) *Comprehensive Group Psychotherapy*, 3rd edn, Baltimore, MD: Williams & Wilkins.

Salvendy, J.T. (1993) 'Selection and Preparation of Patients and Organization of the Group', in H.I. Kaplan and B.J. Sadock (eds) *Comprehensive Group Psychotherapy*, 3rd edn, Baltimore, MD: Williams & Wilkins.

Scheidlinger, S. (1982) 'Presidential Address: On Scapegoating in Group Psychotherapy', *International Journal of Group Psychotherapy* 32(1): 131–3.

—— (1987a) 'On Interpretation in Group Psychotherapy: the Need for Refinement', *International Journal of Group Psychotherapy* 37(3): 339–52.

—— (1987b) 'Rejoinder to the Discussants', *International Journal of Group Psychotherapy* 37(3): 367–9. [Refers to Horwitz; Grahan; and Napolitani, 1987]

—— (1993) 'History of Group Psychotherapy', in H.I. Kaplan and B.J. Sadock (eds) *Comprehensive Group Psychotherapy*, 3rd edn, Baltimore, MD: Williams & Wilkins.

—— (1997) 'Group Dynamics and Group Psychotherapy Revisited: Four Decades Later', *International Journal of Group Psychotherapy* 47(2): 141–59.

Schermer, V.L. and Klein , R.H. (1996) 'Termination in Group Psychotherapy from the Perspectives of Contemporary Object Relations Theory and Self Psychology', *International Journal of Group Psychotherapy* 46(1): 99–115.

Schoenholtz-Read, J. (1994) 'Selection of Group Intervention', in H.S. Bernard and K.R. MacKenzie (eds) *Basics of Group Psychotherapy*, New York: Guilford Press.

Seligman, M. and Marshak, L.E. (eds) (1990) *Group Psychotherapy: Interventions with Special Populations*, Boston, MA: Allyn & Bacon.

Slavson, S.R. (1957) 'Are There "Group Dynamics" in Therapy Groups?', *International Journal of Group Psychotherapy* 7(2): 131–54. Repinted in K.R. MacKenzie (ed) *Classics in Group Psychotherapy*, New York: Guilford Press, 1992.

Smith, P.B. (ed.) (1970) *Group Processes: Selected Readings*, Harmondsworth, Middx: Penguin Books.

Spira, J.L. (ed.) (1997) *Group Therapy for Medically Ill Patients*, New York: Guilford Press.

Spitz, H.I. (1997) 'The Effect of Managed Health Care on Group Psychotherapy: Treatment, Training, and Therapy Morale Issues', *International Journal of Group Psychotherapy* 47(1): 23–30.

Steenbarger, B.N. and Budman, S.H. (1996) 'Group Psychotherapy and Managed Behavioral Health Care: Current Trends and Future Challenges', *International Journal of Group Psychotherapy* 46(3): 297–309.

Stephenson, W.E. (1953) *The Study of Behaviour: Q-technique and its Methodology*, Chicago, IL: University of Chicago Press.

Stern, D.N. (1985) *The Interpersonal World of the Infant*, New York: Basic Books.

Stewart, A.M., Kelly, B., Robinson, J.D. and Callender, C.O. (1995) 'The Howard University Hospital Transplant and Dialysis Support Group: Twenty Years and Going Strong', *International Journal of Group Psychotherapy* 45(4): 471–88.

Stock, D. (1962) 'Interpersonal Concerns During the Early Sessions of Therapy Groups', *International Journal of Group Psychotherapy* 12(1): 14–26.

—— and Lieberman, M.A. (1962) 'Methodological Issues in the Assessment of Total-group Phenomena in Group Therapy', *International Journal of Group Psychotherapy* 12(2): 312–25. Reprinted in G.S. Gibbard, J.J. Hartman and R.D. Mann (eds) *Analysis of Groups*, San Francisco, CA: Jossey-Bass, 1974.

—— and Thelen, H.A. (1958) *Emotional Dynamics and Group Culture: Experimental Studies of Individual and Group Behavior*, New York: New York University Press. Portions of this book have been rewritten and appear as Chapter 5 in M. Rosenbaum and M. Berger (eds) *Group Psychotherapy and Group Function*, New York: Basic Books, 1995.

——, Whitman, R.M. and Lieberman, M.A. (1958) 'The Deviant Member in Therapy Groups', *Human Relations* 11(4): 341–72. Reprinted in R. MacKenzie (ed.) (1992) *Classics in Group Psychotherapy*, New York: Guilford Press.

Stone, W.N. (1992) 'The Place of Self Psychology in Group Psychotherapy: a Status Report', *International Journal of Group Psychotherapy* 42(3): 335–50.

—— (1993) 'Group Psychotherapy with the Chronically Mentally Ill', in H.I. Kaplan and B.J. Sadock (eds) *Comprehensive Group Psychotherapy*, Baltimore, MD: Williams & Wilkins.

Strauss, A. and Corbin, J. (1990) *Basics of Qualitative Research: Grounded Theory Procedures and Techniques*, London: Sage.

—— and Glaser, B.G. (1977) *Anguish: A Case History of a Dying Trajectory*, London: Martin Robertson.

Sultenfuss, J. and Geczy, B. (1996) 'Group Therapy on State Hospital Chronic Wards: Some Guidelines', *International Journal of Group Psychotherapy* 46(2): 163–76.

Tantillo, M. (1998) 'A Relational Approach to Group Therapy for Women with Bulimia Nervosa: Moving from Understanding to Action', *International Journal of Group Psychotherapy* 48(4): 477–98.

Thelen, H.A., Stock, D., Ben-Zeev, S., Gradolph, Il, Gradolph, P.C. and Hill, W.F. (1954) *Methods for Studying Work and Emotionality in Group Operation*, Research Monograph, Human Dynamics Laboratory, University of Chicago.

Toner, B.B., Segal, Z.V., Emmott, S., Myran, D., Ali, A., DiGasbarro, I. and Stuckless, N. (1998) 'Cognitive-behavioral Group Therapy for Patients with Irritable Bowel Syndrome', *International Journal of Group Psychotherapy* 48(2): 215–43.

Tutman, S. (1993) 'Countertransference and Transference in Groups', in H.I. Kaplan and B.J. Sadock (eds) *Comprehensive Group Psychotherapy*, 3rd edn, Baltimore, MD: Williams & Wilkins.

—— (1997) 'Protecting the Therapeutic Alliance in This Time of Changing Health-care Delivery Systems', *International Journal of Group Psychotherapy* 47(1): 3–16.

Van der Hal, E., Tauber, Y. and Gottesfeld, J. (1996) 'Open Groups for Children of Holocaust Survivors', *International Journal of Group Psychotherapy* 46(2): 193–208.

Vannicelli, M.A. (1992) *Removing the Roadblocks: Group Psychotherapy with Substance Abusers and Family Members*, New York: Guilford Press.

Walker, R. (ed.) (1985) *Applied Qualitative Research*, Aldershot, Hants.: Gower.

Wallerstein. R.W. (1990) 'The Corrective Emotional Experience: Is Reconsideration Due?', *Psychoanalytic Quarterly* 10(3): 288–324.

Wender, L. (1936) 'Dynamics of Group Psychotherapy and its Application', *Journal of Nervous and Mental Disease* 84: 54–60.

Whitaker, D.S. (1965) 'The Processes by Which Change Occurs and the Role of Insight', *Acta Psychotherapeutica* 13: 126–41.

—— (1982) 'A Nuclear Conflict and Group Focal Conflict Model for Integrating

Individual and Group-level Phenomena in Psychotherapy Groups', in M. Pines and L. Rafaelsen (eds) *The Individual and the Group: Boundaries and Interrelations in Theory and Practice*, vol. I, New York: Plenum Press.

—— (1987a) 'Groupwork Understandings and Skills Applied to Intervening in Personal Networks', *Journal of Social Work Practice*, May, 93–112.

—— (1987b) 'Some Connections Between a Group Analytic and a Group Focal Conflict Perspective', *International Journal of Group Psychotherapy* 37(2): 201–18.

—— (1989) 'Group Focal Conflict Theory: Description, Illustration, and Evaluation', *Group* 13 (3–4): 225–51.

—— (1990) 'Types of Practitioner Research and Frameworks for Planning and Conducting Practitioner Research', in D.S. Whitaker, L. Archer and S. Greve (eds) *Research, Practice and Service Delivery: The Contribution of Research by Practitioners*, York: Central Council for Education and Training in Social Work and University of York.

—— (1992a) 'Making Research a Part of Group Therapeutic Practice', *Group Analysis* 25(4): 433–88.

—— (1992b) 'Transposing Learnings from Group Psychotherapy to Work Groups': 15th S.H. Foulkes Annual Lecture, *Group Analysis* 25(2): 131–49.

—— (2000) 'Theory-building, Theory-use and Practice in Group Psychotherapy', *Group Analysis* 33(4): 575–89.

—— and Archer, J.L. (1985) 'An Experiment in Helping Social Work Practitioners to Design and Conduct Research', *Journal of Social Work Education* 4(2): 3–8.

—— and —— (1989) *Research by Social Workers: Capitalizing on Experience*, CETSW Study 9, London: Central Council for Education and Training in Social Work.

—— and —— (1990–1) 'Using Practice Research for Change', *Social Work and Social Sciences Review* 2(1): 9–21.

—— and —— (1994) 'Partnership Research and its Contributions to Learning and to Team-Building', *Social Work Education* 13(2): 41–62.

——, —— and Hicks, L. (1996) 'Understanding and Managing Practice in the Helping Professions',Working Paper Series B, no. 2, York: University of York: Social Work Resarch and Development Unit.

—— and Lieberman, M.A. (1964) *Psychotherapy Through the Group Process*, New York: Atherton Press, and London: Tavistock Press: The chapter on 'Strategy, Position and Power' was reprinted in G.S. Gibbard, J.J. Hartman and R.D. Mann (eds) *Analysis of Groups*, San Francisco: Jossey-Bass Publishers, 1974.

White, R. and Lippitt, R. (1960) 'Leader Behaviour and Member Reaction in Three "Social Climates"', in D. Cartwright and A. Zander (eds) *Group Dynamics: Research and Theory*, Evanston, IL: Row, Peterson.

Whitman, R.M. and Stock, D. (1958) 'The Group Focal Conflict', *Psychiatry* 21: 269–76. Reprinted in S. Scheidlinger (ed.) *Psychoanalytic Group Dynamics: Basic Readings*, New York: International Universities Press, 1980.

——, Lieberman, M.A. and Stock, D. (1960) 'The Relation Between Individual and Group Conflicts in Psychotherapy', *International Journal of Group Psychotherapy* 10(2): 259–86.

Williams, M. (1966) 'Limitations, Fantasies, and Security Operations of Beginning Group Psychotherapists', *International Journal of Group Psychotherapy* 16(2): 150–73.

Winnicott, D.W. (1949) 'Hate in the Countertransference', *International Journal of Psychoanalysis* 30: 69–74.

Wolf, A. and Schwartz, E.I.K. (1962) *Psychoanalysis in Groups*, New York: Grune & Stratton.

——, Kutash, I. and Nattland, C. (1993) *The Primacy of the Individual in Psychoanalysis in Groups*, New York: Aronson.

Yalom, I.D. (1970) *The Theory and Practice of Group Psychotherapy*, New York: Basic Books.

—— (1995) *The Theory and Practice of Group Psychotherapy*, 4th edn, New York: Basic Books.

Yalom, I.D. and Vinogradov, S. (1988) 'Bereavement Groups: Techniques and Themes', *International Journal of Group Psychotherapy* 38(4): 419–46.

Yalom, V.J. and Vinogradov, S. (1993) 'Interpersonal Group Psychotherapy', in H.I. Kaplan and B.J. Sadock (eds) *Comprehensive Group Psychotherapy*, 3rd edn, Baltimore, MD: Williams & Wilkins.

Zamanian, K. and Adams, C. (1997) 'Group Psychotherapy with Sexually Abused Boys: Dynamics and Interventions', *International Journal of Group Psychotherapy* 47(1): 109–26.

Zimet, C.N. (1997) 'Coping with the New World of Health Care', *International Journal of Group Psychotherapy* 47(1): 17–21.

Index

Sacks, J. M. 60
safety: maintaining a sense of, as an
instrumental purpose 4, 4–5; feeling too
safe, or unbearably at risk, or safe
enough to take risks 4–5; during the
formative phase 123–4, 167–9; therapist
errors which erode a sense of 217–18,
220–1; therapists' responsibility with
respect to 232
sanctions 79; an example of 87
scapegoating 144, 257–8
Scheidlinger, S. 37, 62, 208–9, 210, 247,
257, 258
Scheidt, S. 88
Schermer, V. L. 138
Schoenholtz-Read, J. 93
Schwartz, E. I. K. 207, 262
selection of members 75–8: and group
composition 75–6; procedures for the
86
self-help groups 91
Seligman, M. 93
short-cuts: 125–6
short-term and time-effective groups:
examples of 82–3, 83–5, 86; literature
on 89–91; pressures to conduct 88–9
silence: in response to the therapist's
opening comment 114, on the part of
individuals 185–6; on the part of the
whole group 114, 220, *see also*
non-participating members
size: decisions concerning 73–4; groups
which dwindle in 136; maintaining an
advantageous 272
Slan, J. B. 76, 236–7
Slavson, S. R. 207, 210
small face-to-face non-therapeutic groups
31–42: goals 31–2; norms and shared
beliefs 32–3; themes, agenda items, and
'hidden agendas' 33; moods,
atmospheres, and emotional contagion
34–5; cohesiveness 35–6; change and
development 36–7; leaders and
leadership functions 38–9; personal
roles, cueing, and altercasting 39;
sociomentric choice and sub-grouping
40; communication patterns 40–1; *see
also* group dynamics; group focal
conflict theory
Smith, P. B. 41
sociometric choice and sub-grouping: as
phenomena occurring in groups 40
solutional conflicts and the 'deviant'

member 52–4; an example of 167–9; *see
also* group focal conflict theory
solutions: developed and maintained by
group members 51–2; developed and
maintained by individuals 48–50;
metaphors which function as 50–1;
'enabling' solutions 51–2, 59–60; norms
and shared beliefs as 59; 'restrictive'
solutions 51–2, 59–60, 115;
homogeneity of behaviour within 52;
role differentiation within 52; *see also*
group focal conflict theory
spectator effects 186, 260–1; *see also*
silence(s)
Spira, J. L. 21
Spitz, H. I. 89
Steenbarger, B. N. 89
Stein, A. 281
Stephenson, W. E. 46
Stern, D. N. 62
stereotyping: 200
Stewart, A. M. 87
Stock, D. 46, 56
Stone, W. N. 21, 61, 62
Strauss, A. 330
Strodtbeck, F. L. 36
structure of programmes: example of 86–7
structure of therapeutic groups: 71–2,
91–2; and therapist's style 72; avoiding
the collapse of, as an instrumental
purpose 4, 5–6; changing the 83–5, 120,
131; combining structures 92; definition
of 5; examples of 81–2, 82–3, 83–5, 85,
86–7; matching to members' needs and
capabiities 91–3; and use of contracts
81–2
style, therapists': conditions under which it
may be necessary to shift 119; as
influenced by a group's structure 71–2;
as influenced by personal preferences
and needs 275–6
Sultenfuss, J. 87, 92, 131

Tantillo, M. 88
termination phase 9; the literature on
137–8; specialized procedures used
during the 82; themes occurring during
the 128–9, 176–8
terminations, literature on 137–8
Thelen, H. A. 46
themes: as properties of groups 33, 253–4;
and agenda items 33; definitions of 51,
57; examples of, in therapeutic groups